Elizabeth Bishop

A Miracle for Breakfast

ALSO BY MEGAN MARSHALL

*The Peabody Sisters: Three Women Who
Ignited American Romanticism*

Margaret Fuller: A New American Life

Elizabeth
BISHOP

A Miracle for Breakfast

MEGAN MARSHALL

Houghton Mifflin Harcourt
BOSTON   NEW YORK
2017

For information about permission to reproduce selections from this book, write to
trade.permissions@hmhco.com or to Permissions, Houghton Mifflin Harcourt
Publishing Company, 3 Park Avenue, 19th Floor, New York, New York 10016.

www.hmhco.com

Library of Congress Cataloging-in-Publication Data is available.
ISBN 978-0-544-61730-8

Book design by Jackie Shepherd
Type set in Chronicle Text

Acknowledgments for permission to publish previously unprinted material
and to reprint previously published material can be found on page 366.

Printed in the United States of America
DOC 10 9 8 7 6 5 4 3 2 1

*for Emily
and for Scott,
then and now*

Every living human being is a biographer from childhood, in that he perpetually studies the souls of those about him, detects with keen and curious thought the resemblances and differences between those souls and that still more present and puzzling entity, his own, and weighs with the most anxious care the bearing and effect of others' thoughts and actions upon his own life.

— GAMALIEL BRADFORD, *"Confessions of a Biographer,"* 1925

SESTINE, SESTINA. — A very elaborate measure invented by the Provençal poet Arnaut Daniel, imitated by Dante and other Italians, tried inexactly by Spenser, and sometimes recently attempted in English.

— GEORGE SAINTSBURY, *Historical Manual of English Prosody,* 1910

SESTINA French. Syllabic. Thirty-nine lines divided into six SESTETS and one TRIPLET, which is called the *envoy.* The poem is ordinarily unrhymed. Instead of rhymes, the six *end-words* of the lines in stanza one are picked up and re-used *in a particular order,* as end-words in the remaining stanzas. In the envoy, which ends the poem, the six end-words are also picked up: *one* end-word is buried in each line, and *one* end-word finishes each line. Lines may be of any length.

The order in which the end-words are re-used is prescribed in a set pattern. . . . What the numerological significance of the set is, however, has evidently been lost since the Middle Ages, though the form is still a popular one.

— LEWIS TURCO, *The Book of Forms,* 1968

CONTENTS

LIST OF ILLUSTRATIONS

CHAPTER 1: BALCONY

page 9: Elizabeth Bishop at six months, baby book photo. Courtesy of Elizabeth Bishop Papers, Special Collections, Vassar College Library.

page 10: Great Village postcard, ca. 1910s. George A. Shepherdson to H. B. Shepherdson. From the Bulmer Bowers Hutchinson Sutherland family fonds, 1997.002.I.i.23. Courtesy of Esther Clark Wright Archives, Acadia University.

page 11: Gertrude Bulmer Bishop, date unknown. From the Bulmer Bowers Hutchinson Sutherland family fonds, 1997.002.II.i.48. Courtesy of Esther Clark Wright Archives, Acadia University.

page 13: Elizabeth Bulmer and William Brown Bulmer on verandah of Bulmer family home, Great Village, Nova Scotia. Photograph ca. 1920s. From the Bulmer Bowers Hutchinson Sutherland family fonds, 1997.002.II.i.95. Courtesy of Esther Clark Wright Archives, Acadia University.

page 15: Elizabeth Bishop on beach at Spencer's Point, Nova Scotia. Photograph ca. 1921. From the Bulmer Bowers Hutchinson Sutherland family fonds,1997.002.II.i.102. Courtesy of Esther Clark Wright Archives, Acadia University.

page 18: Una Layton Frances, Grace Bulmer Bowers, Maude Bulmer Shepherdson, and George A. Shepherdson. Photograph ca. 1910s. From the Bulmer Bowers Hutchinson Sutherland family fonds, 1997.002.II.i.57. Courtesy of Esther Clark Wright Archives, Acadia University.

page 23: Snapshot from Camp Chequesset ("Bishie–Mike–Happy–Buddy–Brownie"). Courtesy of the Esther Merrell Stockton Papers, Special Collections, Vassar College Library.

page 25: Staff photograph of the *Blue Pencil,* 1929. Courtesy of Walnut Hill School for the Arts.

page 33: Elizabeth Bishop, Vassar College yearbook, 1934. Courtesy of Special Collections, Vassar College Library.

page 37: Drawing of birds on the roof by Elizabeth Bishop, from letter to Donald Stanford, April 5, 1934. Courtesy of Donald E. Stanford Papers, Special Collections, Louisiana State University Libraries.

Elizabeth Bishop

A Miracle for Breakfast

John Ashbery was late. The man who'd won, all in a season four years earlier, the three major prizes — National Book Award, National Book Critics Circle Award, Pulitzer Prize — that it had taken Elizabeth Bishop, the poet whose work and life the day's crowd had gathered to honor and mourn, a lifetime of fitful yet painstaking effort to garner, was late and holding up the proceedings.

A Harvard man, Ashbery knew the campus well, though perhaps not this lesser brick building in Radcliffe Yard — Agassiz House — where more than one hundred of Elizabeth Bishop's friends and former students sat on folding chairs in a mahogany-paneled reception room, growing warm in the sunlight from the high windows on an unusually hot Sunday in late October. Waiting. Waiting to hear from a succession of friends and poets, Ashbery most eminent among them, the one assigned to read first. Waiting to sing, accompanied by portable Hammond organ, the hymns — "Rock of Ages," "A Mighty Fortress Is Our God," "Dear Lord and Father of mankind, Forgive our foolish ways!" — that buttressed the poetry but not the faith of Elizabeth Bishop, a resolute "Unbeliever," as she had titled an early poem.

It was not Harvard's usual site for an important funeral. That would have been Memorial Church, or its smaller side chapel, across a broad lawn crisscrossed with pathways from the imposing Widener Library and adjacent to stodgy Robinson Hall, the classroom building where

Elizabeth Bishop had taught eleven aspiring poets, myself among them, through a fall semester three years before in a dimly lit seminar room. That was her last "verse-writing" class at the college, which had let her go in the spring of 1977 when she turned sixty-six, passing the mandatory retirement age for nontenured faculty members. It was the year I graduated. The year Robert Lowell, the poet and friend who had brought Elizabeth Bishop to teach at Harvard, died, just after Labor Day at age sixty. Lowell had been my teacher too, and I'd attended his funeral in Boston's incense-laden neo-Gothic Church of the Advent on Beacon Hill. There had been no amiably consoling program of poets reading and friends reminiscing and Hammond organ quavering that day, but rather a solemn high-church Episcopal requiem, with six hundred mourners filling the cavernous sanctuary and two wives — which of them was former? possibly not even they were sure — dressed in stylish black and seated in the front pew. No one of any importance arrived late.

Now in Agassiz House, Alice Methfessel, Elizabeth Bishop's close friend (Elizabeth would never describe Alice to others as anything but "friend" — not as "lover" or "partner," words that might have begun to seem right had she lived a decade longer), signaled the organist to begin. "We gather together to ask the Lord's blessing," the mourners sang. And then blond, athletic Alice spoke in her steady musical voice, quoting the elegiac last lines of E. B. White's *Charlotte's Web,* saying all she would in public: "Wilbur felt about Charlotte exactly the way I feel about Elizabeth . . . [she was] 'a true friend and a good writer.'" Alice, who was so much younger than Elizabeth, more than thirty years, and had been her close friend for less than a decade, could not have known Elizabeth's pronouncement on *Charlotte's Web* when it was first published. Alice had been scarcely ten years old in 1953 when Elizabeth wrote to the poet Marianne Moore, recalling a visit to "Mr. White" and his wife, Katharine, Elizabeth's editor at the *New Yorker;* Elizabeth had admired the spider webs in the Whites' barn in North Brooklin, Maine, and learned of the work in progress: "I ordered the book but, Marianne, it is so AWFUL." Elizabeth despised sentimentality, particularly about death. She had not wanted a memorial service.

Alice again: "Mr. Ashbery doesn't seem to be here, so I guess we can just move along."

I wasn't there either. In the two years since graduation I'd fallen away from what I once hoped was a calling to write poetry, into magazine journalism and the occasional more literary book review. Solving the riddle of what I might accomplish with such talent with words as I possessed would take decades. I had not been close to Elizabeth Bishop, indeed I had reason to think she might dislike me.

Those decades passed. Biographies, critical studies, volumes of Elizabeth Bishop's correspondence, and new editions of her slender oeuvre — one hundred poems, a dozen stories — were published. In 2011, Elizabeth Bishop's hundredth birthday was celebrated at readings and conferences across the United States. In 2012, Bishop's face — sleepily beautiful, pale and just a bit puffy, topped by a shock of unruly hair — made it onto one of the U.S. Postal Service's ten "Twentieth-Century Poets" stamps. Robert Lowell's did not.

When I told my writing students I'd studied with Elizabeth Bishop, their eyes widened in amazement. Typing "Elizabeth Bishop" into Google's search engine (a phrase the poet never heard) netted more than twenty-five million "results," from "Elizabeth Bishop Society of Nova Scotia" to an entry in a catalogue of "Popular Lesbian and Bisexual Poets" at www.sappho.com. The Internet brought me to a recording of the memorial service in Agassiz House, the one I'd missed.

Sitting at my desk and staring into a dark computer screen (the website offered few graphics), I listened to another of my former teachers, Robert Fitzgerald, translator of the *Odyssey* and the *Iliad,* thirty years dead, recall a humorous encounter with "Elizabeth." Meeting unexpectedly in a waiting room at University Health Services on a day at the height of the 1973 energy crisis, when OPEC had forced gas prices to double or triple, Elizabeth had refused to admit to Robert the least concern about the country's dependence on fossil fuels. She took the long view: "My grandmother in Nova Scotia used whale oil in *her* lamps." I heard Bishop's publisher, Robert Giroux, read a letter in which the author, famously self-deprecating and painfully shy, wrote of learning she'd won the National Book Award in 1970: "It was very nice." No, she couldn't make the trip from the Brazilian countryside to New York City on a day's notice for the award ceremony in early March: "I have nothing to wear . . . nothing with me but summer frocks."

And John Ashbery finally arrived, to read Elizabeth Bishop's sestina "A Miracle for Breakfast." It was the first of two she'd written, sparking a vogue for the ancient form in younger writers. Ashbery had discovered the poem as a college student in the mid-1940s, he explained, ten years after its initial publication in *Poetry* magazine. Bishop's sestina — clever, incantatory, casually epiphanic — inspired him to try one of his own, the first poem he'd written that he considered worth saving. He'd felt "close" to her ever since, though like many of her admirers, he scarcely knew Elizabeth Bishop.

A MIRACLE FOR BREAKFAST

At six o'clock we were waiting for coffee,
waiting for coffee and the charitable crumb
that was going to be served from a certain balcony,
— like kings of old, or like a miracle.
It was still dark. One foot of the sun
steadied itself on a long ripple in the river.

The first ferry of the day had just crossed the river.
It was so cold we hoped that the coffee
would be very hot, seeing that the sun
was not going to warm us; and that the crumb
would be a loaf each, buttered, by a miracle.
At seven a man stepped out on the balcony.

He stood for a minute alone on the balcony
looking over our heads toward the river.
A servant handed him the makings of a miracle,
consisting of one lone cup of coffee
and one roll, which he proceeded to crumb,
his head, so to speak, in the clouds — along with the sun.

Was the man crazy? What under the sun
was he trying to do, up there on his balcony!
Each man received one rather hard crumb,
which some flicked scornfully into the river,
and, in a cup, one drop of the coffee.
Some of us stood around, waiting for the miracle.

I can tell what I saw next; it was not a miracle.
A beautiful villa stood in the sun
and from its doors came the smell of hot coffee.
In front, a baroque white plaster balcony
added by birds, who nest along the river,
— I saw it with one eye close to the crumb —

and galleries and marble chambers. My crumb
my mansion, made for me by a miracle,
through ages, by insects, birds, and the river
working the stone. Every day, in the sun,
at breakfast time I sit on my balcony
with my feet up, and drink gallons of coffee.

We licked up the crumb and swallowed the coffee.
A window across the river caught the sun
as if the miracle were working, on the wrong balcony.

❧ 1 ❧

Balcony

ELIZABETH BISHOP'S BIRTH in her parents' home at 875 Main Street, Worcester, Massachusetts, on February 8, 1911, was recorded in a baby book, handsomely bound in scarlet grosgrain and titled "The Biography of Our Baby" in ornate gilt letters, that she would treasure all her life. The doctor and nurse attending the 10:45 a.m. delivery signed the first page. A birth weight of seven pounds was entered under "Baby's Weight" on a chart illustrated with a comical scene of husband, clad in morning suit and bow tie, dangling baby from a hanging scale as wife, dressed in voluminous flowered robe, reaches out to catch the newborn if she should fall. The cartoon parents, dark-haired and prosperous like William and Gertrude Bishop, are united in a comforting concern for their child — "Our Baby" — that Elizabeth Bishop could scarcely have experienced in her parents, and certainly never remembered.

The weights march down the page, registered weekly through the second month of life, with a satisfying average gain of a half pound at each line. Then the entries shift to a monthly basis — "2d Month: 9 lbs, 14 oz." (The book also provides a "First Photograph" at two months: smiling, plump-cheeked Gertrude grasps infant Elizabeth firmly with both arms.) Third month: 10 lbs., 12 oz. At the fourth month, figures give way to words: *"Mother had to go away with Father & leave Elizabeth for three months."* The alarming sentence crowds the next four lines on the chart ("5th Month," "6th Month," "1st Year," "2d Year"). Then a final entry in black ink: "17½ lbs at 10 months," out of place on the line reserved for "3d Year."

Gertrude and William Bishop, aged thirty-one and thirty-nine at Elizabeth's birth, had enjoyed a lavish seaside honeymoon in Jamaica and Panama only three years before — sailing, swimming in pools and at the beach, picnicking on a riverbank — amply documented in another cherished album, dated 1908, the year of their wedding in New York City's fashionable downtown Episcopal Grace Church. William earned a tidy income working as an estimator for his contractor father, John W. Bishop, whose Worcester base of operations provided access to granite quarries in the center of the state while he maintained offices in Boston, New York, and Providence to supervise the construction of such important buildings as Boston's Museum of Fine Arts and its public library. Born to a ship carpenter with a simple farm on Prince Edward Island, Elizabeth Bishop's paternal grandfather had joined a late-nineteenth-century exodus of Canadians seeking work in the United States to become one of New England's great self-made men. "What it is he made it," read an admiring entry on J. W. Bishop and his company of that name in an encyclopedia of Worcester's prominent citizens, published the year before his son William's marriage, lauding John W.'s unstinting hard work, his "rare judgment . . . foresight . . . unerring decision," and above all his powers of execution: "He reduces every detail to a science, and then studies it in its relation to every other detail, and thus mastering them all comes to know and understand the whole as a man comes to know and understand the five fingers of his hand and how to use them."

But William, the oldest of John W.'s eight children, suffered from Bright's disease, an incurable illness affecting the kidneys, then the fourth leading cause of death in the United States. The younger Nova Scotia–raised Gertrude Bulmer, a lithe ice skater who trained to become a nurse in Boston, seemed to embody the physical health her husband sought. But she could not confer it. Mother's three-month absence with Father, whether in a quest for a cure or a last vacation, ended with a return to Worcester and William's death there in October 1911, when Elizabeth was eight months old. The entries on her baby book's weight chart frame the first tragedy in her life, one she was too young to have the words to describe.

A few pages later, photographs tell the story. Elizabeth is posed for the camera at six months, dressed in a white gown. It is August 1911, the month of her mother's birthday, but she is alone in a broad wicker armchair set outdoors on the lawn. In one view she appears to have toppled over onto her side; immobilized in a nest of blankets, she stares stubbornly in frustration at the camera — or is she about to cry? In another, she is seated ramrod straight, gazing imperiously beyond the frame of the photograph, to garden or woods. Already she is "being brave" — "for years and years . . . my major theme," she would one day write.

Dislocations followed, the sort that startle a child with vivid new impressions and force indelible early memories. For a time she traveled between Massachusetts and Nova Scotia with her grieving mother, the second of five children, four of them daughters, of Elizabeth and William Bulmer — or Boomer, as the name was sometimes spelled — a tanner until the trade died out. Elizabeth remembered learning to walk in

Elizabeth at six months, baby book photo, August 1911

her mother's childhood home, her Bulmer grandparents' house at the corner of Cumberland and Old Post Roads in the center of tiny, primitive Great Village, Nova Scotia: "a homely old white house that sticks its little snub nose directly into the middle of the village square," she would later say. That day, her mother was away — where? — and she toddled over a soft, rose-patterned carpet toward her grandmother's outstretched arms and a "blur of plants" on the windowsill, the indoor greenery her grandmother maintained during the winter months when Elizabeth reached her first birthday. She remembered lying on the bed in the room she shared with her mother, watching Gertrude stand shivering in the washbasin as she bathed herself with water from a pitcher — there was no running water in Great Village. Her mother was beautiful, with long dark hair that she pinned up afterward in a pompadour. Elizabeth let her head hang down over the edge of the bed to view her mother upside down — the pretty curves, the vulnerable, defenseless, naked white body — and felt sad. She was a little older now.

Few memories of her mother were beautiful, or simply sad. Her mother hit her sometimes. Worse was the way Gertrude left her for

Great Village, Nova Scotia, postcard view

weeks or months — repeatedly — or seemed to be absent even when she was there. At three years old, Elizabeth was visiting Bishop relatives with her mother at the shore in Marblehead, Massachusetts, when a fire broke out across the harbor in Salem. It was a hot, dry day and Elizabeth woke in her crib, stood to watch the red sky outside the window, grasped the white bars of her crib as they too glowed red; the crib's brass nobs "held specks of fire." Outside on the lawn below, her mother also watched, her white summer dress turning "rose-red," Elizabeth forgotten. People arrived in boats, escaping the blaze. Her mother joined neighbors offering "coffee or food," and Elizabeth called out to her through the open window "and called and called." Day turned to night, flames engulfed the city across the water, and "I was terribly thirsty but mama didn't hear me calling."

This was 1914, the year the Great Salem Fire consumed more than a thousand buildings and left twenty thousand residents homeless; the year Gertrude Bulmer Bishop was hospitalized for mental illness

Elizabeth's mother, Gertrude Bishop, ca. 1916

at Boston's Deaconess Hospital, where she jumped out a second-story window but was not badly hurt. Gertrude was moved to a private sanatorium in Norwood, Massachusetts, and stayed three months before returning to Nova Scotia and Elizabeth, who had settled there with her Bulmer grandparents. By now Elizabeth had come to view her mother more as one of the Bulmer aunts, and the least reliable of them. Or perhaps not even that — Grandmother and the aunts had become Gertrude's caretakers. Was it before or after this hospitalization that one of them found Gertrude sleeping next to Elizabeth, holding a knife? Not to use against Elizabeth, but perhaps to ward off the demons — or the provincial authorities — she feared would take Elizabeth from her. Gertrude could not stop grieving for William; what if she lost Elizabeth too?

But Gertrude was first to be taken away. Elizabeth was now five years old, a girl who loved the Baptist hymns and Scottish tunes her grandparents sang, the "pure note" of Mate Fisher's hammer on anvil in the blacksmith shop next door, the "flop, flop" of dung dropped by Nelly the willful Jersey cow as Elizabeth drove her through the village and up a hill to pasture in the early morning when "the grass is gray with dew." A girl whose black-and-white patent leather shoes required cleaning before church on Sundays — cleaning with "gasoline" then polishing with "Vaseline," her grandmother explained as she buffed the little shoes. Elizabeth repeated the rhyming words over and over to herself all day, as enchanted by them as by the pulsing lines she sang while wearing the gleaming shoes: "Holy, Holy, Holy — All the saints adore Thee! Casting down their golden crowns around the glassy sea."

Sounds filled her ears, terrifying ones too: her mother's screams, which could be heard in neighboring houses; the slam of a bedroom door; her grandmother's weeping. Did she know her mother — so thin now, wraithlike — had tried to hang herself with a sheet, had grabbed her own mother by the throat? Writing from the distance of several decades, Elizabeth Bishop would recall one unending maternal scream and its echo floating over the village, following her as she drove Nelly to pasture. She would not see her mother or hear her mother's voice again.

What was said to Elizabeth about her mother's disappearance? She was in primer class at the Great Village school, daunted by long columns of numbers she couldn't decipher, although she admired the stacked twin ovals of the number 8, the way it assumed its perfect shape with one twisting motion of the hand. From her grandmother, whose name she shared, Elizabeth had already learned an alphabet that "made a satisfying short song" through the letter *g,* and she'd pressed on to learn the remaining nineteen. At school, "reading and writing caused me no suffering. I found the first easier, but the second was enjoyable." She liked forming the letters with the chalk stylus on her slate.

Elizabeth could read or simply knew the meaning of the indelible purple address her grandmother penciled on the package she sent each week to Gertrude in a sanatorium fifty miles away in Dartmouth, across the narrow bay from busy Halifax. Was it imagining that distance, the land and water to be crossed by carriage or automobile from Great Village to Dartmouth, N.S., that made Elizabeth love the two glossy maps — one of Canada and one of the whole world — that hung on her classroom wall, though she was too young to learn geography? (Only third and fourth graders were given lessons from the geography textbook.) If she wished to see her mother, she didn't say and was not

Elizabeth's Nova Scotia grandparents, Elizabeth and William Bulmer

asked. Her mother's existence — if it could be called that — was shameful. Gertrude was "permanently insane": Elizabeth would say it later, but not yet. Perhaps there was still hope of change for the better.

Elizabeth hid her mother's purple address from Mate the blacksmith, tucked the package she'd watched her grandmother fill with fruit, cakes, wild-strawberry jam, a book of Tennyson's poetry, or a Bible, under her arm, and covered the names and numbers with her hand as she walked to post it in town, the weekly errand her grandmother assigned to her. Was she walking toward her mother as she approached the village post office, small as a horse's manger? Could she forget Mother once the package was received by Mr. Johnson the postmaster, placed on the scale by his two hands with two fingers missing (lost to a threshing machine), its weight recorded and postage calculated? After she had seen there was no return mail in the Bulmer box, number 21?

The routine — sitting in primer class with chalk and slate and lustrous roll-down maps, driving Nelly up to pasture and looking out over Minas Basin's "wet red mud glazed with sky blue" at low tide, delivering the shameful package to Mr. Johnson — ended abruptly. Elizabeth was "kidnapped," or it felt that way, by "god-like" Grandfather Bishop and Sarah Foster Bishop, his American-born wife, the other grandmother whom she'd nearly forgotten, and taken by overnight train to live in their mansion home at 1212 Main Street, Worcester, Massachusetts. John W. Bishop "was another grandfather and I already had one I loved," she wrote thirty years later, confiding in a psychiatrist; along with her mother and aunts, Elizabeth had called her Nova Scotia grandfather, whose cheeks covered in "silver stubble" she happily kissed, "Pa." The Bishops thought to rescue her from all she loved: barefoot summer days, chalk on slate, oil lamps, even the privy out back. The psychiatrist listened to this story and more, and told Elizabeth Bishop she was lucky to have survived her childhood.

And she was. By 1917, five of John and Sarah Bishop's eight children had died, three in childhood, and Grandfather believed it was Sarah's fault — she "didn't know anything about children." Elizabeth too fell ill in the big house, not really a mansion but a sprawling farmhouse at the end of the trolley line, with a billiard room for Grandfather, where he smoked a cigar in the evening, and a many-windowed sewing room for

Grandmother, where she tended her canaries, and a Swedish cook and a maid and kind Ronald the chauffeur, and the broad lawn on which Elizabeth had been photographed in a wicker armchair at six months, the grass kept in trim by a hired man. Elizabeth suffered bouts of asthma and eczema, and Grandmother wasn't the only one who didn't know what to do with her.

Neither Grandfather nor his one surviving son, Jack, knew when a joke became terrifying to a six-year-old girl used to country ways. She'd learned "good manners" from Pa — "always / speak to everyone you meet," answer "nicely" when spoken to — but Grandfather Bishop and Uncle Jack liked to tease and threaten and exclude. Elizabeth was not a bad child, even if she and Evelyn, the girl next door, the only daughter of a bank president, sometimes played at being thieves: Evelyn stole her father's checkbooks and fountain pens from his desk; Elizabeth took a miniature wrench from her grandmother's sewing room and buried it under an elm tree, along with three potatoes nabbed from the kitchen. Elizabeth was never found out, nor could she find the tiny wrench when she dug for it later. She knew stealing from

Elizabeth at Spencer's Point, Nova Scotia, during a
summer visit to her Bulmer grandparents, ca. 1921

Grandmother Bishop was wrong, but she also knew she was "bitterly unhappy and lonely." No one noticed her petty thievery, no one loved her. Elizabeth told Evelyn her mother was dead, like her father. But then she "loathed" herself for lying, for the "hideous craving for sympathy" her lie revealed, the dishonorable longing for a loss she could speak of and mourn.

When Uncle Jack came to stay, he fawned over Evelyn and ignored Elizabeth, except to tease that "someone needed a spanking or a whipping" — for what? — and afterward to "argue argue" with her grandparents at the dinner table, where the frightened Elizabeth rarely spoke: "I was scared to death of him and he didn't like me." That same dining table provided a hiding place, a playhouse beneath the dark mahogany, behind the white folds of tablecloth, reminding her of the flowering syringa bush in Nova Scotia "whose shelter I often shared with a hen." Grandfather Bishop knew when Elizabeth was playing there. "Godlike," he could be generous too. "I wonder if some little girl would like to take piano lessons?" he asked one day of the child hiding under the tablecloth. And soon Elizabeth was "overjoyed" to be taking lessons with Mrs. Darling, although the young pupil teetered on the piano bench, her legs too short to reach the pedals.

Uncle Jack was mean, but Aunt Florence Bishop, who still lived with her parents in Worcester, was "foolish." On a winter day when Elizabeth was out of school, wheezing with asthma and itchy with eczema, she accompanied Aunt Florence to the dentist, and sat by herself in the waiting room. Not quite by herself: there were "others waiting, two men and a plump middle-aged lady, all bundled up." It was February 1918, Elizabeth knew — her seventh birthday was in a few days — and the cover of the latest *National Geographic* she was leafing through said the same. Elizabeth could read well now. The heat of the stuffy waiting room in winter, the mesmerizing yellow lamp on the side table, the frightening images of molten volcanoes and African women in tribal undress in the magazines, her foolish Aunt Florence's cry of pain from the dentist's chair, the false smile of the plump lady seated opposite her — all brought on "a feeling of absolute and utter desolation." Elizabeth felt as if she were falling, "sliding / beneath a big black wave," and another. The journey from Great Village to Worcester had brought her here, to the realization that she was alone — *"myself,"* an *"I, I, I"* — among unreliable, unpredictable adults. Worse, she would be *"one* of them too."* Forever. Never again an unthinking child with barnyard animals for friends, playing under the flowering syringa in Great Village, N.S. *"Why* was I a human being?"

Being human, growing up too fast as the virtual orphan she was now, meant becoming a self divided from the world — "inside looking out" — and suffering ever more divisions: Nova Scotia and Massachusetts, Bulmers and Bishops. The European war was on. In Great Village there had always been "War Work," done by men "dressed up" attractively in kilts and tam-o'-shanters. In Worcester during the winter of 1917–18, the war was new and grim: men walked the streets in drab uniforms, Grandmother Bishop required Elizabeth to learn to knit — "I hated it" — for the war effort. In school, when she was well enough to attend, there was no singing of "God Save the King" or "The Maple Leaf Forever." Saluting the American flag felt like being "a traitor: I wanted us to win the War, of course, but I didn't want to be an American." Grandmother Bishop was horrified when she heard that. What else would Elizabeth need to hide inside while looking out?

Finally, illness permitted a reprieve. She'd been sent home from first grade with terrible sores, a humiliation she would not forget, and the long days that followed at 1212 Main Street brought on asthma so severe she kept to her bed, scarcely able to breathe, feeling herself "aging, even dying." A private nurse was no help, and John W. Bishop feared his little granddaughter, so pale and small, would die "in another two months" if she stayed in Sarah's household. Gertrude's sister Maud, one of the Bulmer aunts, had married George Shepherdson, the principal of the Great Village school, and followed him to Boston. Grandfather Bishop helped to fund an apartment for the Shepherdsons by the ocean in working-class Revere, an enclave of Italian and Irish immigrants near Lynn, where Uncle George found work as an accountant for General Electric. The sea breeze might do Elizabeth good. When kind Ronald the chauffeur carried weak and wheezing Elizabeth up the stairs to the Shepherdsons' second-floor apartment and all the way to her new room, the back room of five, Aunt Maud burst into tears at the sight. But Elizabeth was happy. Soon cheerful, steadfast

Aunt Grace Bulmer, Elizabeth's favorite, a trained nurse as Gertrude had been, joined the family to work in Boston. Elizabeth's breathing improved.

And yet the aunts could not be Elizabeth's deliverance. Sometimes she forgot, and sometimes she remembered, how in those first weeks Uncle George Shepherdson insisted on drawing her bath, how he fondled her until — "suddenly very uncomfortable" — she knew he wasn't simply giving her "an unusually thorough washing," and she twisted away from his probing fingers. He stopped giving her baths then, or she remembered no more of them.

She didn't forget the time Uncle George, a "very tall man," grabbed her by the hair and dangled her over the railing of the second-story balcony. All in "good clean fun." Elizabeth was a slip of a girl and her brown hair unusually thick and wiry. "Maybe lots of people have never known real sadists at first hand," Elizabeth supposed, writing about Uncle George to her psychiatrist thirty years later. "I got to thinking that they [men] were all selfish and inconsiderate and would hurt you if you gave them a chance."

Living in Revere with the Shepherdsons, Elizabeth still suffered from asthma, enduring Aunt Maud's nighttime injections of adrena-

Aunts Grace Bulmer and Maud Shepherdson (in white)
with Uncle George Shepherdson

line, missing days and weeks of school, eventually falling behind her class by a full year. But now she was "wheezing and reading" her way through her aunt's bookcases, reading "harder & harder" in bed in the early mornings when Uncle George's temper erupted and he shouted at Aunt Maud before he left for work, or when he threatened Elizabeth with beatings for "answering back" or being "impertinent." Sometimes she blamed herself for their quarrels, felt she might deserve those threatened beatings: she was the unwanted child who drew her aunt's attention away from Uncle George. His rages dissipated as quickly as they burst forth, then Uncle George turned sentimental, tearing up over his wife's ministrations — "everything was done for his comfort and enjoyment, nothing for anyone else." Uncle George's "dreadful sentimentality" — hypocritical and manipulative — was as painful for Elizabeth to witness as his "streak of cruelty," although Aunt Maud, "small, worried, nervous, shy," pardoned it all with "Oh you know how men are."

Elizabeth's aunts Maud and Grace thrived on another kind of senti-ment — the verse epics of Longfellow, Tennyson, Robert and Elizabeth Barrett Browning, which Elizabeth found on the bookshelves or im-bibed as her aunts recited passages they had come to cherish in village reading circles through long Nova Scotia winters. The aunts played the piano too, and Elizabeth kept up her lessons. They also painted in watercolor and oils, having learned from an uncle whose rather "bad" portraits and landscapes intrigued Elizabeth, and they took her to the Boston museums. But poetry was "the most natural way of saying what I feel." At age eight she began to write, adding her own words to the store of memorized poems that was growing to become "an uncon-scious part of me." Aunt Grace read Elizabeth's early efforts, counseled her to accept criticism gracefully and work to improve her poems, but none survive. An essay on "Americanism" written at age twelve brought her first pay as a writer — a five-dollar gold piece, first prize in a contest sponsored by Revere's fledgling American Legion post, founded at the Great War's end. Perhaps she wrote the essay sitting in a classroom of children whose parents she knew as "aliens, dreamers, drunkards," she would later recall, many of them Sicilian immigrants hoping to gain American citizenship; and six years in the United States

may have eroded her once-vehement loyalty to Canada. Yet her opening words — "From the icy regions of the frozen north to the waving
palm trees of the burning South" — preserved only in Elizabeth's memory, hint of Nova Scotia's enduring claim on her imagination.

Along with her classmates Elizabeth memorized whole poems, required by their teachers for recitations. James Russell Lowell's "The
First Snow-Fall" haunted her for years. She could still recite its singsong opening stanza word-for-word in later life —

> The snow had begun in the gloaming,
> And busily all the night
> Had been heaping field and highway
> With a silence deep and white.

And she could easily rattle off the remaining nine quatrains, which
turned macabre as they told of Lowell's barely suppressed grief that
winter day as he imagined the first snow falling on the grave of his infant daughter in the cemetery nearby, while an adored surviving child
stood at his side:

> Then, with eyes that saw not, I kissed her;
> And she, kissing back, could not know
> That my kiss was given to her sister,
> Folded close under deepening snow.

Perhaps the poem reminded her of Gwendolyn Patriquin, a frail,
beautiful girl she had played with in Nova Scotia, who died of untreated
diabetes not long after spending a night with Elizabeth. Or another
early-fixed memory: she could not have been more than four years old
when her mother lifted her up to "say good-bye" to her little cousin
Frank, laid out in a child's coffin in her Bulmer grandparents' winter-
cold parlor, "his eyes shut up so tight / and the roads deep in snow."
Now her mother was gone, although not dead; she had never stood beside her father to receive his kiss. How to imagine a father's grief — or
love — for his child? Who would miss Elizabeth, so often scarcely able
to draw breath, if she died?

Better to read harder and harder. Elizabeth read the tales of Grimm and Andersen and imagined she was no mere orphan, but a fairy princess living in squalid Revere "just temporarily." She read *Hans Brinker, or The Silver Skates,* a winter's tale with a happier ending, so many times she knew most of it "by heart." And though she still faltered in math at school, she loved the science she learned on her own in books. The British physicist C. V. Boys's *Soap Bubbles and the Forces which Mould them,* with its foldout diagrams and illustrated experiments for children — requiring "no apparatus beyond a few pieces of glass or india-rubber pipe, or other simple things easily obtained" — enchanted her. The book, composed of lectures delivered "before a juvenile audience" in London, began: "I do not suppose there is any one in this room who has not occasionally blown a common soap-bubble, and while admiring the perfection of its form, and the marvellous brilliancy of its colours, wondered how it is that such a magnificent object can be so easily produced." Elizabeth Bishop would one day tell a young aspiring writer, "Observation is a great joy." To write one's observations, record such wonderings, the greatest joy of all.

The year Elizabeth won her five-dollar gold piece, Aunt Grace returned to Nova Scotia to marry, and Uncle Jack became Elizabeth's legal guardian when her elderly Worcester grandparents died less than a week apart. Grandmother Bishop may never have learned of Elizabeth's prize-winning patriotic turn. Mercifully, Jack Bishop and his wife, Ruby, although childless, wanted little to do with their niece; she could stay on in Revere, "dreaming deliberately," turning a deaf ear to Uncle George's tantrums, willing away his transgressions. And stern Uncle Jack was surprisingly liberal with the Bishop family money. Perhaps he'd imbibed the country's postwar mood of extravagance: he established a $10,000 trust fund for Elizabeth beyond the share of the family fortune set aside for her at her father's death. Now she could go to sailing camp on Cape Cod in the summer and a good boarding school when she was ready for it, and then college. The Nova Scotia Bulmers knew nothing of such camps or schools or colleges for women, and when Elizabeth rode the train to Cape Cod the first summer with another girl going to the same camp, she gave in to shyness and never spoke for the entire trip. The girl thought her "an idiot child," but soon learned otherwise.

Camp Chequesset, to which Elizabeth returned for five happy summers, opened a new life. Small for her age and still inclined to cough and wheeze, she nevertheless became an athlete, a "tomboy," she would say: swimming, sailing, exploring beaches and woods near the camp in Wellfleet. She made friends with "other children as bright as *me*," and found she could talk with them about her interests — poetry, above all. One girl gave her Harriet Monroe and Alice Corbin's anthology of modern verse, where Elizabeth learned from Monroe's introduction that "the new poetry strives for a concrete and immediate realization of life," and is "less vague, less verbose, less eloquent" than the Victorian poetry she had read and recited with her aunts or public school classmates: it seeks "absolute simplicity and sincerity." There were nearly as many women writers as men represented in the book, their poems gathered by *Poetry* magazine's two female editors, whose own work appeared in the volume. Elizabeth discovered Robert Frost, Ezra Pound, William Carlos Williams, Wallace Stevens, Hilda Doolittle (who published as H.D.), among dozens of others, arranged alphabetically from Conrad Aiken to Edith Wyatt. *The New Poetry,* as the volume was titled, became hers.

On a trip to Provincetown, the haven for artists and writers at the farthest end of Cape Cod, she located a secondhand bookshop, and returned to spend her allowance on the poetry of George Herbert and Gerard Manley Hopkins, both priests (Anglican and Jesuit) who had lived over two centuries apart. They swiftly became her favorites, Herbert for the "simple dignity" of the language he used to express "very deep emotion," and Hopkins for the unconventional means — "sprung rhythm" — he'd devised to accomplish the same. Herbert and Hopkins used rhyme, but not the way James Russell Lowell or Longfellow or Tennyson did — never singsong, never disrupting the natural flow of speech. There was newness in the old of Herbert, and Hopkins had studied the Anglo-Saxon of *Beowulf* to originate his densely accented sprung rhythm, counting stressed syllables rather than regular metrical feet in each line. Elizabeth still loved the rhymes and rhythms of childhood, and put them to use composing camp songs and skits, becoming "extremely popular," even "showing off." When it was her turn to keep the cabin log, she wrote in verse.

The girls at Camp Chequesset had a habit of falling in love with one another, forming naive crushes that, over the course of long days and nights together, sometimes turned physical. The summer Elizabeth was fourteen she admired from afar the camp's swimming instructor, a young woman everyone called Mike, a favorite with campers, and she felt the thrill of Mike's interest in return. Elizabeth — known here as "Bishie" — was one of Chequesset's best swimmers; with her gamine look and wild hair cropped short, of course she attracted Mike's attention. She was a favorite too, and precocious, yet under all that, lonely, an orphan, not likely to write letters home reporting a counselor's trespass. A year later she told a fellow camper, "I haven't any family whatever — excepting a few aunts and uncles . . . and its glorious not to feel you'll have to turn out well or you'll break someones' heart." That summer, at fifteen, Elizabeth was assigned to Mike's cabin, a forty-seven-foot sloop in dry dock called the *Ark;* she was pretty sure Mike arranged it that way.

Elizabeth and Mike on the *Ark* with Camp Chequesset cabin mates

Some nights Mike climbed into Elizabeth's bunk and stayed there, kissing her, exciting her, while the other girls slept. Elizabeth was pleased to have been remembered for an entire year, glad to be chosen, to be kissed. Had *she* seduced Mike with her pointed interest? she later wondered. Did she have such power? But Mike, ten years older, "should have known better" than to get in bed with a teenager, even one who had read Havelock Ellis, finding his treatise on "sexual inversion" — same-sex love — on the bookshelf in Revere among the nursing texts that had belonged to her mother and Aunt Grace. Mike gave Elizabeth a copy of Kahlil Gibran's *The Prophet;* Mike whispered plans for a "rendez-vous" the last night of camp, then "didn't show up at all." Elizabeth was left to wonder, until she heard that another counselor had discovered the plan and talked Mike out of it. Angry now and unexpectedly "feeling ashamed," Elizabeth refused to answer any of Mike's letters and tried to forget. The nighttime hours together in her bunk had been a secret anyway. Elizabeth hadn't liked Gibran's syrupy aphorisms on love and friendship; now she detested the book.

Despite her early reading of Havelock Ellis — who described homosexuality as a naturally occurring variant in human behavior — and her strong attraction to Mike, Elizabeth didn't think of herself as an "invert." She simply loved the people she loved, and mostly they were women or girls of her own age. She loved Aunt Grace, who had been visiting Revere the night twelve-year-old Elizabeth's first menstrual period arrived. Aunt Grace found Elizabeth in her room, terrified that the bleeding signaled complications from the appendicitis that had recently sent her to the hospital for emergency surgery. Aunt Grace showed her what to do and then held Elizabeth on her lap in the bathroom to calm her. "There was a white bathmat and as she talked she drew pictures of ovaries etc in the pile of the mat," Elizabeth remembered, a map of a mystifying, scarcely comprehensible interior. Aunt Grace slept with Elizabeth that night, holding her close, and Elizabeth was happy.

Elizabeth loved Aunt Maud too, believed her aunt would have taken her in even without the Bishop money, which the Shepherdsons sorely needed. Uncle George had been laid off at General Electric. One night

Elizabeth woke to find Aunt Maud kneeling by her bedside, praying. Had Uncle George been rough with her? Elizabeth wondered. Once he'd squeezed Aunt Maud so hard she'd broken a rib. Lately he'd taken to pawing Elizabeth, "always trying to feel my breasts" when she walked past, when Aunt Maud wasn't looking. She pulled away, telling him "Don't," but he was "so very large and strong," she still sometimes got "caught." This too she willed herself to forget or excuse, following Aunt Maud's example; she tried not to understand "exactly what it was he was doing." She was glad to leave Revere for boarding school at the end of the summer she was fifteen, after the failed rendezvous with Mike.

Walnut Hill School, a college preparatory school for girls on the outskirts of Natick, Massachusetts, was like camp, only better. It lasted longer, September to June. Except for a bout with asthma that com-

Blue Pencil staff, Walnut Hill School, 1929. Frani Blough and
Elizabeth are seated in second row, center and right.
Judy Flynn is standing, wearing the dark blouse.

promised her freshman year, Elizabeth stayed on until she graduated at nineteen. School was school, drudgery at times — especially algebra and geometry — but there were plays every semester to act in (she loved dressing up as the male villain), concerts to attend at nearby Wellesley College and in Boston (she saved the program for Prokofiev's Wellesley recital after shaking the composer's hand), hymns to sing every morning at chapel, a Glee Club to join, and a literary magazine, the *Blue Pencil,* to write for and finally to serve as its editor in chief. There were teachers who loved her, maybe too much, but they didn't paw her or climb into her bed. And there were friends — to confide in, to write skits for, to play four-hand piano with, and a few to kiss and hold in her arms, to be kissed by and held. She truly loved one girl — the deep-voiced Judy Flynn, tall with red hair so dark it was almost black, cut in a bob that drew attention to her graceful swanlike neck. Elizabeth attended Catholic Mass with Judy for the chance to gaze at the "beautiful girl … on her knees with a rosary." With the others, Elizabeth simply "liked to feel rather naughty and mischievous."

Walnut Hill School had been founded in 1893 by two Wellesley College graduates, Florence Bigelow and Charlotte Conant, who shared a house near the campus, living in what was sometimes called a Boston marriage until Conant died in 1925, the year before Elizabeth entered the school. This had been the way of many girls' schools and women's colleges in their founding years, as a few bold women asserted the right to higher education for all and forged long-lasting affectionate partnerships in reform. While questions were raised at times now by faculty members about whether intense student friendships were "normal," Miss Bigelow still presided over Walnut Hill in the late 1920s with her younger assistant principal, Miss Helen Farlow, who took a lenient, possibly uncomprehending, view of girls who paired off. Miss Farlow sometimes took Elizabeth and Judy on drives and picnics, encouraging the friendship.

The fifty-acre campus was wooded and hilly, with playing fields and tennis courts and a long, sloping, grassy bank as its central green, where students skied in the wintertime. To her Walnut Hill friends, Elizabeth was "Bishop," and when she was mischievous or joking — such as the time she and a friend dressed up in bedspreads, put baskets on their heads, and walked down the main road toward Wellesley, perhaps mocking a school regulation that required hats on outings to town — the nickname was ironic; when she was solemn, judgmental, or enigmatic in her continued bouts of shyness, it suited her perfectly.

In 1926 the Shepherdsons had moved a short distance to a "dreadful little house" in the Cliftondale neighborhood of Saugus, leaving behind the carnival atmosphere at Revere, where the mighty Cyclone, the longest and fastest roller coaster in the world, had been installed a year before, attracting thrill seekers from miles around. But neither town was on the typical itinerary of Elizabeth's new friends from camp or Walnut Hill School, mostly daughters of professionals and businessmen, several of whom owned summer homes on New England's more secluded shorelines. Elizabeth confided the fact of her mother's hospitalization to a new friend, Frani Blough — a live wire, small, thin, and bold, who shared Elizabeth's birthday though a year older. But that painful truth seemed more remote, less immediately distressing, than her "dreadful" residence with timid, tender-hearted Aunt Maud and brutish Uncle George in Saugus. When Judy Flynn stopped in without advance warning at Cliftondale during a school vacation, Elizabeth burst into tears at the kitchen table, uncertain how to introduce her beautiful friend to her unrefined aunt and uncle. Yet she had no wish to move into Uncle Jack Bishop's plush household north of Worcester; and on one visit to her aunt Florence's new home in Stockbridge, she'd run away, with a few dollars and two books of poetry stuffed in her pocket — hitching a ride to the station, boarding a train to Framingham, then walking back to school — rather than stay for a dance party organized by foolish Aunt Florence. With her Bishop relations she always felt "on more or less visiting terms," longing to be elsewhere.

Elizabeth clung to Walnut Hill and to her friends there, cadging invitations to their homes whenever possible for vacations and holidays. More than most of her classmates, Elizabeth found a safe haven in the insular world of girls and women, interdependent and mingling easily despite the regimentation of morning room inspections and dressing for dinner, where silver napkin rings engraved with each girl's name waited at round tables covered in starched white linen. Teachers donned period costumes to join students in theatricals, enjoying the lark of playing male roles as much as "Bishop" did. It was the actual boys Aunt Florence had wanted her to meet that caused Elizabeth to panic and run away back to school; she'd spent a rainy night huddled in the woods up on the "Ridge," a favorite retreat, until daylight when she found her way to her English teacher Miss Mulligan's house across the road, to be cosseted with warm blankets and a breakfast of scrambled eggs. Visiting Judy Flynn at her home in New Hampshire was heavenly, except for the older brother who picked them up by car from school.

Much supervision came in the form of rules or grades for posture and neatness. (Elizabeth rated poorly at times in the former, a consistent A-plus in the latter.) Yet Miss Farlow also took note of the childish pranks and of what Elizabeth would later call her "*social* terrors," and arranged for her to see a psychiatrist in Boston, expecting Elizabeth to confide about her mother's mental illness. Jack Bishop had informed Miss Farlow of Gertrude's "insanity" when registering Elizabeth for school, assuring the assistant principal there was "no hereditary tendency" to fear in Elizabeth's case, and asserting that "no one" had ever spoken to his niece about her mother. He requested the Walnut Hill staff to follow suit. Elizabeth could not bring herself to speak at the sessions, and they soon ended. But she remembered Miss Farlow's concern with gratitude, especially one ride back to school from the psychiatrist's office during which Miss Farlow had defied Uncle Jack and asked Elizabeth whether she "worried" about her mother "a lot." Elizabeth was "so overcome," startled that Miss Farlow knew about Gertrude, that she could only cry — and then wonder afterward if she'd used her tears to elicit Miss Farlow's sympathy. She didn't know her mother well enough to worry about her. She didn't know how she ought to feel.

Elizabeth would not speak to a psychiatrist, but she wrote unstoppably at Walnut Hill School — stories, book reviews, essays, poetry, and plays that were published in the rigorously edited *Blue Pencil* as early as her sophomore year and performed on the school's improvised stages. The Christmas pageant she wrote with Frani Blough served as the school's holiday program for decades, and a fanciful twelve-line lyric, "Behind Stowe," referring to one of the school's two principal dormitories, remained popular with students as well. "I heard an elf go whistling by" and "heard a cricket sing," the poem began:

> *His singing echoed through and through*
> *The dark under a windy tree*
> *Where glinted little insects' wings.*
> *His singing split the sky in two.*
> *The halves fell either side of me,*
> *And I stood straight, bright with moon-rings.*

At Walnut Hill, the remembered sound of her mother's screams hovering in the air over Great Village diminished, and music "echoed through and through" her new world. The sky might split in two around her, but Elizabeth stood straight and bright, crafting her own song in words, playing with rhyme and meter.

At Walnut Hill she grew strong enough to write an essay, "On Being Alone," admitting to a "fear of all those innumerable quiet hours alone that are ahead of all of us," but proposing that in solitude "the mind can do what it wants to": "find the islands of the Imagination" and befriend "the companion in ourselves who is with us all our lives ... the rare person whose heart quickens when a bird climbs high and alone in the clear air." The self "inside looking out" that she'd discovered since that dizzying day in the dentist's waiting room in Worcester could experience joy as well as suffering. The girl who had once dangled by her hair at the mercy of her brutish uncle could write now about "Roof-Tops," as Elizabeth titled another *Blue Pencil* essay — the "many-slanted, many-shingled planes" we have "longed to rise up" and "heave" off, leaving "open every building to the blue sky and the wind."

Elizabeth planned to major in music at Vassar, following the lead of Frani Blough, who'd gone to college a year ahead. Piano study at Walnut Hill, where her teacher had trained with the English pianist Myra Hess, had been more rigorous and rewarding than childhood lessons with Mrs. Darling. As a senior she'd taken a yearlong course in harmony and was secretary of the Glee Club. Most of all, she'd loved the hours spent improvising on favorite hymns at the piano with Frani, singing at the top of their lungs, when rainy days kept them indoors. If she could write poetry and plays, perhaps she could compose music as well.

But Vassar College wasn't Walnut Hill School. While she joined the choir and sang happily again with Frani, the advanced music theory class she signed up for as an overconfident freshman was beyond her capabilities, and piano instruction proved equally daunting. In an early group recital she suffered a memory slip and couldn't finish her piece; she left the room and never performed in public again. At lessons her teacher found her "handicapped by an unusual degree of muscular tension," and Elizabeth mastered only one of the four pieces assigned during her first semester, a Bach three-part invention. She complained "feelingly" of limited time and noisy practice rooms. Her teacher worried that Elizabeth didn't have the stamina for Vassar, noting her difficulty in "adapting her quick and imaginative, but too self-conscious self to college conditions." In Frani's view, Elizabeth was a "good musician," but "very particular, as she was with writing poetry." She lacked the "carefree abandon" necessary to perform with confidence, or to keep pace in her piano studies.

For Elizabeth, who had no place to go but school, the stakes were high. Elite private women's colleges took pride in enforcing rigorous academic standards, and many first-year students did not return. One of Elizabeth's new friends, the paper-company heiress Louise Crane, struggled academically for three years and never graduated. Unlike Louise, who could return home to a Fifth Avenue apartment shared with her widowed mother, a founder of the Museum of Modern Art and the progressive Dalton School, Elizabeth resorted to renting cheap hotel rooms in Boston or inexpensive beach houses for vacation and holiday stays when she couldn't wangle invitations from friends, avoiding both her Cliftondale and Worcester relatives as much as possible. Perhaps hoping to dodge hard-to-answer questions about her mother, she'd listed both parents as deceased on her information card when she enrolled at Vassar. She considered herself "independent" now.

Fortunately, Elizabeth's freshman English teacher responded differently to her pupil's "too self-conscious self." She saw Elizabeth as "enormously cagey," but admired the quietly willful nineteen-year-old "who looked at authorities with a suspicious eye." Elizabeth seemed "quite capable of attending to her own education," and, with her penchant for metaphor even in term papers, was evidently "doomed to be a poet." While Vassar offered no classes in verse writing — no colleges did — Elizabeth took every opportunity to prepare herself to become a writer.

The college had been founded in 1865 by a devout Baptist philanthropist and brewer, Matthew Vassar, who considered himself, along with Abraham Lincoln, one of the country's "Two Noble Emancipists — one of Woman — [the other] of the Negro." With a cloistered campus eighty-five miles up the Hudson Valley from New York City in Poughkeepsie, Vassar was the second of what eventually became the "Seven Sisters," the first to make its start as a full-fledged college. (Mount Holyoke began as a seminary in 1837.) A next generation of wealthy Baptists, the Rockefellers and Pratts of Standard Oil, funded the massive neo-Gothic stone library, chapel, art building, and crenellated gatehouse that gave Vassar its fortresslike air of secluded — and exclusive — privilege.

But the 1930s brought a restless mood to campus. During Elizabeth's freshman year in the spring of 1931, Vassar's experimental student theater director, Hallie Flanagan, soon to lead the New Deal's Federal Theatre Project, staged *Can You Hear Their Voices?*, a social realist drama contrasting the plight of impoverished southern farm families with the frivolous world of debutante balls so familiar to Vassar students. Yet many students were hurting financially as family fortunes shrank or disappeared in the Depression. Talk in dormitory smoking rooms turned to socialism and Communist Party politics, and Elizabeth found herself caught between an instinctive populism, derived from her childhood in Nova Scotia and among the working poor north of Boston, and a yearning for the stability and comfort she'd glimpsed in the fine homes of her Walnut Hill School friends. She might turn her back on Bishop hospitality, but she relied on her trust fund, conservatively invested in blue chip stocks that withstood the '29 Crash, as on little else but her way with words.

At Vassar Elizabeth called herself a socialist, wore a pea coat rather than stylish camel hair or furs in winter, and adopted a vegetarian diet.

But she hung back in smoking room conversation, and not just out of shyness. When she joined the leftist staff of the twice-weekly Vassar *Miscellany News* her junior year, she found her niche as editor of "Campus Chat," the humor column, poking fun at the campus scene, often in verse. Elizabeth valued wit in friends like Louise Crane and serious intellectual engagement — Frani Blough's dedication to music, a new friend Margaret Miller's devotion to art as a painter and critic for the *Miscellany News* — over what she saw as political posing. The "really 'red'" students on campus were "too silly"; covering their activities as a reporter for the college paper held no interest.

The battle Elizabeth was prepared to wage was over literature. Her circle had grown to include the sisters Eunice and Eleanor Clark and brassy, brilliant Mary McCarthy, a true orphan whose parents had died in the flu epidemic of 1918. Along with Elizabeth, Frani Blough, and the gifted Margaret Miller, most had suffered rejection by the stodgy campus literary magazine, the *Vassar Review,* and they joined forces to found a rival journal, *Con Spirito* — the title devised by Elizabeth as a pun on the musical term, suggesting the conspiracy among the six. The idea was born in a speakeasy off campus in the waning months of Prohibition, and the first issue celebrated with a legal bottle of wine in February 1933. *Con Spirito*'s stories and poems were published anonymously to conceal the conspirators' identities, but the publication won praise from the *Miscellany News.* After three issues, Elizabeth was welcomed on board at the *Vassar Review* for her senior year.

In *Con Spirito* Elizabeth voiced her ambivalence about Depression-era politics with an ironic tale, "Then Came the Poor," about a wealthy family hastily packing up its valuables to escape a rampaging "red" mob. At the last minute, the narrator stays behind to mingle with the marauding crowd, ultimately taking up residence with the squatters in his own house, agreeing with a wink to his new roommate's summation: "Seems like home already, don't it." But Elizabeth took the people's side emphatically in a mocking "Hymn to the Virgin," one of four poems she contributed to the fledgling journal. The speaker addresses a statue of the Madonna — "wax-faced, wooden-bodied," stored away for years among "sacramenting moths" — and demands more than "smell-stale incense" and "dusty grandeur" from the "petulant and cranky princess": "Turn not aside Thy pretty-painted face, parade and meet our audience-eyes you must." Elizabeth was imitating Gerard Manley Hopkins in alliterative lines packed with stressed syllables; she would later dismiss her collegiate experiments with sprung rhythm as failures. But in evoking a female deity, she'd adapted Father Hopkins's spiritual questioning to her own circumstances. In place of his Jesuit community, she'd had a girls' camp and boarding school, now a women's college, where unbelievers and "reds" debated issues of faith and justice. The poem was personal too. On arrival at Vassar, Elizabeth had banished her own mother, listing her as deceased, yet she still must have wished for the impossible, a miracle: Gertrude's return to meet Elizabeth's eyes after so many years locked away.

During her senior year, Elizabeth sold "Then Came the Poor" and "Hymn to the Virgin" to a new literary monthly, *The Magazine,* for $26.18, a princely sum in those dark times. But the greater reward for her *Con Spirito* efforts had come in the spring of her junior year, with T. S. Eliot's visit to campus for Hallie Flanagan's premiere of his first

ELIZABETH BISHOP
Great Village
Nova Scotia

Elizabeth's senior photo,
Vassar College yearbook, 1934

verse play, *Sweeney Agonistes,* in May 1933. Elizabeth's reputation as poet and upstart literary editor earned her an assignment from the *Miscellany News* to interview Eliot, who was in the United States for the year to deliver the prestigious Norton Lectures at Harvard.

Despite her jittery nerves and the formal setting in the founder's suite on a hot spring day — Eliot, who "looked exhausted and sat mopping his brow" after giving a lecture, was seated in one of Matthew Vassar's plush velvet armchairs, and Elizabeth, dressed in a light summer suit and spectator pumps, settled as best she could on an immense horsehair sofa, her short legs dangling, trying hard not to slide off — she pursued the questions most on her mind. What did Mr. Eliot think of "spontaneous" campus publications like *Con Spirito*? Elizabeth, who had been considering soliciting manuscripts for the journal, was reassured by the poet's pronouncement, based on "his experience at Oxford and Cambridge," that such magazines were "more interesting and had more character the fewer the editors and the fewer the contributors." Eliot, who praised Flanagan's production of *Sweeney,* a one-room one-act play featuring prostitutes and the burly Sweeney as its lead characters, explained his theory that the "rhythmic forms, and rhymed verses" he'd employed, picking up on jazz syncopations, had a more promising future on the modern stage than blank verse, the province of Shakespeare and his contemporaries.

The mood in the founder's suite must have lightened; Eliot asked if he could loosen his tie. Something emboldened the shy but puckish Elizabeth to gently tease the poet: had Mr. Eliot "ever done a girl in" — murdered a woman? She was referring to Sweeney's sinister lines, "Any man has to, needs to, wants to / Once in a lifetime, do a girl in." No, the forty-five-year-old author of *The Waste Land* replied — was he amused? — "I am not the type."

A year later Elizabeth was once again seated on a bench, the left-hand one in the grand hallway outside the New York Public Library's second-floor reading room, and "scared out of my wits." She'd taken the train into the city to meet another poet, one she admired more deeply than Eliot, Marianne Moore. Moore was Eliot's contemporary, but she was not well known on the Vassar campus, or much at all beyond the circle of writers she'd edited at the modernist *Dial* in the late 1920s: Ezra Pound, Eliot, E. E. Cummings, William Carlos Williams. Elizabeth had been forced to make a determined effort to find Moore's poetry in small magazines. The college library didn't yet own a copy of her first book published in the United States, *Observations,* though Vassar's librarian, who by lucky chance knew Moore's family, had arranged this meeting.

Perhaps it was Moore's densely worded commentary on Eliot's *Sweeney Agonistes* in *Poetry,* quoted in the *Miscellany News* the same week Elizabeth's interview was published, that caught her attention: "Mortal and sardonic victims though we are in the conflict called experience, we may regard our victimage with calmness." Elizabeth would soon strive to emulate Marianne Moore's equanimity, her "impersonal" approach to literary reputation: she "goes right on producing perhaps one poem a year and a couple of reviews that are perfect in their way," despite being "practically unread." But for now what mattered was Moore's thrilling originality. "I hadn't known poetry could be like that," Elizabeth marveled at the "miracles of language and construction" in the copy of *Observations* the college librarian loaned her. "Why had no one ever written about things in this clear and dazzling way before?" Moore wrote odes "To a Snail," "To a Steam Roller," and on "Those Various Scalpels." Her terse disquisition in verse, "Poetry," began as irreverent conversation: "I, too, dislike it." In "An Octopus," about a mountain range not the sea animal, Moore argued for "relentless accuracy" and the "capacity for fact." Moore had gone beyond Hopkins to practice a metrics based on syllable counts alone, and her rhymes were often so well hidden as to be undetectable on a first or even second reading. Here was a woman writing poetry with a complete absence of sentimentality, who could win praise in the pages of the *Dial* for creating "the self-portrait of a mind . . . not as a model, and not as beauty, but as experience."

On this April day in 1934, Elizabeth was dressed impeccably in a black jacket trimmed with sealskin, pearl earrings, and white gloves. The forty-six-year-old Moore wore a blue tweed suit with a black bow tied at the broad collar of her white blouse, her fading red hair wound around her head in one long braid — "quaint . . . but stylish." If Elizabeth had known that Moore had chosen the public library as a meeting place so she could escape easily if she found Elizabeth dull, the college senior would have been even more terrified. But to the surprise of both skittish women, "it went very well." Elizabeth's "ability and technical interest," her "concentrated and selective" taste, Moore said later, were already evident in the list of questions she carried with her in a small notebook and that the older poet happily answered: "It is almost scary ... to find a college student with so much sense." The year before, at his request, Elizabeth had sent Mr. Eliot copies of *Con Spirito,* and he'd written back a note conveying favorable impressions. At this first meeting with Marianne Moore, Elizabeth didn't mention her own writing, and she would not show her a poem for more than a year. They spoke instead of their mutual fondness for Hopkins, and for the circus. Elizabeth didn't yet know where she would live after graduation from Vassar, or what she would do. But she would take Miss Moore to the circus when it next came to town.

Vassar had not been like Walnut Hill School, but Elizabeth found a home there despite her initial failures in music, despite the disturbing reappearance of Mike from Camp Chequesset as a gym teacher at the college. Elizabeth learned that Mike was "having affairs" with students. Mike wasn't "a bad woman just very unfortunate," it seemed to Elizabeth, now that she was no longer a "tomboy" and safely identified as a poet and an "intellectual." Elizabeth herself may have begun a flirtation with Louise Crane while at Vassar; the woman she loved was Margaret Miller, but she did not tell her so. She had dated several men, but no one attracted her as Walnut Hill's Judy Flynn had, as Margaret did now.

By senior year Elizabeth had become an editor of the college yearbook and a minor campus celebrity, thanks to publication in *The Magazine.* She'd even resumed music study with a yearlong course, Music as a Literature. She lived in a coveted tower room in a suite she shared with Margaret Miller. "A ladder goes up out of our living room," Elizabeth wrote with satisfaction to a new friend, Donald Stanford, a Harvard graduate student and aspiring poet introduced to her through the mail by Ivor Winters, an editor of the avant-garde journal *Hound & Horn,* which had recently awarded Elizabeth honorable mention for poems she'd entered in a young writers' competition. "Once up among the elaborate Victorian iron railings," she continued, "it's a very nice spot to smoke a dishonest cigarette." With Stanford, Elizabeth established her first serious correspondence about poetry and the writing life, which, like all such later correspondences, would be more about life — *observing* life — than about poetry. "The chimney pots here (my exclusive view from one window) are shaped rather like a merry-go-round," she wrote as her last year in school drew to a close, "and all winter long the birds have come and sat in them to warm themselves. First they sit with their tails inside, then they switch around and warm their heads. It's a very amusing sight. I'll even draw you a picture of it."

April 29, 1975
NINTH-FLOOR CONFERENCE ROOM, HOLYOKE CENTER

I was the worst kind of student poet, nearly illiterate in contemporary poetry and writing to relieve an immobilizing sadness that had overtaken me the year before as a junior at Bennington College. And I wasn't a student. My depression had led me to drop out of college — schoolwork, even at Bennington, which gave no grades, felt like too much pressure — and move to Cambridge, taking a room in a communal apartment at $27 a month (heat not included) and a secretarial job at Harvard, working in the college registrar's office in Holyoke Center, just one floor below the conference room where I was now sitting. Getting a position in one of Harvard's many administrative offices, I'd heard, was an easy matter if you could pass the typing test.

That was the winter of the energy crisis, 1973–74, a particularly cold one, and the cost of heating oil had skyrocketed, making the low rent a doubtful bargain. From my room on the top floor of a River Street tenement, which swayed in the wind blowing up off the Charles, I checked the temperature on the electrified Coca-Cola sign across the river each morning before venturing outside and passing a long row of cars puffing steam as their drivers waited in line for the cheapest gas in town, at the Arco station up the street. The first glimmer that my depression was lifting arrived as a fleeting sense of joy that I wasn't living in Southern California, where I'd grown up, dependent on a car to get anywhere, or Bennington, where it was so much colder. Still, I walked the mile to work at Harvard's new ten-story concrete-and-glass administration building at the center of Harvard Square, saving bus fare so I could afford the steeply discounted therapy sessions that anchored my days.

My job required me to type information gleaned from the application folders of the incoming freshman class onto permanent record cards, on which student grades would be entered over the next four years. Into my humming IBM Selectric typewriter I rolled a stiff 8½-by-11-inch white card printed horizontally, with blanks for name, birth date, home address, high school, and SAT scores along the top, and spaces for eight semesters of grades below. Next I opened an application folder and soon became lost in the drama of an accepted student's personal essay, letters of recommendation, and the admissions committee's notes. "GOOD HARVARD SON" appeared with predictable frequency, scrawled across an application's first page. Although women (a new self-appellation for college girls in the 1970s) were granted admission in those years to a combined Harvard-Radcliffe, the enrollment ratio stood at 3 to 1 in favor of men, and the legacy preference went unquestioned.

It pained me to read the heartfelt words of those academically well-fed young men and women so close to my own age, the praise that poured forth from their teachers. I typed out unfamiliar names — The Pingree School, The Groton School, New Trier High School, Milton Academy — many times over. No one from my high school in Pasadena, a relatively new one built to accommodate baby-boom teenagers, had ever attended Harvard; I'd been turned down when I applied. But I couldn't stop reading, even when my supervisor chided me for taking so long with what should have been a simple task.

Occasionally I was asked to go to the "vault," where the record cards were stored, and retrieve a card to make a grade change (accomplished by my supervisor with careful application of single-edged razor, fountain pen, and black ink). I was nearly fired the day I lingered too long in the windowless room lined with dark metal file cabinets after realizing I could look up my father's card, class of '42. I wasn't surprised by the scramble of A's and E's (Harvard's F's), or the college-mandated leave of absence that just happened to coincide with my father's wartime service in the merchant marine, but the stark confirmation of whispered family secrets shocked me all the same. I wondered if another story my mother had told me could also be verified. When my father succumbed to a second major depression shortly after their wedding and failed to complete his senior year, the college psychiatrist had ordered my mother, a panicked newlywed who hadn't known about my father's first collapse, "You have married a genius, stand by him!"

I was thinking about my father, now fifty-four years old and a puffy yet still handsome version of the dark-haired, hollow-eyed youth in the black-and-white photo clipped to the card, wondering which of three typical moods he was in back home in Pasadena—comatose with depression, manically spouting urban-renewal schemes, passed-out drunk—when the registrar swooped down and pulled me into her office, threatening dismissal if she caught me looking at my father's record card again. I cried and promised I would not. My father's frightening example was why my sad feelings scared me, why I was in Cambridge and not California. Why I did not tell my long-suffering mother what was going on in my life. I needed to keep my job.

Maybe it was then I started to become a shadow student, began to wish for college again. I learned which dorms I could enter by following a student closely and catching the door, which cafeterias I could access through an unguarded exit and help myself to yogurt and cereal at breakfast, or the salad bar at lunch or dinner. I wasn't earning much, but that wasn't the only reason I sometimes sat alone with my stolen meal in the company of Harvard students in the high-ceilinged Freshman Union or at the sleek modern tables in Quincy House; my roommates on River Street were all grad students in their late twenties, caught up in radical politics, and I felt even more a stranger there. One of them invited me to attend a session of her consciousness-raising group on a Saturday morning in our apartment, cautioning me that I would not be invited to join.

So I auditioned for the new Harvard-Radcliffe choir for mixed voices, established two years before when the dorms had gone co-ed and open to faculty and staff as well as students, but I hid my secretary status from the other altos when I got in. I'd read the application file of one of them: Beaver Country Day School. A piano practice room at street level in Adams House caught my eye, and soon I was writing my name on the sign-up sheet and spending an hour at the Steinway grand whenever I could.

Losing music had been part of my sadness. When I'd first arrived in Cambridge in January, I'd scheduled a visit to the converted warehouse near Lechmere Sales where Bill Dowd built harpsichords. That's where I should have looked for work. I'd been playing the instrument for five years, after switching over from the piano in high school because I loved Bach; the early music revival was on, and Bach could no longer be played on the piano in good conscience. I learned to appreciate the quirkier styles of Couperin and Rameau, Scarlatti and Soler, and I excelled in the tricky ornaments — trills, mordents, turns — that embellish baroque keyboard music. I can't say whether it was the heightened demands of preparing for a solo career on the harpsichord — the persistent terror of performing from memory, the requirement to master the irksome tasks of tuning and repairing so sensitive an instrument — or the teachers I'd traveled from Bennington to study with each week that put me off. I never auditioned at Yale for Ralph Kirkpatrick, the great Scarlatti cataloguer and Bach specialist, who sometimes accepted students from other colleges; I'd heard he hid behind a screen or in a closet when women came to play for him. Instead, I spent a semester with a Miss Havisham–like protégé of Wanda Landowska who lived in the defunct diva's country house in Connecticut and taught me to play each piece precisely as *la Maîtresse* had. Next came lessons with a young Manhattan phenom, who greeted me in the hallway outside his Upper West Side apartment with open-mouthed kisses and massaged my back while I played, leaning in for more, reaching for my breasts. I could hear his opera-singer wife warming up with scales in an adjacent room. That's when, if not why, I quit.

But though I left the Dowd factory in Cambridge without speaking to the master builder, I bought a second-balcony ticket to one of Arthur Rubinstein's last Boston concerts soon after. The gilt glory of Symphony Hall, the lush sounds that reached me from the distant piano, brought tears — the first not shed in my therapist's office or before my boss that winter. When I sneaked into the Adams House practice room I was carrying Chopin and Schumann scores checked out of the music library with my staff ID card. The pieces I played felt as illicit as my use of the piano. The crashing chords, the swelling pedal, the singing melodies — I'd left them all behind in my years at the harpsichord, and mercifully they came back to me when I needed them to revive my capacity for emotions other than sadness. To give shape to my sadness.

I began to write again too. My mother had taught me to love poetry, reading aloud at bedtime from children's anthologies; her mother had sung to me settings from Stevenson's *A Child's Garden of Verses* while I lay on my parents' bed after school and watched her iron my father's shirts that my working mother didn't have time to press. My grandmother's songs blotted out the fact of my father's disturbing presence in the house. He was often asleep in a faded wing chair downstairs in the spare room, once the family TV room, that passed as his office since he'd been fired from yet another city-planning job. I'd begun writing poetry at age eight, and my mother helped me mail one of my rhymes to the editor of the children's page at the local paper, earning publication and a few dollars in prize money.

The poems I submitted a dozen years later for admission to Robert Lowell's workshop class in January 1975 were written out of ignorance, out of sorrow numbed by fear. I'd quit the job at Harvard to work as a research assistant and typist for a famous writer in Boston. He wrote at night and slept during the day, and our meetings took place at dinnertime in his townhouse apartment. He liked my work. He liked me. I'd come to expect this sort of thing; it had happened with music teachers, professors, a camp counselor. The attentions of a famous writer are flattering. I slept with him and told him I enjoyed it, half believing it was so; I needed to keep my job. Yet where could this lead?

I'd saved enough money to pay for three courses as an unenrolled "special" student at Harvard, two literature seminars on English novels and the Romantics and Lowell's workshop, if I could get in. I'd applied to the class not having read a line of his poetry. Still, in an uncanny way, I'd written poems that aped his style, or appealed to Lowell's sensibility. One, titled "November 9," evoked my frozen mood by describing the few items in my sparsely decorated room on that day in 1974. Another, "Through-Composed," employed the term for a piece of music without repeated themes or cadences as a metaphor signifying the challenge of living into an unknown future. When I read my name on the list of ten accepted students posted on the ninth-floor conference room door in early February, I quit working for the famous writer, who punched me in the shoulder and then stomped on my foot on the brick sidewalk in front of his apartment building as I left. I could get along for the next four months on my savings and food stamps, and look for a summer job after that.

Professor Lowell, rumpled and wild-eyed, shuffling in his loafers as if they were bedroom slippers, was an irregular participant in his own class that semester. Sometimes his protégé Frank Bidart appeared in his place, explaining a mix-up in the poet's medications. Family members sat in: the poet's third wife, Lady Caroline Blackwood, bright blond and thin in the way of chain smokers; his teenage daughter, Harriet, sullen, restless.

I'd been studying Lowell's poems assiduously since gaining admission to the class. I liked "Eye and Tooth" ("I am tired. Everyone's tired of my turmoil") and "Home After Three Months Away," reading the melancholy stanzas as if they were my own father's apologies for his illness. On his good days, Lowell read his favorite poems out loud — William Carlos Williams's "The Yachts," or Donne's "The Relic" and "A Valediction: Forbidding Mourning" — marveling at excellent lines and turns of phrase, making us love them too. But none of this prepared me for the lure of a poem titled simply, "Poem."

On an April afternoon I entered the classroom to find a small older woman with short, stiff white hair, clad in an elegant light-wool suit and carrying a thin black binder, taking a seat across the conference table from mine. Professor Lowell introduced his friend Elizabeth Bishop — *"Miss Bishop,"* he purred in his southern-tinged Boston Brahmin drawl. Now it was our guest's turn to read. She smiled obligingly, somehow both coy and businesslike, and took a sheaf of photocopies out of her binder, handing around "Poem," as it had appeared in the *New Yorker* several years before.

The scene "Poem" evoked contrasted strikingly with the cityscape captured in the picture windows behind the writer's bowed head as she leaned over the page — Harvard's brick dormitory rooftops, the campanile of St. Paul's Church. "About the size of an old-style dollar bill":

she was introducing a tiny landscape painted in oils by her uncle — no, really her "great-uncle," she corrected herself in the poem, taking us back a generation, and then one more, to a Nova Scotia pasture — a "water meadow" — populated by "minuscule" geese and cows, with the brown and white houses and green shade trees of a country town in the background, storm clouds overhead. She read in a low, hoarse smoker's voice, smoothed out with the buttery *r*'s of New England's upper crust, yet given to flat inflections, the plain language of country folk. Or was it plain?

> *A specklike bird is flying to the left.*
> *Or is it a flyspeck looking like a bird?*

The painting was old — more than seventy years old — and hadn't been cared for by the descendants of the great-uncle with dubious talent. Still, a white-and-yellow wild iris in the foreground appeared to be "fresh-squiggled from the tube."

Then — "Heavens, I recognize the place, I know it!" — the speaker affirms. "Poem" was not about the miniature scene, but about a miraculous coincidence: "I never knew him" — the great-uncle — yet "We both knew this place . . . looked at it long enough to memorize it, / our years apart." It was about the ways this small family heirloom, "useless and free," collapsed "life and the memory of it" into each other. "Which is which?" the poet asked —

> *Life and the memory of it cramped,*
> *dim, on a piece of Bristol board,*
> *dim, but how live, how touching in detail*
> *— the little that we get for free,*
> *the little of our earthly trust. Not much.*
> *About the size of our abidance*
> *along with theirs: the munching cows,*
> *the iris, crisp and shivering, the water*
> *still standing from spring freshets,*
> *the yet-to-be-dismantled elms, the geese.*

⤜ 2 ⤛

Crumb

OW CAME TRAGEDIES Elizabeth could have written about, but didn't. Two weeks before commencement, in late May 1934, her mother died at age fifty-four in the sanatorium in Dartmouth, Nova Scotia, where she'd lived since 1916. In a letter to Frani Blough, one of the first friends in whom she had confided about Gertrude years ago at Walnut Hill, Elizabeth offered the news in a terse postscript at the end of several chatty pages about summer plans — "I guess I should tell you that Mother died a week ago today. After eighteen years, of course, it is the happiest thing that could have happened."

"Apoplexy," the result of a cerebral hemorrhage or stroke, was the cause recorded on her mother's death certificate, with "Chronic Psychosis" listed as the "contributory" factor. Elizabeth would not read these words for more than a decade, and she may not have been told anything at the time beyond the fact of Gertrude's death. If she attended the burial at Hope Cemetery in Worcester, where Gertrude was interred next to William — her parents joined for the first time since Elizabeth was a baby — she told none of her friends. More likely she stayed at Vassar, where, she confided later to her psychoanalyst, she had been prone to crying jags that spring, often following a night of drinking in Poughkeepsie with Louise Crane, who'd abandoned her college studies but still took the train or drove up from New York City to visit friends. Elizabeth's mother was on her mind "constantly" as

she looked toward the months and years ahead that seemed frighten-
ingly blank without the community and structure of school.

Perhaps when she wrote to Frani that her mother's death was "the
happiest thing," Elizabeth hoped she might be able to put an end to
her persistent anxiety; there was no need any longer to imagine her
mother's daily life on a locked ward, in a walled garden. The death she
had sometimes lied about, even wished for, was finally real. But could
that make any difference now? Uncle Jack Bishop believed firmly that
there was "no hereditary tendency to insanity" in the family, as he'd
told Miss Farlow, but Frani understood that for Elizabeth the "fear of
inheriting her mother's illness was a horrible thing" she "consciously"
willed herself to suppress. During the year after her mother's death,
she jotted down a rhyming poem in one of her notebooks that started
out cheerfully enough but ended starkly:

> *The past*
> *at least*
> *is polite:*
> *it keeps out of sight.*
>
> *The present*
> *is more recent.*
> *It makes a fuss*
> *but is unselfconscious.*
>
> *The future*
> *sinks through water*
> *fast as a stone,*
> *alone alone.*

Rhyme, Elizabeth wrote in her journal around the same time, is "mystical." Such poems, perhaps all her poems, were charms against the
loneliness they often expressed.

When she wasn't thinking about her mother that last spring at Vassar, she was thinking about Margaret Miller — slim, raven-haired, soi-
gné, everything that plucky Elizabeth, still something of a tousled kid

in appearance, despite her smartly tailored suits and pearl earrings, was not. And Margaret, a scholarship student, had a mother to whom she was close and with whom she could share a modest New York City flat after graduation. It wasn't just Margaret's inclination to shrink from Elizabeth's few gestures of physical affection during the year they'd spent together as roommates at Vassar that told her a romance would not work out. Margaret's emotions were even more contained than Elizabeth's — Margaret never broke down in tears, never drank herself into a state of oblivion, although she was usually patient with Elizabeth when she did, sat beside her on the floor and patted her head when she was "howling away about my mother," the only way Elizabeth could safely release in Margaret's presence the dread she felt at their impending separation.

Elizabeth had tried to distract herself by dating Bob Seaver, who'd fallen in love with her soon after they met, the summer before she'd entered Vassar. Bob was an older friend of a girl in Elizabeth's Walnut Hill School circle; he'd already graduated from Hamilton College and was attending business school at Harvard. A survivor of polio in his early teens, Bob walked with crutches and relied on wit and a wide literary reference to charm women; he rarely lacked for female companionship. His physical limitations may have made Bob seem safe; Bob may have sensed that Elizabeth's extreme shyness made her more accepting of an unconventional male. They talked easily. When Bob left

Margaret Miller

Harvard to take a teaching job in a school near his hometown in Pittsfield, Massachusetts, seventy miles north of Poughkeepsie, and later a position in a Pittsfield bank, there was nothing to stop Elizabeth from joining him for an occasional unchaperoned weekend. He gave her his fraternity pin. During the winter of her senior year, they spent a "wonderful, romantic" week on Nantucket at Christmas, Elizabeth would say later, and after graduation she rented a cottage for most of July on sparsely populated Cuttyhunk Island, on the edge of Buzzards Bay, and invited Bob to stay with her for several days.

It was the last vacation Elizabeth spent with Bob. She was happier after he left, when she could indulge the "island feeling" of "making this do for that, and contriving and inventing." More vivid to her in recollection was the weekend house party at Louise Crane's summer home in Dalton, Massachusetts, just before Bob had joined Elizabeth at Cuttyhunk: sharing a room there with Margaret Miller for what seemed like the last time, sobbing and finally telling her how much she'd miss living with her. This time, in the Cranes' big house, Margaret shushed her.

When Bob asked Elizabeth to marry him, she could not accept. She would never marry anyone, she told him, hoping the rejection would hurt less, and it must have seemed to her the truth. He turned fierce, berating her. Bob guessed, or somehow knew, although Elizabeth never spoke to him of her love for Margaret or any woman, that "I'd like him better if he were a girl"; she seemed to "have it in for" men. The accuracy of the first of his charges, which Elizabeth would not dare admit, was no comfort in close quarters with someone she cared about, although not in the way he'd hoped. She liked Bob — he was one of the few men she *did* like — and wasn't afraid of him, and yet she felt trapped, chained to the bed listening to his accusations in the "cheap hotel" where they'd gone for a night to find a future that left each of them alone.

A year later Bob shot himself. His suicide note was directed to the "girl" who had refused his marriage proposal, a postcard she received while staying at the Hotel Chelsea, one of several residences she adopted in the 1930s and '40s in or near Greenwich Village, choosing to live close to Margaret in New York City rather than hide away in

Boston as she had once planned: "Elizabeth, Go to hell." The message struck at the helplessness and shame she'd often felt when imagining her mother's fate, yet there could be nothing "happiest" about the way this failed romance reached a conclusion.

Mary McCarthy found Elizabeth her first apartment, at 16 Charles Street, two small rooms that Elizabeth planned to fill slowly on her slim budget, acquiring one piece of furniture each month. Nobody except Louise in her grand Fifth Avenue apartment, where her mother lived at one end and Louise at the other, with a salon for concerts and parties in between, had much space or adequate furnishings. Mary, orphaned at age six and, like Elizabeth, raised by a succession of relatives, had graduated from Vassar a year ahead and quickly married Harold Jonsrud, a playwright. Elizabeth remembered a visit when she slept in a cot at Mary's place, while Mary and Harold shared another.

After "figuring up my standing at the bank, my debts, my prospects" in July 1934, Elizabeth was reassured that her funds, soon to be augmented by her mother's portion of the Bishop estate, would cover rent and necessities. She would not need a job any time soon, and she could save toward travel if she lived economically. By September she'd purchased a desk, bookshelves, a table, and two chairs. For entertainment there were parks nearby — Washington Square and Union Square — and the pleasant distraction of "riding around aimlessly on trollies and buses" after a morning spent typing up poems and sending them off to their "ill-fated destinations" at magazines and quarterly journals. Elizabeth did not expect success right away, although she'd begun collecting names of poetry editors at publishing houses. To remind herself of the discipline she hoped to practice — to "get to work" promptly each day — she would ask Margaret to paint a beautifully lettered sign for the foot of her bed bearing John Donne's lines: "But as for one which hath a long taske, 'tis good, / With the Sunne to beginne his business."

The city that fall was on the rebound from the bleakest years of the Depression, when one in four New Yorkers were unemployed and shantytowns sprouted up along the East River. There was hope for better times under the newly elected mayor, Fiorello La Guardia, who energetically courted New Deal sponsorship of relief programs and ambitious public works projects. During Elizabeth's Vassar years, the Empire State Building and Rockefeller Center were completed, monuments to pre-Crash excess that nevertheless gave the Manhattan she moved to a sense of confident — if deferred — prosperity and enterprise. The George Washington Bridge now spanned the Hudson, breaching the city's insularity.

But Elizabeth's Manhattan was Greenwich Village, with its three- and four-story row houses on narrow streets with names instead of numbers, where rent was cheap and artists and intellectuals could get by on freelance pay, where the New School offered classes like the seminar in Early Keyboard Music that Elizabeth attended in the winter of 1934–35, taught by a brilliant young harpsichordist just her age, Ralph Kirkpatrick. She took notes on composers and ornamentation — appoggiatura, slide, inverted mordent — and planned to buy a clavichord, the much smaller and more portable precursor to the modern piano, softer in tone than a harpsichord, when she could afford it.

Elizabeth lived two blocks from Christopher Street, where Bonnie's Stone Wall Inn advertised itself to those in the know as a bar welcoming lesbians, as female "inverts" were increasingly called, by taking the title of the autobiographical confessions of the pseudonymous Mary Casal for its name. Elizabeth may never have visited the place. She may not have read *The Stone Wall,* published in 1930. But she had probably heard of the melodramatic tale, one of the first such narratives published in the United States, in which Mary's "sex desire for woman" leads her to propose marriage to her beloved Juno. After enacting a private wedding ceremony, the two women live happily together in what appears to others to be "an ideal friendship," supporting themselves in the city as an artist and a schoolteacher: "No one knew of the real union, of our bodies." Despite years of harmony, Juno strays; recriminations and recombinations with other lovers follow. "When at its best, as was ours for so many years," Mary writes, "I still believe the love between two women to be the highest type now known. At the same time, I believe that it may lead to the most intense suffering known to woman."

Elizabeth may not have believed that love between women was of the "highest type" — that notion belonged to the era of the Walnut Hill

School's founders—but she understood the "intense suffering" that same-sex love could bring. Both passion and loss had to be concealed. To speak or write openly was impossible; to resist the implicit notion that her love for women was shameful took courage that Elizabeth didn't always have, or that sometimes required alcohol to bolster. In later years she confided to her analyst that all her love affairs had begun while she was drunk. Elizabeth was never one to join the cause of sexual liberation or to identify herself publicly as a lesbian, but in the 1930s there was safety in an urban neighborhood like Greenwich Village, where an establishment like Bonnie's Stone Wall could thrive, hidden in plain sight.

For a while Elizabeth's love for Margaret, still unattainable, and her refusal of marriage to a man she did not desire, left her free for New School classes and private French lessons, to work her way through an ambitious reading list she set for herself at the public library when she found it impossible to write at home every morning, to try out a job as a writing teacher with a correspondence school that she gave up after two weeks. And to establish a friendship with Marianne Moore, who may have drawn her to the city as much as Margaret Miller did.

Although Moore had graduated from Bryn Mawr College twenty-five years before, she remained intriguingly girlish, with her slender figure, coiled braid, and undying passion for the amusements of childhood. Like Elizabeth, she had never known her father, who had been hospitalized for mental illness at the time of her birth and was committed to an asylum soon after. Moore's closest attachment was to her mother, a retired English teacher who vetted all of the poet's work and with whom she shared a two-bedroom apartment in Brooklyn, the second bedroom given over to books and papers. At first Elizabeth felt an awed reluctance to impose on Miss Moore, as she addressed her in person and in letters for several years, until Marianne requested that she use her first name; but not so much that she didn't follow through on her plan to escort the poet to the circus at Madison Square Garden just weeks after their first meeting, arriving early to feed the elephants. Elizabeth wrote often after that, suggesting books — *The Animal Mind,* by a Vassar professor of animal psychology, and *English Handwriting* by Roger Fry — and carefully planned outings: a viewing of the anthropologists Osa and Martin Johnson's documentary on baboons, a drive to Coney Island with Louise Crane for supper and rides on the merry-go-round. Mrs. Moore could come along.

Elizabeth soon learned the route by subway to the Moores' apartment on Cumberland Street — a name that may have recalled her grandparents' Cumberland Road house in Great Village — where her hostess kept a bowl of nickels on a bookcase by the front door to cover her guests' return fare. Marianne Moore was close in age to Elizabeth's favorite aunt, Grace, and watched over the fledgling poet with a similar attentiveness. Elizabeth watched closely too, as her mentor advanced in public reputation that year with the appearance of a second book, *Selected Poems,* introduced by T. S. Eliot, and a promotional portrait by the celebrity photographer George Platt Lynes printed in the New York papers. Elizabeth was enough of a Moore family insider by then to praise the type size in the new book and the "very nice" photograph when it was published in the Sunday *Herald Tribune.*

In the years ahead, Elizabeth would send drafts of her poems to Marianne Moore, waiting to receive her inevitable criticism and praise before sending them out for publication. But in the early days of their acquaintance, Moore's sense of vocation was the prime lesson she

Marianne Moore,
photograph by George Platt Lynes, 1935

took, even if only some aspects of it stuck, chiefly in matters of craft. Elizabeth would never imitate, but her range of subjects grew to include singular objects and animals, even a fish, perhaps in answer to Moore's famous "The Fish," which opened as a school of fish "wade / through black jade." She would always share with Moore a near obsession with accuracy of detail and precision of language. Form intrigued both poets, though Elizabeth's poems more often adopted traditional figures, while Moore, as a pioneering modernist, invented shapes on the page. Above all she learned from Moore "never to try to publish anything until I thought I'd done my best with it, no matter how many years it took — or never to publish at all."

Marianne Moore led a highly disciplined life with her mother in Brooklyn, ascetic and abstemious, unaltered by such fame as she earned by publication. On her own, Elizabeth tried to follow suit, "pulling her mind up to the surface" each morning, as she wrote in her journal at Charles Street, "like a bucketful of water out of [a] well." Often she came up empty. She jotted observations and ideas in notebooks she carried with her, so that she seemed to others always to be writing. But the process was never efficient and could be "painful," she once explained to a friend: "she first wrote a poem in her head, but the act of writing, putting it down, was usually a letdown, so then she either put it away, destroyed it, or rewrote it." Drafts were covered with crossouts, often emphatic ones, and severe judgments like "TERRIBLE." Days passed with little to show for her efforts. "I've always felt that I've written poetry more by *not* writing it than writing it," she would one day reflect. Occasionally poems came to her fully or partially formed in dreams, or at odd hours of the night or early morning. These were gifts.

One of these arrived on New Year's Eve after five months in New York, after a combination of flu and asthma had kept her mostly in bed for two weeks at the end of December 1934; she'd fled Christmas dinner with Margaret Miller and her mother, wheezing from an asthma attack. Elizabeth had amused — or distracted — herself on this solitary night, when she might have been at a party with her old *Con Spirito* friends Eleanor Clark and Mary McCarthy, by dialing MEridian 7-1212, the number New Yorkers called to find out the time, to listen for any change of tone in the recorded voice when the New Year came. There was none. But she spent much of the evening poring over a framed map of the North Atlantic, studying Canada's easternmost coastline, the boundaries of Newfoundland and Labrador, where she'd taken a walking tour one college summer. She puzzled over the colors and markings, and constructed a poem, "The Map," that would be the strongest she had written so far, one that was itself framed by two stanzas of eight lines each, arranged in a mesmerizing pattern of rhymes and repeated end words:

> *Land lies in water; it is shadowed green.*
> *Shadows, or are they shallows, at its edges*
> *showing the line of long sea-weeded ledges*
> *where weeds hang to the simple blue from green.*
> *Or does the land lean down to lift the sea from under,*
> *drawing it unperturbed around itself?*
> *Along the fine tan sandy shelf*
> *is the land tugging at the sea from under?*

While at Vassar, Elizabeth had written to Donald Stanford that she believed a poem ought to convey the effect of being "in action, within itself." Here she had found a way to do it. Statements, refined and expanded by questions that follow, would become a characteristic means of drawing the reader into her process of thought. As Marianne Moore wrote some years later in an admiring review of Elizabeth's work, "tentativeness can be more positive than positiveness."

Had Elizabeth asked herself "The Map"'s questions as long ago as the days in Great Village School, when she'd gazed at Canada's meandering outline and envied the older children their study of geography: Are those shadows or shallows? Is the land tugging at the sea? An imaginative girl who could not ask what was most on her mind — will my mother come back? — might have let her mind wander this way. In the poem's interior stanza of eleven unrhymed lines, the yellow of Labrador appears "oiled," like the glossy pull-down maps of childhood. And what of the map Aunt Grace had traced in the nap of a white bathroom carpet? The aunts, who'd taken Elizabeth along on their daily errands, are here too: "These peninsulas take the water between thumb and finger / like women feeling for the smoothness of yard-goods."

Elizabeth's poems of the decade after graduation from Vassar were rarely autobiographical, but they drew on personal experience and asked questions, sometimes obliquely, that were her own: "Are they assigned, or can the countries pick their colors?" Shouldn't their hues be determined by "what suits the character or the native waters best"? The search for belonging, for home, could hardly find a better metaphor than a map. She considers the map's printer, who has allowed the names of seaside towns to "run out to sea," the names of cities to "cross the neighboring mountains / . . . experiencing the same excitement / as when emotion too far exceeds its cause." Knowing how, and how much, she ought to feel had so often troubled Elizabeth. "The Map" gathered force from her own "tugging" from under, and the poem earned her prominent publication in an anthology, *Trial Balances,* in which established poets introduced younger ones. Marianne Moore served as her sponsor, describing Elizabeth's work as "archaically new" and praising its "rational considering quality" as well as her "flicker of impudence."

A second gift of inspiration came ten days later — "A Little Miracle," as Elizabeth titled her account of the incident in her Charles Street journal. She'd woken to find she'd forgotten to buy bread and had only a "dry crust" for breakfast. Resigning herself to orange juice and coffee and "no more," she was startled by a ring of the doorbell and the subsequent appearance on the stairs of a "weary-looking woman," a representative of Wonder Bread bakeries, which had begun marketing sliced bread nationally in the 1930s. "I don't want to *sell* you anything — I want to *give* you something," Elizabeth heard the woman call up the stairs, and she was soon the recipient of "a small box containing three slices . . . all fresh, a rye, a white, and whole-wheat," as well as a "miniature" loaf unsliced. Instead of the dry crust, "I breakfasted on manna."

Elizabeth's composition of "A Miracle for Breakfast," the sestina that had its origins in that morning's surprise, was more characteristic of her halting progress than the swiftly composed "The Map." Two summers would pass before she found the form and voice with which to realize the incident's potential and enclosed the finished poem in a letter to Marianne Moore. During that time she'd given up her apartment on Charles Street for a year in Europe, spent mostly with Louise Crane.

On the voyage over, begun in late July 1935, before Louise joined her in the French countryside and then in a luxurious Parisian apartment rented for the two younger women by Louise's mother, Elizabeth had been overcome by the sharpest sadness she had felt in years — a condition she could only describe as profound "homesickness," she wrote in her notebook: "It is as if one were whirled off from all the world & the interests of the world in a sort of cloud-dark sulphurous grey of melancholia." At dinners on board ship, despite the companionship of a college friend, Hallie Tompkins, she found herself unable to "speak, swallow, scarcely breathe" under pressure of this "awful, awful feeling of deathly physical, and mental illness, — something that seems 'after' me." She tried to talk herself out of her depression; at age twenty-four, she felt, "I really have no right to homesickness at all." And what home could she be missing? Her Bulmer grandparents had died in their

Elizabeth's passport photo, 1936

eighties, one after another, in 1930 and 1931, and she had not been back to Great Village since. But the feeling dogged her through a period of sightseeing in Antwerp and Brussels, where paintings in the exhibition rooms at the world's fair "wouldn't stay still — the colors moved inside the frames, the objects moved up closer & then further back."

She found her bearings in a small hotel in Douarnenez, a fishing village in Brittany whose "picturesqueness is just like the water in Salt Lake, you simply can't sink in it," she wrote to Marianne Moore. The seaside town and its inhabitants were both quaint and familiar, reminiscent of Nova Scotia. She stayed for over a month, reading and writing in bed most mornings, until Louise joined her and the two traveled on to Paris. Just when their romance began is uncertain, but there was a quality of child's play, of boarding school hijinks, to the affair at first. They bought a pair of doves from a street vendor to enliven their seven-room apartment on the Rue de Vaugirard, furnished with antiques and staffed by a cook and maid. They joked about having flowers sent to themselves to prevent the maid from pitying their lack of male suitors. Elizabeth began a poem in her notebook that she left unfinished:

> *I looked for the kiss all night*
> *It shone all night through the forest . . .*
> *Like the white crumbs or pebbles the foresters' children*
> *followed home from the heart of the forest.*

> *This morning I found it in my mouth.*

Yet Louise, like nearly all the women Elizabeth fell for, was more grown-up than she: a worldly sophisticate who, unlike Margaret Miller, could match Elizabeth drink for drink and was ready to answer her desire. With Louise, Elizabeth felt cared for — and she was. At Christmastime she caught a cold that brought on acute mastoiditis, requiring surgery and a three-week hospital stay; the Cranes covered much of the cost and supplied a Russian nurse during Elizabeth's convalescence. Elizabeth happily fell in with Louise's high style, though she prided herself on traveling inexpensively — her Atlantic crossing and return on a German freighter had cost only $155. Economizing had permitted her to purchase the clavichord she had wanted using the bulk of a small bequest she'd received when Uncle Jack Bishop, the guardian she'd feared as a child, died the previous spring. The small keyboard instrument, shipped in its convenient carrying case from the Dolmetsch workshop in England, arrived in Paris in time for her to take a half-dozen lessons at the Schola Cantorum with Ralph Kirkpatrick's teacher. She'd acquired a typewriter as well, so she could send off finished drafts to Marianne Moore, who now played her agent, providing introductions to magazine editors; passing along a compliment from another of the eminent *Dial* poets, William Carlos Williams; even sparking interest in an editor at Harper & Brothers, who asked if Elizabeth had enough material for a book. Yet with scarcely more than a handful of polished poems so far, the project could not go forward.

In Douarnenez Elizabeth had been reading and translating Rimbaud, continuing a fascination with the origins of French surrealism, spurred by her library studies and French lessons in New York. She was naturally drawn to surrealism, a movement in literature and the arts roughly contemporaneous with American modernism. She could sympathize with its practitioners' efforts to render in their works "the actual functioning of thought . . . in the absence of any control exercised by reason," as the founding poet and critic André Breton wrote in his "Surrealist Manifesto" of 1924. Elizabeth visited Breton's

Louise Crane and Elizabeth

gallery in Paris and had sightings of the artists Max Ernst and Alberto Giacometti. She made notes for a trio of poems about sleep and the inversion of waking and dream states: "thoughts that were recumbent in the day / rise as the others fall, / stand up and make a forest of thick-set trees."

But Elizabeth's wide-ranging curiosity (she had been reading Isaac Newton's *Optics* as well as Rimbaud) and her disorienting bout of "homesickness" held her back from full commitment to a particular style, especially one marked by skewed or hallucinatory perception. "Some surrealist poetry terrifies me," she wrote in her journal, "because of the sense of irresponsibility & *danger* it gives of the mind being 'broken down' — I want to produce the opposite effect." Poetry — read, recited, written — had long served Elizabeth as a safeguard against such danger. What she preferred, she later wrote, was the "surrealism of everyday life, unexpected moments of empathy" when it is possible to "catch a peripheral vision of whatever it is one can never really see full-face but that seems enormously important." In Douarnenez she had tacked to her wall several pages from Ernst's *Natural History,* images made from pencil rubbings done on strongly grained floorboards so as to reveal strange birds, trees, and forests. Elizabeth saw the series of plates as a comic homage to Darwin; the images were more playful than threatening, and Ernst had used simple, "everyday" materials to glimpse — and capture — the fabulous, to suggest the large and scarcely visible truths of nature.

Only when she was back in the United States, staying in another inexpensive rental, on Cape Cod, for the summer of 1936, did fragments of the past two post-Vassar years of study and experience coalesce in the sestina. And even then, "A Miracle for Breakfast" came close to being cast aside, along with Elizabeth's hopes for becoming a poet. In late August, after a lonely and mostly unproductive two months punctuated by visits from Frani Blough and Margaret Miller, who worked intently on several impressive canvases in a style that united early Picasso and the Pre-Raphaelites, Elizabeth confessed to Marianne Moore that she had sent away for applications to medical school: "I cannot, cannot decide what to do. . . . I feel that I have given myself more than a fair trial, and the accomplishment has been nothing at all." She would rather work hard at "Science . . . or even something quite uncongenial" than devote herself to "POETRY" if she could produce nothing better than "my contemporaries." She apologized for the "great imposition," but asked Moore for a "severe" assessment of her capabilities. She signed herself for the first time simply "Elizabeth."

After all Marianne Moore had already done for her, Elizabeth may have felt she could expect an encouraging reply — and she received one. Moore assured Elizabeth that her work so far was "enviable" and appealed to her sense of calling: "interesting as medicine is, I feel that you would not be able to give up writing." She recognized in Elizabeth, because she knew it in herself, an undeniable and lifesaving need for expression in verse. In the future Elizabeth often despaired of her slow progress and slight output, but she never again considered abandoning her vocation. By return mail she now offered her mentor "A Miracle for Breakfast," the poem that, perhaps more than any other she'd written so far, confirmed Moore's judgment of her protégé's work as "archaically new," while establishing a key element of Elizabeth's own aesthetic: "something needn't be large to be good."

Elizabeth had discovered the sestina form in *The Countess of Pembroke's Arcadia,* Sir Philip Sidney's sixteenth-century masterwork of poetry and prose, and likely knew of more recent attempts by Ezra Pound and W. H. Auden. Sidney's remarkable double sestina in alternating voices employed ordinary — or "colorless," as Elizabeth described them — end words: mountains, valleys, forests, music, morning, evening. The six words could slip easily into the poem's dialogue, their repetition evident but not distracting. Elizabeth chose instead a mix of both "colorless" and "unusual" end words — coffee, crumb, balcony, miracle, sun, river — heightening the challenge of achieving fluidity in the rigidly structured form. Years later she identified "A Miracle for Breakfast" as "my Depression poem," with its opening image of breadlines that began to form early each morning in New York City: "At six o'clock we were waiting for coffee, / waiting for coffee and the charitable crumb." When Elizabeth returned from Europe in 1936, almost 20 percent of the city's residents were still receiving public assistance. Yet the river that reappears in each stanza more clearly resembles the Seine than the Hudson; there is little of the newsreel to the scene and

more Old World noblesse oblige or communion rite. The poem's sup-
plicants await the appearance of an official on a balcony above them to
provide "charitable" sustenance — "like kings of old, or like a miracle."

Disappointed when a man finally arrives with only a cup of coffee
and a roll, which he proceeds to crumble and dispense to the hungry
crowd as "one rather hard crumb" each, the narrating "we" turns into
an assertive "I" who performs — or envisions — her own miracle. With
"one eye close to the crumb," the poet's perspective expands in a surrealism of beneficence rather than breakdown; the crumb becomes a
"mansion" glowing in the sun, with "galleries and marble chambers"
giving off the alluring "smell of hot coffee." The poem nearly ends with
this deliverance:

> ... *Every day, in the sun,*
> *at breakfast time I sit on my balcony*
> *with my feet up, and drink gallons of coffee.*

But it is not to be. In the sestina's concluding three-line envoy, the
world returns to its proper dimensions, "I" shrinks back into anonym-
ity, and the poem finishes on a note of longing:

> *We licked up the crumb and swallowed the coffee.*
> *A window across the river caught the sun*
> *as if the miracle were working, on the wrong balcony.*

Although "A Miracle for Breakfast" had its genesis in the free sample of Wonder Bread that had brightened a bleak winter morning in
Greenwich Village, it had taken the "homesickness" of a first Atlantic
crossing, the grandeur of Europe, the luxury of Louise Crane's em-
brace, and Elizabeth's return to the empty Cape Cod house that was
not a home to complete the sestina. If everyday surrealism was at work,
what had been glimpsed in that dizzying close inspection of a crumb
that was so "enormously important"? Not only home and nourish-
ment and confident autonomy, but beauty — the transforming miracle
of art. One night in Paris the winter before, Elizabeth and Louise had
entertained Vassar classmate Hallie Tompkins and her fiancé, and the

quartet had fallen into a debate about beauty — was it subjective or absolute? Hallie's fiancé had argued forcefully that beauty "is in the eye of the beholder." Elizabeth turned emotional, defending the opposite position as best she could until she abruptly left the room. Hallie and Louise found her in the kitchen, "weeping in frustration over a glass of gin." For Elizabeth, her friends learned, "beauty was one of the eternal absolutes."

Despite her recent appeal for guidance, Elizabeth was confident that she had "done my best" with the sestina; it would mark her debut in *Poetry* magazine the following year. Paradoxically, Marianne Moore's swift endorsement seemed to give Elizabeth the courage to challenge her mentor on several points, to begin to move out from under the senior poet's protective wing. "Gallons of coffee" was too colloquial for the fastidious Miss Moore, and "crumb" and "sun" were so nearly alike in sound they created a kind of dissonance. But Elizabeth resisted the criticism. She liked the "boisterousness" of "gallons," she replied with that "flicker of impudence," and as for the clash of "sun" and "crumb," the poem could not have been written without them. There are "certain things," Elizabeth wrote, that "without one particular fault they would be without the means of existence."

Three months after Elizabeth sent Marianne Moore "A Miracle for Breakfast," Bob Seaver mailed Elizabeth his suicide note, then shot himself. Just two years after her mother died, Elizabeth felt the shock of a second distant death, now of a friend and former beau who wanted to blame her for it. Louise took Elizabeth away for the winter to the Keewaydin Club, a resort on the west coast of Florida, and then planned a second European tour for them both, leaving late in the spring of 1937.

They crossed the Atlantic together on a luxury liner, with Louise's car stowed in the hold. Elizabeth had persuaded Margaret Miller to join them for a midsummer excursion in the French countryside, brushing aside Margaret's qualms about Louise's driving. At least Margaret remembered telling Elizabeth she'd been afraid to ride with Louise at the wheel. Margaret's fears were confirmed when Louise's speeding car was forced off the road by a passing vehicle near the small town of Montargis. The car rolled; Elizabeth and Louise emerged unhurt, but Margaret's right arm, which she'd been resting on an open window, was severed just below the elbow. A nearby field worker applied a tourniquet, saving Margaret's life. The driver of the other car ferried Margaret and Louise into town; Elizabeth stayed at the roadside to answer questions from officials, alone with her fears for Margaret, reliving in her mind the "freakishly cruel" accident, the sight of the severed arm.

At first it seemed Margaret might recover almost fully, that "what resides in the right hand is in the left too," and she might paint again. Elizabeth tried to believe the three women could continue their travels after a period of healing. "To keep 'going' is the main thing," she wrote to Frani Blough in New York, "not to let her feel that there has been the slightest interruption in her work, once she is out of the hospital." But there were complications with skin grafts and ongoing pain from damaged nerves. Margaret's mother arrived, knowing only there had been an accident; when Elizabeth told her about Margaret's arm, Mrs. Miller fainted. "I know now what it feels like to be a murderer," Elizabeth told Frani.

If Elizabeth failed to recall Margaret's initial reluctance to make the trip, she could not forget her friend's first words when they met again in the hospital room. Margaret wished she had died in the accident, "it

Louise Crane and Elizabeth in Paris
after the car crash

would have been better" that way, she said. Elizabeth blurted out her love for Margaret: "how could I possibly live without her." For once, Margaret didn't seem to mind. But several weeks later, when Margaret was well enough to walk the streets near the hospital, Elizabeth reached out a hand to steady her and Margaret pushed Elizabeth away, saying "don't." Elizabeth gave up any remaining hope of receiving the love of her adored friend.

Louise Crane's auto insurance provided Margaret with a substantial settlement, and the Cranes may have found Margaret the job as editor in the publications department at the Museum of Modern Art that she kept for many decades. But Margaret did not paint again. She stopped answering Elizabeth's letters for a time, and the friendship was never the same. Elizabeth and Louise turned to each other for solace, traveling to Italy later in 1937 in hopes of alleviating the asthma that had overcome Elizabeth once again, landing her in the same hospital in Paris where Margaret had undergone her surgeries. Both were haunted by the accident. Elizabeth recorded a dream Louise confided: Louise had been released from a prison, dressed in red and "condemned to death . . . at a certain hour," when she became a target for anyone to shoot. Elizabeth had less reason to feel responsible, but it was hard to shake her fear that the people close to her were somehow destined for tragedy, that her presence in their lives was a liability.

Did a shared sense of culpability — deserved or not — keep Elizabeth and Louise together? Both possessed a powerful urge for distraction; they spent hours playing billiards during the weeks they'd waited for Margaret's recovery. They traveled well together, whether touring museums and drinking at cafés in Europe or, the previous winter, fishing on Florida's Gulf Coast; to friends at the Keewaydin Club they were "Lizzie and Louise," or "L and L." But in most ways they were a mismatched pair: Louise socially adept and spontaneous, Elizabeth painfully shy. Louise was free to go where she wished, live as she pleased; Elizabeth could keep pace only as long as Louise paid most of the bills.

The winter after the accident, they returned to Florida, where the island community of Key West, at the southernmost tip of the peninsula, enchanted them both. They bought a house together at 624 White Street, bankrolled by Louise, a simple two-story wooden "eyebrow" house standing alone on its block midway between the town's two sheltered bights where fishing boats moored, and "perfectly beautiful to me, inside and out," Elizabeth wrote to Marianne Moore. The interior was painted a stark white and sparsely furnished, although it was soon filled with books and records. A broad roof (the eyebrow) shaded the front porch, keeping the house cool. Lush gardens in front and back contained "1 banana tree, 2 avocados, 1 mango, 1 *sour-sop*, 1 grapevine . . . and 2 magnificent lime trees, one loaded with large limes." But Elizabeth was more inclined to settle in than Louise, who traveled frequently between New York City and Key West, returning with new friends, provoking Elizabeth to rent rooms elsewhere so she could write. Louise was following her mother's lead by turning arts patron, directing a series of "coffee concerts" at the Museum of Modern Art featuring jazz and Latin musicians who became her friends, some of them lovers, Elizabeth would later learn. In Key West that winter of 1938, Elizabeth wrote a story called "In Prison" that won a prize and publication in *Partisan Review*. "I can scarcely wait for the day of my imprisonment," the story began. "It is then that my life, my real life, will begin."

The fanciful tale, reminiscent of Poe, another writer-orphan whose work she had been reading closely, was not about guilt or punishment, but rather expressed a longing for confinement, routine, and seclusion: "Many years ago I discovered that I could 'succeed' in one place, but not in all places, and never, never could I succeed 'at large.'" The narrator expects to "attract to myself one intimate friend" from among the other prisoners "whom I shall influence deeply," and to add "inscriptions" to the "Writing on the Wall" of the prison cell: "brief, suggestive, anguished, but full of the lights of revelation." There is no hint of the dark side of incarceration, such as her mother had known or Louise's nightmare had revealed, although her own missing mother may have been on Elizabeth's mind as she watched Louise join forces with the indefatigable Mrs. Crane and ceded Margaret to her mother's care. Elizabeth was again turning a crumb — the imagined whitewashed cell, "twelve or fifteen feet long, by six feet wide," with one high window and an iron bed — into a mansion, where one day she might write "a short, but immortal, poem."

The two women parted ways in 1940. Louise left Elizabeth the White Street house to rent or sell; they'd lived in it together only sporadically during the two years of joint ownership. "We hadn't meant to spend so much time / In the cool shadow of the lime," Elizabeth began an unfinished poem; "I can't stand your arrangements anymore." She had tried living with Louise in Manhattan during the summer of 1939, but the city overwhelmed her nearly as much as her shock at walking in on Louise and one of her musician friends — Elizabeth sometimes told others it had been Billie Holiday — making love in their bedroom. They had not pledged themselves to each other, but for Elizabeth the outright infidelity was unforgivable. In another unpublished draft, she admitted hurt and the longing she still felt after the breakup for Louise, whose "huge blue eyes" she would always miss:

> See, here, my distant dear, I lie
> Upon my hard, hard bed and sigh
> For someone far away,
> Who never thinks of me at all
> Or thinking, does not care. . . .

The major poem Elizabeth finished writing during the winter of 1939–40 and sent to *Partisan Review,* where it found easy acceptance, had its beginnings three years before, back when Louise had taken her to the Keewaydin Club as solace after Bob Seaver's suicide. Elizabeth had pulled a sixty-pound amberjack out of the Gulf waters, then several nights later dreamed of swimming after a large fish, "scaled, metallic . . . a beautiful rose color." "We met in water," Elizabeth wrote of the dream-fish in her notebook, and "he led the way . . . glancing around at me every now and then with his big eyes to see if I was following." But Elizabeth wrote "The Fish" at the end of her affair with Louise, whose big blue eyes she could no longer follow; after she'd lost Margaret's friendship; and at the waning of a third significant relationship of the 1930s. "The Fish" would also mark the distance Elizabeth had come since she first sought Marianne Moore's guidance as a college senior. Now both women had written poems of the same title. Only Elizabeth's was really about a fish.

Moore's fish, a school of them, leave her poem after the opening lines, as the poet's attention turns to a rocky cliff on the Maine coast, encrusted with barnacles, dashed by waves, pocked with tide pools where crabs, jellyfish, and "submarine / toadstools, slide each on the other":

> *All*
> *external*
> > *marks of abuse are present on this*
> > *defiant edifice —*

Elizabeth meant no criticism when she set out to write an entirely different sort of fish poem. She was simply writing her own, expressing wonder and then sympathy for the barnacled sea creature she never lets out of her gaze:

> *I caught a tremendous fish*
> *and held him beside the boat*
> *half out of water, with my hook*
> *fast in a corner of his mouth. . . .*
> *He hung a grunting weight,*
> *battered and venerable*
> *and homely. . . .*
> *I looked into his eyes*
> *which were far larger than mine. . . .*
> *They shifted a little, but not*
> *to return my stare.*

Moore's subject is the dynamic force of sea on land over time; for Elizabeth, time is experience, *personal* experience such as she recognizes in the "venerable" fish when she counts five big hooks remaining in its mouth, "Like medals with their ribbons / frayed and wavering, / a five-haired beard of wisdom / trailing from his aching jaw." The fish's jaw, bearing so many external "marks of abuse," is the "defiant edifice" of Elizabeth's poem — a living one.

Elizabeth's powers of description rival her mentor's —

> *I thought of the coarse white flesh*
> *packed in like feathers,*
> *the big bones and the little bones,*
> *the dramatic reds and blacks*
> *of his shiny entrails,*
> *and the pink swim-bladder*
> *like a big peony.*

But close inspection leads to an intimate encounter, an "unexpected moment of empathy" — Elizabeth's everyday surrealism — in a revelatory meeting on the water:

> *I stared and stared*
> *and victory filled up*
> *the little rented boat,*
> *from the pool of bilge*
> *where oil had spread a rainbow*
> *around the rusted engine*
> *to the bailer rusted orange,*
> *the sun-cracked thwarts,*
> *the oarlocks on their strings,*
> *the gunnels — until everything*
> *was rainbow, rainbow, rainbow!*
> *And I let the fish go.*

The release granted at the close of the poem, the rainbowed victory after long struggle, belong to both ancient fish and youthful poet-angler. "The Fish" was Elizabeth's declaration of independence — from Marianne Moore's direct influence on her poetry, from her own fresh wounds of experience, from guilt.

Yet victory was fleeting. Turning thirty alone in Key West in February 1941, Elizabeth was convinced she'd accomplished "nothing." Slowly she had accumulated more than two dozen publications in small journals and prominent magazines like *Partisan Review* and the *New Yorker,* where she'd placed her first poem, "Cirque d'Hiver," about a horse-and-dancer windup toy, in January 1940, but she'd had no success in securing a major book publisher. Against Marianne's advice she'd refused New Directions editor James Laughlin's offer to turn her collection into a pamphlet in his "Poets of the Year" series, perhaps annoyed by another of Laughlin's invitations: to contribute to an anthology of five young poets, providing needed "Sex Appeal" to the otherwise all-male group.

Key West was changing too, as a rising "militarism" took hold of the once-sleepy town, still in recovery from the devastating effects of the Depression and the 1935 hurricane that wiped out a new railway line connecting the island to the mainland. Now an improved roadway brought automobile traffic to annoy Elizabeth on her daily circuit of the island on her bicycle, "more and more Navy ships" docked in the harbor, and a "tremendous airplane hangar" was under construction as the United States prepared to join the war in Europe. American intervention seemed inevitable, but Elizabeth, who'd thrilled as a little girl to the sight of Great Village's kilted regiment on parade during the Great War, felt only dread at the prospect: she now knew that "almost every boy in that tiny place, from 18–22, was killed in one of the big battles." Scarcely two decades later, another small town she'd come to love was threatened, and the Europe she'd traveled freely not long ago was under siege.

During the fall of 1940, as Mussolini's army invaded Greece and Hitler's Nazis bombed London and claimed Paris, where Elizabeth had once lived happily with Louise and their two pet doves, she'd worked on a poem, "Roosters," describing a typical Key West backyard cock fight, whose combatants "command and terrorize the rest," aiming to "tell us how to live." The allegorical antiwar poem also prompted Elizabeth's decision to quit sending early drafts to Marianne Moore for approval. When Marianne returned a "purified" version of "Roosters," bearing the marks of both the poet and her mother, with significant alterations in everything from the poem's title — Marianne preferred "The Cock" — to its meter and rhyme scheme, Elizabeth knew she'd outgrown her teacher. She wrote back defending an "important 'violence' of tone" in her triple-rhymed three-line stanzas, and refusing to adjust the poem's "rather rattletrap rhythm" or eliminate its "sordidities." (Marianne had deleted Elizabeth's reference to a "water-closet door.") Her "cranky" letter closed the years of apprenticeship. The correspondence continued, and Marianne never stopped supporting Elizabeth with letters of recommendation and reviews when the opportunity arose, but when asked in later years about their longtime connection, Elizabeth always emphasized the friendship, and expressed annoyance at suggestions of the older poet's influence beyond "perhaps some early preferences in subject matter."

Insistence that her art was self-originating came naturally to the orphan girl now grown. It was the same stubborn self-reliance her English professor at Vassar had recognized in the "enormously cagey" freshman. Yet in turning away from Marianne, Elizabeth had also set herself adrift. "Roosters," which appeared in the *New Republic* in March 1941, would be the last poem she completed for publication in nearly four years.

In the months after her grim thirtieth birthday self-assessment, Elizabeth began an affair with Marjorie Stevens, a recovering tuberculosis patient who'd moved to Key West for her health, leaving behind a husband in Boston who preferred an open marriage. Alcohol brought the two women together. Elizabeth remembered the first night "I took Marjorie home with me" from the bar where they'd met: "I was so drunk I kept falling off my bicycle and once I didn't want to get up again." Marjorie had been only "a little drunk herself," but told Elizabeth that night she'd "never seen anything so beautiful in my life as you lying there in the gutter with the street lamp shining on your face." Key West was a hard-drinking town, and passing out after a night at a bar was no immediate cause for alarm. Early in her residence there, Elizabeth had noted appreciatively the erratic work schedules of the locals, for whom "drunkenness is an excuse just as correct as any other." Marjorie could not yet have known how much Elizabeth welcomed the camouflage.

Elizabeth found Marjorie beautiful too. Her long dark hair, when she let it down at night, reminded Elizabeth of her young mother bathing in the bedroom they'd shared in Nova Scotia, and so did the vulnerability of her pale white body, though Marjorie was taller and thinner than Gertrude as Elizabeth preferred to remember her, before mental illness ravaged her mother's body and mind. Marjorie soon took on a caretaking role with Elizabeth; fragile as she was in health, Marjorie had a practical side. It was Elizabeth who prized the hot early mornings during their first summer together, when she woke to find the whole yard white with a heavy dew that "would drip on the screens and the palm branches just outside the window," and embraced Marjorie, whose "back was wet with perspiration and it all seemed part of the dew." Elizabeth wrote a love poem, never published, beginning: "It is marvellous to wake up together / At the same minute. . . ." The hour before dawn, when it is "just starting to get light," Elizabeth would confide to the psychoanalyst she sought out for help later in the decade, is "about the time I usually start drinking, or writing a poem, or come to think of it . . . when I liked best to make love to someone."

Elizabeth rented out the White Street house for the income and moved into Marjorie's apartment on Margaret Street behind the Caroline Shop, a fabric store Marjorie ran with Ernest Hemingway's second ex-wife, Pauline Pfeiffer. But their idyll ended abruptly in December 1941 when the United States finally entered the war after the Japanese attack on Pearl Harbor, another remote port city with a navy base. Key West's population rapidly doubled with the arrival of fifteen thousand servicemen and their families; the vacant lots surrounding Elizabeth's house on White Street were taken for military housing. A favorite bar

Marjorie Stevens (standing) and
Pauline Pfeiffer Hemingway, Key West, 1940s

was torn down to make room for a naval air station and submarine base to defend against torpedo-bearing German submarines in the Florida Straits. Blackouts curtailed nightlife. Key West was no longer a place where two drunken women could fall in love on a street corner without anyone taking notice. The Caroline Shop closed its doors.

While Marjorie found work as an accountant for the navy, the tense atmosphere pushed Elizabeth toward leaving the country. She wanted to study Spanish and brought Marjorie along with her on a tour of Mexico that stretched to six months as they traveled first to the Yucatán, where a chance meeting with Pablo Neruda at a hotel near the pyramids at Chichén Itzá led to a stay with the Chilean poet-diplomat and his second wife in Cuernavaca. The thirty-seven-year-old Neruda, initially a poet of private emotions, had become politicized while posted to Madrid in the 1930s, joining the Loyalists in defense of the Republic at the outbreak of the Spanish Civil War. After the capture and execution of his friend the poet and playwright Federico García Lorca, he'd written *España en el corazón* (*Spain in Our Hearts*), a sequence of defiant war poems printed and distributed in 1937 to soldiers at the front. Neruda's partisan role ended his diplomatic service in Spain. Elizabeth and Marjorie visited Cuernavaca in the spring of 1942, just after their host received the news of the death of a second close friend, Miguel Hernández, another poet turned Loyalist soldier, in a Spanish prison. That spring, too, Mexico declared war on the Axis powers after German submarines sank Mexican oil tankers in the Gulf. The two women traveled on to Mexico City, Puebla, and the "translucent-looking" mountains and "quilted" hillsides of Oaxaca, but they found no peace there. Elizabeth could write no better in Mexico than in Key West.

Returning to the United States, Elizabeth braved New York City alone in October 1942, staying in a room at the Murray Hill Hotel near Grand Central Terminal and hoping the city's vitality, even when dampened by wartime, would transfer to her work. She met Marianne for an afternoon at the Metropolitan Museum and revived a friendship with Loren MacIver, the artist wife of the poet Lloyd Frankenberg. Loren had taken a long working vacation in Key West three years before, staying with Elizabeth in an effort to console her after the breakup with Louise, briefly becoming her lover. Now Loren painted Elizabeth's portrait, filling more of the hours that Elizabeth found herself unable to use for writing. Within two months of her arrival in Manhattan, Elizabeth gave up and returned to Margaret Street, where she followed Marjorie's lead and looked for work at the navy yard.

Elizabeth landed a job as trainee in the navy's optical shop, taking apart binoculars and reassembling them after their working parts had been repaired. She'd resisted placement as an office worker among women who "seem to comb their hair and file their nails most of the time," preferring the company of the optical shop's tattooed sailors, who worked in their undershirts in the steamy Florida heat grinding lenses for "magnificent optical instruments" — sextants and periscopes as well as binoculars. But eyestrain and an eczema flare-up brought on by the chemicals used for cleaning prisms caused her to quit after five days. She'd enjoyed drinking "very strong Navy coffee all day long" and practicing her French with two Swiss watchmakers in the crew. The view of the busy harbor from the navy yard had been magnificent. "The water is jade green, the gray ships looked bright

Elizabeth's portrait by Loren MacIver, 1942

blue against it," Elizabeth wrote to Marianne Moore. But she doubted she'd have lasted long in the shop even if she hadn't gotten sick. No one else seemed to care about "the *theory* of the thing, *why* the prisms go this way or that way." The "lack of imagination" of the navy men, who seemed content "*fiddling*" endlessly with their "delicate, maddening" little tools, would only have gotten "more and more depressing."

At the same time, Elizabeth felt herself growing "stupider and stupider and more like a hermit every day" — the reason, along with her dwindling funds, she'd taken the job in the first place. She had almost given up on completing the "six bedraggled old poems and a couple of short stories" she'd carried with her from Key West to Mexico to New York City and back. On too many days, Elizabeth started drinking long before Marjorie returned home from work. Whether Elizabeth's drinking was the root cause of the breakup that now loomed is impossible to determine, but Marjorie's letters from the time show she no longer found an inebriated Elizabeth attractive. Marjorie didn't mind being the household wage earner, but she expected Elizabeth to write every day and have something to show for it. Like many of Elizabeth's lovers, and Elizabeth herself in her early years as a poet, Marjorie didn't understand that inspiration could not be summoned through regular application. In the fall of 1944, with the help of Loren MacIver, Elizabeth rented a small apartment on King Street in Greenwich Village and tried once again to live on her own.

In the final months of the war, Elizabeth responded to a surprise invitation from an editor at Houghton Mifflin, the venerable Boston publishing firm, to enter its first annual Poetry Prize Fellowship competition. She sent off a "lovely brand-new set of mss.," she wrote to Marianne, who readily served as one of her recommenders, under the title *North & South,* reflecting the diverse settings of a collection that opened with "The Map." In May 1945 she received a telegram with the news that her "mss." had been chosen for the prize out of a field of 833 submissions. In June a check for $1,000 arrived.

Yet what should have been cause for celebration soon turned to a source of tension as Elizabeth worked under pressure of deadline to expand the manuscript by a half-dozen poems in order to satisfy her editor, Ferris Greenslet, and herself that she had a complete volume. The several new poems worried the question of love, as her romance with Marjorie finally unraveled. "Wading at Wellfleet" and "Chemin de Fer" recalled girlhood summers at Camp Chequesset: the "scenery" of "scrub-pine and oak," a walk down the tracks of an abandoned railway line, the ritual visit to the local hermit's shack. "Love should be put into action!" the hermit screams at the close of "Chemin de Fer," and across the pond "an echo" — perhaps from the young Elizabeth, newly awakened to her body's yearnings — "tried and tried to confirm it."

Elizabeth wrote "Anaphora," the final poem in *North & South,* for Marjorie. The setting is the Mexican city of Puebla they'd visited in 1942, where morning begins "with birds, with bells, / with whistles from a factory." In the first of two opposed stanzas, the sunrise that had once awakened their pleasure instead summons "intrigue" and "mortal / mortal fatigue"; in the second, sunset — "the fiery event" of closure — ends "every day in endless / endless assent," the final word's ironic pun underscoring the sense of defeat. By the spring of 1946, with the book's publication a few months off, Marjorie was writing to Elizabeth that there was no point in returning to Florida or "trying to make something work that doesn't."

North & South appeared in print in August 1946, while Elizabeth was traveling in Nova Scotia for the first time since her Bulmer grandparents died. If she had fled to Canada now, spurred by anxiety about the book's reception, she soon had little to worry about. A first review in the *Atlantic Monthly* was stingy, but *Poetry,* the *Saturday Review,* the *New York Times,* and others followed swiftly with unequivocal admiration for "Miss Bishop's almost perfect artistic acumen." Prominent voices weighed in: Louise Bogan in the *New Yorker,* and a poet-critic of the rising generation, Randall Jarrell, who praised her work as "honest in its wit, perception, and sensitivity" in *Partisan Review* — "all her poems have written underneath, *I have seen it.*" Writing in the *Nation,* Marianne Moore concluded her glowing review of "this small-large book of beautifully formulated aesthetic-moral mathematics": "At last we have someone who knows, who is not didactic." Marianne had even singled out the unrevised "Roosters" for compliment, and she wrote, with qualified admiration, of "The Fish": despite its too-graphic description of the fish's entrails ("one is not glad of the creature's every perquisite"), "the poem dominates recollection." "The Fish" was the book's strongest offering, critics agreed, and for many years it was Elizabeth's most anthologized poem.

Good news kept coming. The *New Yorker* granted Elizabeth a coveted first-read contract with a 25 percent premium for poems accepted for publication. Randall Jarrell's review led to a dinner party in January 1947 at his New York apartment, where Elizabeth found the courage to stay and meet Jarrell's friend and fellow Kenyon College alumnus Robert Lowell, whose Pulitzer Prize later that year for his second book, *Lord Weary's Castle,* would confirm the thirty-year-old's status as American poetry's *enfant terrible.* The dinner, in turn, led to Lowell's review of *North & South,* along with new books by Dylan Thomas and William Carlos Williams, in the summer issue of *Sewanee Review.* Lowell deemed Bishop "one of the best craftsmen alive" and "about equal" to Thomas in achievement so far. He analyzed the "simple and effective" structure of "a Bishop poem": "It will usually start as description or descriptive narrative, then either the poet or one of her characters or objects reflects. The tone of these reflections is pathetic, witty, fantastic, or shrewd. Frequently, it is all these things at once." The technique worked to "unify and universalize," and in this she resembled Robert Frost. Lowell counted ten of Elizabeth's poems "fail-

Robert Lowell, 1940s

ures" and ten more "either unsatisfactory as wholes, or very slight," but he pronounced "Roosters" and "The Fish" "large and perfect": the "best poems," aside from Marianne Moore's, "that I know of written by a woman in this century."

Fiercely competitive, Lowell had a compulsion to rate and rank, yet while she disliked the qualifier — "by a woman" — and preferred not to be linked with Marianne Moore, "her most important model" Lowell surmised, his frank assessment of Elizabeth's successes and failures won her trust. This was praise she could learn from. She had liked him too. Elizabeth would always remember the younger poet's endearingly "rumpled" dark blue suit and the "sad state of his shoes" on the night of their first meeting, how handsome he was despite needing a haircut, and, most of all, "that it was the first time I had ever actually talked with some one about how one writes poetry." Elizabeth forgot her shyness; trading thoughts about their craft became "strangely easy" — "like exchanging recipes for making a cake."

For a time, however, the acquaintance with Robert Lowell seemed to hold less promise than the psychoanalysis with Dr. Ruth Foster that Elizabeth finally committed to during the winter of 1946–47. There are "certain things," she had written to Marianne Moore over a decade before, defending her choice of end words in "A Miracle for Breakfast," that "without one particular fault they would be without the means of existence." By age thirty-six, Elizabeth's own existence was painfully linked to a number of faults — shyness, dependence on alcohol, chronic asthma — that, along with her deepest concern, the faltering pace of her poetic output, seemed possible to ease, perhaps even cure, through psychoanalysis.

"Every magazine or paper I pick up has an article proving that asthma is psychosomatic," Elizabeth observed to Dr. Anny Baumann, the German émigré physician she'd begun to see in New York for her breathing troubles after settling into the King Street apartment, and who may have provided the referral to Dr. Foster. As long ago as her second trip to Europe, she'd been advised by Marianne Moore's friend the avant-garde novelist Bryher, whom she'd met in Paris following her hospitalization for asthma, that psychoanalysis could help. More tantalizing, Bryher had promised that a Freudian analysis "makes one write better and more easily." But Marianne had shared Elizabeth's initial skepticism, her worry that psychoanalysts viewed the poet "as a neurotic working off his complexes," as Elizabeth had written to Marianne back then, quoting the literary critic Christopher Caudwell, and in the course of analysis tampered with "symbols that are peculiarly private," impeding the poet's work. When Elizabeth met several times with the renegade German analyst Karen Horney in the fall of 1940, as she'd despaired of her future in the wake of Louise Crane's betrayal, Marianne, a staunch Presbyterian, had counseled instead "the quiet heroisms of faith." Elizabeth quit the analysis and moved back to Key West.

In stepping away from Marianne's influence, Elizabeth opened herself to the possible benefits of the talking cure. She made her first appointments with Dr. Ruth Foster in the spring of 1946, and by February 1947 was firmly attached to the tall, blue-eyed analyst who saw patients in the apartment where she lived alone at 110 East 87th Street. Elizabeth called Dr. Foster "Ruth," and, in the first of a remarkable series of letters written between analytic sessions that February, told her "I really do love you very much . . . all transferences aside." Elizabeth was sure she would have loved Ruth regardless of the process by which a patient was expected to "transfer" the powerful emotions of childhood into the analytic relationship. And she might have.

Almost twenty years older, Ruth Foster was a native New Englander with a girls' private school background like Elizabeth's. Her choice to take up a profession had left Ruth Foster estranged from her proper Bostonian family even as she'd become one of the earliest American women to train and practice as an analyst. That education had been hard to come by; she'd specialized in neurology at the University of Maryland's medical school, graduating in 1931, before the founding of any American psychoanalytic training institutes, and she'd coauthored a paper on one-sided paralysis to establish her credentials as a neurologist. But in Baltimore, and later in London and New York, she'd interned and practiced in clinics founded by Freud's acolytes, then established her own private practice in 1937, preferring to treat patients who lived on the margins: creative people, and the poor children of Harlem served by the newly founded Northside Center for Child Development. Elizabeth may have known little of Ruth Foster's background beyond the upper-crust lineage she could easily intuit, but she did know, because Ruth told her, that her analyst was writing a paper now on color in dreams. Elizabeth found that fascinating. She began a poem, "Dear Dr. Foster": "Yes, dreams come in colors / and memories come in colors / but those in dreams are more remarkable."

Elizabeth's letters to Ruth Foster were filled with dreams. In one of them she relived the car crash in Montargis. Ruth rather than Louise was with her and Margaret on the roadside afterward — "you didn't seem responsible in any way," Elizabeth assured Ruth in her letter. She woke from the nightmare bewildered and frightened, and with the "not very good" first line of a sonnet on her lips, expressing relief that Ruth had survived — "Alive alive and with blue eyes." The letter also supplied details of Elizabeth's desperation that winter, despite the critical success of *North & South*. Elizabeth had wanted to tell Ruth her dream right away, recite the line to her while it was fresh in memory, and she'd been too drunk that night to stop herself from picking up the phone and dialing the number Ruth had given her in case of emergency. But it was after midnight; there was no emergency; she shouldn't have called. Elizabeth apologized to Ruth by letter that morning: she'd been "in my cups — kegs" for five days straight, starting to drink on a Thursday and making the drunken phone call late Sunday night.

Dr. Foster seems to have asked Elizabeth for a written account of her sexual history. Elizabeth wasn't seeking help in shifting the direction of her attraction away from women; she'd selected the two unmarried female analysts she consulted in the 1940s, pioneers in a predominantly male profession, knowing they would not find her love for women a perversion demanding a cure. Horney was already famous for rejecting Freud's theory of penis envy as demeaning to women. But such intimate confessions lay at the heart of psychoanalytic work, and Elizabeth *was* troubled by loneliness. She told Ruth Foster about Mike at summer camp, about her passion for Judy Flynn, about sadistic Uncle George; about her unrequited love for Margaret Miller, Bob Seaver's accusation that she "had it in" for men, and Marjorie's more recent one, that she didn't really love women — "it was all some sort of revenge on my mother." Elizabeth described for Ruth her early childhood: her parents' departure when she was "a few weeks old," her father's illness and death, her mother's hospitalization. Elizabeth guessed she must have been bottle-fed as a baby: "Heavens do you suppose I've been thinking of alcohol as mother's milk all this time and that's why I pour it down my throat at regular intervals? Or bottle feedings, or what?"

Elizabeth's physician, Dr. Baumann, had suggested that her craving for whiskey (she could drink three quarts in one days-long binge) might have been cyclical — a premenstrual symptom. But Elizabeth knew better. She'd long associated drinking with her mother's absence — she began in earnest the year her mother died, she told Ruth Foster — and the love she sought in replacement. Getting drunk had allowed her to cry in Margaret Miller's arms, to keep pace with hard-drinking Louise Crane, to win the affection of Marjorie Stevens when she collapsed under the street lamp in Key West. And she drank alone, too — to blot out painful feelings, but also for inspiration, for the vivid dreams that came after a boozy evening or morning, precious to her despite the inevitable "hours of hangover ahead" and the worry she confided to Ruth Foster: she'd become "that dreadful thing an 'alcoholic.'"

Elizabeth's trip to Nova Scotia in the summer of 1946 had been more than a flight from the bad reviews of *North & South* that never came; it had been a voyage of discovery set in motion by her early sessions with Ruth Foster. She had summoned the courage to find out what she could of her mother's history. The trip began inauspiciously, with a week's stopover in Keene, New Hampshire, during which Elizabeth was "more or less drunk all the time." When not "at the hotel unconscious or trying to read detective stories," she had boarded buses at random, riding them for miles in various directions to the end of the line and back in a sodden haze. But one of the bus rides had yielded a dream "in which everything was very wild & dark & stormy," she wrote to Dr. Foster, "and you were in it feeding me from your breast." In the dream, Elizabeth had shrunk to the size of an infant and felt "very calm inside the raging storm," drinking "not milk" but "some rather bitter dark gray liquid" from her analyst's breast. Transference, both Elizabeth and Ruth Foster must certainly have concluded this time.

Elizabeth made her way to Halifax and the Department of Health, where she sought out the records of her mother's hospitalization and death two decades before. Her letters to Dr. Foster don't say what she uncovered; a cousin Elizabeth visited while in Halifax later recalled that "I had the feeling that she didn't learn a lot, but she didn't say it had been a failure." Perhaps all Elizabeth found was her mother's death certificate, with its unsurprising verdict of "chronic psychosis," disturbing nonetheless in its stark confirmation of the little she'd already been told. Or she may have read more: her mother's case files, describing strange behavior — tossing her clothes and favorite possessions out the window, eating plaster from the hospital walls, singing through the night though she "seldom speaks." And delusions: that she would be hanged as a witch, that she was the cause of the Great War. Elizabeth might have gleaned from her mother's intake interview a startling fact: she, Elizabeth, had been delivered by forceps in a procedure that lacerated her mother's cervix; both her parents had been unwell at the time of her birth. But Elizabeth may have learned little or none of this. Perhaps she had not been allowed to see her mother's hospital records and returned to her room at the Nova Scotian Hotel disappointed. It was there she began to write the poem "Dear Dr. Foster," summoning up her analyst's reassuring presence, the colors of dreams.

As often happened, an incomplete draft opened the way for a different finished poem, "At the Fishhouses," one of Elizabeth's best. It took time: Elizabeth's return to New York City, more analytic sessions, the feeling that she loved Ruth Foster, who cared for her and was "so nice." Elizabeth had given Ruth a copy of *North & South*. Dr. Foster read the book and offered an opinion: there was a way in which many of the poems, so finely crafted, some written in constricting verse forms, were "tight." Elizabeth agreed. But with all the talk and all the letters, she was finding release. "I've lost the fear of repeating myself to you," she wrote to Ruth. "And I feel that in poetry now there is no reason why I should make such an effort to make each poem an isolated event, that they go on into each other or over lap . . . and are really all one long poem anyway." To "regard every single poem as something almost absolutely new" had become crippling. Elizabeth would never fully escape this demand of herself; the surprising variety in her relatively small oeuvre derived from her compulsion to make each poem somehow radically different from the last, to address a new problem or situation each time she wrote. In his review, Robert Lowell had registered his "excitement" in reading her poems: "Few books of lyrics are as little repetitious as *North & South*."

But for now there was release — and the new poem written in free-flowing iambs. She gave Ruth Foster a copy of "At the Fishhouses" to read in draft; she planned to dedicate it to Ruth. "The day I saw this poem I was in Lockeport," Elizabeth wrote, a coastal town south of Halifax with a white crescent of beach facing the open ocean. She'd been drinking less since leaving the Nova Scotian Hotel, but she had given in the night before and woke up "feeling dreadful." She'd ridden her bicycle a dozen miles, "sort of by way of punishment," along a "very hilly gravelly road" to a small harbor, where she sat down on the rocks and "cried for a while."

A "big old seal" surfaced out on the water and, Elizabeth wrote later, in the poem, seemed "curious about me." She rode farther on, reaching a row of fishhouses with "steeply peaked roofs / and narrow, cleated gangplanks . . . / for the wheelbarrows to be pushed up and down on," where fishermen scaled and gutted their catch; a forest of "dignified tall firs" rose up behind the shacks. By now, she wrote Ruth Foster, she had "started feeling very exhaltedly happy." The seal that "regarded me / steadily, moving his head a little," had reminded her of Ruth, the steady attention that invited Elizabeth's confessions, that made her feel loved. (Unlike Elizabeth's enormous fish, this sea creature looked back at Elizabeth and met her eyes.) The word "seal" has a "double meaning," she wrote to Ruth. "I suppose a kiss is always considered a sort of seal." And she "connected the appearance of the water" in which the seal swam "with my dream on the bus," the dream of drinking a bitter gray liquid from Ruth's breast. In the closing lines of the poem, "there is . . . a sort of interchange between kissing & feeding," Elizabeth told Ruth, "or is this all too obvious to you and I don't need to bother to pt. it out at all?"

"Cold dark deep and absolutely clear," begins the magisterial final stanza of "At the Fishhouses," describing the northern ocean, which the poet has stopped to contemplate after conversing with one of the

fishermen: "element bearable to no mortal, / to fish and to seals. . . ."
The speaker approaches the "gray icy" water, imagining what it would
be like to taste it — "it would first taste bitter, / then briny, then surely
burn your tongue."

> *It is like what we imagine knowledge to be:*
> *dark, salt, clear, moving, utterly free,*
> *drawn from the cold hard mouth*
> *of the world, derived from the rocky breasts*
> *forever, flowing and drawn, and since*
> *our knowledge is historical, flowing, and flown.*

"Knowledge is historical" referred to the process of psychoanalysis,
Elizabeth explained to Ruth, the self-understanding reached by exam-
ining one's personal past, by making lonely voyages of discovery under
the watch of a tall, blue-eyed analyst. As she set down the last lines, the
words came so fast "she hardly knew what she was writing," Elizabeth
told a friend years later, though she "knew the words were right." It
was an exultant feeling, as if she were ten feet tall.

When "At the Fishhouses" appeared in the *New Yorker* in August 1947,
the first of Elizabeth's poems to be published under the new contract,
she heard from Robert Lowell right away. It was the second letter she'd
received from him since the dinner at Randall Jarrell's in January,
the first in which he addressed her as "Elizabeth" rather than "Miss
Bishop" — "you must be called that," he insisted. "I'm called Cal, but I
won't explain why. None of the prototypes are flattering: Calvin, Caligula, Caliban. . . ." He'd been made "very envious" by the new poem:
"Perhaps, it's your best." Cal's only "question" was "the word *breast* in
the last four or five lines — a little too much in its context perhaps."

Elizabeth didn't answer that question. There was much she
wouldn't tell him about her life or, as in this case, her work, the way
the two intertwined. In her letters to Cal at the time, Ruth Foster was
simply "a psychiatrist friend of mine" who is "writing an article on
color in dreams." But Cal Lowell soon became Elizabeth's chief supporter, outdoing even Marianne Moore in his efforts to further her ca-

reer and befriend her. And Elizabeth admired his work in return: "your poetry is as different from the rest of our contemporaries as, say, ice from slush." She could play the ranking game too, or perhaps she let Cal draw her in. The two grew to be the most astute appreciators of each other's work, using their letters to refine their own conceptions of poetry's demands. "There's a side to writing that's like a little bird swooping in to snatch a piece of bread," Cal once wrote to Elizabeth, "only there are so many birds bustling about, and I suppose the bread is always vanishing, so that only by miracle can the bird get it." He was always aware of those other birds — the other poets. But perhaps because Elizabeth was a woman and not, in his view, a direct competitor, Cal could admit that she often got the crumb: "if one is very lucky and talented, there's a way of writing that is actually believable, and beyond that, a way that is rich and interesting, and beyond that, a way that really gets the bread — then a bell rings and a poem is what we call immortal. That's what you've done."

Elizabeth's good fortune had continued with the receipt of a Guggenheim Fellowship that spring of 1947. The funds allowed another summer trip to Nova Scotia and prompted her return to Key West for the winter and beyond. Marjorie had arranged the sale of the White Street house, so Elizabeth could afford an apartment on her own, while still maintaining the King Street rental in Greenwich Village if she wanted to spend time in New York. Her friends now were the Pfeiffer sisters: Pauline, Marjorie's onetime partner in the Caroline Shop, who'd retained the rambling house in Key West she'd shared with Ernest Hemingway before their separation in 1939, and Jinny, who had a lover in Rome, an Italian violinist turned documentary filmmaker, Laura Archera.

Elizabeth stopped seeing Ruth Foster when she left the city in 1947. Perhaps she felt she'd gained enough to give up treatment, or she may have foreseen an itinerant life in the years ahead that simply couldn't support regular sessions. Possibly, despite the breakthrough with "At the Fishhouses," she'd given up in frustration: both asthma and alcoholism have since proven beyond the reach of psychoanalysis. And Elizabeth's shyness — her extreme self-consciousness — may have been the "fault" her existence as a poet depended upon.

Living on her own in the years after the breakup with Marjorie left her vulnerable to lapses from the sobriety she strove to maintain. There were sustaining benefactions from Cal, including an appointment from September 1949 through the summer of 1950 as Poetry Consultant at the Library of Congress, the post Lowell had held two years before, now known as Poet Laureate. And on either side of Elizabeth's year in Washington, there were stays at Yaddo, the artists' colony in Saratoga Springs, New York. But Elizabeth often gave in to binge drinking, out of loneliness she sometimes said now, and there were drying-out stays as well: two months in Connecticut's Blythewood Sanitarium, where a Freudian version of the Alcoholics Anonymous program was practiced, emphasizing surrender of the ego; and then at Saratoga Hospital near Yaddo, during her second residency, after her hands had begun to "shake so I can't sign my name." Each time she told herself she "had to stop" — "It can be done." Yet her 1946 trip to Nova Scotia had reminded her how much drinking ran in the family. In Great Village, her mother's only brother was a lifelong alcoholic, and the Bishop men, including her father, she'd heard, also drank to excess.

Nearly everyone Elizabeth knew drank heavily. Social life, whether

Elizabeth at work as the Poetry Consultant, Library of Congress, ca. 1949–50

in summer communities on the Maine coast, where she'd stayed in Wiscasset and Stonington during 1948, at Key West, or in the "literary" scene in New York and Washington, was a matter of cocktail parties and well-lubricated lunches and dinners. Elizabeth frequently drank alone in advance of such events, perhaps initially to brace herself, ultimately to remove herself from the fray. The year before she took over as Poetry Consultant, she never made it to a dinner Cal organized in Washington for visiting poets T. S. Eliot and W. H. Auden; instead, after draining all the bottles in her host's liquor cabinet, she was rushed to the hospital. She'd been braver, and steadier, as a junior at Vassar, interviewing Eliot in the founder's suite.

The post at the Library of Congress, which she'd been hesitant to accept, brought worries Elizabeth didn't mention in letters or perhaps even articulate to herself. Her term in office came at the midpoint of a postwar decade during which the federal government determined to rid itself of the "constant menace" posed by homosexual employees. Six thousand workers were fired between 1945 and 1956 in a crusade for "morality and decency" nearly as visible as the concurrent hunt for Communist Party members and sympathizers. From her office at the library, Elizabeth looked out on the capital's buildings, "all those piles of granite and marble," which failed to impress the granddaughter of John W. Bishop, contractor. The solidity of her surroundings masked the unsteady foundation of her appointment, and that of any homosexual employed by the federal government at the time. During the spring of her Washington year, in a campaign that became known as the "purge of the perverts," security officials in the State Department boasted of firing one homosexual per day, twice the rate of firings for political disloyalty. Most of those who lost their jobs were men, but government work was one of few options for professionally ambitious women, who could fall under suspicion simply for dressing unconventionally, sharing an apartment with another woman, or socializing in bars known as meeting places for lesbians. Perhaps the loneliness Elizabeth suffered so acutely in Washington, where she lived for most of the year in a women's boarding house in Georgetown, was due to the need for more than usual secrecy about her private life, a concealment that amounted to suppression.

And yet the Poetry Consultant appointment, Elizabeth's first job lasting more than a few weeks, was a highly visible position. Many of the requirements chaffed. She considered her lone public reading in Washington a "terrible flop," and bitterly resented the obligatory visits to Ezra Pound, institutionalized at St. Elizabeths Hospital after suffering a breakdown while imprisoned in Italy on charges of treason. She had little sympathy for Pound, who had written and broadcast anti-Semitic propaganda in Mussolini's Italy during the war; here was an actual traitor. But with the support of Eliot, E. E. Cummings, and others, he'd received the Library of Congress's first Bollingen Prize for Poetry in 1949, just as Elizabeth took office — for the *Cantos* he'd begun writing in prison. Pound's supporters had hoped the recognition would win his release from St. Elizabeths. Instead, it brought dishonor to the prize, which afterward was administered by Yale.

Elizabeth's duties also included scheduling public readings and setting up recording sessions for visiting poets, and she fought her shyness each time. She arranged a party honoring Carl Sandburg and Robert Frost, two poets she imagined would have much in common, but they sat at opposite ends of a couch receiving their admirers, not exchanging a word; Elizabeth had been helpless to draw them out. With the kowtowing to eminences, and "all this recording & reading," she wrote to Randall Jarrell, who'd remained a supporter and held out the hope of taking the Library of Congress job himself next, she'd begun to feel "sick of Poetry as Big Business." (In the end, the position went unfilled for six years after Elizabeth's term expired. William Carlos Williams was selected, and first was too ill to move to Washington, then was rejected as a Communist sympathizer for his postwar poem "Russia.")

Asthma kept Elizabeth away from work for weeks during the winter of 1949–50, and she refused invitations to read at the YMHA Poetry Center and the Museum of Modern Art in New York during the spring. Even the help of a vocal coach couldn't rid her of the sense that she was "hopeless" at the podium. Audiences, she imagined, could tell she was suffering stage fright, "and I don't think people enjoy seeing someone miserable." But she counted the public reading she organized for Dylan Thomas that spring, at the start of his triumphant American tour, "the high point of my incumbency," she wrote to Cal. The two poets could not have been more different in their public personas. But they'd both had village childhoods, and Dylan's ebullience and informality (they were instantly on a first-name basis) put Elizabeth at ease. At a gala party in Dylan's honor, they locked themselves in the butler's pantry to drink and talk. Dylan had asked how Elizabeth would manage after the Poetry Consultant's pay ran out — would she "go back on the parish?" She figured on "going back on Yaddo."

This time Elizabeth brought her clavichord along to the artists' retreat for a five-month stay beginning in October 1950, and set herself three simple pieces to practice each day in the studio at East House, one of the smaller outbuildings on the estate's grounds. For her first Yaddo residency, a year earlier at midsummer, she'd been assigned a tower room where, often too nervous in the proximity of more prolific authors or too drunk to write, she'd passed idle hours on her balcony, blowing bubbles from a clay pipe dipped in a cup of soapy water and watching the translucent spheres drift away on the breeze. She planned to spend her days more wisely now, and was writing a story about her mother, working "so fast I expect to be rich before long." The *New Yorker*'s per-line rates meant prose was a vastly more profitable enterprise than poetry. She quickly made friends with another poet in residence, May Swenson, two years younger and with one book already in print. But there was a "sort of 'Pub' down the road," with a half-grown colt out back, near Saratoga's racetrack. And on a stopover in New York City on her way to Yaddo, she'd learned that Ruth Foster had died, alone in her 87th Street apartment. Ruth was fifty-six, the *New York Times* obituary stated, survived by her mother and three brothers in Boston. The cause was pancreatic cancer. Elizabeth had not seen her since the spring of 1947.

Perhaps Elizabeth no longer loved Ruth Foster. Her New York physician, Dr. Anny Baumann, who had also tended to Ruth Foster through her illness, had become Elizabeth's confidant instead. Dr. Baumann dispensed a variety of anti-anxiety and asthma medications long-distance — Theoglycinate and Bellargel pills, adrenaline shots, sulfate cartridges for an inhaler that made her feel like the caterpillar smoking a hookah in *Alice in Wonderland* — and treated Elizabeth like a friend when she appeared in the city. Elizabeth wrote Dr. Baumann letters too, addressing her as "Anny" — not recitals of dreams or childhood memories, just simple statements: "for about a week I've been feeling very depressed"; "having a terrible fight to keep from drinking"; "I did drink for two awful days — no damage done"; "I feel some sort of cycle settling in & I want to stop it." By early 1950, Elizabeth was begging Dr. Baumann for *any* remedy "this side of going to a psychiatrist, which I never want to do again," for the asthma that left her choking and gasping for breath most nights, unable to lie down to sleep. Had she told Ruth Foster too much? Much of what Elizabeth confided to Dr. Foster would never be uttered again.

Yet Ruth's death, so young — scarcely older than Elizabeth's mother had been when she died — stunned her. Dr. Foster had "helped me more than anyone in the world," Elizabeth wrote to Marianne Moore now. "It was so sad, she was so nice — I wish you had met her." Dr. Baumann reassured Elizabeth that her intense grief was normal, and the loss could feel worse for a patient who had terminated treatment. Still, Elizabeth drank herself into a five-day hospitalization, remembering afterward, she wrote to Dr. Baumann, how Ruth had once told her, "Well, go ahead, then — ruin your life." And "I almost have," she admitted.

Through the fall and winter months at Yaddo in late 1950, Elizabeth worked fitfully on the story about her mother, now called "Homesickness," and a poem of the same title. There was a nugget of family history at the heart of both. At sixteen, Gertrude had taken a job as schoolteacher a day's ride from Great Village. Gertrude had been overcome by loneliness — a homesickness so acute it may have been the first indication of her later illness. She could not afford to give up the job and return home, but her father drove up by wagon to leave the family dog with her for comfort. In the story, Elizabeth named the large brown dog Juno: "She had been promiscuous," running off after squirrels or other small prey, "and yet there was something very settled and domestic in her manner ... a character to turn to with confidence in life's darker moments."

Had Elizabeth's own "homesickness," the frightening sensation she'd had of being "whirled off from all the world" on her first trans-atlantic voyage, recurred as, more lonely than she'd been since leaving college, she mourned her confessor, Ruth Foster? Elizabeth labeled her journal for 1950 "worst year." She would not finish the story in which Juno was meant to accomplish a rescue. Could she have longed, without being able to say so, for a Juno, the promiscuous but passionate lover in *The Stone Wall*? The poem trailed off, an unfinished fragment —

> *... not even realizing she was weeping*
> *her face   nightgown   drenched —*
> *It was too late — for what, she did not know. —*
> *   already —, remote,*
> *irrepair able . . .   irreparable.*
>
> *Beneath the bed the big dog thumped her tail.*

I had known homesickness — unjustified, unwarranted. How could I miss a home where I could not bring friends, where I felt lonely or fearful except at the piano or behind the pages of a book? But still, when I left California for Vermont, as the unfamiliar trees turned red and yellow and dropped their leaves, when a foot of snow fell on Thanksgiving Day and I woke alone in the white clapboard dormitory, I felt something like homesickness — though I was glad to be far away on the holiday and did not miss my home, I told myself, trying to explain away the otherwise unexplainable feeling that I was lost, misplaced.

I latched on to my roommate, a millionairess eight times over, with a desperate admiring love. She was nineteen, I was seventeen; she'd skipped from boarding school to boarding school, I'd skipped a grade. She was generous, laughing at my cheap white Orlon gloves and buying me soft leather mittens with wool liners like the ones she wore skiing at Killington and Stowe. She offered to buy me a winter coat, and a harpsichord better than the clunker in the basement practice room in Jennings, the gray stone mansion that was Bennington's music building.

She owned a car, her third Saab 99E; two others had been totaled in accidents not her fault, and she had not been hurt. Before classes started, she drove into town to buy stereo components — amplifier, turntable, Bose speakers — and returned with furniture as well. We cast out the battered student desks that had made me feel like I was in college, where I wanted to be, in favor of a single weathered drop-leaf table that could be opened out for entertaining. We balanced our typewriters precariously at either end, her Smith-Corona electric, my Olivetti manual, to write our class papers on smudgy Corrasable Bond.

On fall weekends we drove to the vacant country houses her family owned, one on Cape Ann, north of Boston, and another on an island off the coast of Maine. She was driving fast. A childhood friend richer than she rode up front beside her. I was in back, peering out between their heads, watching the pickup truck approach slowly from a distance, at the speed of a country road at dusk and a driver not expecting to meet a whizzing carload of college students shaving hours off a full-day's ride. Slowly, the pickup turned across our path, and we were upon him, then swerving to avoid the collision, off the road, rolling, miraculously land-ing upright on dry grass. A roll bar–style headrest from one of the front seats had come off in my grasping hands.

My roommate's quick reflexes and her Saab 99E had saved us, she said over and over. Except that her friend's neck and shoulder ached. An ambulance arrived, the friend was flown to a hospital, then home. She would be fine, she might miss a semester at Vassar, but she would be fine. This Saab 99E wasn't totaled. It stayed in the shop until the end of term, though, and by spring my roommate had a boyfriend who drove the car, and things were different.

Maybe the homesickness I shouldn't have felt grew into the sadness that made me want to leave Bennington. But I was making a home in Cambridge, first in a new apartment on leafy Ellsworth Avenue shared with just one roommate, another music student from Bennington, en-rolled in a piano tuning and repair course at Boston's North Bennet Street School. On campus he'd made a point of going barefoot through the winter and wearing a white chorister's surplice instead of a shirt. But he'd turned practical the year we roomed together, and he left the apartment each morning in work boots, work shirt, and jeans like ev-eryone else.

During the spring of Robert Lowell's class, I applied to transfer to Radcliffe and was accepted, joining the class of students whose appli-cation folders I'd read as a secretary. By now they were college juniors, no longer recognizable as the fresh-faced preppies and high school valedictorians whose photos I'd studied enviously more than a year before. Could the famous writer's letter of recommendation have made the difference for me this time? He'd been sorry about hitting me and wanted to help. He asked me to marry him and hoped, at least, I'd come back. I didn't trust myself to let him know I'd gotten in and would not be leaving Cambridge for Vermont.

My acceptance at Radcliffe was conditional, though. I'd have to live off campus. There was a shortage of dorm rooms, and since I would turn twenty-one that summer, the college wasn't obliged to house me. I would be one of ten "older women students," the other nine much older than me, in an admissions experiment intended to bring women whose educations had been stalled by marriage and child-rearing back to school. The financial aid was the same Bennington offered, and I said yes, eager for even this partial resumption of student life. All summer long, as I worked a new job as cashier in a secondhand bookstore on Mass. Ave., I looked forward to choosing my courses in the fall, finding my way to classrooms where I would belong, drafting poems in spiral-bound notebooks with the Radcliffe shield on the cover. I bought a used paperback copy of Elizabeth Bishop's *Complete Poems* with my employee discount, not minding the acid-burned pages or inked underlines of the previous owner, and looked for "Poem." It wasn't there. I understood, as I hadn't before, that I'd heard something brand-new that day in Professor Lowell's class, from the small woman who'd bowed her head and read to us from the pages of a slim black binder.

Maybe I fit the description "older woman student" well enough. I'd been on the outside supporting myself, cooking plain meals with the worn cast-iron pan, battered aluminum colander, and tarnished but still-whirling eggbeater I'd picked up at Goodwill for a few dollars. I felt more than one year older than my classmates — or most of them. When, after a semester, I pressed for admission to a newly co-ed dorm in the Radcliffe Quad and met the two Vietnam vets who lived in one of the top-floor suites at Cabot Hall, I felt ashamed of my sense of superiority. They never spoke of what they'd seen or done as soldiers, or of the indignity of living now among relative children who had never had to worry their draft numbers might be called. Like me, they seemed grateful for the regression to coddled dormitory life, for the chance to make Friday-afternoon booze runs to the New Hampshire state liquor store an hour's drive north, returning with tax-free cases of Rolling Rock and Marlboro Reds to drink and smoke through endless bridge games played with the two senior women who shared the dorm's fifth-floor aerie. Their smoke and occasional laughter wafted down the staircase to the fourth floor where I sometimes sat on the hall carpet just outside my room, notebook propped on my knees, working on a poem for class, happy to be in the midst of other students' comings and goings, to forget myself as I remembered.

I was following what seemed the direction of poetry then, which also suited my need for retrospection. Robert Lowell had given me an A-minus (I tried not to feel the nick) for poems about my father, about my season of depression. One of them, he wrote on the strip of paper clipped to my sheaf of final pages, "has all the litheness and control of good prose." I did not understand this then as praise for a poem, but I kept on each semester in writing classes for which I applied and was accepted out of a few dozen aspirants, relieved each time I saw my name among the ten posted on the classroom door — uncertain what I'd have done if I had not. Jane Shore, a poet just a half-dozen years older than me, beloved by students, gave assignments: write a poem based on a fairy tale, write a poem inspired by a work of art, write a sestina. I chose "The Ugly Duckling" (my anxious childhood) and Claes Oldenburg's soft sculptures (a one-night stand that fizzled). Only my sestina, with the names of players on the winning 1975 World Series Cincinnati Reds — Gullett, Bench, Rose, Morgan, Concepcion, Geronimo — threaded through the stanzas, brought unqualified praise from classmates and professor. But I knew the poem was merely clever. I hadn't really cared about the widely mourned Red Sox loss in Game Seven. If I had, I wouldn't have written about the Reds.

Still, one or more of these poems earned me admission to Elizabeth Bishop's class in the fall of 1976, my senior year. Like Robert Lowell's workshop, into which I'd stumbled as a lucky beginner, this was a graduate-level course, and the competition for admission had to have been stiff. In early September, Lowell had suffered a breakdown, his third in little over a year, causing him to withdraw from teaching that semester and thrusting Bishop into his spot on three days' notice. She

never taught workshops — "verse-writing classes," she called them
— the same semester as Lowell, not wishing to compete for students.
I didn't know, and she wasn't sure either, that this would be her last
verse-writing class at Harvard. She was hoping for an extension to her
contract, and her colleague and friend Robert Fitzgerald, a tenured
professor with a named chair and considerable clout, had made inquir-
ies on her behalf.

Would more students have applied, knowing this was a last chance?
Probably not. Lowell was Harvard's headliner, and he would teach
again in the spring; Octavio Paz and Seamus Heaney were waiting in
the wings. Elizabeth Bishop was not a big name like those men, and
not an outspoken feminist like Adrienne Rich or May Swenson — icons
on campus, revered by students beyond the English department. Nor
was she a histrionic beauty like Sylvia Plath or Anne Sexton. Some of
us had heard Anne Sexton read at Harvard in 1974, the year of her suicide. Perched on a stool like a nightclub performer in an A-line shift
and knee-high boots, she'd recited her poem "The Fury of Cocks," first
warning her electrified audience in Sanders Theatre, "And I don't
mean *roosters*."

About thirty students crowded the seminar room on the first floor
of Robinson Hall, the history department building at the far north-
east corner of Harvard Yard, on a Wednesday afternoon at the end of
September. Why we were meeting here no one, least of all our professor, knew. It didn't matter that most of us had to stand through the
brief advisory issued by Miss Bishop, a grimmer, grayer, possibly even
smaller woman than I'd remembered from her guest appearance in
Robert Lowell's class eighteen months earlier, dressed smartly but
uncomfortably, it now seemed, in another tailored suit — a delicate
tweed. She dismissed us soon enough, after giving instructions to hand
in our sample poems at the English department office, then return to
Robinson Hall next Tuesday, the day before the next class meeting,
to check the roster posted on the classroom door. For homework we
should complete three stanzas of a ballad rhyming *abcb* or *abab*, our
choice.

Did some give up then, put off by the somber, sallow Miss Bishop
or by her assignment to write verses in rhyme? If there was one thing

never encouraged by any of our workshop professors and uniformly derided by my classmates, it was rhyme. And a ballad? I could think only of poems in the children's anthology from which my mother read aloud at bedtime, or the French folk tunes my father sometimes picked out on the piano. As a little girl I'd begged him to play over and over a favorite song, "Ragotin," about this clownish fellow's *"pots de vin,"* whose title my father translated for me as "Tipsy." I hadn't known what any of those words meant, just liked their sounds and the playful ditty that accompanied them. I'd almost forgotten this was where my love of poetry began, with rhythmic melodies and pulsing story-poems whose rhymes pinned their plot lines in memory like messages tacked to a bulletin board: "Paul Revere's Ride," "O Captain! My Captain!" "Barbara Allen," "Barbara Frietchie." Hadn't I memorized Robert Frost's "Stopping by Woods on a Snowy Evening" in fifth grade, enchanted by the hushed midnight scene, the hint of wisdom at the poem's close, and aided by subtly recurring sounds at each line's end?

That night in my room at Cabot Hall, I paged through the yellowed leaves of my *Complete Poems.* How could I not have noticed the elegant rhyme schemes of "The Map" and "The Colder the Air," whose message seemed to mock my inattention —

> *We must admire her perfect aim,*
> *this huntress of the winter air*
> *whose level weapon needs no sight,*
> *if it were not that everywhere*
> *her game is sure, her shot is right.*
> *The least of us could do the same. . . .*

— or "Chemin de Fer" (*abcb*), "Sleeping Standing Up" (*abcacb*), "Cirque d'Hiver" (*abcbb*), and "Roosters," with its emphatic *aaa* triplets? But this was "her game," her magic that my not noticing certified. On Tuesday I was back in Robinson Hall checking the roster, finding my name, and then the next day in the room with the lucky ten — eleven, with one auditor — for the start of class.

Miss Bishop seemed no happier. "I don't believe poetry *can* be taught," she started in, looking straight out at us, yet somehow managing not to meet anyone's gaze. *Her level weapon needs no sight.* "But we'll do what we can with the time we've got." A tentative smile. Should we have laughed?

She passed around a photocopied sheet with each week's assignment listed: ballads to be finished by next class, at least twenty lines of iambic pentameter, the same of rhymed couplets, and "Please try your hands at a *Christmas* poem" for December. These alternated with "free" dates: "Anything you want to submit, but only one poem, please — no longer than one single-spaced page or two double-spaced pages."

At the end came more rules, in all-caps: "PLEASE USE PAPER CLIPS OR STAPLES!" and "PLEASE DON'T HAND IN POEMS THAT HAVE ALREADY BEEN HANDED IN AND DISCUSSED IN OTHER CLASSES. THIS IS A WASTE OF EVERYONE'S TIME." It seemed that wasting time — one's own, one's classmates', one's professor's — was a cardinal sin for Miss Bishop. Perhaps the class itself was a waste of everyone's time. But here we were. We would make the best use we could of the hours we had.

⟡ 3 ⟡

Coffee

S HE COULD SMELL coffee beans even before the SS *Bowplate,* the Norwegian freighter she'd boarded in New York in November 1951, landed at the Brazilian port of Santos. There had been open-air coffee stands on street corners in Key West, releasing the pungent aroma of brewed coffee to drift on warm sea breezes. But this was different, the acrid scent of roasting beans that greeted her as she descended from the *Bowplate*'s upper deck amid dozens of cargo ships loaded for export with the odorless fresh beans, still green. She would later say you could smell coffee everywhere in Brazil, either roasting in factories outside cities and towns, or the subtler fragrance of coffee plants in flower on the mountainsides she grew to love, as she did the rich dark liquid that ushered in each day — not in gallons but in tiny cupfuls, *cafezinhos.*

Elizabeth hadn't meant to stay. She hadn't meant, at first, to travel to South America at all. When she'd pocketed a $2,500 writer's fellowship from Bryn Mawr College, bestowed on her the previous spring at the urging of Marianne Moore and her editor at the *New Yorker,* Katharine White, both graduates, she'd planned on spending a year in Europe before returning to deliver the requisite lecture on campus. Cal Lowell was traveling in Italy with his new bride, the acerbic critic and novelist Elizabeth Hardwick, and he'd invited her to visit each time the couple settled in for a stretch. In Florence he promised a "large apartment and maid . . . waiting for you," and he painted the scene of "a smallish sand and wind-swept cottage" on the island of Ischia that all three would share. But an unexpected "tax tangle" and a finally unmet desire to complete the manuscript of a second book that was "85% at Houghton Mifflin" stalled her departure until the fall when, she wrote to Cal from the *Bowplate,* there had been no cheap tickets to Europe. The prospect of a "crazy trip" around the South American continent, stopping at various ports until the next passage of the freighter line, began to appeal to her.

She had hardly seen Cal since a summer day in Maine in 1948 when the two had been stranded awkwardly together at the guesthouse in Stonington, on Deer Isle, where she'd rented a room for several weeks, inviting friends to join her. Still not officially divorced from his first wife, the novelist Jean Stafford, Cal had arrived to meet his girlfriend, Carley Dawson, only to rudely dismiss her, leaving Elizabeth to offer comfort to his rejected lover on the morning of her departure. Later that day, swimming, lounging on the beach, and trading stories with Cal, Elizabeth couldn't be certain he understood she loved women. It wasn't something she made clear to most people, least of all to men, and Cal, who hadn't known her when she'd been involved with Louise Crane or Marjorie Stevens, might have had the wrong impression. She'd been dallying with a mutual friend, Tom Wanning, inviting him along on vacations like this one. Marriage was something she'd always instinctively resisted — "But no! I would be no man's wife," she'd written as a girl in a string of humorous couplets, "family life is not for me. / I find it leads to deep depression / And *I* was born for self expression." Still, she was nearing forty, and other women she knew had married simply to have children, or to provide cover for a romantic life they felt constrained to hide. But Tom's drinking was as bad as hers, and when the opportunity arose to send him off to the train station with Carley, Elizabeth pushed him away too.

While later Elizabeth would say she might have wished to have a child with Cal, it wasn't hard to see that the habitually disheveled Adonis of American poetry needed more nurture than she could give. A thoroughbred Boston Brahmin, six feet tall and with a mass of dark ringleted hair, Robert Traill Spence Lowell IV had long cultivated nicks in the Yankee veneer, leaving Harvard for Kenyon College in Ohio, adopting a southern drawl in imitation of his mentors Allen Tate and John Crowe Ransom. Elizabeth knew at least some of Cal's romantic history—the car wreck in Boston before his wedding to Jean Stafford that had put her in a coma and left her beautiful face scarred, her nose misshapen; the house on the Maine coast in Damariscotta Mills purchased with the proceeds of Jean's first novel, a bestseller; the night near the end of the marriage when he'd nearly strangled his young wife in a jealous rage. The episode figured dramatically in Cal's third book, *The Mills of the Kavanaughs*. Elizabeth had delayed responding to the manuscript when he'd sent it to her for critique during her second stay at Yaddo, and she struggled still to find ways to praise the book when it came out in the spring of 1951. In manuscript she'd found the collection "harrowing," and she objected, she finally told its author, to a line near the end: "a girl can bear just about anything." She was dismayed by Cal's attempt to capture — *appropriate* — Jean's angry, injured voice in dramatic monologue. Jean wasn't a close friend, but they shared an editor in Katharine White, and, for several months before leaving for South America, Elizabeth had stayed in the same New York rental where Jean had written her most recent novel.

Then there were Cal's breakdowns and hospitalizations, which had begun less than a year after the 1948 Maine holiday and which hadn't kept Lizzie Hardwick from marrying him. Elizabeth had felt the heat that drew women to Cal despite his erratic behavior, felt it that day alone with him in Maine. But such a man could never have consented to a sham marriage. She read it in his letters from Florence, where he wrote derisively of the tourists who crowded the city: "mostly fairies, people of taste and students from Chicago," producing a "certain blank." He needed to be aroused.

And so did she. The "crazy trip" was not so crazy, not at all. Her first stop would be in Rio, visiting Mary Morse and Lota de Macedo Soares. When she'd met the couple in New York four years earlier, she'd been drawn to Mary Morse, a former dancer, and confided as much in Dr. Foster. She'd made a drunken phone call to Mary—"a very nice tall bony Boston type" — confessing her love, and instantly regretted it; she didn't want to risk Lota's fury by acting on her attraction. Lota — small, olive-skinned, and quiet, perhaps because she was amid English-speakers; something in Lota's manner warned of fierceness, or passion. Backing off, Elizabeth told Ruth Foster it was only Mary's looks and startlingly "frank conversational style" she cared for; she hardly knew her. She hoped Mary and Lota hadn't caught on to her drinking problem.

Now she would be seeing them both for the first time on their home turf — Lota's, really. Mary Morse had fallen for Lota when the two met on a steamer from Rio to New York a decade before. Lota was traveling with her teacher and friend the muralist Candido Portinari, who'd been commissioned to paint wall frescoes in the Hispanic Reading Room at the Library of Congress. Mary had just completed her last tour as a dancer. Once the murals were finished, she followed Lota back to Brazil and, except for an extended visit the couple made to New York at the end of the war, never left — living with Lota in a penthouse apartment in Rio overlooking Copacabana beach and on the Soares family estate fifty miles outside the city, in the mountain village of Petrópolis, the summer retreat of Rio's elite.

It had been a year since the shock of Ruth Foster's death. Aboard the *Bowplate* Elizabeth took heart from a new acquaintance, Miss Breen, a retired police officer who'd presided over Detroit's women's prison for twenty-six years; she spoke "a lot to me" of her "roommate," a lawyer named Ida, Elizabeth recorded in her journal. Miss Breen was tall with bright blue eyes, like Dr. Foster, and "extremely kind," but at almost seventy, a survivor. Elizabeth wrote of Miss Breen to Cal as "very gentle and polite," modest about her crime-solving capabilities; she'd been featured in *True Detective*. She may also have reminded Elizabeth of the intrepid women who founded and ran Walnut Hill School and occasionally traveled to England on holiday, writing back enthusiastic journal letters for publication in the *Blue Pencil*. Miss Breen entertained "day-dreams" like her own, Elizabeth wrote to Cal, then wintering with Lizzie in Amsterdam, of "going down through the Straits & up the West coast" of South America.

She wrote about Miss Breen once more, three months later in her first poem from Brazil. Elizabeth had traveled with the older woman to São Paulo for two days, touring the massive, Versailles-inspired National Museum before taking the night train alone to Rio. There Lota's apartment, hers for the month while Mary and Lota withdrew to Petrópolis, was "all very luxurious." She was surrounded by "Calders" — Lota was a collector — "Copacabana, Cariocans, Coffee, etc." But the city seemed a "*mess,*" like Miami and Mexico City combined, and with "men in bathing trunks kicking footballs all over the place" beginning at sunrise. She made plans to move on to Buenos Aires, taking the next freighter. Elizabeth's feelings about Brazil would change, however, when, to her surprise, as she concluded the poem "Arrival at Santos," she found herself "driving to the interior" — with Lota.

All it took was two "very sour" bites of a cashew fruit, the bulbous, persimmon-colored stem that bears the nut, rarely eaten anywhere but in Brazil. Elizabeth's face blew up until she could no longer see. Her hands ballooned; she couldn't type or even hold a pencil. Her ears were two "large red-hot mushrooms." Up in the mountains at Samambaia, the property in the village of Petrópolis named for a giant fern on which Lota was building a glass-walled house in the shape of a butterfly, its wings spread open to the sun, she lay in bed, except when Lota drove her to the hospital each day for injections of calcium.

When did they first touch? Perhaps Lota stroked the suffering Eliz-

Lota's Samambaia house, Petrópolis

abeth's stiff wild hair with its ripples of gray. On the back of a draft of her unfinished story "Homesickness," Elizabeth scribbled "A love letter," written at five a.m.: "Lota! — (if I may call you so . . .) Come scratch me again! I am madly in love with you." She could not have written this while stricken with the "fearful and wonderful allergy," but soon, when she took out her manuscripts and began to work again. "I call to you every morning. Don't you hear me? It is from the heart."

She'd come to Samambaia to watch the workmen raise the roof of Lota's new house; she'd learned that Mary Morse was leaving Lota to build her own separate residence farther down the mountain. Perhaps there was an opening to fulfill one or more of the aims Elizabeth had listed in her travel journal in a fervent litany, headed "I believe" —

> *that the steamship will support me on the water,*
> *& that the aeroplane will conduct me over the mountain,*
> *that perhaps I shall not die of cancer,*
> *or in the poorhouse,*
> *that eventually I shall see things in a "better light,"*
> *that I shall continue to read and continue to write,*
> *that I shall continue to laugh until I cry with a certain few friends.*
> *that love will unexpectedly appear over & over again,*
> *that people will continue to do kind deeds that astound me.*

It wasn't long-limbed Mary, but small, impulsive, and imperious Lota — not at all quiet in her mix of convent-school French, native Portuguese, and improvised English — whose love appeared unexpectedly. Whose kind deeds astounded Elizabeth, not just in nursing her back to health — when Elizabeth fainted one morning, Lota collapsed too, in sympathy — but in offering to build an *estudio* where Elizabeth could write if she would stay on at Samambaia. Never in her life had anyone "made that kind of gesture toward me." Elizabeth felt as if she'd "died and gone to heaven without deserving to." She stayed.

Even before the studio was completed, while the two women lived in Lota's unfinished house open to the elements, amid heaps of construction materials, lighting their way at night with oil lamps, Elizabeth was writing as she never had before — stories, not poems, of her childhood in Nova Scotia. Although she would never finish the story "Homesickness," about her mother, she found she could write about her own early terror at her mother's screams echoing over Great Village — "alive forever" in memory — because she could also recall "those pure blue skies," the "leaning willows" along the riverbank that were her comfort, and the villagers — seamstress, blacksmith, postmaster — who knew her so well, as she settled into another country village in a differently vivid, "unbelievably impractical" landscape of black granite cliffs, waterfalls, purple-flowered Lent trees, and "brilliant, brilliant blue" skies. "I am a little embarrassed about having to go to Brazil to experience total recall about Nova Scotia," she wrote to Katharine White, who gratefully accepted "In the Village," Elizabeth's tale of childhood in Great Village, for the *New Yorker:* "geography must be more mysterious than we think." She could write a story called "Gwendolyn," about the death of her frail girlhood playmate; Elizabeth herself was safe and cared for. "You have an ally here in the friend I am staying with," she would tell Katharine White. Lota had given her a gold ring with the date of their impetuous pledge to live together — "20-12-51," less than a month after Elizabeth's arrival in Rio — inscribed in it. Elizabeth would be "no man's wife," but she and Lota had started a marriage.

At Walnut Hill School Elizabeth had written of her longing to "open every building to the blue sky and the wind." Now in Brazil — "or my perpendicular stretch of it," as she wrote to Katharine White in letters carefully introducing her decision to extend her stay in Petrópolis with "my hostess" — at the very top of a thickly forested property that Lota was selling off in parcels to support her construction project, Elizabeth lived in a house where a cloud might be "coming in my bedroom window right this minute," or a large yellow and black hummingbird had to be shooed out of the pantry with an umbrella. Her view was of a steep green valley rimmed by mountains with thick mists spilling over them "like waterfalls in slow motion."

And she lived with Lota, a woman "much too attached to material possessions ... in a careless country like Brazil" — the Calders and other works of art she collected, the Saarinen and Aalto furniture with which she filled her homes, the expensive fabrics she had made up into suits and shifts she wore in the city — but who, at Samambaia, was "rarely without a measuring stick, a trowel or a screwdriver" and nearly always, like Elizabeth these days, dressed in blue jeans and an old, man-tailored shirt. Lota, who had once triumphed in samba competitions partnered by men of her newspaper-editor father's ruling class, but who used her inherited property and prestige to live as she pleased — always with women. Lota, who instinctively knew that Elizabeth needed "getting used to be happy and sleeping well, and less scared," as she added in a postscript to one of Elizabeth's letters back to America; who would repeatedly assure Elizabeth how "wonderful you are" and how "amusing" and "likeable," and never tire of shooing away Elizabeth's "inferiorities," like so many hummingbirds from the pantry.

Elizabeth was slow to admit to her American friends that she wasn't coming back. Her letters mentioned plans to continue her circuit of South America by steamer at the end of February, and then early March. But Lota had given her the ring on her birthday, February 8,

Lota de Macedo Soares at Cabo Frio, Brazil

and a party the night before with cake and champagne and gifts from neighbors — a "real" banana-eating, "very tame and mischievous" toucan was Elizabeth's favorite. It had been her "lifelong dream" to own one. She told no one of the ring, but could Marianne Moore or Dr. Anny Baumann or Cal Lowell or anyone to whom she described Uncle Sam, with his "electric-blue eyes," red-feathered stomach, "bright gold bib," and sleek black body, think she could leave the bird behind? The name she chose "in a chauvinistic outburst," she told Cal, both recalled her old home and celebrated the new one: in everyday speech the bird was "Sam," the shorthand Lota used in referring to her Petrópolis estate, or "Sammy."

For Lota's birthday, March 16, when Lota turned forty-two to Elizabeth's forty-one, Elizabeth painted a watercolor of the Aladdin kerosene lamp they read by at night, inscribed "For Lota":

> *Longer than Alladin's burns,*
> *Love, & many Happy Returns.*

———

In late April they traveled to New York, staying for more than a month at the Hotel Grosvenor, on Fifth Avenue in Greenwich Village — "Lota likes luxury," Elizabeth already knew — to gather books, clothes, and the clavichord, and pack them for shipment to Brazil. Elizabeth gave her talk at Bryn Mawr. Few students appeared, but she assured the college president, Katherine McBride, by letter that "the last six or seven weeks have been very good ones for me and I am feeling very grateful."

In Manhattan they visited mutual friends — the painter Loren MacIver and her husband, the poet Lloyd Frankenberg. Loren had painted Elizabeth's portrait; Lota collected Loren's paintings. They saw the duo pianists Arthur Gold and Robert Fizdale in their two-story studio apartment at Carnegie Hall. Elizabeth introduced Lota to Marianne Moore, who at almost sixty-five had received both the National Book Award and the Pulitzer Prize for her *Collected Poems* and was on the brink of late-life celebrity. Moore had picked out the black tricorne hat that became, with flowing cape to match, her signature garment and wore it atop her pinned-up white braids to the National Book Award ceremony that spring of 1952; her lovably eccentric appearance in the news photo ushered in her era of fame. At the *New Yorker,* which had previously rejected any poems she submitted, Katharine White begged Elizabeth to use her influence to press Marianne to send new manuscripts. Shortly after her return to Brazil with Lota in July, Elizabeth complied, finessing the awkward fact that she'd been first to join the *New Yorker*'s stable of writers by telling Marianne that William Shawn, the new editor, "is really interested in trying to get good, better, best poems, for a change."

Katharine White had been out of the city during Elizabeth's New York stay and did not meet "the friend with whom I am living here," the most Elizabeth would venture to say in letters about her connection to Lota. Perhaps missing the opportunity to introduce Lota this time was fine with Elizabeth. She was leaving a country where same-sex love was more than ever taboo, where the American Psychiatric Association's first *Diagnostic and Statistical Manual of Mental Disorders,* newly released in 1952, was to categorize homosexuality as a "sociopathic personality disturbance." Had she consulted a psychoanalyst now, confided as she had in Ruth Foster five years before, Elizabeth might not have found acceptance. Elizabeth was well aware that the *New Yorker*'s editorial department insisted on strictly verifiable facts and refused to print certain curse words or "functional references," even in poetry and fiction. She may not have known that the magazine maintained an equally strict code of suitable topics, which Katharine White, wife of the magazine's longtime contributor E. B. White, upheld: homosexuality was "definitely out as humor, and dubious in any case."

Within a year of her return to Brazil with Lota, Elizabeth would read Lizzie Hardwick's dismissive review of Simone de Beauvoir's *The Second Sex* (which Elizabeth had read earlier in French and "fundamentally" agreed with) and take in Hardwick's approving surmise that the French feminist at least was not "a masochist, a Lesbian, a termagant, or a man-hater." Lizzie had done "a fine job" with the review, Elizabeth wrote to Cal, who'd stayed on with Lizzie in Amsterdam, in the same letter in which she informed him, tersely, that she'd settled down with Lota — "she wanted me to stay; she offered to build me a studio." A year later, the first chapters of Mary McCarthy's *The Group* began to appear in *Partisan Review,* leaving Elizabeth aghast at her old schoolmate's ability to write such "fantastic" prose, yet "without one shred of imagination" — and most of all worried that Mary might expose Elizabeth as one of the sex-obsessed grown-up Vassar girls she caricatured in the novel.

Elizabeth would not tell Cal outright that she loved Lota. But that first Brazilian summer of 1952 she did tell him, and everyone else she wrote to, how happy she was, "happier than I have felt in ten years," or twenty, or ever. "It is so much easier to live exactly as one wants to here." Brazilians in general may have been no more overtly welcoming to homosexuals in the 1950s than Americans, but the country had a long history of tolerance. In 1830, a few years after gaining independence from Portugal, following the lead of Napoleonic France and its colonies, Brazil was the first nation in the New World to repeal anti-sodomy laws. As in Key West, a mix of races and ancestries contributed to what Elizabeth called "the really lofty vagueness of Brazil," which extended to mail delivery, "seasons, fruits, languages, geography, everything." It was "nice & relaxing" to live in such "complete confusion." Her choice of housemate hardly seemed to matter, and the Brazilian people, she told Cal, are "extremely affectionate, an atmosphere that I just lap up — no I guess I mean loll in." For Elizabeth, who struggled with the Portuguese language and was just as happy that Samambaia's remote location meant visitors arrived only on weekends, those "people" were Lota.

They were rarely apart. Days in Samambaia were framed by an hour or more of reading each morning and evening; it was "wonderful" that Lota "likes to read as much as I do and begins at 6:30 a.m. usually," Elizabeth wrote to Marianne. Once her books were unpacked, Elizabeth estimated that between them they owned three thousand volumes. The hours of work — Elizabeth writing, Lota supervising the "mens" who arrived to lay flooring or pave the driveway — were punctuated by *cafezhinos* and meals prepared by a cook or by Elizabeth herself, whom Lota promptly nicknamed "Cookie." The coffee was always "superb," and Elizabeth was well aware "how good it is for me to live in a country where one scarcely ever dreams of drinking anything else." She told her doctor, Anny Baumann, who increasingly served as Elizabeth's confidant and confessor as well as clinician, that she was shedding the thirty pounds she'd gained in recent years and had reduced her nights of drunkenness to "once or twice a month, and I stop before it gets really bad." Both drinking and working had "improved miraculously," thanks to Lota's "good sense and kindness." Elizabeth simply didn't "think about it any more"—whether or not to drink—"or go through all that remorse" on the few occasions when she succumbed. She no longer feared, as she wrote to Cal, that she'd "wander around the world in a drunken daze for the rest of my life."

Some days the landscape and weather were "so beautiful" it was hard to stay indoors and work. Some days Lota's workmen were noisy and distracting, or the two women drove down the mountainside in Lota's "rather elderly" Jaguar to shop at the village market. One weekend Lota's friend Rosinha Leão, another of Candido Portinari's former students, arrived from Rio with buckets of paint, and the women covered one wall of the "enormous" new bathroom with multicolored diamonds, "harlequin-tights style." When Elizabeth's studio, "way up in the air behind the house," was finished at the end of December, in Brazilian midsummer, she spent hours gazing in disbelieving gratitude at the gray-blue mica-flecked rock that Lota had found for the small building's exterior, the whitewashed walls and herringbone-patterned brick floor, the tiny bathroom and kitchenette with stove for making

Elizabeth in the pool at Samambaia

tea, the view of "stupendous mountain scenery" in the distance, the vegetable garden up close. Although she'd had no formal training in architecture or landscape design — few women did — Lota had a genius for everything from siting a building to sculpting its outdoor spaces and outfitting its interiors, which her projects at Samambaia, where she was at liberty to experiment on her own remote mountainside, abundantly displayed.

Lota also had a way of knowing what mattered most to Elizabeth. Next she dammed a natural pool at the base of a small waterfall that ran beside the house to make Elizabeth a "neck-deep" swimming pool that filled right away with *delicious*, ice-cold, pale green water "straight down off the top of the mountain." A cat, Tobias, "black with white feet and vest," joined the household soon after Elizabeth spoke of wanting one to curb the mouse population. "Wishes seem to come true here at such a rate one is almost afraid to make them any more," Elizabeth wrote to Dr. Baumann.

Before the pool was finished and a "super-bathroom" installed in the big house, the two women relied on tin basins for bathing, as in the long-ago days when Elizabeth had watched her mother wash herself in the bedroom at her grandparents' house in Great Village. But now Elizabeth and Lota reveled in Samambaia's unending supply of "running, rushing water" outdoors, using the garden hose. Elizabeth offered to wash Lota's long, straight hair, black with wide silver streaks on either side; the shampooing of Lota's hair became a ritual they couldn't give up. The ritual became a poem, the second Elizabeth wrote in the early months of her stay in Brazil; its interlocking pairs of rhymes spoke her love for Lota, her gratitude for Lota's impulsive invitation to stay on at Samambaia:

> *The still explosions on the rocks,*
> *the lichens, grow*
> *by spreading, gray, concentric shocks.*
> *They have arranged*
> *to meet the rings around the moon, although*
> *within our memories they have not changed.*

And since the heavens will attend
as long on us,
you've been, dear friend,
precipitate and pragmatical;
and look what happens. For Time is
nothing if not amenable.

The shooting stars in your black hair
in bright formation
are flocking where,
so straight, so soon?
— Come, let me wash it in this big tin basin,
battered and shiny like the moon.

Lota and Elizabeth were an interlocking pair — in love, in their lives together. A decade later, when Elizabeth had collected a volume of poems all written in Brazil, *Questions of Travel,* she would dedicate the book to Lota with an epigraph in Portuguese, the final couplet of a sonnet by the sixteenth-century poet Luís de Camões: "Giving you what I have and what I may / The more I give you, the more I owe you." Elizabeth gave Lota what she had and what she made — this new poem and others to come.

She sent "The Shampoo" to the *New Yorker,* but unlike "Arrival at Santos" and the stories "In the Village" and "Gwendolyn," it came back. "This sort of small personal poem perhaps doesn't quite fit into the *New Yorker,*" wrote Katharine White apologetically. "It won't make literary history," Elizabeth complained to a friend, "but I did think it was easy enough to understand." Too easy, perhaps. She sent "The Shampoo" to *Poetry,* and it was returned as well. "I never thought I'd see the day when we would reject a poem of yours," wrote *Poetry's* editor, Karl Shapiro, "but we do so daringly today." Marianne Moore, to whom Elizabeth had mailed the earliest finished draft in August 1952, never mentioned "The Shampoo" in return letters. Elizabeth confided to the poet May Swenson, with whom she'd formed a fast bond at Yaddo that "winter . . . when I thought my days were numbered," her worry that there was "something indecent about it I'd overlooked." May also lived with a woman, Pearl Schwartz, in a relationship sanctified by rings engraved with the date of their commitment; she knew what Elizabeth was asking. Finally, three years later in 1955, the *New Republic* published "the little poem Mrs. White couldn't understand."

Elizabeth struggled, even in Lota's paradise, to complete what she'd once estimated as the remaining 15 percent of the manuscript expected by Houghton Mifflin and meant to become her second book since *North & South* appeared in 1946. There had been "a good spell of work and then a long bad one," during which the "old bronchitis-asthma cycle" recurred, along with circling thoughts: was asthma the reason she couldn't write, or did her fear that "poetry is all over forever" provoke the asthma? The two stories she'd written early on at Samambaia, "In the Village" and "Gwendolyn," had been accomplished while under the influence of cortisone, a new medication that cleared her lungs but also left her feeling hopped up, and afterward worn out. She quit using the drug, triggering the letdown in mood, and returned to it only intermittently in later years, always pleased with the energy she gained on the "ride" — *"this euphoria is wonderful,"* she once wrote Cal — but disliking the frenetic state cortisone put her in, the surges of emotion the steroid caused.

Disrupted sleep was no help. She woke several times a night gasping for breath, lit the oil lamp so she could see to administer a shot of adrenaline, then waited for the effects to take hold. She guessed that "intimacy with clouds" might affect her lungs adversely, she wrote to Marianne Moore, but she would not consider moving from Samambaia — "I like it so much." To her delight, Elizabeth had earned more than $1,200 for "Gwendolyn" and more for "In the Village," far exceeding any sums she'd received for poems from the *New Yorker*, with its per-line rates. Expecting to sell more stories, she bought a car, a year-old MG two-seater, black with red leather upholstery, and began learning to drive, eager to "stop being the passenger-type I've been all my life" and take over the shopping in Petrópolis for Lota, who disliked the chore. Here was a way she could help save "emotional wear & tear" in the household. "I don't like arguments," Elizabeth would always say, and she strove to avoid them in even small matters with Lota, a Brazilian for whom "argument . . . is the favorite occupation." Dependence on Lota, in a country where Elizabeth couldn't speak the language and had no friends of her own, felt risky at times. But learning to operate the car's finicky gearshift proved too difficult on mountain roads in Brazil, where female drivers were a rarity and the sight of a woman at the wheel could provoke shouts of "Well done, daughter!" or "Go back to the kitchen!" Perhaps, with a traumatic car crash in memory, Elizabeth was destined to remain a passenger, and she admitted to Cal a residual fear that any of "the few people I'm fond of may be in automobile accidents." The disappointment added to her sense, as she wrote in a letter of apology to a second editor at Houghton Mifflin, Paul Brooks, that she was someone "who just can't 'produce.'" Finally she resorted to telegram: "CANNOT PROMISE ANYTHING IMMEDIATELY. . . . HOPE YOU WILL CONSIDER PUBLISHING BOOK AS IT IS NOW."

Elizabeth was "getting used to be[ing] happy." She wondered, could happiness itself cause her to "never write a line" again? And Lota was getting used to Elizabeth's pace, her yen for distraction. "Elizabeth is the slowest personne in the world," Lota informed their friends Gold and Fizdale, after a year together. "You should see the mail she gets asking, begging, etc. and nope, she is cooking a cake!" The new life, the feeling of being "so at home" for the first time since early childhood, may have made it hard for Elizabeth to look back at the poems she'd written before, when she'd been at "dead low tide." In the new book, which she planned to title *A Cold Spring* after a poem describing a season that "hesitated" into being, there would be "At the Fishhouses," with its bitter draught of knowledge, and "The Bight," written to mark a birthday at Key West when she'd despaired of both the year past and the one ahead. The poem began with a bleak description of Garrison Bight, a sheltered harbor for small craft:

> *At low tide like this how sheer the water is.*
> *White, crumbling ribs of marl protrude and glare*
> *and the boats are dry, the pilings dry as matches.*

At low tide, the water "doesn't wet anything." In the sky—

> *Black-and-white man-of-war birds soar*
> *on impalpable drafts*
> *and open their tails like scissors on the curves*
> *or tense them like wishbones till they tremble.*

The soaring man-of-war birds with their scissoring tails threaten, yet they too are wishing, trembling, in tension. On shore, shark tails for the "Chinese-restaurant trade" hang out to dry on chicken wire; a dredge thrums a steady beat, bringing up more marl from the bay's sandy bottom; and small white boats, damaged by a recent storm, lie on their sides, "stove in" or "piled up / against each other . . . / like torn-open unanswered letters." The whole "untidy" scene reflected her state of mind, "awful but cheerful," as she had faced down a lonely birthday in February 1948.

"The Prodigal," a double sonnet, was inspired by an encounter with one of her aunt Grace's stepsons, who'd offered her a drink early one morning during her 1946 trip to Nova Scotia. He'd been standing in the pigsty when he held out the bottle of rum, and if Elizabeth wasn't drunk or hung over herself, there had been many mornings that summer when she was. He'd recognized that in her, and she felt it; he was her double. "O Breath" captured her battle with asthma. Even "Insomnia," a small, personal love poem the *New Yorker* published happily in 1951, just before Elizabeth left for South America, must have brought confused feelings as she read it over in her newfound Eden. Although "Insomnia" told of abandoned constraint, of staying awake all night for the sake of love in a "world inverted / where left is always right," Elizabeth understood, in the wake of "The Shampoo"'s rejection, that the first poem's lovers had been suitably ambiguous, need not have been, to most readers, two women. Had the subterfuge been intentional? Most likely. But Elizabeth knew now, if she hadn't before, how closely her words were scrutinized for hints of the secret life she managed to live by hiding in plain sight.

In the end, Houghton Mifflin took her suggestion; there would be no more unmet promises for new poems. But rather than publish a slim volume, the editors proposed a "collected poems," combining *North & South,* now out of print, with *A Cold Spring.* "The Shampoo" provided the conclusion for what Elizabeth described sheepishly to Marianne Moore as this "misbegotten book." Proofs left Elizabeth's desk in July 1955. The book's simple cover was designed by Loren MacIver: a brilliant yellow-green leaf ascending on a field of white and blue; the title, *Poems: North & South — A Cold Spring,* displayed modestly in typewriter type. Elizabeth would not presume to use the word "Collected" in her title; she was not yet forty-five, twenty years younger than Marianne had been when she issued her prize-winning *Collected Poems.*

Yet now, with the pressure to produce lifted, Elizabeth pushed a dozen new poems through to completion in 1955 and '56. "Squatter's Children," "Manners," "Filling Station," "Questions of Travel," "Sestina," "Manuelzinho," "The Armadillo," and "Sunday, 4 A.M." all went to the *New Yorker* and found swift acceptance. More poems filled her notebooks in draft. She'd begun translating the diary of a Brazilian girl — Helena Morley, she would be called in the finished book — a vivid portrayal of life in a remote diamond-mining town in the mid-1890s. So far the project seemed to help rather than hinder her progress with poetry, and allowed her to reckon with her newly adopted country's language without the strain of rapid conversation. Finally, as Elizabeth wrote to Katharine White, she could state truthfully that Samambaia was "the best, or maybe first, place I've found to work in steadily." Her health rebounded, Elizabeth told Dr. Baumann, and she was "maybe gradually making up for some of my misspent youth-and-early-middle-age." She had "almost a new book of poems," she wrote to Randall Jarrell, with whom she'd carried on an occasional correspondence since he'd introduced her to Cal back in 1947. Randall, who could be a vicious critic of his contemporaries, had told her she was doing something both "theoretically and practically impossible": writing nothing but good poems. "Exile seems to work for me," she concluded. In the midst of this unprecedented burst of productivity, a reporter from *O Globo* in Rio called in early May 1956 to tell Elizabeth that *Poems* had won the Pulitzer Prize.

It wasn't the first award that had come to the women at Samambaia. Six months after she'd settled in Brazil, Elizabeth had received the Poetry Society of America's $800 Shelley Memorial Award. The year before *Poems* was published, the design for Lota's house, which had already been featured in several international magazines, took first place in a competition judged by Walter Gropius for architects under age forty; Sergio Bernardes, who'd drawn up the plans in collaboration with Lota, was the named winner. And the Pulitzer wasn't the only award *Poems* would bring. During the year following the announcement, Elizabeth received a Ford Foundation grant of $2,700 from *Partisan Review* and an Amy Lowell Traveling Scholarship. "Never has so little work dragged in so many prizes," she quipped. But the Pulitzer Prize, which she had won out of a field including Jarrell and Auden, put Elizabeth on film in Brazil's weekly newsreel and in a photo in *O Globo*, where she was recognized by the vegetable man in Petrópolis, who congratulated her at the market. Most important, Elizabeth would say, the prize certified her worth as a poet to Lota's circle of friends.

Elizabeth's sense of being "so at home" could vanish when the artists and writers and politicians who were Lota's lifelong compan-

Elizabeth on the patio at Samambaia

ions arrived for weekend stays or dinner parties at Samambaia. Some seemed "pointedly uninterested" in or attacked American culture; others grew tired of the effort to communicate with Elizabeth in English or French, or were jealous that Lota's affection had been won by an American. Elizabeth's shyness returned, forcing questions: "what am I doing *here?*—*who* am I, anyway—did I *ever* have a personality?" Mary Morse had drifted off to Rio, where she was dating men; she wanted a child. And although Elizabeth enjoyed Rosinha Leão and the poet Manuel Bandeira (despite disliking his poetry), she felt most comfortable practicing her limited Portuguese with the cook, who named her new daughter after Elizabeth.

In Elizabeth's view, Brazil suffered as a country with "NO MIDDLE CLASS," she wrote to a friend, in which the "ruling" and "intellectual" elites were drawn from a small group of people who "all know each other and are usually all related." There was no competition from below to challenge the few anointed writers and artists, and press them to do better. Political power was both entrenched and vacillating, and all too closely allied with the military. When Elizabeth arrived, the country was under the rule of a former dictator, Getulio Vargas, elected as president after six years out of power. Lota's close friend the publisher Carlos Lacerda had waged a relentless campaign against Vargas in his newspaper and narrowly escaped assassination. The failed plot to kill Lacerda gave the military a pretext for demanding Vargas's resignation; Vargas stepped down and then committed suicide, setting off a period of instability that enabled Lacerda to enter the political arena himself, putting Lota and her friends close to the center of power. Lacerda had bought one of the lots on Lota's estate and was a near neighbor on weekends and holidays; he loved to drop by to talk politics, art, and literature with Lota and Elizabeth.

The severe imbalance of rich and poor, obvious to any visitor in the 1950s at a first glimpse of Rio's luxury apartment buildings lining the beach and slum neighborhoods, *favelas,* climbing the mountainside behind, both disturbed Elizabeth and fired her imagination. Elizabeth herself was born of such an imbalance, an unusual hybrid of the extreme ends of the social spectrum: an orphan heiress who'd spent her happiest childhood years among tradespeople, a Vassar girl whose home address was a dingy working-class suburb. Traveling in luxury in Europe with Louise Crane, Elizabeth had formed a close bond with the Russian nurse who cared for her after a surgery. In Key West, she'd grown attached to the matronly housekeeper at White Street, Hannah Almyda, and drafted a poem about her that she revised many times but never finished. She'd completed poems about two other domestic workers, black women she'd met in Key West, honoring their complicated lives in "Faustina" and "Cootchie," both published in her prize-winning *Poems*.

Now in Brazil, Elizabeth lived among the wealthy, but as an outsider, a dependent whose trust fund met only basic expenses, and she sometimes chose as subjects people and situations that must have seemed commonplace to Lota, her benefactor and mate. "Squatter's Children," the first poem she sent to the *New Yorker* in 1955, grew out of Elizabeth's sympathetic identification with neglected children, and recalled the imagery of "A Miracle for Breakfast." Viewed from a great distance, a "specklike girl and boy" play alone near a "specklike house," dark crumbs scattered on the "unbreathing sides of hills" — the *favela*. The sun hangs in the sky, a "suspended eye," and while there is no river, the children "wade" in "gigantic waves of light and shade." The image magnifies to reveal the children playing with their father's tools in the hard dirt, dropping the heavy mattock with a clang. Their laughter blooms, joining their mother's sharp cries to come inside as thunderheads rise and rain begins to fall on the "unwarrantable ark," the squatter's shack that is their tenuous home. The storm, like the Oz-bound tornado that swept up an orphan Dorothy Gale and her flimsy Kansas homestead and deposited them in a vibrant new world, provides a "threshold" beneath the children's "muddy shoes" over which they can step into a wider world, free to enter "mansions" (another image drawn from "A Miracle for Breakfast") of their own choosing, "rooms of falling rain." This new realm is neither miracle nor fantasy, however, but the natural world where the "rights" of children are guaranteed and their "lawfulness endures," even if in "soggy documents." It is the new world of 1955, where a handful of Negro schoolchildren in Topeka, Kansas, had just won, at least in court documents, the right to cross thresholds into classrooms previously closed to them. Would Brazil act to secure the natural rights of its dispossessed children too?

Cold War politics had played into the 1954 *Brown v. Board of Education* decision: how could the United States present itself as an exemplary democracy if it denied racial minorities equal treatment? Elizabeth may have heard such accusations in dinner party conversation at Samambaia or in Rio as the landmark case worked its way to the Supreme Court from 1951 to 1953, and might have wished to turn them back on her host country. She published "Squatter's Children" first (in English) in the progressive Brazilian monthly *Anhembi,* where it followed the serialization of Vinicius de Moraes's "verse tragedy" of *favela* life, *Orfeu da Conceição,* from which the movie *Black Orpheus* was later derived.

Elizabeth followed the American scene as closely as she could — subscribing to the Sunday *New York Times* and the *Nation* as well as *Partisan Review* and the *New Yorker* — even as she pressed Lota, who frankly preferred traveling in Europe or the United States, to explore Brazil with her. Lota thought her beloved Cookie was suffering from "bi-localization." One weekend in April 1953 they made a journey in the old Jaguar, carrying spare cans of gasoline and Lota's revolver, along mountain roads transformed into a "deep river of red mud" by equinoctial rains to the nearly deserted former gold-mining town of Ouro Prêto. Lota's expertise in changing a flat tire *"in a jiffy"* impressed Elizabeth almost as much as the baroque Basílica do Bom Jesus in neighboring Congonhas, with its *Twelve Prophets* by the mulatto sculptor Aleijadinho, the "little cripple." Aleijadinho, a leper, had completed the works with hammer and chisel strapped to his fingerless hands. Lota had changed the tire while clad in a wraparound skirt that fell open as she bent over to jack up the car, oblivious to the stares of passing truck drivers. Elizabeth could not have been surprised by Lota's "precipitate" practicality; she'd also seen "my hostess" direct the early-morning dynamiting of an enormous boulder in her bathrobe.

Lota resisted the exotic river trips Elizabeth longed for, but starting in 1957 they spent Christmas and New Year's in the quiet seaside village of Cabo Frio, with its high white dunes and "secret beaches," two hours from Rio by car, where they fished, swam, ate the local lobster, shrimp, and pineapples, read and napped in string hammocks. Every year, Elizabeth and Lota attended Carnival, usually in Rio. Elizabeth, who struggled with conversational Portuguese, nonetheless picked up the new samba songs — "living poetry," she called the lyrics composed by rival samba schools to sing as they danced in elaborate costumes through the streets at night. She treasured the ironic humor of some:

> *Rio de Janeiro,*
> *My joy and my delight!*
> *By day I have no water,*
> *By night I have no light.*

A favorite love song echoed her own "Shampoo":

> *Come, my mulatta,*
> * Take me back.*
> *You're the joker*
> * In my pack,*
> *The prune in my pudding,*
> * Pepper in my pie,*
> *My package of peanuts,*
> * The moon in my sky.*

The song's mulatta lover could have been Lota, with her "beautiful colored skin"; Lota turned darker in the sun while Elizabeth remained pale, even as her "Anglo-Saxon blood" was "gradually relinquishing its seasonal cycle." Carnival was the epitome of the "underdeveloped-yet-decadent" Brazil that Elizabeth settled into contentedly at age forty-five, writing May Swenson, who thought Elizabeth looked "wise" in her recent author photo, that in fact she had "never felt foolisher." Elizabeth "loved" this photo, in which she had posed against "my rocks" at Samambaia wearing "an old shirt," and she wished May — who'd become one of Elizabeth's most reliable correspondents since her move to Brazil, providing literary news along with the occasional pair of Lee jeans, high-powered binoculars for bird watching, or a pink skirted bathing suit from Saks — could slide down the waterfall into the pool with her and Lota, join them for an outdoor lunch of fresh figs and prosciutto. Elizabeth didn't much like Rio except at Carnival time, but where else, she wondered, could you find a billboard advertising a new gas stove showing a "young Negro cook, overcome by her pleasure . . . leaning across it toward her white mistress . . . as they kissed each other on the cheek."

In "Manuelzinho," another poem of 1955, the same year she produced "Squatter's Children," Elizabeth captured the effort at connection across class lines she found so remarkable in Brazil and reminiscent of her village childhood. She recorded Lota's frustrated dealings with the inept gardener, "half squatter, half tenant (no rent)," whose right to live at Samambaia with his family on land farmed by his ancestors Lota never questioned. "You helpless, foolish man, / I love you all I can," she finished in Lota's voice. "Or do I? / . . . Again I promise to try." When Howard Moss, the *New Yorker*'s new poetry editor, wrote to Elizabeth praising the poem, she rolled a special sheet of paper, a memento of Carnival season, into her typewriter to answer him. Hand-lettered across the top of the page in bright pink, green, and silver glitter, the colors of Rio's popular Mangueira samba school, were the words UNIDOS SEREMOS FELIZES. "United we shall be happy," she translated her "motto" for Moss; "so *true,* don't you think?"

Although many of the new poems of the mid-1950s featured Brazilian subjects, Elizabeth was still imaginatively engaged in her Nova Scotia and New England youth, seeking the roots of her present happiness in several unfinished works about her early erotic life. A poem, called simply "Judy," revived her passion for Judy Flynn at Walnut Hill School: "I still am proud / that then I stared so hard / upon this best of Beauty. . . ." She remembered the high school classroom where pupils "sat in rows" and "we were all / helpless before it even / our old martinet principal." Another story, incomplete or perhaps never begun, but mentioned in a letter to May Swenson, derived from a favorite book by Gene Stratton-Porter. Aunt Maud had read Stratton-Porter's *A Girl of the Limberlost* aloud to Elizabeth when she was sick with the measles, and the two had cried over the tale of the fatherless teenager who earned enough money to stay in school by selling rare moths she collected in the wilderness. But it was *The Keeper of the Bees* that inspired Elizabeth now, with its child hero, Little Scout, who "no one knows whether is a boy or a girl," she explained to May, apologizing for her awkward syntax in describing such an unusual character. May would understand her fascination with a tomboy far more insistent on her androgyny than Elizabeth had dared to be. When asked outright, "Are you a girl or a boy?" the child replies, "If you can't *tell,* it doesn't make a darn bit of difference, does it?" Little Scout dresses as a boy and belongs to a Boy Scout troop, but is still capable of planting "the hardest, hottest, sweetest little kiss" on the lips of the novel's protagonist, a shell-shocked World War I veteran recuperating on a seaside ranch in California. There he observes the impish child in a moment of abandon: "on bended knee . . . with eyes rolled heavenward, ecstatically sucking" honey from the pistils of Madonna lilies.

Perched amid a flowering wilderness, Elizabeth and Lota could have been taken for "little scouts" — almost child-sized women, dressed all day in slacks and work shirts, still rare feminine attire in the 1950s. In fun, Lota had gone shopping in a local priests' clothing store and come back with a pair of bishop's socks of a "particular bright magenta," Elizabeth told May, "just the thing with blue jeans." Which was the greater breach of convention, wearing men's clothes or a bishop's socks? Elizabeth was proud that Lota could give orders to carpenters and bricklayers, drive the jeep or Jaguar as expertly as a man, kill a five-foot snake with one shot of her .22. Elizabeth herself, who'd "combined being asthmatic with also being athletic" since childhood, had taken hold of a "hydraulic cannon" at a mine in Diamantina, where she'd gone to research her translation of the young Helena Morley's diary, and "brought down a few tons of landscape." When Elizabeth had flown out of the small town — a desolate place, a "wild Atlantic Ocean of rocks" that felt as far off as the moon — she'd been one of only two women on the small plane, the other an expectant mother of twins on transport to a city hospital for the delivery.

In the poetry world, it was the same. While she had learned from and leaned on Marianne Moore, and, in recent years, encouraged May Swenson with letters of recommendation and line-by-line critiques, she was pleased to have been "on parade with such a slew of men," as May described the photo gallery of Pulitzer Prize winners published in the newspapers, and to learn that she'd been featured, along with Robert Lowell, Theodore Roethke, and Richard Wilbur, on a WNYC radio program, *Poets Since 1945*. Elizabeth seemed amused rather than daunted by her despised aunt Florence Bishop's repeated "crack," remembered now, at a safe distance in Brazil, that "being a writer makes a woman coarse, or masculine." Although she wrote love poems on occasion, Elizabeth was nettled by what she perceived as the *New Yorker* poetry critic Louise Bogan's expectation that women poets should confine themselves to "feminine" or sentimental subjects. Elizabeth could not have been happy to hear from May that she'd been acknowledged, along with Bogan, at a reading at the Museum of Modern Art, as among "our best women poets," despite the moderator's clumsy effort to clarify he'd meant "women *poets*," not "*women* poets."

But at Samambaia, Elizabeth could indulge in the conventionally feminine when she wanted to. Elizabeth and Lota were not just building but also decorating and furnishing a house together, and there were trips to tile makers and decisions to make about upholstery and linens.

May Swenson,
photograph by Erich Hartmann

In the kitchen, Elizabeth supervised the cook or made her own lasagna, chicken tetrazzini, and stuffing for the Christmas turkey. She perfected recipes for jams and marmalades using local fruits, and taught herself to work with yeast so she could offer guests English muffins made from scratch. "When the muse gives up the ghost," she joked to May, "I can set myself up with a little shop in Rio, an impoverished gentlewoman, selling doughnuts and brownies." There were children to look after too — the cook's baby and, in the hot summer months, Lota's young grandchildren escaping the heat in Rio. Long before Elizabeth arrived in Brazil, Lota had adopted the son of a garage mechanic who'd been repairing her car. She'd noticed the boy, Kylso, nearly hidden behind the service station's high counter, his legs crippled by polio, and asked his father's permission to take him to a hospital. Several operations enabled the boy to walk with the aid of a cane, and then Lota supported his education at a boarding school. Now Kylso was grown, working as an architect's draftsman, and married with children of his own.

Perhaps Lota's benefaction was in the back of Elizabeth's mind as she wrote "Filling Station," another poem of 1955, set in a gas station on one of Brazil's highways, although she later placed it in the "Elsewhere" section of her 1965 volume, *Questions of Travel,* implicitly transposing the scene to Canada. "Oh, but it is dirty!" the poem begins. "Father wears a dirty, / oil-soaked monkey suit / . . . and greasy sons assist him / (it's a family filling station)." Yet the grimy roadside establishment is furnished with a "comfy" if battered wicker sofa, and an "extraneous" begonia plant sits atop a side table draped with a large handmade doily. These humble decorative touches, hints of femininity and craft or art, yield a closing benediction: "Somebody embroidered the doily. / Somebody waters the plant, / . . . Somebody loves us all."

"Love's the main thing always" in child-rearing, Elizabeth was learning from her experience tending little "Elizabetchy," the cook's daughter, and Kylso's toddler children, although Lota did the bulk of the work when Kylso left his "babies" at Samambaia for weeks on end. Lota was "magnificent with child-problems," Elizabeth conceded. "I suspect it's because she's had so much practice with me." She remembered the saving love of her Bulmer aunts and grandmother, and as she listened one day to Kylso's youngest, Lotinha, "discovering her voice ... amusing herself trilling away by the hour, all alone," Elizabeth was grateful she had not missed this: "see[ing] so much more of children than I ever had before." Perhaps she had not been ready to see this way, but now it occurred to her that the "best results" of psychoanalysis, her sessions with Ruth Foster in the 1940s, had "come with the years," enabling explorations of her childhood and adolescence in poetry and prose.

One of these arrived in the form of a sestina, originally titled "Early Sorrow," in which Elizabeth turned again to the scene of her mother's removal to the asylum. It is a too-quiet afternoon like many following the night of screams and the slammed door; mother is gone. Grandmother and child sit at the kitchen table, taking comfort in the familiar objects around them — the hot Marvel stove, the singing teakettle, the almanac dangling on its string within easy reach for reference or jokes. But sorrow can't be hidden. The grandmother weeps into her teacup. The child — like Little Scout, neither girl nor boy in this poem — draws crayon pictures of "inscrutable" houses one after another. The child is too young to write, but already finds in art "a way of thinking with one's feelings," as Elizabeth defined poetry in a letter to May Swenson in September 1955, the month before she sent "Sestina" to the *New Yorker*.

May Swenson wasn't the only American friend who missed Elizabeth and wondered whether she was planning to stay in Brazil *"forever."* After a spell of itinerant teaching on his return to the United States in 1953, Cal had taken a job at Boston University in 1955 and settled in the Back Bay with Lizzie, who would soon give birth to their daughter Harriet. Cal never stopped urging Elizabeth to visit — he'd make a trip to New York City to see her, put her up in Boston or near his elderly cousin Harriet Winslow's house in Castine, Maine, where the Lowells spent the summer months in a converted barn on the property. Sometimes Elizabeth's reasons for staying away seemed clear. In New York, "everybody is so intent on using everybody," there was "no room or time for friendship any more." She'd always been too shy for this sort of "inter-communication," she wrote to Cal, "and I was miserably lonely there most of the time."

But when she heard about a spate of verse plays scheduled to open in the city, Elizabeth asked May Swenson to report on them, and guessed that before long she would "start sounding actually wistful" about all she was missing. Elizabeth admitted to May that "sometimes I get awfully homesick for *cold* salt-water," and for spring: "I'd like to hear a robin on a rainy evening, and see some maple trees budding." She missed bicycling, "the way I got around in Florida," impossible now in both vertiginous Petrópolis and crowded Rio. Still, five years after her arrival in Brazil, in October 1956, Elizabeth told May she was sorry she couldn't vote for Adlai Stevenson in his run against President Eisenhower in the coming election, because she had no residence in the United States. "Sorry I can't vote," she specified, "I don't mind about not having a residence."

The impending publication of her translation, *The Diary of "Helena Morley,"* provided a reason to return to New York for six months during the spring and summer of 1957 to review the proofs of the nearly four-hundred-page manuscript, a product of several years of "finicky" work rendering the young teenage girl's late-nineteenth-century Portuguese idioms into fluid English. She rented a sublet on East 67th Street, and Lota came along to shop for the now almost completed house at Samambaia. They would return to Brazil in the fall with twenty-six pieces of luggage, as well as three barrels, four large crates, and seven trunks, packed into the ocean liner's hold. The pianists Gold and Fizdale hosted a "bang-up party" in their new apartment on Central Park West, with Marianne Moore, E. E. Cummings, and Elizabeth's Vassar classmate Eleanor Clark and her husband, the poet and novelist Robert Penn Warren, on the guest list. There were several social calls on Katharine White in New York, where Elizabeth was observed to be "svelte and chic and free of asthma," and Lota remained "Donna Lota" to Mrs. White. The two women saw more of Cal and his family — Harriet was born in January 1957 — first in Boston and later in Maine for a troubling several days in August as their host began to show the excitability that warned of a breakdown. He'd gone "almost off the rails at the end," he admitted afterward.

Elizabeth and Cal's intellectual affinity, and their affection for each other, had deepened through the mail during the years both lived out of the country and after Cal's return to the United States. Linked in the popular imagination since Elizabeth's first book, *North & South,* and Cal's second, *Lord Weary's Castle,* appeared during the same publishing season in 1946, the two had more in common than even they sometimes acknowledged. Both had trust funds inherited from New England forebears that allowed them to get along without teaching, although Cal began to take jobs in the 1950s, as much to exercise his critical powers in the classroom and "inter-communicate" with fellow writers on the circuit as to contribute to the support of his new family. Cal suffered no shyness; in sociability he was Elizabeth's opposite. Yet Elizabeth and Cal shared an aesthetic — ranging across literature, art, and music, and strengthened by trading impressions in their correspondence — that made them each other's best reader, and that ensured, as Elizabeth wrote to Cal in June 1956, "I think of you every day of my life." Their key terms of approbation were "real," "genuine," and "new" — or "firmly new," as Cal described a recording of Charles Ives — in a midcentury modernism that took the stripping away of artifice and sentiment on an inward course toward personal narrative of the sort Cal had toyed with in *The Mills of the Kavanaghs,* his oblique account of his failed first marriage.

By the early 1950s, Elizabeth at Samambaia was leading the way with her autobiographical stories, a new means to accomplish what she'd always found easier in verse: "to get things straight and tell the truth." Cal was entranced by "In the Village" when he read it in the *New Yorker,* by its "great ruminating Dutch landscape feel of goneness," so powerfully convincing "I could weep for the cow," he wrote to Elizabeth. He knew she'd worked hard over it, but the story read "as though you weren't writing at all, but just talking in a full noisy room, talking until suddenly everyone is quiet." Could she develop the piece into a Nova Scotia "growing-up novel," Cal wondered, or, as he thought back over the half-dozen tales she'd published since her first residence in Florida, fill out a collection? Elizabeth pursued the idea of a book of stories long enough to get a rejection from Houghton Mifflin, which also turned down her translation of *The Diary of "Helena Morley."* In early 1957 she finally broke with the publisher to take a chance on a new editor at Farrar, Straus and Cudahy, Robert Giroux, who offered contracts for both *Helena Morley* and Elizabeth's next collection of poems. Her recent productivity suggested a third book of verse might not be far off.

Perhaps discouraged by Houghton Mifflin's rejection, Elizabeth finished no more stories through the 1950s, but her example set Cal in motion. The December before her 1957 trip to New York, Elizabeth read his childhood memoir, "91 Revere Street," in *Partisan Review,* feeling afterward as if she'd just "sat through one of those Sunday dinners," she wrote to Cal, and marveling at his account of being "thrown out of the [Boston Public] Garden, just like Adam." She referred to the story's tragicomic set pieces, but Cal had, like Elizabeth, rendered a devastating portrait of his originating family drama: the overbearing mother and emasculated father tearing at each other in arguments the boy thrilled to overhear late at night in the not-fashionable-enough Beacon Hill townhouse, lacking "purple panes" and "delicate bay," that could never satisfy his mother, though it stood "less than fifty yards from Louisburg Square . . . the Hub of the Hub of the Universe." The high-pitched "*Weelawaugh, we-ee-eelawaugh, weelawaugh*" of his mother's unending complaints and his father's sputtering "*But-and, but-and, but-and!*" borrow from Elizabeth's use of onomatopoeia to establish a child's perspective and echo her mother's hovering scream. The fraught situation for young Cal, an only child like Elizabeth, inspired his grade school bullying of other boys and, in the suffocating atmosphere of matriarchal oppression at home and at the Brimmer School, a desire for the "freedom to explode" that never really left him.

In her turn, Elizabeth urged Cal to "*keep it up,*" extend the narrative beyond his early school years. She imagined it wouldn't be difficult: "your life being more all of a piece than — well, mine." Elizabeth was exercising her customary self-deprecation, but she could also have been daunted by the extensive genealogy that filled the story's opening pages; the cameo appearance of his eminent relation the poet Amy

Lowell; the casual reference to Henry James as possible family chroni-
cler; or the simple fact of Cal's two living if embittered parents. In Cal's
young life, clamorous as it was, there had been no severing from parents or beloved grandparents and first remembered home; Cal's favorite, his autocratic grandfather Winslow, lived just blocks away. Elizabeth would work intermittently on a story to follow "In the Village"
about her own oppressive childhood on a very different Revere street,
"in the upstairs apartment of a two-family house on the outskirts of an
old but hideously ugly city north of Boston." But the story, "Mrs. Sullivan Downstairs," into which Elizabeth tried to inject some of the fond
humor of her Nova Scotia memoir by depicting neighborhood characters, was never finished. The problem of how to "get things straight
and tell the truth," how to represent with honesty her surrogate parents, sadistic Uncle George and timid Aunt Maud, may have been too
difficult to solve.

Despite urging each other on, neither Cal nor Elizabeth continued
their autobiographical projects in prose for publication. Still, the twin
accounts broke ground for future poems and drew on the poets' shared
experience of psychoanalysis. Like Elizabeth, and for equally pressing
reasons, Cal had begun "psycho-therapy" in the late 1940s, a process
he found "rather amazing — something like stirring up the bottom of
an aquarium — chunks of the past coming up at unfamiliar angles, distinct and then indistinct." Those chunks of remembered feeling and
incident served as material for "91 Revere Street" and much to follow.
His aquatic analogy recalled Elizabeth's 1947 "At the Fishhouses,"
the poem she'd written near the end of her treatment, in which the
icy ocean water, a revelation of "what we imagine knowledge to be" —
knowledge of the self gained through psychoanalysis, she'd explained
to Ruth Foster — is "dark deep and absolutely clear," qualities that
could also describe the poem itself and Elizabeth's aim as a poet.

Although Elizabeth did not confide in Cal about her romantic life,
each knew enough to worry about the other's vulnerabilities, their
"similar difficulties," in Cal's phrase: the binge drinking or periods of
derangement that had sent them to hospitals more than once in the
past. In late 1953, as each had reacted to the shocking news of their
mutual friend Dylan Thomas's early death, which no one could sepa-

rate from his chronic heavy drinking, Cal had written to Elizabeth, "Thomas wanted to live burning, burning out." He hoped neither of them would follow suit: "I want to live to be old, and want you to." Elizabeth had been distressed, she told a friend, by the way so many in Cal's inner circle, like Dylan's, seemed to "really just *love* the spectacle of the poet destroying himself and they're filled with rotten romanticism about it." If Elizabeth hadn't so dreaded proximity to mental illness, with its reminders of maternal neglect and abandonment, she might have drawn closer to Cal — visited him in Europe as she once planned, traveled sooner to the United States when he returned. It was Cal who bemoaned the distance between them — "Oh what a gap and blank and sorrow that you are so far away" — and put it into words. "We seem attached to each other by some stiff piece of wire," he'd written in the same letter mourning Dylan Thomas, "so that each time one moves, the other moves in another direction. We should call a halt to that." He'd adapted a lyric of Donne's that both Cal and Elizabeth knew well, "A Valediction: Forbidding Mourning," in which the poet conceives himself bound to his absent lover as the two legs of a compass: "Thy soul, the fixed foot, makes no show / To move, but doth, if the other do."

When they met again after nearly seven years, it was not for the consummating reunion Donne described in his "Valediction," although Cal may have half wished for that. When Elizabeth and Lota visited Boston early in their sojourn en route to paying a duty call on Aunt Florence in Worcester, Cal heard Elizabeth read one of her new Brazilian poems, "The Armadillo," scheduled to appear in a late-June issue of the *New Yorker*. As he had after reading her Nova Scotia tales, Cal felt challenged by the poem's clarity of image and diction to find his own new way of writing, less "armored heavy and old-fashioned," and saw in himself something of the armadillo that scuttles away at the end of the poem, "glistening" and "rose-flecked," yet "head down, tail down." Now he was set on "breaking through the shell of my old manner," and "The Armadillo," which he later carried in his billfold, seemed to point the way. By the time Elizabeth and Lota arrived at the Lowells' summer home in Castine, to stay with the young family for several weeks in August, Cal was wound up with inspiration for new poems he began to write almost as soon as they left, and with what Elizabeth felt to be an amorousness that set the two women packing nearly as soon as they arrived.

Precisely what transpired can't be known. There was discussion, initiated by Cal, of a visit to Brazil — he hoped to travel alone and stay with Elizabeth and Lota. Elizabeth quashed the plan with Lizzie Hardwick's support; if Cal were to come at all, he should bring his family and rent an apartment in Rio. Lizzie may not have told Elizabeth about the Renoiresque beauty in Cal's class at Boston University with whom he'd had a fling the previous fall, when Lizzie was six months pregnant, but thanks to a chatty letter from Randall Jarrell, Elizabeth knew all about the "Italian girl," Giovanna Madonia Erba, a producer of opera recordings Cal had met in Europe and for whom he'd nearly broken up his marriage the previous year. With imploring love letters that crossed the Atlantic, some written from hospital rooms, Cal had succeeded in persuading Giovanna to leave her husband, only to change his mind about the affair on his recovery. Cal's amorousness toward women not his wife, Elizabeth understood, signaled his ascent into mania. She left Castine wishing, she wrote Cal later, they'd managed a "more constructive and hopeful" conversation, and bearing Cal's gift of his grandfather's handsomely bound two-volume set of George Herbert, Elizabeth's favorite poet since summer camp, inscribed "with ALL his heart by Robert T. S. Lowell (4th)" followed by a line from Herbert's famous elegy "Death": "Thy mouth was open, but thou couldst not sing." Cal had pressed the books on Elizabeth over her protests, and would not take them back.

A nearly four-thousand-word apology, more alarming than the visit itself, reached Elizabeth days later, explaining Cal's quotation from Herbert. Much of the letter was given over to a "scherzo" rendition of a sail, "rich in undramatic mishaps," on Mount Desert Island's Somes Sound with poets Richard Eberhart and Philip Booth and their wives, as well as the "second ex-" Mrs. Kenneth Rexroth, "red-haired, figury, black-sweatery." Cal was still in a state of arousal, despite the "anti-manic pills" — Sparine — he claimed had put him "in reverse." At last he came to the point. Elizabeth's visit to Maine had cast him back to that summer day in Stonington ten years before when they'd exchanged confidences after sending away their unwanted paramours.

Cal had felt then, he now revealed, that "our relations" had "reached a new place": "I assumed that [it] would be just a matter of time before I proposed and I half believed that you would accept." His mouth had opened, but he couldn't, or wouldn't, sing: "I didn't say anything then." And soon after, he'd met "my Elizabeth" — Hardwick. The moment passed, leaving him to reflect over the intervening ten years — with regret? longing? Cal didn't say — on "*the* might have been for me, the one towering change, the other life that might have been had."

Could Elizabeth credit this seemingly earnest confession? Scarcely a week before she'd arrived in Castine, Cal had written that he'd quit drinking, as he had several times in the past without ever managing a clean break. "Oh heavens, all the lives one wants or has to lead," he'd mourned. She knew Cal's inclination to think of life in terms of roads not taken; he'd once described his father's decision to quit the navy, under pressure from his wife, as the source of the senior Lowell's "one great might-have-been — a first-rate Naval career." A different choice could have prevented the "terrible dim, diffused pathos" that was his father's lot. But this was Cal's fantasy. Nothing indicated his father had been in line for martial glory.

Then, too, Cal's admiration of Elizabeth as a writer had escalated since he'd read "In the Village," and he'd been "delighted" by the confirming Pulitzer Prize. "I read you with more interest than anyone now writing," he told Elizabeth early in the summer of her visit, and her direct influence on his work proved the feeling genuine. What "might have been" more splendid to Cal, in his inflamed state of mind, than a marriage of two Pulitzer-winning poets? Or even a near miss of a marriage, documented in a letter? Along with the rest of the literary world, Cal had been titillated by the revelation of Lytton Strachey's impulsive and immediately retracted proposal of marriage to Virginia Stephen, made public for the first time in a 1956 edition of the Strachey-Woolf correspondence. In light of his retrospective version of the day in Stonington, Cal suggested to Elizabeth, "we might almost claim something like apparently Strachey and Virginia Woolf."

How was Elizabeth to sort out the heartfelt from the hypomanic in this rambling letter? With Cal's mention of Strachey and Woolf, he strayed toward the question of sexual preference. Strachey had withdrawn his marriage proposal for a reason widely quoted in reviews of the correspondence — "the whole thing was repulsive to me." Strachey loved men. And Virginia, Strachey had been relieved to learn, was "not in love" with him. Cal acknowledged, in an oblique reference to Elizabeth's preference for women, that "of course there was always the other side, the fact that our friendship really wasn't a courting . . . really led to no encroachments. So it is."

So it was. Only with Elizabeth traveling safely in the company of Lota, whose presence Cal seemed to welcome and may even have stirred his competitive amorousness, would Cal "sing." He could make and unmake his proposal knowing that "all has come right since you found Lota," and unburden himself of the "great block and question mark" that had disturbed everyone's peace at Castine in August 1957. His message delivered and read — but never to be answered — Cal rested content that "everyone loves, admires and approves of everyone else and are happier than a month ago."

Elizabeth was not happier. She canceled readings she'd agreed to when she'd felt more sure of herself and returned early with Lota to Brazil, where, she had once written to Randall Jarrell, "distance makes the heart grow tougher."

Years later she wrote to Dr. Anny Baumann about Cal, "As you must know I love him, next best to Lota, I suppose — if one can measure love & affection or compare it." She had not wanted the comparison forced on her. Elizabeth was not one for "might-have-beens." Life, or its most significant events, had rarely seemed to her a matter of choice, they just happened — both tragedies and windfalls. Cal's declaration was another blow, leveled blithely by the one man she did love, if not as a romantic partner, then as her soul mate. Had there really been "no encroachments"? This was one.

Better to return to Brazil, where before long she received a sheaf of new poems from Cal, one of them, "Skunk Hour," dedicated to her and set in the Castine of the past August. There was rugged Nautilus Island across the harbor, where Cal had pointed out grazing sheep, and the slopes of Blue Hill to the east covered with a "red fox stain" signaling a turn toward autumn: "The season's ill." There too, as Cal would later acknowledge, were the "short line stanzas," "drifting description," and culminating image of a single wild animal she'd originated with "The Armadillo." Could Elizabeth ignore all that, along with the "fairy decorator" working late at his shop in town, who'd "rather marry" than rearrange the unsold baubles in his display window? Yes, she would. The poem, Elizabeth could see, was the "best" of the new group, a nocturne on the theme of Cal's mental distress one late-summer night — "My mind's not right" — relieved finally by the appearance of a line of skunks marching up Main Street past the white-spired Trinitarian church, kittens led by a mother who "will not scare."

The new poems, Elizabeth wrote to Cal, "all seem real as real — and getting more so." By now, although she didn't know it yet, he was in the hospital again, falling in love with a young Bennington graduate doing psychiatric fieldwork. Elizabeth was despairing too. "Oh heavens, when does one begin to write the *real* poems?" she asked Cal from her *estudio* in December 1957. "I certainly feel as if I never had." She would not publish another poem for more than two years.

We met under the clock in front of the Coop in Harvard Square, one junior boy from the class and three "older" women — my best friend, Linda Lord, a transfer from Bryn Mawr who'd also served time in Harvard's secretary pool; Millie Nash, a grad student at the ed school who'd enrolled in a master's program expressly to take Miss Bishop's class; and me. Our teacher had invited us to a semester's-end party at her new apartment in the North End, and none of us had been sure how to get there.

Red Line to Park Street, Green Line to Haymarket. I'd done that plenty of times on Saturday mornings before I'd moved into the dorms, to take advantage of cheap produce at the market stalls where fruit sellers yelled and refused to do business if you tried picking up a peach or plum to test for ripeness. And I'd crossed under the elevated expressway into the North End for cannoli on Hanover Street at Mike's Pastry, where the crisp curled shells were filled to order from white squeeze-bags of sweetened ricotta; Mike's cannoli were never soggy. But none of us had been to the neighborhood's waterfront, where dilapidated brick and granite warehouses were fast being transformed into office buildings and condominiums, a new term in the city. It was a cold night and we imagined dark alleys paved with broken cobblestones leading to Boston's waterside urban frontier.

But I was terrified of this trip for another reason. I was not certain I would be welcome. I thought I'd been doing well in Miss Bishop's class, although it was hard to be sure. Two semesters of poetry workshops after Lowell's had given me the confidence to drop out of the English department's honors track, with its onerous requirements, to make room for two writing courses in the fall of my senior year. (I'd been troubled, as well, by my adviser's critique of my junior qualifying paper on Emerson and Dickinson: "Again and again I look for confirming details or for necessary definitions — of 'Transcendentalism,' for instance — that do not appear.") I'd passed a tricky entrance exam to gain admission to a graduate course on prosody taught by Robert Fitzgerald, the celebrated translator of the *Odyssey* and the *Iliad,* and I'd made the cut for Miss Bishop's Advanced Verse Writing. Between the two classes I'd discovered a passion, maybe even a knack, for rhyme and meter.

Fitzgerald and Bishop were both short, soft-spoken, gray-haired, almost elfin creatures, dwarfed by the immense black-oak seminar tables that dominated our classrooms, but there was a palpable difference in atmosphere. We leaned forward to catch Professor Fitzgerald's wry jokes, esoteric explanations, and occasional praise of the exercises in Sapphic or Alcaic stanzas we turned in each week, receiving grades in a scoring system designed to induce humility: NAAB, or Not At All Bad, was tops in a gradual descent through Not Bad, Not Very Bad, Not Too Good, ending at PB, Pretty Bad. Professor Fitzgerald selected passages from among the NAABs to read out loud in class, never naming the student writer, but I'd been quietly proud to have had two of my samples chosen.

Miss Bishop's assignments, along with her own poetry, revealed an affection for verse forms too, and my rhymed couplets on the French baroque composer François Couperin came back with only one minor correction. She'd been absent, recovering from periodontal surgery, on the day we discussed our twenty lines of iambic pentameter, but Frank Bidart, the young friend who filled her place, took my poem seriously. I described the full-moon night in June when my family had gathered to celebrate my twenty-first birthday on a California beach; the grunion were running at high tide, and all of us, parents, uncle, cousins, raced through the waves to catch the slithery spawning fish in our bare hands. "What is this cruel feast you've made me, Father?"

I'd asked in the poem. "I watch you slit each fish I've caught, scrape /
the innards — vermilion eggs washed back to sea, / their scaly parents
sputter buttery on the fire." Reading that line was great fun, Frank had
said, before referring me to Miss Bishop's "At the Fishhouses."

Frank (we called him that, though he was a professor at Wellesley),
tall, lanky, and impassioned, appeared at the head of the seminar table
several more times that fall. Perhaps it was ongoing dental work that
gave our teacher a pained look more often than not when she arrived to
lead discussion, although asthma brought later absences. Miss Bishop
really did seem to wish she wasn't there.

On November 3, the day after Jimmy Carter took the presidency
from Gerald Ford, she asked us to write election-inspired poems in
class. Trying her own hand at the assignment, she gave up without
reading her jottings to us, declaring our doggerel better than the serious idea she "couldn't get started." Occasionally she forgot herself and
told a story — once about the time Marianne Moore stole her line. Our
teacher's voice grew stronger, more musical, as she warmed to the tale,
especially when recalling the line. "There goes the bell boy with the
buoy balls," she'd thought when checking into a bustling hotel on Cape
Cod one summer in the 1930s, catching sight of a bellhop carrying another guest's purchase of colored glass balls dangling in rope netting.
Then she'd repeated the line for Marianne Moore's approval when
they met several days later in New York City. We could go read it for
ourselves, now, in "Four Quartz Crystal Clocks," she told us, seemingly
still piqued at the theft forty years later. Miss Moore had dropped the
plural *s*.

At such times, despite an inflection combining a Vassar purr with
Nova Scotia plain speech, Miss Bishop reminded me of my aunt Sally,
a diminutive home ec major at the University of Oregon who'd left college at nineteen, during World War II, to marry. Aunt Sally wore the
same smartly tailored suits when she dressed to attend meetings of
the women's Wednesday Club in La Jolla and, while raising five children, waged successful campaigns to stop high-rise development in
the quiet beachside community and protect an ancient grove of Tor-
rey pines on a two-thousand-acre reserve north of town. There was a
power in these quiet, compact women, nearly always hidden, that one

couldn't name. Was it femininity? Surely neither of them would have raised a clenched fist at a Take Back the Night rally, but they did what had to be done. I'd always been a bit afraid of Aunt Sally, who sternly enforced a cleaned-plate rule at mealtimes and handed out what she called "sitting violations" to children, her own or visitors, who sat reading indoors when they might be outside playing.

In mid-November I studied Miss Bishop's assignment sheet carefully. We'd reached Assignment 6, a "free" week, "Anything you want to submit, but only one poem, please — no longer than one single-spaced page or two double-spaced pages." I read over again the message typed in all-caps at the bottom of the page: "PLEASE DON'T HAND IN POEMS THAT HAVE ALREADY BEEN HANDED IN AND DISCUSSED IN OTHER CLASSES." I'd written an exercise in Catullan hendecasyllabics for Professor Fitzgerald that he'd never mentioned in class and had not yet been returned to me with his marks. It felt like more than an exercise to me, a poem. I wanted Miss Bishop's opinion. I turned it in on a day she was out with asthma.

Was it a good poem? I called it "The Change of Philomel," and surely my version of the Greek myth had nothing on Eliot's terse encapsulation in *The Waste Land.* But the strict eleven-syllable metrical scheme, devised two millennia before by Catullus, in which each line began and ended with double-stress spondees, had captured my imagination. First there was Professor Fitzgerald's enchanting one-line mnemonic demonstrating the rhythm, recited to us in a vatic whisper: "Make strange all that you want someone to hear well." And then he'd gone to the blackboard to show us how Robert Frost's poem "For Once, Then, Something" followed, more or less faithfully, the prescribed meter:

$$- \; - \; / \; - \quad \smile \; \smile \; / \text{-} \; \smile \; / \; - \; \smile \; / \; - \quad -$$

Others taunt me with having knelt at well-curbs
Always wrong to the light, so never seeing
Deeper down in the well than where the water
Gives me back in a shining surface picture
Me myself in the summer heaven godlike
Looking out of a wreath of fern and cloud puffs.
Once, when trying with chin against a well-curb,

I discerned, as I thought, beyond the picture,
Through the picture, a something white, uncertain,
Something more of the depths — and then I lost it.
Water came to rebuke the too clear water.
One drop fell from a fern, and lo, a ripple
Shook whatever it was lay there at bottom,
Blurred it, blotted it out. What was that whiteness?
Truth? A pebble of quartz? For once, then, something.

I'd never seen a well. I knew wells only as props in fairy tales or nursery rhymes. But Frost put me alongside him, kneeling to peer down into one, seeing himself reflected in the water "godlike" along with the sky, and then seeing beyond or beneath that reflection to — what? "What was that whiteness? / Truth? A pebble of quartz?" In fifteen eleven-syllable lines he'd done what it took Herman Melville an epic novel to accomplish. This was a great poem, and my new knowledge of its internal structure gave me the faint hope that someday I might make something worthy too.

My poem was not great, but because of the borrowed meter it pulsed with the rhythms of greatness, and I needed to know where and how it fell short. And I wanted to hear it from a woman. "Weave your tapestried message, Philomela," my poem began. "Not with words nor by force will savage kings die." I told the story from Ovid's *Metamorphoses* of the beautiful Philomela, kidnapped and raped by her sister Procne's husband, King Tereus, and the bloody revenge the sisters took, in turn repaid by the transmutation of all three into birds:

Weave and dream, wretched sisters, transformations:
Blazoned scarlet with murder, marked for change, you
Take flight, larks with a freedom earthbound creatures
Can't know. Spin till the nightmare king is banished —
Rendered last, as a feathered warrior, helpless.

A week later I read the poem in class. There was little to say, it seemed, aside from Miss Bishop's observation that I'd written the piece in Catullan metrics, which she defined for the class: spondee, dactyl, trochee, trochee, spondee. And then we reached Thanksgiving break and the final classes in December. Miss Bishop held me back after the last session, stony-faced, her arms already full of satchel and pocketbook. I'd written well, she said, but she'd have to lower my grade for handing in an assignment from another class. She turned, a slight but determined figure, and walked out of the room.

Now one of us was ringing the bell at a plain oak door down the hall from the fourth-floor elevators in the Lewis Wharf condominiums. It had been dark when we left Harvard Square on this winter evening, and darker still when we arrived at Haymarket station and made our way through a maze of narrow streets, finally crossing broad Atlantic Avenue to the hulking granite structure. Too dark to do more than sense, in the damp, brisk breeze, Boston Harbor lapping at the far end of the enormous pier that once sent coastal steamers to Nova Scotia.

The door opened on a brilliantly lit room, or so it seemed compared with the dim hallway. A party was in full swing, people we didn't know — dark-haired, bearded men in V-neck sweaters and corduroys — sipping at drinks. I'd never seen exposed-brick walls before, and there were two of them, hung with unfamiliar objects: a gleaming Venetian gilt mirror and a long, brightly painted paddle polished to a high sheen. Suspended from the ceiling was a horned beast, the figurehead of some Amazonian craft, I guessed, blue-eyed, yellow-haired, open-mawed. A third wall was given over to tightly stuffed bookshelves. Beyond sliding glass doors I glimpsed a deck and the flickering lights of East Boston across the water. Chairs had been set in a circle, and I slipped into one opposite a dark wooden rocker in which our teacher reclined, dressed in slacks, white blouse, thin cashmere sweater — smiling, girlish, pretty. Among friends.

We all took seats. At Miss Bishop's invitation, one of the dark-haired men, Ricardo Sternberg, Brazilian, pulled papers from a briefcase to read several new poems. I listened, unable to take in his words. I could see only Miss Bishop, seated next to Ricardo, with Frank Bidart on her right. So differently warm, yet indifferent to the students she'd invited to her home, perhaps regretting it now. Or had we come as an audience, one she could trust to be admiring?

In the weeks since our last class meeting, we knew, her book *Geography III* had been published, and she'd been honored with a double session at the annual Modern Language Association meeting in New York City. She'd read a handful of her own poems and then, while scholars presented papers on her work, fled the conference center for a meal of corned beef hash with Frank Bidart and her old friends, the duo pianists Gold and Fizdale at the Stage Deli across the street. Fortified, she'd returned for the performance of Elliott Carter's *A Mirror on Which to Dwell,* a setting of six of her poems for chamber ensemble with soprano soloist, which capped off the evening.

Now Frank was urging Miss Bishop to read from the new book, and she was waving him away. "'One Art,'" he persisted. At last she took up the slim taupe volume, the book those white pages in the black binder I'd seen two years before in Robert Lowell's class had become, and put on her glasses, large plastic frames.

"My god, Elizabeth, these lenses are almost opaque," Frank exclaimed, taking the glasses from her to polish with a handkerchief. Our lore on Harvard's celebrity poets extended to a long-ago reading at the Guggenheim in New York where Robert Lowell had introduced Elizabeth Bishop as "the famous eye." Miss Bishop had risen to the podium and tweaked Cal: "The famous eye will now put on her glasses."

She put them on and began to read. A slim younger woman appeared in the hall that led to the kitchen. Blue eyes, dirty-blond hair cropped short. Was that Alice, the woman we'd heard was Miss Bishop's lover?

> *The art of losing isn't hard to master;*
> *so many things seem filled with the intent*
> *to be lost that their loss is no disaster. . . .*

⚔ 4 ⚖

River

E LIZABETH HAD FAILED so far at every attempt to write the kind of literary travel piece that was a staple at the *New Yorker*. Finally she would be forced to admit, "I am NOT a journalist." But in the meantime there was serious money to be made in prose, in contrast to the few dollars per line she earned for poetry, and Elizabeth knew how to capture Katharine White's interest with a proposal letter.

She'd spent months that stretched to years drafting and redrafting an account of a 1951 voyage to Sable Island, a desolate twenty-five-mile crescent of sand dunes and beach grass lodged in the Atlantic between Nova Scotia and Newfoundland known as the "Graveyard of the Grand Banks" — a place that "has haunted my imagination most of my life," with its race of wild ponies, its unique Sable Island sparrow ("the or-nithologists' delight"), and "wonderful ghost stories" of shipwrecked sailors. Elizabeth's own great-grandfather had gone down with all hands on a West Indies schooner off Sable Island's shores. Her idea to "combine personal reminiscences" with the "best parts" of the island's history, "plus a first-hand account of it now," seemed a sure-fire plan, and as late as 1956 Katharine White still hoped to receive the article, along with several other "projected fact pieces" Elizabeth had sug-gested on locations in Brazil. Eventually Mrs. White stopped asking about Sable Island.

Yet now, in August 1958, Elizabeth was flying off in a Brazilian air force DC-3 with the celebrated British novelist Aldous Huxley, a denizen of Hollywood since the 1930s, and his younger Italian wife, Laura Archera, to explore a remote Indian post on the Xingú River, after several days spent touring the new capital city of Brasília, with the aim of writing up the trip for the *New Yorker* as a combination travel piece and profile. Lota's fortune was tied to her Samambaia properties, and Elizabeth believed it was "up to me to earn a lot of $$$$$$ somehow," as inflation, fueled by government instability, drove the price of necessities in Brazil ever higher. Lota and Elizabeth deplored the relocation of the nation's capital from nearby Rio to Brasília, a modernist City of Oz "created from scratch" out of previously uninhabited jungle lands in the country's interior, not least for its diversion of enormous sums to the quixotic scheme. Still, when invited to join the Huxleys on a tour sponsored by the Brazilian government, Elizabeth had accepted. Trailing the aging author of *Brave New World* through the spare beginnings of the planned city, the green-tinted Ray-Ban glass panels scarcely in place on the first of Oscar Niemeyer's sleek public buildings, followed by a meeting with the Uialapiti, a tribe under government protection from "missionaries, land speculators, etc.," as Elizabeth wrote May Swenson on her return, would surely yield marketable copy. Huxley was enjoying a new wave of fame since the 1954 publication of *Doors of Perception,* his record of a refulgent California afternoon on mescaline, a hallucinogenic compound found in the peyote cactus used in religious rituals by certain tribes in the American Southwest. William Maxwell, taking over as Elizabeth's prose editor from Katharine White, who had recently retired to full-time residence in Maine, telegraphed his boss William Shawn's instructions to "go ahead" with the Brasília piece, with the caveat that "we can't be sure it will work."

The air force transport, retrofitted with blue plush seats, bore its "rather highbrow" passengers northwest over "the River of Souls, and the River of the Dead, to a branch of the *Xingú* — if you have a map!" Elizabeth wrote to May Swenson, describing "my best trip in Brasil, so far." There, a village of thatched huts "rushed to meet us" as the plane landed on a small strip of asphalt in the jungle, not "the green Amazonian jungle — just immense waste lands, with palms and small rivers" where, Elizabeth soon observed, the Uialapiti swim and fish "off and on all day — they are very clean."

Huxley had been a frustrating companion and interview subject, Elizabeth later complained to Bill Maxwell, speaking only of mescaline at any length; "medicine, mysticism, and God are his present themes," she wrote to Cal. But she knew Laura Archera, a documentary filmmaker and lay psychotherapist, from Key West days. Laura had been the lover of Pauline Hemingway's sister Jinny Pfeiffer before marrying the widowed Huxley in 1956. Elizabeth herself had been attracted to Jinny, with whom she'd spent a ten-day vacation in Haiti in 1949, easing her loneliness after the breakup with Marjorie Stevens. Lota and Elizabeth entertained the Huxleys at Samambaia in the Brazilian winter of 1958 when they first arrived, and now Elizabeth and Laura, two friends who had once loved the same woman, mingled with the Indians — "all quite naked" except for strings of beads and, for the women, a palm-leaf *cache-sexe, "cache*-ing nothing." The "rounded behinds and childishly smooth legs, in both sexes, are remarkably pretty," Elizabeth wrote in her draft for the *New Yorker.*

Laura had brought along a Polaroid camera, perhaps the same one Jinny, Laura's partner in filmmaking, had purchased for the Haiti trip, and it proved an immediate attraction. Elizabeth took her own photos of Laura as she worked, a "small, trim" northern Italian blond in

Aldous and Laura Archera Huxley with Elizabeth
in front of her *estudio,* Samambaia, 1958

stylishly draped slacks among the dark-haired indigenous Brazilians. Later, on the riverbank, while some in the tour group swam, the "tall, pale, and thin" Aldous Huxley, strikingly handsome with "well-modeled" features, pulled a magnifying glass from his pocket and leaned over "from his great height" to examine "a mass of pale yellow Sulphur butterflies . . . quivering, in the wet mud at the river's edge, like the start of a yacht race," Elizabeth wrote in her *New Yorker* draft.

The party toured a "manioc patch" a half mile from the village, the tribe's "only attempt at agriculture," they were informed by the Cambridge University graduate student who served as guide to this "most primitive people left in the world," except for Africa's Pygmies. The Uialapiti "do no work at all, as we consider work," he told them, though fishing, done with bow and arrow in the flowing, waist-deep Xingú, was a refined art: "they rarely miss." Inside a longhouse, where men swayed in hammocks and women "messed about with manioc and clay pots" on the dirt floor, the tourists were besieged with requests for cigarettes. Elizabeth obliged by giving each man a cigarette from her own pack and lighting it. At the far end of the shelter, hidden by a fence of

Laura Archera Huxley (with Polaroid camera) touring
a Uialapiti village, photograph by Elizabeth Bishop

"twigs and palm leaves," a young girl was held in isolation, required to remain "silent and invisible" for a months-long puberty ritual. Elizabeth was invited to peer through the fence: "this isn't the really secret part," the guide explained.

After a siesta, followed by a wrestling match with no declared winners or losers — "they are gentle with each other" — the travelers departed for the airstrip, but not before a Uialapiti widower, fascinated by Elizabeth's earrings and watch, inquired whether she was unmarried. Would she stay behind to wed him? "This produced a great deal of tribal merriment," Elizabeth wrote in her *New Yorker* draft, wryly working in a quotation from *Othello:* "although I was vain of having been singled out, I was afraid he merely did not want to be the Indian who threw away the pearl, richer than all his tribe." Laura Archera may have taken this moment to confide in Elizabeth the fact that her own marriage to a widower had been nearly as precipitate, the ceremony performed on a whim at a roadside chapel in Yuma, Arizona. The newlywed Huxleys took up residence in the Hollywood Hills, in a house a few hundred yards up the road from the one Laura had shared for years with Jinny, the two households becoming one family, including two young children Jinny adopted in the early 1950s. Certainly both Lota and Elizabeth took note of the Huxleys' arrangement; it was a model they would soon follow when Mary Morse gave up on men and determined to adopt the babies she longed to raise.

What killed the piece for the *New Yorker* were the passages on Brasília. This time Elizabeth composed and delivered her travelogue within two months of the journey, but she had trouble rendering the ingenious "swooping" pillars of Niemeyer's futuristic Palace of the Dawn: like "a chain of huge white kites, poised upside down, then grasped by giant hands and squeezed on the four sides until they are elegantly attenuated." The labored architectural descriptions stalled the narrative; after that, "everything 'tails off badly,'" Bill Maxwell wrote, reporting the "factual department" editors' verdict. And, as Elizabeth had feared, "Huxley doesn't come through." She had been no more able to penetrate this famous writer's reserve than she had Frost's or Sandburg's in her days as reluctant Library of Congress doyenne. But in the end, Elizabeth scarcely minded the loss of money and time, and felt only "rather *dumb*" to have worked so hard again on something outside "my natural bent." As she wrote to May, she'd gotten a poem out of the experience, a long one, "The Riverman," her first in two years — "what a relief to begin again."

The months after her return from New York City, before the Brasília trip, had been difficult. Brazil seemed "dingy and dark and grease-stained" that November of 1957, in contrast to the "rich, gleaming, deodorized U.S.A." She missed the "bright cleanness," and Lota's ret-rospective complaints about Maine's diminutive rocky beaches and the fir trees she insisted must have been artificially planted dampened Elizabeth's customary enthusiasm for "Nature . . . so bright & fresh" in Brazil. She wanted to travel abroad again, but there was no money for it. Without telling Lota, she began to consider the old Bulmer house in Great Village as a place to retire someday. "I wonder if that's where I shouldn't be, after all," she wrote to Cal of her sometimes acute long-ing for Nova Scotia.

In late March 1958, Elizabeth's cherished toucan died, the result of a tragic mistake. She'd applied an insecticide to control the ant swarms in the courtyard where Sammy's cage hung, having been as-sured by the sales clerk that the poison was "inoffensive" to animals, only to find Sammy supine on the floor of his cage a few hours later, claws — or "feet," as Elizabeth referred to them in recounting the di-saster — raised to the offending air. The ode to Sammy she began writ-ing that day joined a cache of others already devoted to the bird and never completed, though she quoted a fond first line to Cal when she sent him the news: "Most comical of all in death. . . ." The lines she kept to herself and added in later drafts were more self-recriminat-ing and anguished: "I killed you! I didn't mean to, / of course; I cried & cried —." She mourned Sammy's "neon-bright blue eyes, / looking at me, sidewise" and his love of "shiny things, bright things." She'd feared his life was "boring," but "*You* cheered me up. . . . I loved you, and I caged you." The *New Yorker*'s 1962 serialization of Rachel Car-son's indictment of commonly used pesticides, *Silent Spring,* would come too late for Sammy.

Lota refused to consider acquiring another toucan, and in any case the two women were "up to our necks in babies," caring for Kylso's expanding brood during the hot summer months of February and March. At Easter, Elizabeth staged an egg hunt for the older children and her three-year-old namesake, the cook's daughter, hiding dozens of tiny eggs (quail eggs most likely) wrapped in colored foil all around the terrace, in the MG she'd never learned to drive, among the spines of a ceiba tree. But she wasn't writing. Her asthma returned, the result of anxiety over her meager output, she was convinced. Cal's recent productivity, despite hospitalizations, put her to shame. The breakthrough inspired for both of them by "In the Village" had yielded a book's worth of poems first for Cal. Elizabeth envied him this "stretch" of fluent composition, a time, she imagined, such as she had only rarely experienced, "when everything and anything suddenly seemed material for poetry — or not material, seemed to *be* poetry, and all the past was illuminated in long shafts here and there, like a long-waited-for sunrise." That "rare feeling of control, illumination" — *that* was "the whole purpose of art, to the artist." She craved it for herself.

Was it Cal's "assurance" that made the difference? As she paged through the manuscript he'd sent, the sheaf of poems that would be published a year later as *Life Studies,* she marveled: "all you have to do is put down the names! And the fact that it seems significant, illustrative, American, etc., gives you, I think, the confidence you display about tackling any idea or theme, *seriously,* in both writing and conversation." There were poems titled "Last Afternoon with Uncle Devereux Winslow" and "Commander Lowell," or situated in the Winslow-Stark family burial ground in Dunbarton, New Hampshire, and the Beverly Farms "cottage" — Brahmin code for rambling summer house — that was Cal's father's last residence. These weren't reverential elegies or patriotic odes. "Terminal Days at Beverly Farms" concluded with his father's prosaic last words: "I feel awful." But Cal's family background put him in a league with T. S. Eliot and Henry James, to whom Elizabeth compared him in a blurb for the book, not to mention his own Lowell relations, Amy and James Russell, whose poem "The First Snow-Fall" she had memorized in grade school and could still recite.

Elizabeth knew Cal's illness was hardly enviable, but his breakdowns, too, had found their way into his writing, with "Waking in the

Blue," "Home After Three Months Away," and "Skunk Hour." It was not just that Elizabeth's family seemed inconsequential by comparison to Cal's. She had so much to hide that was central to her experience. "It is hell to realize one has wasted half one's talent through timidity" was how she phrased her dilemma for Cal. Her intractable and deeply painful shyness stood for it all, indeed served as a protective screen she could never give up, shielding her from public scrutiny even as it limited her professionally. Elizabeth could not chat up Huxley or Frost. She could never write an autobiographical poem called "Man and Wife," as Cal had. She had ventured to write about her mother's madness, obliquely, in "In the Village," but she would never make poetry or prose of her own hospitalizations for the drinking binges that continued sporadically even in paradisal Brazil. These last, though originating decades earlier in panicky shyness and feelings of difference — her orphan state, her attraction to women — merited only silence, evasion, shame, now that they'd become habitual, and produced only unmet promises to Lota to "behave" better in future.

At such times, Lota was forced to act as more than Elizabeth's caring spouse. She became her keeper, checking Elizabeth into the hospital, insisting she take the Antabuse pills newly prescribed by Dr. Baumann, who "seems to feel my pulse all the way across the Equator," Elizabeth thought. This was aversion therapy; the pills made Elizabeth violently ill if she drank while under their influence. Lota told herself she was helping "um grande poeta." She loved Elizabeth and nothing else mattered. But Elizabeth was increasingly aware, as she wrote to their friends Gold and Fizdale shortly after the *New Yorker* turned down her Brasília piece, that "my natural melancholia taxes her severely." The admission served as a veiled apology to Lota, who read Elizabeth's contribution to this shared letter before it was mailed.

Lota read most of the letters Elizabeth sent and received; she was "a great letter-snoop," Elizabeth explained early on to May Swenson, reporting Lota's fondness for May's letters. At first Elizabeth had enjoyed sharing her epistolary friendships with Lota. Cal, May, Marianne Moore, all seemed closer if Lota knew them too. But as Elizabeth struggled, with herself most of all, to make room in her life for poetry, she began to regret the loss of privacy. She looked for opportunities to post outgoing mail on her own, and asked her correspondents not to refer to comments she occasionally made about her "dear friend" in their return letters, knowing Lota might read them. She felt hemmed in, at times, by Lota's intense devotion, impatient of the dependence she'd once reveled in, even as her reliance on Lota for everything from daily companionship to rides to the market and a house to live in was nearly complete.

Lota hated "The Riverman," Elizabeth told Cal and May and everyone to whom she mentioned her "anthropological number." Elizabeth wasn't sure she liked it herself, though she was grateful for a poem that reached the page in nearly finished form. The year preceding her 1958 trip to the Xingú had produced nothing but jottings, "just crumbs that always fail to shape themselves back into the loaf again," she complained to May. In "Manuelzinho," another poem with which she'd broken through a creative logjam, Elizabeth had adopted Lota's voice to tell the story of her gardener, a tenant farmer on the mountainside where his family had lived for generations. Now she wrote as an Amazonian Indian, a shaman-in-training, conjured up with the help of the anthropologist Charles Wagley's 1953 study *Amazon Town,* which she'd read in advance of her meeting with the Uialapiti.

"The Riverman" begins in the middle of the night, when a river god in the form of a dolphin calls the riverman to the shore:

> *I waded into the river*
> *and suddenly a door*
> *in the water opened inward, . . .*
> *I looked back at my house,*
> *white as a piece of washing*
> *forgotten on the bank,*
> *and I thought once of my wife,*
> *but I knew what I was doing.*

The riverman already practices as a *pajé,* a medicine man dispensing folk remedies to the sick, but he would like to be a truly great shaman, a *sacaca.* By the 1950s, as Elizabeth learned from Wagley's book, no *sacacas* remained in villages along the Amazon. But elders recalled the

famous mystics Joaquim Sacaca and Fortunato Pombo, whose super-
natural powers enabled them to enter an enchanted kingdom beneath
the river by means of "ports," disappearing into a hollow tree trunk at
the river's edge or walking barefoot down a thorny log into the water.
They returned hours later with fantastic tales of meetings with the
river gods and underwater journeys along secret passageways to the
mouth of the Amazon at Belém and back in the blink of an eye. "Why
shouldn't I be ambitious?" Elizabeth's riverman asks.

In Elizabeth's poem, the riverman experiences such a journey, after being plied with *cachaça,* the strong Brazilian liquor distilled from
sugarcane juice, and "green cheroots" — "my head couldn't have been
dizzier." A "tall, beautiful serpent / in elegant white satin" appears,
showering the riverman with compliments in an unfamiliar language
that he must master as part of his training. This serpent is Luandinha,
the most powerful of all, the goddess who bears him up and down the
Amazon, "travelling fast as a wish."

The riverman will take more midnight journeys, whenever the dolphin calls, in search of knowledge, cures "for each of the diseases": "it
stands to reason / that everything we need / can be obtained from the
river." He resists his wife's efforts to break the river gods' spell, tossing
out "behind her back" the "stinking teas" she brews for him when he
returns in the morning, his skin yellow, his scalp muddy, his feet and
hands cold. He will not give up his newfound secret freedom:

> *You can peer down and down*
> *or dredge the river bottom*
> *but never, never catch me. . . .*

Elizabeth had not yet visited the world's largest river when she
wrote the poem, and she felt troubled that she had no firsthand experience of her subject. But Katharine White, filling in for Howard Moss
on leave, loved "The Riverman," considering it a "magical poem that
casts a spell — one of your very best." It had been three years since Elizabeth submitted a poem to the *New Yorker,* and "I can't tell you how
happy we are — all of us — to have it." Elizabeth wrote back acknowledging the "long arid stretch" and promising "if not exactly an Ama-

zon of verse, at least a small steady trickle." Perhaps Katharine White's compliments would work their own magic, as Luandinha's had on the riverman. Elizabeth promised to dedicate the poem to her. And when, after reading "The Riverman" in the magazine, Cal called it "the best fairy story in verse I know," Elizabeth was relieved. It was a "very powerful initiation poem," he wrote again later of her "forsaken Merman."

Elizabeth never said why Lota disliked the poem. Could she have been troubled by Elizabeth's identification with the riverman, who drank the intoxicating *cachaça,* tossed away his wife's medicinal teas, and escaped at night to consort with a tall, shining goddess, turning his back on home? Was she envious of the door that "opened inward" for Elizabeth, her regular disappearances into an imaginative realm to pursue her ambitions, though Lota herself had constructed that portal, Elizabeth's *estudio?* Or perhaps the answer was as simple as the one Lota gave each time she turned aside Elizabeth's suggestions of travel to remote destinations in Brazil: she wasn't interested. Any vacation that required slow boats or "roughing it" was out of the question for Lota, and she "refuses to have anything to do with anything Brazilian or 'primitive,'" Elizabeth explained to Cal.

Elizabeth pleaded now with May Swenson to fly to Brazil and make the journey down the Amazon she had been longing for since her arrival almost a decade before. But May already had plans to tour Italy and France with Pearl Schwartz on an Amy Lowell Traveling Scholarship. Finally, in February 1960, two months before "The Riverman" appeared in print, but long after it had been set in type, Elizabeth boarded an Amazon River steamer with Lota's friend Rosinha Leão, who'd promised the trip to her sixteen-year-old nephew. Still Lota refused to go along.

They'd flown inland to Manaus, where the dark, lucent Rio Negro joined the turbid Amazon, its rushing waters "like weak *café com leite.*" Elizabeth telegraphed Lota news of her safe landing: "RIVER VERY BIG . . . MISS YOU VERY MUCH." They would travel downstream — the current flowing faster than the boat, which hugged the shore — all the way to Belém, stopping at eighteen villages over five days to let on passengers bearing livestock to market: chickens, turkeys, alligators, and turtles, stowed in one of the ship's two lifeboats filled with river water. The human population on board swelled from 250 to 700 passengers along the way. Most brought their own hammocks or slept on deck, while Elizabeth, Rosinha, and the teenage Manoel enjoyed relative comfort in cabins *de luxo* reserved for tourists at the bow.

Yes, Elizabeth wrote to Cal afterward, there were dolphins in the Amazon, pods of them, gray ones and pink ones with gray spots. She'd brought along a beach ball and tossed it out to the dolphins — the females, larger than the males, could be readily identified — and watched them play. "Pink ones are lucky." She'd gotten everything right in her poem.

One evening at dusk near Santarém, at the halfway mark in their journey, where the Tapajós flowed into the Amazon and cows and zebus stared at the passing steamer from flat green meadows, Rosinha spotted an enormous dead tree with more than a hundred white herons roosting in its silver-gray limbs. The vision, "against a dark blue stormy sky," was "unearthly": "I have never seen a lovelier wild sight."

At home in her studio at Samambaia, Elizabeth would immediately start in on an "authentic, post-Amazon" poem. But more than that,

Landing at Gurupá on the Amazon, photograph by Elizabeth Bishop

she told Cal, "I want to go back to the Amazon. I dream dreams every night" — "I . . . am living to go back there again."

While on the river, Elizabeth had written letters to Lota on the type-writer she brought along for note taking, letters far longer than the journal entries she hoped to turn into a magazine article someday. She promised Lota she really would make money now. She missed Lota, wished she had come along. Elizabeth told her to go ahead and read "all" the mail that arrived while she was away. She worried about Lota's driving, begged her to be careful. She hoped Lota would enjoy her "rest from *me*" — the trip, with several plane rides and excursions in Manaus and Belém, kept Elizabeth away for nearly three weeks, their longest separation so far. Elizabeth's traveling companion, Rosinha Leão, looked healthier than ever: "we think that the rough and rigorous life is what she's needed all along." Wouldn't Lota like to accompany Eliza-beth on a return trip, a twenty-five-day voyage up the Amazon from Manaus to Iquitos, over rapids and into Colombia and Ecuador, where the river narrows? Before boarding the steamer at Manaus, Elizabeth had examined the smaller ships that took the upriver route — "not too bad," she reported — and she interviewed one of the captains. "We must go back"; it is "my dream." She signed her letters "Love, love, love," and "Love and devotion, Elizabeth."

She returned to Samambaia with a prized souvenir, one of the lol-lipop-shaped paddles she so admired, used by men and boys in the smallest boats on the river, the paddler perched in the bow, the stern "sticking up in the air — against all principles of aquadynamics" she'd learned as a teenager at sailing camp. This one was lacquered to a high sheen and painted with the Brazilian and American flags on either side. She'd bought it from a boatman who'd paddled close to the steamer, ferrying a wooden armchair he hoped to sell to one of the passengers. He'd been confused by Elizabeth's bid for his paddle, but when she of-fered more than he'd expected for the chair, he handed it up to her, then shuttled back across the great river using his young son's much smaller paddle. The brightly painted paddle found a place on the walls of Samambaia, along with the Kurt Schwitters collage Elizabeth had given to Lota seven years before on her birthday in 1953, the second they'd celebrated together.

"On the Amazon" was the authentic poem Elizabeth worked on after her return, but this one would join her ode to Sammy among the unfinished. Instead, in her new mood of elation, when "everything seems nearer the surface, or the possible, than usual," as she wrote to Cal, Elizabeth pulled out some older drafts — "cleaning up the attic," she called it. By June 1960 she was able to send Katharine White "Song for the Rainy Season," a poem Elizabeth had begun six years earlier, she told May, not long after she'd given Lota the Schwitters. It was a love poem in syncopated "*rumba* rhythm," put aside as "The Shampoo" shuttled from one editor to another, enduring repeated rejection.

The finished version was even more oblique than "The Shampoo," but brimming unmistakably with Elizabeth's passion for her new life with Lota in Brazil:

> *Hidden, oh hidden*
> *in the high fog*
> *the house we live in,*
> *beneath the magnetic rock,*
> *rain-, rainbow-ridden,*
> *where blood-black*
> *bromelias, lichens,*
> *owls, and the lint*
> *of the waterfalls cling,*
> *familiar, unbidden.*

Five more ten-line stanzas follow, rhyming easily, irregularly, celebrating the giant fern; the singing brook; the owl that lands on the roof each night and stamps five times, proving "he can count"; the "fat frogs that, / shrilling for love, / clamber and mount." At Samambaia with Lota she had rediscovered the pleasures of early-morning lovemaking in the tropics, first experienced at Key West: "House, open house / to the white dew / and the milk-white sunrise. . . ."

Did Elizabeth resurrect and complete the poem now to show Lota her commitment to their life together, a necessarily hidden yet deliciously shared life? She would not leave their home behind like laundry drying on a riverbank. Yet was it possible to make such a promise — for Elizabeth, who had once recorded in her travel journal her belief that "love will unexpectedly appear over and over again"? For Lota, who had written in the shared letter to Gold and Fizdale, responding to news of a couple's breakup after nine years, "I always thought a strange trait in the human nature — the desire for the permanent, when in realité we are always changing."

At its conclusion the poem allows for the possibility of such change, conveyed not in personal terms, but in meteorological ones, as in the final lines of the more explicit love poem she had once written to Marjorie Stevens, "It is marvellous to wake up together," a draft of which Elizabeth had brought with her to Brazil:

> The world might change to something quite different,
> As the air changes or the lightning comes without our blinking,
> Change as our kisses are changing without our thinking.

Marjorie Stevens had died several months before Elizabeth's Amazon trip, weakened by the tuberculosis that brought her to Key West. In "Song for a Rainy Season," in stanzas added to finish the poem, Elizabeth imagines climatic catastrophe, a time "without water" in a "later era" when:

> the great rock will stare
> unmagnetized, bare,
> no longer wearing
> rainbows or rain,
> the forgiving air
> and the high fog gone;
> the owls will move on
> and the several
> waterfalls shrivel
> in the steady sun.

Katharine White, still covering for Howard Moss, wrote within a month from Maine to say "we are delightedly buying 'Song for a Rainy Season'. . . It is perfection, really." She asked only that Elizabeth alter the title, or add a subtitle to convey the poem's setting in Brazil. At this, Elizabeth balked. She'd already confided in Cal her concern — "one of my greatest worries" — that she might be pegged as a poet "who can only write about South America." She answered Katharine White: "I don't want to become a local color poet any more than I can help." The poem, Elizabeth argued, wasn't "specific"; it could refer to "any rainy season, any place that there was a big rock and a brook and a waterfall or two." Mrs. White conceded the point.

But Lota knew which house Elizabeth had in mind; she complained that the poem made Samambaia seem "too damp." Lota had not agreed to Elizabeth's proposed trip up the Amazon from Manaus, but she'd taken time off from real estate negotiations in late May 1960 for a brief vacation with Elizabeth in Ouro Prêto, the mountain town three hundred miles north of Rio to which Lota had bravely driven Elizabeth in 1953, changing a flat tire while passing drivers gawked. Now there was a direct highway, and inland travel was easier.

Although Ouro Prêto boasted a Grande Hotel designed by Oscar Niemeyer, the couple stayed near the main square at a small inn, the Pouso do Chico Rey, owned and managed by Lota's friend Lilli Correia de Araújo, the Danish widow of a prominent Brazilian artist, Pedro

Lilli Correia de Araújo

Correia de Araújo, who'd died in 1955. Elizabeth described Lilli to May Swenson as "twice as tall" and "even blonder" than May, who came from a family of blond, blue-eyed Swedes. The "Danish Viking" wore her hair like May's too, in a blunt bowl cut. Children sometimes asked, "Is she a *blonde* Indian?"

On departure, Elizabeth signed the hotel register with a rhyming quatrain, her first gift to Lilli:

> Let Shakespeare & Milton
> Stay at a Hilton —
> I *shall stay*
> At Chico Rei —

The thermometer stood at 100 degrees in Rio. There was no water for its two million residents, and still Elizabeth and Lota remained in the city in March 1961, relying on four quarts of spring water they'd brought from Samambaia to brush their teeth, and sea water, carried up from the beach by the apartment building's janitor, to flush the toilet. For dinner and baths they would visit a friend with a well. "It rains and rains," Elizabeth wrote to May Swenson; there was no water shortage. But Rio's public utilities were in a shambles. There had been blackouts, stalling apartment elevators all over the city in the evenings — you could hear the angry howls. And now no running water. A state of emergency was declared, but "what good does that do?" Elizabeth wondered.

When the two women had met again in Brazil in the early 1950s — Lota astonished to find that Elizabeth's hair had gone gray since they'd last seen each other four years earlier in New York, Elizabeth dazzled by the twin streaks of silver in Lota's dark mane — Lota announced that she had "retired" from "society" and had no interest in Rio. In the intervening years, Elizabeth and Lota visited the city only at Carnival time or for dress fittings and dentist appointments; nearing fifty, both women had recurrent need for extractions and fillings, between which their dentists (they preferred different ones) plied them with sweet *cafezinhos*. Lota used her Rio apartment so rarely that she rented it out to boost her income.

But even as the city's aging infrastructure was taxed to the breaking point, a building boom was on. Elizabeth would soon be disturbed by the sounds of a demolition crew tearing down a rare colonial-era villa at the end of her street to make way for more high-rise apartments. Lota had been called to Rio to spearhead the most ambitious project of all, a new city park on several miles of waterfront landfill, vacant now except for Affonso Reidy's angular concrete-and-glass Museum of Modern Art anchoring the northernmost edge of the fill. Lota's friend Carlos Lacerda, the newly elected governor of the state of Guanabara, which included Rio, had been watching Lota closely on his weekends in Petrópolis, where he'd built a summer home on land purchased from her, and marveling, along with Elizabeth, at Lota's gift for design and skill at managing her crew of "mens." Nothing fazed Lota, and he could count on her loyalty. Lota had been the one to counsel him on the ways in which the massive public works initiative could revitalize the city after the federal government's move inland from Rio to Brasília, and ensure Lacerda's legacy as governor — perhaps even propel him to the presidency. Improbable as it seemed, the job was hers.

As Elizabeth wrote in separate letters to Cal, May, and Marianne Moore, the year had begun with two transforming events. First was the arrival of Mary Morse's three-month-old "darling baby," Monica, by means of an off-the-books adoption several years in the planning; mother and daughter took up residence at Samambaia until Mary's house down the road could be completed. Imagine "three old maids, hovering over this new infant," Elizabeth wrote to May, admitting her preference for newborns and children under age three. The little girl was "cunning," easy to soothe, and best of all, she "wakes up laughing." Lota and Elizabeth had gone to examine the baby first, knowing Mary would fall in love instantly with any child, and agreed with the doctor's report: Monica was "healthy as a young horse."

But soon Elizabeth and Lota were traveling to Rio each week so that Lota could spend the "useful days," as Brazilians termed Monday through Friday, supervising development of the *aterro,* the landfill. The second of the year's "big excitements" was Lota's appointment as "Chief Coordinatress," and it was "just the kind of job I've always dreamed of for her," Elizabeth wrote to May, work such as she might have done years ago in another, less "*macho*" or "backyards" country, as Lota said in her endearingly scrambled English. As always for Elizabeth, Lota — whether changing a tire on the roadside, firing her .22 to kill a snake, or dancing a samba — was "wonderful in action." In April 1961, Elizabeth had watched Lota keep a roomful of engineers, all men, laughing while winning them over to her plans for public beaches, playgrounds, cafés, dance floors, and a two-lane road set back from the shore instead of a four-lane whizway at the water's edge. To have Lota "doing something at last, using her brains and helping poor dirty dying Rio at the same time," was more wonderful still.

But already Elizabeth could see that the mix of egotistical architects and conniving bureaucrats Lota would have to manage was a combustible one — "everyone involved is too crazy and there are too many cross-purposes," she summarized for May. The "semi-revolutions" and even an "anti-revolution revolution" — none of them "very bloody" — that Elizabeth occasionally mentioned in letters had brought Lacerda into power for the moment, and given Lota a job at last. Yet Elizabeth foresaw a precarious future, in which Lota might either "find herself *in* politics . . . or else she will get too fed up with the fearful jealousies, maneuverings, etc.," and retire again from public life.

Lota's new position, for which she had refused pay to show she was beyond influence, brought Brazil's shifting political scene into sharper focus. In late August, Lota and Elizabeth huddled by the radio to follow news of the abrupt resignation of President Quadros, Lacerda's ally. Quadros was replaced by his vice president, "a real old crook from the dictator gang," loyalists to the Vargas regime that had once sent Lacerda into exile. Fear of civil war ran high for more than a week. "We might even leave Brazil — who knows?" Elizabeth wrote to Aunt Grace, the last of her mother's sisters still living in Nova Scotia; she did not seem disturbed by the prospect. Yet before long, life "as usual" resumed: a "strange" new "up & down life," with weekdays down in Rio, where the phone started ringing for Lota at 7 a.m. and evening conferences lasted until after midnight, and rushed weekends with Mary and baby Monica up at a scarcely more peaceful Samambaia.

Elizabeth often had trouble gauging just how bad things were in Brazil, where, as she wrote Cal early in her stay, "the word for even a small accident . . . is *'desastre'*" — "I often have false alarms." She tried to get used to Rio, a city of "beaches & mts. jumbled together, frequently connected by unexpected tunnels with cars whishing through them, or aqueducts with trolley cars swaying over them . . . all quite fantastic," she'd written to May. Rio was a city that "changes every week or so." Eventually water ran through the pipes again, but the blackouts continued. Elizabeth strove to maintain an "awful but cheerful" attitude, captured in the samba song she'd learned about Rio, "My joy and my delight!" — "By day I have no water, / By night I have no light."

The new schedule kept Elizabeth away from her *estudio*, but worse, she was forced to postpone indefinitely a car trip across Europe, starting in Lisbon and ending in Greece, that she'd planned in great detail with maps from Esso and consultations with May, who'd just returned to her Greenwich Village apartment from a rejuvenating six months abroad with Pearl. Heeding Elizabeth's pleas for travel funds, Cal had performed his usual "amazing first aid" and wangled a $7,000 fellowship from the Chapelbrook Foundation. She would have to bank the check for later, because Lota was to have done the driving.

Dependence ran in both directions. Lota "hates to be alone," Elizabeth told May more than once. Lota had never learned to type and didn't know how to cook: "Brazilian 'ladies' are not trained in the household arts." She conscripted Elizabeth to compile an "anthology" of excerpts from urban design texts — "hunks of Lewis Mumford" and Edward Higbee's *The Squeeze: Cities Without Space* — for use in persuading Governor Lacerda, who "doesn't have time to read any book properly," to augment the *aterro*'s public beaches and promenades with an amphitheater, a *trenzinho* (train ride) for children, and a small airfield for launching model planes. On those rare occasions when Lota stayed by herself in Rio, Elizabeth was sure to get a despairing phone call in the morning asking how to assemble the Italian coffeepot, after Lota had "made her coffee upside down again."

Elizabeth was "sick of cooking, or supervising other people's cooking," she'd written to May, and had been looking forward to a spell of hotel living during her European car trip, turning aside her friend's advice on money-saving campgrounds. Making jam or baking brownies and English muffins, an apple pie on request for Lota's birthday, or an ornate wedding cake when Lota's oldest nephew got married, was a pleasure. But too often Elizabeth had to stop writing a letter or revising a poem to "go down and heat up the lasagna" or "get busy cooking a chicken" for dinner. May had remarked that Elizabeth "seemed to have one hand on the oven door while typing with the other." Now, marooned in Rio, where Lota had begun skipping weekend trips to Samambaia, Elizabeth was planning and preparing dinners for Lota's brain trust of architects and landscape designers, and joining the effort to charm or mollify them at table, struggling to overcome her shyness for Lota's sake.

In June Elizabeth had boldly canceled her first-read contract with the *New Yorker,* still troubled by Katharine White's rejection of a poem long in the works, "From Trollope's Journal." Elizabeth sometimes apologized for the poem, saying she'd borrowed most of the language from Anthony Trollope's account of his stay in Washington, D.C., during the Civil War. But she suspected that its implicit criticism of Eisenhower's Cold War politics, as the 1960 election drew near, had prompted the *New Yorker*'s refusal — for "fear it could be badly misinterpreted," as Katharine White explained. Cal had been struck by Elizabeth's ingenious means of posing her critique when he read the poem in manuscript: "You are about the only poet now who calls her own tune." The poem easily found publication in *Partisan Review,* whose editors didn't have to worry about offending "their Republican readers," as Elizabeth complained to May of the *New Yorker.* By then, however, Eisenhower's vice president, Richard Nixon, had already lost the election to John Kennedy, and the poem, Elizabeth's means of casting an absentee ballot, lacked a target.

The deeper reason for canceling the *New Yorker* contract was strategic. Despite so many domestic distractions, Elizabeth still had "several poems crowded on my one-burner stove." If she wasn't traveling, she could at least finish those poems to fill out a new book that, she told Cal, was "almost ready." In advance of the book's release, she hoped to expand her publications to the literary journals where Cal, who never published in the *New Yorker,* had made his reputation, and where poems too hot for Katharine White to touch would fare better. But in the end, Elizabeth finished only two poems in the next few months, not enough to make a book, and she sent them to the *New Yorker* anyway. They would be the last she completed for three years, as the "excitements" of 1961 accelerated and Elizabeth took on a "job" of her own.

By the time "Sandpiper" appeared, in July 1962, almost a full year after she'd sent it to Katharine White, the poem must have seemed prophetic. Cal Lowell was visiting Lota and Elizabeth on a Congress for Cultural Freedom tour, giving lectures and readings in Brazil and Argentina, and weren't they all "obsessed!" — "looking for something, something, something" along the shore, like the "poor" bird of the poem? Years later, Elizabeth would compare herself to the sandpiper, who "runs to the south . . . / in a state of controlled panic," and, as "a student of Blake," pays close attention to each grain of sand between

Cal and Elizabeth on Copacabana Beach, Rio de Janeiro,
photograph by P. Muniz, 1962

his toes, "no detail too small." But now it was Lota who had her "fini-cal" (finicky) designer's eye trained on a particular stretch of beach, engaging in "bitter telephone fights about the dimensions of the trees" to be planted in "her park" and debating countless other details, none of them too small to ignore.

And Cal—he'd arrived in Rio with Lizzie, five-year-old Harriet, and a "Radcliffe girl" to tend the child, only to turn garrulous and caustically opinionated, gathering velocity for yet another "attack of pathological enthusiasm," as he preferred to view his "violent manic seizures." There had been five breakdowns in ten years, by Cal's reckoning, and the pattern was predictable. Elizabeth, Cal, and Lota had spent a glorious afternoon together at Cabo Frio, perched on the "very dangerous" edge of a cliff above a crater formed by jagged rocks — "just like Inferno" — mesmerized by the sight of a pair of seabirds, possibly boobies, "diving right into the wild seething foam" as the surf spilled over into the crater at high tide: "It didn't seem possible they could fly against that wind, or see *anything* in that raging sea or dive so far from so high quick enough to catch anything." When wife, daughter, and babysitter left on an ocean liner bound for New York at the end of August, Cal traveled on alone to Buenos Aires, where his mania became full blown. After tearing off his clothes and mounting equestrian statues in a city square, proclaiming himself Argentina's Caesar, he was put in restraints and then on a plane back to the United States, heavily sedated, accompanied by a doctor and nurse and the friend, Blair Clark, who'd flown down from New York to bring him safely home.

The bond that sustained the two poets as they worked had never been enough to pull Cal back from the brink of madness. No human bond, nothing, could do that for him, though he had once hoped that through psychoanalysis, "the knot inside me will be unsnarled." Cal's breakdowns continued, as did Elizabeth's drinking, beyond the reach of "psych-a," in Elizabeth's new shorthand: "Before one gets bored with it there seems to be a very good stretch when anything seems possible." Yet in the same letter in which she dismissed "psych-a," Elizabeth praised Cal's rare ability among poets of their generation to demonstrate that "poetry does have some connection with emotions."

Despite what Cal described as "the seemingly dispassionate coolness" of her poems, Elizabeth had, since childhood, regarded poetry — reading it, writing it — as a release for emotion, "the most natural way of saying what I feel." Psychoanalysis had been a way station in a lifelong pursuit of insight and mastery of emotion. Writing was the only consistent means of achieving the elusive moments of illumination she sought, and Cal's new work in *Life Studies* had spurred her to "think I may be able to write a few simple but *gripping* lines myself."

She had answered his poems of boyhood with "First Death in Nova Scotia," the other poem published in 1962, which reached Cal before he'd left for Brazil. Calling it an "elegy," he'd praised Elizabeth's account of the wake she attended as a young girl for her little cousin Frank (named Arthur in the poem) as "lovely and pathetic, the best in the language of its kind . . . a piece on a real little child, memorialized from your own memories." This was another poem dusted off from Elizabeth's "attic" of drafts; she'd referred to "First Death" several years before in a letter to Cal as a poem "about snow in Nova Scotia." Did Cal, or Elizabeth for that matter, consider its resemblance to an earlier Lowell's poem memorializing a "real little child," James Russell Lowell's elegy on his infant daughter, "The First Snow-Fall"? In Elizabeth's poem, she stood by the child-sized coffin, "a little frosted cake," alongside her mother — the mother who had "laid out Arthur," "all white, like a doll," then lifted up tiny Elizabeth to place a lily in her dead cousin's hands, to see "his eyes shut up so tight" on a winter day when roads were "deep in snow." This mother had never protected her daughter, had shown her death up close and offered no words of comfort or explanation; Gertrude herself would soon be dead to Elizabeth. She was left alone, asking "how could Arthur go"? Though Elizabeth mocked it as sentimental when she rattled it off in a letter to a friend back in Key West days, the poem by James Russell Lowell that she had memorized so long ago must have lodged in her mind as an expression of parental love she could scarcely imagine: the poet, standing by the window with his surviving daughter, kept his grief from her as they watched the season's first storm "heaping field and highway," answered her questions, gave her the kiss he wished he could bestow on her dead sister, buried under "deepening" snow. Elizabeth had rewritten Lowell's poem, making it "real" for her, earning Cal's highest approbation. The poem, he told her, was "immortal."

Yet Cal, even at his sanest, could not help Elizabeth either, as she entered the most "*distrait*" and distressed period of her adult life. She would not confide in him, except to say, "I have been minding my loneliness here more lately, I'm afraid." Although she wrote to Cal and others of her worry over Lota's steadily intensifying obsession with the *aterro,* she always praised Lota's hard work and emphasized her concern that Lota would be devastated if her efforts came to naught, or if she was pushed out of her role as coordinatress. Elizabeth was "lost in admiration" of Lota, and proud that she was rapidly becoming Rio's most famous woman, featured in South American *Time* and news stories, interviewed on television. Elizabeth confided in no one her frightening sense that Lota was a different person, a stranger overtaken by a kind of mania, offending both opponents and supporters with her vehemence, breaking ties with her adopted son, "shrieking" at Elizabeth

Flamengo Park, Rio de Janeiro, photograph by Marcel Gautherot, ca. 1966

when she was slow in dressing for an important dinner engagement. Or was this the same Lota, but with a new, exclusive object, "her park"? Either way, Lota was unable to see that her obsession threatened the project she so dearly loved, and the love she counted on from Elizabeth. Nor did Lota notice, until too late, that Elizabeth had stopped taking Antabuse. When Lota was out all day on the *aterro,* Elizabeth did not need a driver to reach the corner bakery where *cachaça* was stocked along with bread and pastries. She told her friends nothing of this either.

Once Elizabeth saw that Lota would not leave Rio for Europe, she accepted a job with Time Inc., writing a volume on Brazil in the LIFE World Library series. Time offered $9,000 and a month's stay in New York to work with editors on revisions. The LIFE series books were lavishly illustrated, but 35,000 words of text were required, including a summary of the country's history and a comprehensive overview of present-day Brazil with an emphasis, Elizabeth learned to her dismay, on politics and commerce. She'd imagined the book as an extended letter home from her adopted country, with commentary on birds, animals, and plants; the samba songs she loved; the remote villages she hoped to visit on Time's travel allowance. But writing progressed so slowly she had no chance for travel. Elizabeth arrived in New York in the late fall of 1961 short on copy and accompanied by Lota, who hated to be left alone and could not resist the lure of shopping in Manhattan.

While Lota indulged her passion for "material possessions," spending money at an alarming rate on plates and towels and sugar bowls for the Rio apartment she planned to remodel as her base of operations, Elizabeth worked long hours in the Time offices, feeling "homesick," she later wrote, for "the New York I *didn't* see." Her days were so rushed "I can't see or hear or think." There was scarcely a moment for old friends, but together with Lota she paid visits to Dr. Baumann, "so blue-eyed and balanced"; Marianne Moore, fragile at almost seventy-five; the Lowells; May Swenson; and, in a meeting she would have reason to regret, Mary McCarthy. Little could distract Elizabeth, though, from the seemingly endless "fight with LIFE" over the editors' "ghastly 'slanting'" of every aspect of the book, from chapter titles and text to photographs and captions, "to make it seem as if the be-all & end-all of life is 'industrialization' — and happy, American-style homes." Time Inc., she realized, had wanted her name but not her voice, had always planned to "present their own undisturbed pre-conceptions" of the country. The series' editors were not interested in "sloths, boa constricters . . . ant-eaters, morfo butterflies, orchids — 4,000 varieties of fish," she fumed, even as she watched them gleefully select color photographs of lions and zebras for a volume on Africa, "because they already *know* lions live in Africa."

The wrangling continued by telex after Elizabeth's return to Brazil. By the time it was published in the spring of 1962, *Brazil* had become for her "that blasted book." There were no photographs of wildlife, few of Indians (Time Inc. was "afraid of nakedness"), and seven of her ten chapters had been altered beyond recognition. In a chapter called "Groups and Individuals," which Time renamed "A Changing Social Scene," she'd written of Brazilian women: "marriage at seventeen or eighteen and the grim race of procreation are the lot of even the rich and educated." In the final *"LIFE*-slicked book" there was no "grim race," only "customary" early marriage and motherhood. She had lost nearly every battle, and "I have no confidence left whatever," Elizabeth wrote to May on Valentine's Day, worried that "I can't seem to stop haranguing" and that her black mood "carried over into private life." She spent long days going through the stack of finished books Time sent her, making corrections in green ink before giving them to friends, as Lota resumed her frenetic pace of meetings on the *aterro.* "I've never seen the point of, or been able to endure, much argument," Elizabeth had once written to Cal, remembering the bickering Bishops of her childhood and her yet more cruel Uncle George. But for more than a year, her life had been filled with contention. In the small apartment, where she couldn't help overhearing Lota's phone calls, carried on at such high volume Lota became hoarse, Elizabeth found herself longing for silence — "what I like best of all." Or a river trip, on the less traveled Rio São Francisco, she thought now, "if I can leave Lota for a couple of weeks."

In the months after Cal's July visit, Elizabeth spent so little time in Samambaia that a house wren, a *cambaxirra,* nested in the Mexican mask, a relic of her travels with Marjorie Stevens, that hung on the wall of her studio. At her desk in Rio she managed to give line-by-line criticism on manuscripts by Cal, who dedicated to her the almost too-loose translations in *Imitations,* his anthology of European verse from Sappho to Pasternak; and by May, who asked Elizabeth's advice in paring down a collection of ninety poems to make her third book. She composed jacket blurbs for them both, lengthy prose poems in themselves. And she translated several stories by the Brazilian writer Clarice Lispector, whose tales she considered better than Borges's, finally placing them in the *Kenyon Review* after the *New Yorker* and *Encounter* turned them down. In contrast to "Practicing Poets" like Cal and May, Elizabeth had come to think of herself as a "Practical Poet" — answering her friends' requests, looking after Monica while Mary Morse traveled to New York to see a rich aunt, typing and cooking for Lota, but writing scarcely a word of her own. By October 1963, Elizabeth confided in May, "I can't write at all anymore." She had not uttered those words before, only feared it could be so. It was a grim admission for a writer who had counseled others, and herself, in hard times: "Work's the thing."

In the same letter, Elizabeth told May that she'd finished reading Mary McCarthy's *The Group,* her new novel retailing the private lives of a thinly disguised "group" of Vassar classmates after graduation in the 1930s. It was Mary's tenth book and, with its "set-fire-works-sex-pieces," an instant bestseller. Reading the early portions of the novel in *Partisan Review* and the *New Yorker,* Elizabeth could not have predicted the explosive ending, in which Lakey, the elegant and supercilious class intellectual, returns to New York after several years in Europe to attend the funeral of Kay, the novel's protagonist, accompanied by a "foreign woman," her lover. Lakey's shocked friends slowly realize, as the pair settles in at the Elysée Hotel, "This woman was her man." The next sentences must have jolted Elizabeth: "This was why Lakey had stayed abroad so long. Abroad people were more tolerant of Lesbians." Mary had even poked fun at "the convention by which the Baroness was 'my friend,' like a self-evident axiom." Trying their best "not to think" of what the female couple "did in bed together," the Vassar women were uniformly of the opinion that "what had happened to Lakey was a tragedy."

Most readers assumed the book was a *roman à clef*. Elizabeth readily identified Helena — a "short sandy-haired girl with an appealing snub nose" and a "habit of walking around nude" — as her friend Frani Blough. "Mary lets her off lightly!" she told May. Elizabeth had been a year behind Mary and Frani at school, and it was easy enough to make a blanket denial: "I was not in her 'group' (thank heavens)," and more firmly, "I'm thankful not to be in 'The Group.'! My poor friends...." Lakey bore a closer physical resemblance to the willowy Margaret Miller, as Mary would later admit, than to Elizabeth. But, except for the fact that she was "stocky," Lakey's lover, the short, mannish Baroness Maria d'Estienne, dressed in tweed suit and Cuban-heeled pumps, was a carbon copy of Dona Maria Carlota Costallat de Macedo Soares when she and Elizabeth had visited Mary in Manhattan. Lota — who worked eighteen-hour days and was hardly ever at home, except to sleep and shout into the phone.

Elizabeth did not criticize Mary — that would have revealed too much. "I admire her *gall*," she wrote to May, but "I dislike the age we live in that makes that kind of writing seem necessary.... We're all brutes." Nearly as much as she despised having Lota and herself caricatured, Elizabeth envied Mary's "commercial success," although, as she noted slyly in a letter to Cal, "it entails that bitterness that it's not for what she deserves it for." Compared to Mary's *Venice Observed* and *The Stones of Florence,* both critically acclaimed, *The Group* was tacky.

The same month Elizabeth learned of *The Group*'s publication, Laura Archera Huxley's *You Are Not the Target: A Practical Manual of How to Cope with a World of Bewildering Change and Uncertainty* arrived in the mail as a gift to Lota and Elizabeth. "What DOES California do to people's brains?" Elizabeth asked Cal, marveling over Aldous Huxley's unctuous preface, and Laura's advice, presented in the form of "recipes for living and loving" with titles like "Dance Naked with Music," "Bubble Freedom," and "Be an Animal." Laura's book, too, became a bestseller.

Elizabeth traveled north to Ouro Prêto in January 1965, for the quiet and for the company of Lota's friend Lilli Correia de Araújo, and soon she was writing again. Not poems she would publish. This writing didn't feel like work. Work was no longer "the thing." In late 1964, she'd confessed to May Swenson her desperate "craving for a good long 3 or 4-day day-dream," the kind of uninterrupted reverie "that enables one to stay with something and get it done." She had become, at best, a "Sunday poet," and not a productive one: "after a week of doing other things strenuously and talking Portugese and worrying about politics here — I get very uneasy." Would there be "no escape"? She had to make a change: "self-preservation's the thing." Without writing, she was scarcely living.

And so she turned her back on it all. She'd already tried taking refuge at Samambaia by herself for a week at a time — Lota hardly seemed to notice, now, "whether I'm there or not." But Elizabeth's loneliness in what had been their shared dream house, falling into disrepair without Lota's vigilant presence, was overwhelming: "I don't mind being alone when I'm happy — when I'm not, *then* it is unbearable." She was lonely even in Rio with Lota, whom "I scarcely seem to see ... any more." There had been no time, or goodwill, for lovemaking in — how long? Instead of spending early mornings in bed together, Lota was out the door, leaving Elizabeth to a solitary 7:30 a.m. swim on the beach, the only bodily indulgence of her Rio days. To cheer herself up, Elizabeth had acquired a pair of canaries, both female, but without mates they wouldn't sing. "We're all silent together," she wrote to May. "This *isn't* my world," she asked Cal, puzzling over her confinement to a high-rise apartment in a city she despised, "or is it?"

The world she'd left behind more than a decade ago — Cal's world — had become nearly as foreign. Not only Cal, but also the once-timid Marianne Moore, had read their poetry to audiences numbered in the thousands on the Boston Common. Cal and his family had moved to New York City, buying an apartment near the new Lincoln Center, a mid-Manhattan Brasília for the performing arts. Soon after, he and Lizzie Hardwick had joined a group of 170 writers and artists invited to the White House for President Kennedy's inauguration. "I feel like a patriot for the first time in my life," Cal confessed. (He'd served a jail term as a conscientious objector during World War II rather than join the military.) The most Elizabeth could do to indulge the newly vigorous American spirit was stand in line for a glimpse of the *"capsula"* in which John Glenn had splashed down near the Bahamas after orbiting the earth, on exhibition in a park in Rio. And then Kennedy's assassination in November 1963 left her weeping with sympathetic taxi drivers and shopkeepers for weeks, even as a *"golpe,"* or coup, threatened in Brazil.

That same season of mourning, Lota had been hospitalized with an intestinal occlusion requiring surgery, then she'd contracted typhoid fever. Elizabeth had spent every night with Lota in the hospital, helping to drain an "awful brown slime" out of her stomach into an enamel pan after the surgery and "scared to death" over her high fever, only to have Lota emerge too weak to drive and "FURIOUS!" at having been sick in the first place. Shaken by the experience and likely drinking to excess, Elizabeth checked into a hospital for a week, a "rest home" run by hymn-singing Seventh-day Adventists, teetotalers who skipped coffee but served good meals — she sent May one of the menus. The view from the Hospital Silvestre, situated near Rio's "awful" *Cristo Redentor* on Corcovado, the "hunchback" peak overlooking the harbor, was "magnificent." A precedent had been set: Elizabeth would seek her own cures from now on.

In a journey that would provide memories of their last peaceful hours together, Elizabeth and Lota managed an abbreviated version of the old plan to travel in Europe, spending three weeks driving through northern Italy in May 1964, lingering in Venice before Lota felt she must fly back to the *aterro,* recently named Flamengo Park after one of the beaches on its shoreline.

There were no more flamingos in Rio, Elizabeth explained to May, though they could be seen by airplane over the islands at the mouth of the Amazon, "great low pink clouds of them flapping below you." Lota had good reason to be preoccupied with the fate of the park; one month before the women left the country, the feared *golpe* had taken place. Lota had spent a frightening night barricaded in Rio's Guanabara Palace with Carlos Lacerda and his loyal troops and staff, one of two women on the premises. But the forty-eight-hour siege, a "real" revolution that unseated the leftist President Goulart, did Lota no immediate political damage and permitted her a month's vacation following the regime change. Both Lota and Elizabeth tried not to worry about the imprisonment of a group of intellectuals, not of Lota's protected social class, who'd protested the installation of a military leader as president, Humberto Castelo Branco, who'd made quick use of emergency powers enabling the suppression of dissent. Brazil had survived dictators before; in the unstable nation, another might soon be gone.

Elizabeth pressed on alone that summer for an intended two months in England and Scotland, only to cut short her stay after five weeks. She was lonely and "acutely anxious," despite visits to old friends from Yaddo days. She forced herself to attend several parties — "YE GODS the gentility" and "Oh so many poets" — but turned down all offers to give readings. "I wish you were here so much," she wrote to Lota in one of her frequent typewritten aerograms, filled to the margins. "Oh, I'd like to bring you here and just give you $1,000 to spend all by your little self!" She shopped for Lota anyway, searching out the right "GORGEOUS" tweed for a new suit and a monogrammed silver cigarette lighter at Dunhill's that was "light as a feather." Would she like a gun, a Webley revolver, "excellent for ladies' use," about $48? Lota wrote too, shorter handwritten letters, sending "a thousand little kisses" and reminding Elizabeth to "take your pills" (Antabuse twice a week) — "my love, come back soon." But crossing the Atlantic by "slow boat," Elizabeth dreaded the return. To Cal she wrote, "I am dying to see Lota —" And then it was "back to the Brazilian madhouse." Nothing had changed. Lota was as irritable and distracted as ever, lashing out at Elizabeth on her return from work — irrational, possessed, Elizabeth sometimes thought. What had become of the dear friend, *"minha querida,"* who had once shooed away Elizabeth's "inferiorities" and assured her she was "wonderful" and loved?

In Rio, Elizabeth would have received from her clipping service a copy of the interview she'd done for the London *Times* shortly before her departure. The reporter, Edward Lucie-Smith, dwelled on her connections to Mary McCarthy and *The Group* by way of Vassar, and to Robert Lowell, who'd been enjoying "near-canonisation" in England; and he queried Elizabeth on her least favorite subject, women poets. She answered only that women "get discouraged very young." In the accompanying photograph Elizabeth herself appeared defeated — ashen, sad, an old woman at fifty-three.

In the New Year, Elizabeth hadn't hesitated. Traveling with a young male Fulbright scholar, Ashley Brown, whose yen for sightseeing provided cover, Elizabeth left Lota for two weeks in Ouro Prêto. How soon after her arrival, in January 1965, did she write a poem for long-limbed, Scandinavian Lilli?

> *Dear, my compass*
> *still points north*
> *to wooden houses*
> *and blue eyes,*
>
> *fairy-tales where*
> *flaxen-headed*
> *younger sons*
> *bring home the goose,*
>
> *love in hay-lofts,*
> *Protestants, and*
> *heavy drinkers . . .*
> *Springs are backward,*
>
> *but crab-apples*
> *ripen to rubies,*
> *cranberries*
> *to drops of blood,*
>
> *and swans can paddle*
> *icy water,*
> *so hot the blood*
> *in those webbed feet.*

— Cold as it is, we'd
go to bed, dear,
early, but never
to keep warm.

She marked a star in her calendar on January 21, 1965 — the night Lilli, mercifully, had not been "reluctant" when Elizabeth turned to her, so full of need, and Lilli took Elizabeth to bed.

In the back pages of a small notebook dated December 1961 to May 1965, the years that saw the unraveling of Elizabeth and Lota's marriage, Elizabeth kept a list of books she meant to buy (prices were sometimes noted) or had read. She entered stars alongside some of the titles: *Selected Letters of Rilke, Poetry and Prose of Heinrich Heine, Guy Domville, The Life of Mary Wortley Montague* — and *The Problem of Homosexuality*. The last, published in 1958, may be the only informational book on homosexuality Elizabeth ever mentioned in writing, aside from a reference to having read Havelock Ellis as a teenager in a letter to Ruth Foster. (Fiction was different: she'd read Djuna Barnes's "good old" *Nightwood* soon after its publication in 1938, and told May Swenson she regretted having lost the book in her move to Brazil; she would not have been startled by *The Group*'s conclusion if it were not for the possibility that readers might take Lota for the Baroness.) Although she'd lived primarily in Rio during the years 1961–1965, Elizabeth eventually labeled the notebook "Ouro Prêto," and ideas she could have gleaned from *The Problem of Homosexuality* may have supported the choices she began to make in 1965 that led her away from Lota. Perhaps she sought out the book for help in justifying behavior that felt natural to her — as natural as her homosexuality — even as her actions were almost certain to hurt Lota if discovered.

The Problem of Homosexuality had two authors, both psychiatrists, and only the first of them thought homosexuality was a problem. Clifford Allen threw down the gauntlet: "If happiness is of any value ... then homosexuality should be eliminated by every means in our power." Allen argued the premise, enshrined in the American Psychiatric Association's diagnostic manual since 1952, that homosexuality was a "psychological deviation" to be cured by psychotherapy. But Charles Berg, the second author, made a different case altogether. If there was a "problem" with homosexuality, it was in the minds of those who thought so. Why, he wondered, do "we make such a fuss about it"? The answer, he believed, "is to be found in the precarious balance of forces in our own repressed unconscious." Railing against the "psychopathology of our often stupid and morbid and injurious reactions against" homosexuality, Berg proposed that "'bi-sexual' potentialities within the psyche," so often repudiated when same-sex attraction emerged, actually form "the basis of inter-personal relationships": the "holding together of our social structure" depends on attraction to and identification with both one's own and the opposite sex. Drawing on anthropological studies to demonstrate tolerance of homosexuality in other cultures, Berg quoted a passage from Wilhelm Reich's writings on the Trobriand Islanders that may have meant more to Elizabeth in her loneliness than Berg's defense of her chosen way of loving. "The socially accepted form of sexual life," Reich wrote, "is spontaneous monogamy without compulsion, a relationship which can be dissolved without difficulties; thus, there is no promiscuity." Elizabeth, of course, was not really married to Lota, although the two women mingled their incomes and had written each other into their wills. Whatever rules they made for themselves were extralegal, spontaneous. Could the rules be broken — dissolved — without difficulty?

Elizabeth's love poem "Dear, my compass" was a sub-rosa gift to Lilli. Elizabeth wrote out the lines by hand while visiting Ouro Prêto, and decorated the page with watercolor sketches of a goose, a swan, a hayloft, and an antique four-poster with two pillows at the headboard. By late September she'd written another poem for "My dear Aurora Borealis," "Darling Lilli" — one that was safe to offer to the *New Yorker,* though too late to include in *Questions of Travel,* the book Elizabeth had finally sent to press in the early months of 1965, energized by her stay with Lilli. The book reached a plausible length with the addition of her story "In the Village," following Cal's lead with *Life Studies,* in which he had included his memoir, "91 Revere Street"; and it was still inscribed to Lota ("The more I give you, the more I owe you"). Lota—

who was "killing herself with work," Elizabeth wrote to her *New Yorker* editor Howard Moss when she mailed the new poem she planned to dedicate to Lilli, "Under the Window: Ouro Prêto." *Questions of Travel* would be published by Farrar, Straus and Giroux in October, during Elizabeth's third and longest stay with Lilli.

She had felt "mean abandoning Lota" for two weeks in January, Elizabeth told May, not letting on just how far she had strayed. Elizabeth wrote only that she'd gotten a lot of work done, and felt "much better — a better altitude." Ouro Prêto — with its ten exquisite eighteenth-century churches scattered across the hillsides, "THE Baroque town," in Elizabeth's description — was a thousand meters higher than Petrópolis and considerably more remote, hundreds of miles north in the landlocked state of Minas Gerais. Elizabeth wasn't staying at Pouso do Chico Rey, where Ashley Brown, her Fulbright-scholar friend who'd done the driving, spent his nights, but at Lilli's own house high above the village on the road east to Mariana, the region's oldest city, whose name brought pleasant associations with Marianne Moore. Up on the hillside Lilli kept a flower garden and a "strange assortment of poultry": chickens, geese, guinea hens, white fan-tailed doves, and a pinkish, snake-eating, heronlike bird to protect them all, which Lilli had tamed by leaving bits of meat in a dish on her kitchen floor each morning.

Although Lilli was reserved in temperament and different from Lota in appearance, she was an immensely capable woman too. Elizabeth had been in awe of Lota's ability to "do all kinds of things to cars, install telephones and repair electrical gadgets." Now Elizabeth loved Lilli's "hard hands," strong from gardening and innkeeping and refinishing the antique furniture she collected and planned to sell in a shop in town. She was four years older, but Lilli was "my dearest blue eyed fair-headed child with muscles and *carrapatas* & everything with a soft soft name," Elizabeth wrote to her after a second visit, alone, in May 1965. This time Lilli had come to Rio on business, then driven Elizabeth back with her to Ouro Prêto — Lota could hardly mind. They were all friends.

Carrapatas — or *garrapatas* — were the ticks that Lilli's dog, Danny, brought in, or that Elizabeth may have plucked from her lover's body in the evening after a ramble in the hills above Lilli's house. Elizabeth was in the grips of a passion that made almost anything associated with Lilli — ticks, hard hands, a torn nightgown, her Danish accent — lovable. "Tell me," she urged Lilli, "something beginning with 'w'" — "You are a weak and wanton woman but I want you. . . . Could you say that?"

It was on this second weeklong stay that Elizabeth set down the impressions that led to "Under the Window: Ouro Prêto." To May Swenson she wrote of the "small water-fall right under my bedroom window" at Lilli's house — "and it is good water, so every passerby, every car and truck almost, stops for a drink of water." From her second-story window Elizabeth loved to "lean out and eavesdrop" on conversations — "mostly talk of sicknesses, funerals, babies, and the cost of living." In the poem, and in fact, the small waterfall is diverted into "a single iron pipe," from which "a strong and ropy stream" of cold water runs, attracting pedestrians and motorists: "they veer toward the water as a matter / of course," where once there was an ornate soapstone fountain, "here where all the world still stops."

The poem records the "simple" talk of women in red dresses and plastic sandals who pause to give their babies drinks, "lovingly / from dirty hands"; of old men and younger ones, some driving trucks. A shiny new Mercedes-Benz "arrives / to overawe them all" with its body "painted / with throbbing rosebuds" and its bumper sticker, "HERE AM I FOR WHOM YOU HAVE BEEN WAITING." Had Elizabeth tinkered with a bumper sticker she'd seen in Petrópolis several years before and passed along to May as a specimen of Brazilian machismo, "*Women! Here I am!,*" turning its slogan into a message of gratitude to Lilli? If so, no one could ever guess. Elizabeth had tinkered with the scene itself until it became, with donkeys and swaddled babies, a parable like "Filling Station," with its final hymn-style blessing: "Somebody loves us all." "Under the Window: Ouro Prêto" ends with another vision of redemptive beauty in an apparently godforsaken place, recalling, too, the rainbow in the oil slick at the close of "The Fish." If Time Inc. would not allow an iridescent morpho into the pages of *Brazil,* Elizabeth could pin one to a poem in the *New Yorker:*

The seven ages of man are talkative
and soiled and thirsty.

                    Oil has seeped into
the margins of the ditch of standing water

and flashes or looks upward brokenly,
like bits of mirror — no, more blue than that:
like tatters of the Morpho *butterfly.*

———

"I feel human and slightly giddy and silly again," Elizabeth wrote to Lilli, thanking her for the weeklong tryst in May, using a post office box she'd rented in Ouro Prêto. Elizabeth addressed the envelopes to herself, but Lilli had the key and knew to open the letters and read them. Since their affair began, Elizabeth had been "full of poetry" — "all kinds of bits of things that *may* turn into something — the first time in three or four years I've felt normally bright." Could she help it that "I need love"? "It is the way I am made." Some people, she wrote to Lilli, "seem to function all right without it — or else they 'sublimate' — a chemical process I've never believed in for a moment." Lilli would have known Elizabeth had too-busy, irritable, ailing Lota in mind. Elizabeth asked Lilli to burn her letters: "I wake up frightened at the damage they might do but seem to keep right on writing you." There had been no one to talk to for so long, and she would not stop now.

Elizabeth confided in Lilli the eerie feeling that Lota had developed a "split personality." She was impossible to live with in Rio, but her agitation, the frenetic orders to Elizabeth to compose and type letters to Lota's supporters, to dress rapidly for dinner, to take her pills, subsided as they drove out of the city for infrequent weekends at Samambaia. Elizabeth mourned the early days in Brazil, "after NY," when "I used to wake up every morning so happy just because I was away from that constant pressure — phone-calls interruptions things that *have* to be done, — and because that feeling of a lump of lead in the stomach had finally disappeared after years of it." Now, living with Lota in Rio, dread overtook her again, and "it only disappears on the rare occasions

I get back to S[amambaia], or — when I am with you." Lilli — "my lovely hot and cold snowdrift" — "my appletree still blossoming as prettily as ever" — "who gives everything away and feeds the cats and the hens and anyone who comes along." Lilli — the "dear danish pastry" Elizabeth wished she could eat for breakfast.

At her desk in Rio, trying to resist the ever-present temptation to daydream about Lilli, Elizabeth often felt "hideously guilty," but she refused to admit the feeling for long. She silenced her qualms by "studying" John Crowe Ransom's poem of illicit love, "The Equilibrists": "Full of her long white arms and milky skin / He had a thousand times remembered sin." And "so have I," she told Lilli, yet her memories were all happy ones. How could finding love again when she needed it be a sin? In the months preceding her first visit to Lilli, Elizabeth had been reading the letters of Jane Carlyle, whose marriage to the nineteenth-century British writer Thomas Carlyle was famously unhappy. Making notes toward a poem she planned to call "The Carlyles," Elizabeth had written, "We speak of shipwrecks — why not housewrecks?" In a later draft she wrote, "Oh white seething marriage!" Elizabeth saw herself as the long-suffering, subservient Jane; Lota with her park — which finally promised to do as Carlos Lacerda had hoped, rejuvenate the city — was the caustic, vituperative, bullying genius. Elizabeth could not tell even Lilli, who after all was Lota's friend, just how bad it was — that Lota was "abrupt and rude" with almost everyone now, that her "violent . . . manner" frightened Elizabeth. She had let Lota be "bossy" until "I can't stand it anymore." She had to "get away."

And yet, even if she'd been wronged and neglected, Elizabeth knew her pleasure was taken selfishly, at Lota's expense. Along with Ransom's poem, she studied Thomas Hardy's "The Self-Unseeing" and considered writing her own version; the mysterious scene of revelry rising out of barrenness now resonated with her own willful, unbidden behavior:

> *Here is the ancient floor,*
> *Footworn and hollowed and thin,*
> *Here was the former door*
> *Where the dead feet walked in.*

She sat here in her chair,
Smiling into the fire;
He who played stood there,
Bowing it higher and higher.

Childlike, I danced in a dream;
Blessings emblazoned that day;
Everything glowed with a gleam;
Yet we were looking away!

Elizabeth had to be a "self un-seeing," had to look away, in order to carry on as she was, choosing rebirth in Lilli's arms.

Lota suspected nothing, not even when Elizabeth ran off to Ouro Prêto again in September 1965 and stayed through October and into November, until Lota "finally came and *got* me," making a nine-hour drive — "so I felt she really wanted me back!" Elizabeth wrote to May Swenson. She was hinting at the rift, the pain that had prompted her wandering and that she might inflict on Lota if she wasn't careful. Elizabeth did not tell May that she'd bought a rundown house, among the oldest in Ouro Prêto, across the road from Lilli's, formulating a secret plan to spend several months each year in the town. Perhaps she could have both Lota and Lilli. As if by a miracle, Lota, who "is always very happy when there is some construction going on," entered into the renovation project and stayed on for several days, taking measurements for blueprints.

Elizabeth offered Lilli a 15 percent contractor's fee for overseeing roof repairs and the installation of modern plumbing and electricity; Lili had ably restored both the inn, Pouso do Chico Rey, and her own house, with its "big old-fashioned Brazilian courtyard" of black and white brook stones laid out in daisy patterns. And Elizabeth implored Howard Moss to waive a new ban on dedications at the *New Yorker* and retain her inscription, "for Lilli Correia de Araújo," when the magazine published "Under the Window: Ouro Prêto": "it is almost the only return my friend Lilli will let me make for endless hospitality and kindness.... I can't bear to disappoint her." Moss complied.

But there had been scenes at Lilli's house in Ouro Prêto too. Elizabeth drank too much some nights — "and it makes me feel especially bad that I was such a fool with *you.*" Perhaps Elizabeth needed to test Lilli's loyalty as well; or, as likely, her thirst for alcohol under the stress of leading a double life, no matter how pleasurable, was beyond her control. Would Lilli forgive her bad behavior? "At least I do know it and admit it and feel awful remorse for it. . . . I'll try hard never to be that way with you again." Elizabeth wanted to believe their love was "not just a fling; it's real." Before leaving Ouro Prêto with Lota, she promised to find a ring, one with a lapis lazuli stone to match Lilli's blue eyes, a gift to mark their first anniversary in January. Would Lilli join her on the river trip on the São Francisco Elizabeth still dreamed of?

Back in Rio, Lota resumed her nagging. Elizabeth and Lilli had looked like "fat round pigs" when Lota arrived in Ouro Prêto, she ridiculed them. Elizabeth *had* gained weight after two months of dining in Lilli's "lavishly run kitchen." She had also enjoyed making love with

Lota, Elizabeth, and Lilli inspecting Elizabeth's
recently purchased house, Ouro Prêto, 1965

"nice and big and warm and blonde and *heavy*" Lilli. Now, under Lota's watchful eye, she resumed taking Antabuse, and added diet pills and Metrecal (Danish Coffee flavor) on her own. She could not squeeze into her best dress when *Time* sent a photographer to take her picture for the magazine's review of *Questions of Travel.* She had to conceal the gap with a sash. Elizabeth worried, she told Cal, that she looked like "both my grandmothers put together" in the resulting portrait. The book itself, she apologized to Howard Moss, was "pretty thin."

Yet *Questions of Travel* received positive reviews from the start, even in *Time,* which had never reviewed a book of Elizabeth's before and had dismissed her poems as "cool, eely" and "sometimes repellent" in a 1962 roundup on contemporary poets. Now *Time*'s reviewer allowed that she had written "some of the finest descriptive poetry" since World War II; six of the twenty poems in the volume were "egregiously good," rendering images that "blazon the retina long after the book is closed." In the *New York Review of Books* Elizabeth was "one of the shining, central talents of our day," and the poet Richard Howard, writing in *Poetry,* considered her sequence of Brazil poems "perfect." In the new year, 1966, the book was nominated for the National Book Award.

With her affections vacillating wildly — Lota, who "*loves* it when I am famous, a 'celebrity,'" Elizabeth reported to Lilli, was paying attention to her again — the praise scarcely registered. She had been "feeling too many things at the same time" for so long she'd become "*stuck,*" Elizabeth had written to Cal as her domestic situation grew fraught, not naming the feelings. Frightened and wary and seeking release, Elizabeth still had not stopped caring for Lota, whose stewardship of Flamengo Park, now fully open to the public, was threatened under President Castelo Branco's rule. Lota was suffering from ailments small and large — "gumboils" and ulcers and bronchitis and dizzy spells — but she refused to rest: "now she's had a taste of public life, she'll never be able to retire from it." Elizabeth loved Lilli, her "soothing presence," and the "great comfort and idleness" of Ouro Prêto that made writing possible again.

And she worried for herself. In late October Elizabeth learned that Randall Jarrell, the poet-critic and friend who'd been among her first champions, had walked into oncoming traffic on a highway near campus at the University of North Carolina, where he taught in the Women's College. Elizabeth considered Jarrell's death an "accident of an unconscious-suicide kind, a sudden impulse when he was really quite out of his head." As she gave in to her own impulses, life-affirming ones she believed, Elizabeth remained "determined," she wrote to Lilli, "that I am one poet who's going to stay sane till the bitter end." She had written to Randall just six months before, complimenting him on his new book of poems, *The Lost World,* and telling him of her reviving love for Brazil's inland towns where "some of the Lost World hasn't quite been lost" — "I gather up every bit of evidence with joy, and wish I could put it into my poems, too." She had, in "Under the Window: Ouro Prêto."

Just as the completion of *Poems* in 1955 had released a torrent of new verse, so *Questions of Travel* freed Elizabeth from years of feeling "stuck," this time to face daunting questions that the book itself, its contents divided in two under the headings "Brazil" and "Elsewhere," seemed to pose. Where (and with whom) should she live? Would she remain "passive forever," the submissive wife in her marriage to Lota, or would she find some way to prove "I am not a helpless child anymore and can't be treated like one"? The issue that pressed Lota and Elizabeth toward "housewreck" in November and December 1965 wasn't jealousy — not yet. It was Elizabeth's decision to accept a job as poet-in-residence at the University of Washington in Seattle for five months during the winter and spring of 1966. She had already turned down a similar offer from Rutgers the year before when Lota would not come along. This time Lota refused even to visit, and she argued — often at the top of her lungs — that Elizabeth would fail in the position. She would drink, she would be too shy to teach, she would "make a fool" of herself.

Lota issued one warning after another and "keeps telling me how sorry I'm going to be," Elizabeth complained to Lilli. There had been a "sad scene" between the two of them, lasting most of one night. It was up to Elizabeth to summon "the courage to make this step," and to think of the benefits — "it will be good for me to be surrounded by lots of strangers for a change," she told Lilli, "also be admired, and al-

lowed to talk all I want to, in English, about my own narrow interests!"
The alternative, staying in Rio with Lota, would only make Elizabeth
"more & more of a recluse": "If I allow this life to go on any longer I'll
be totally lost." She could take driving lessons in Seattle and courses
in Portuguese to increase her fluency in conversation; both would give
her greater independence when she returned. She could "get some of
my own work done" too. Although Elizabeth had always said teaching was "not my line at all," everything else about the plan seemed
designed to bring the liberation she sought, the respect and adulation
she'd forfeited for so long by living in Brazil.

Elizabeth purchased a plane ticket for December 30, and Lota and
Elizabeth called a Christmas truce. Lota made "lists and lists" of furnishings for Elizabeth to buy, while Elizabeth wrote repeatedly to Lilli,
assuring her "I don't want anyone else." On arrival in Seattle, knowing
she had crossed Lota by leaving, Elizabeth thought almost exclusively
of Lilli, to whom no one she'd seen on the journey or met at the English
department's New Year's Eve party could compare: "How wonderful to
know that I really know the most beautiful blonde in the hemisphere
and that I feel she is my own property — maybe you aren't, but I pretend you are — you and the house together." Elizabeth could hardly
wait to "get back there and overlook that enchanting dead town and
write a poem, very very slowly, and be with you without having to make
conversation at all." She envisioned a blue-painted balcony where the
two of them would sit, drinking tea and taking in the view.

The secret satisfaction carried Elizabeth through her first days on
campus. "I go around so sedate and neat and *sober* (yes — absolutely),"
she wrote to Lilli, "everyone treats me with such respect and calls
me Miss B — and every once in a while I feel a terrible laugh starting
down in my chest — also a feeling of great pride because nobody knows,
— And how different I am from what they think, I'm sure — and how
wonderful and contradictory life is, and how little appearances tell."
In a neighborhood shop she found the lapis lazuli stone — a "wonderful
rich just-before-dawn blue" recalling their hours of lovemaking — and
had it set "in plain gold, rather heavy, like a man's signet ring," telling
the elderly jeweler it was "for a *small* man (like him)." She thought of
having it engraved for Lilli, then decided that wasn't safe.

But soon she was overcome by a "strange" hollow feeling, she told Lilli, "sick to my stomach — I think it must be homesickness — I never had it before." Elizabeth had forgotten, or did not want to remember, the lost feeling she'd had just after college on her first Atlantic crossing, the feeling she'd called "homesickness" then, and associated with her mother's early bouts of insanity.

Lilli seemed too far away even to miss. The driving lessons and Portuguese classes and "my own work" were set aside. It was all Elizabeth could manage to teach two courses, she was so terrified. She drank, though not as often as Lota predicted. She had a terrible case of the Asian flu, requiring hospitalization. She sambaed alone in her apartment on Carnival night. She was passed over for the National Book Award. And one evening, at a dinner party hosted by the poet Carolyn Kizer, she fell in love with a pixyish blond, blue-eyed twenty-three-year-old, the newly pregnant fifth wife of a forty-eight-year-old Seattle artist.

It was Roxanne Cumming's love letters, not Lilli's, that Elizabeth tossed into the swirling waters of the Rio São Francisco from the deck of a paddle-wheel steamer a year later when she took her last river trip in Brazil, alone. Roxanne was so young, not practiced in deception, and Lota had found them out.

My grade was a B, the first I'd received since high school chemistry, and then I'd been proud — my B-minus was the highest grade in a tough class. I didn't mind this B so much as the knowledge that Miss Bishop thought I'd cheated. A feeling of shame, edged with anger, burned in me every time I recalled her accusation, burned so that I couldn't think. I knew there was no arguing with her. Another student had defended her use of "dime" in a poem set in British Jamaica; the student had heard English schoolchildren use the word as slang, referring to a tenpenny piece, and she was making a point about American cultural hegemony. Before the next class meeting, Miss Bishop had phoned a friend in London to check the usage and reported back, almost gleefully, that the student was wrong. My sin had been far greater in her eyes, I was sure. Had she told Professor Fitzgerald?

There had been no more poetry workshops or Advanced Verse Writing courses left to take by the spring semester of my senior year, and I'd persuaded Professor Fitzgerald — "Fitzy," we called him fondly, never to his face — to supervise an independent study. I wanted to keep on writing poetry, or thought I did. Each time we met in his spartan office in Harvard's new, underground Pusey Library, I wondered what Elizabeth Bishop might have said to him. Had she attempted to verify her hunch that I'd double-dipped with an assignment from his class? Or had she merely assumed (correctly) that no student would have written Catullan hendecasyllabics of her own free will? I still wished I knew what she thought of the poem, and I didn't seem to be able to write much more now.

Professor Fitzgerald, too, seemed diminished, no longer the twinkle-eyed tale-spinner who'd held us captive with recitations of Chaucer and Virgil in his smoker's *sotto voce*. When I saw him pacing ahead of me through Harvard Yard — its patches of winter-brown lawn cordoned off and strewn with grass seed to make them green again in time for commencement — and turning off toward Pusey, his waterproof canvas book bag slung over a stooped shoulder, I slowed my steps and let him reach the building first.

Pusey Library wasn't really a building. It was a bunker, constructed below ground to house overflow books from the immense, many-columned Widener Library next door, and opened just a year earlier. One of Alexander Calder's black steel stabiles, *Onion,* marked the otherwise easy-to-miss glassed-in entryway, seeming to advertise the subterranean world beyond, down a short flight of steps — a bibliophobe's Hades. Sometimes I reached Professor Fitzgerald's office from the bowels of Widener, taking a rickety elevator down seven stories from the fourth-floor entrance to the stacks and following a path marked in crimson footprints through steam tunnels, then emerging into a surprisingly bright shelving area on Pusey 2, one floor below ground level.

Professor Fitzgerald may have liked his new office, one of twenty neat compartments bordering a sunken interior courtyard, open to the sky, where plantings had yet to grow but sunlight streamed in. I didn't know where his office had been previously, but he seemed to me out of place, tucked away amid volumes on sociology and economic theory, and his own shelves were bare. I'd owned a paperback copy of his translation of the *Odyssey* since taking a course on epic narrative at Bennington, and early in this semester I'd acquired the blush-red clothbound *In the Rose of Time,* a collection of his poems, some of them first published in the 1930s when Fitzgerald was a Harvard undergraduate. "What should you know at last when / Spirit's spun from you, bobbin of bone, ghostbody in the sun?" he'd asked in "Elegy." No answer would come from the books in this new neighborhood.

I had never seen the large stucco house on Bryant Street where he'd lived with his family of six children until recently either, only the drab faculty apartment he'd moved to on Fernald Drive, near the Radcliffe Quad, after leaving his wife of twenty-five years for a young professor of English literature at Yale. I'd taken him a loaf of banana bread I baked one week, in lieu of a poem, and handed it to the slim, dark-haired woman who answered the door and welcomed my gift.

I'd changed living quarters too. I had a new boyfriend, a senior English major descended, like me, from Harvard men, but unlike mine, his father and grandfather had left college with degrees and made something of themselves. Finished with his courses at midyear, he moved to an apartment near campus where he'd write his thesis on Wallace Stevens and begin a career as a freelance magazine journalist. I was in love, and my boyfriend's offer to share his modest trust-fund income with me until I graduated in June, enabling me to forfeit the scholarship that covered my dorm fees, shocked me into accepting his invitation to move in with him. His spontaneous generosity felt like — *was* — love.

We shared an ancestor, I would later learn, Thomas Dudley, a colonial governor of Massachusetts who'd built the first house in Cambridge. My boyfriend's branch of the family stayed on the East Coast and prospered; mine headed west to risk and ruin. Still, that trace of common DNA may have contributed to the feeling I sometimes had that he was an adorable little brother, though he was a month older. I liked his playful, impulsive nature. He hadn't lived out in the world as I had, and for a time he relied on my superior wisdom — the Morgan Memorial for secondhand furniture and kitchenware, recipes from *The Vegetarian Epicure.* We would not qualify for food stamps, as I had before returning to college two years earlier. The ten dollars an hour I charged several Harvard students for elementary piano lessons and two English literature PhDs, beleaguered mothers of young children, for help in revising their dissertations for publication, made me feel rich.

My plans for the future were vague. I'd applied for a Michael Rockefeller grant from a lavish travel fund honoring the "brief but intense" life of the twenty-three-year-old son of Nelson Rockefeller who'd disappeared on an anthropological expedition in New Guinea in 1961. It was Harvard's only substantial post-baccalaureate fellowship that didn't require academic work, and I'd proposed a year in Paris where I'd write poetry. Freedom beckoned. Maybe my boyfriend would come along if I won the competition.

I signed up for the LSAT and GRE, but took neither one. For a psychology course that semester I'd interviewed a young female associate at a prestigious Boston law firm, one of the first women hired to her position. She had time for the interview because she was home on a two-month maternity leave. The fatigue in her eyes and my own sleepiness kept me in bed on the Saturday morning of the LSAT. As for grad school in English, my work for the middle-aged PhDs had been alarming. Both had been off the job market for so long that their professors, eminent men of letters, had retired or forgotten them. The grad students in my seminar classes seemed to feel nearly as hopeless; there would be no jobs for most of them either.

I was happy living the life I had, studying psychology and early American literature, taking piano lessons for another self-directed course and practicing seriously for the first time in years. I was in love and I felt loved. Perhaps this was why I suddenly had nothing to say in verse. My only problem was disappointing Professor Fitzgerald. Each week when I had little to show beyond revisions of old poems, he nodded sympathetically. Why not try writing *poésie trouvée*? — found poetry, he explained, the poetry of the street, derived from newspaper headlines, billboard texts, graffiti. He urged me to find beauty, form, grace in what was given to me.

I thought of my piano teacher Patricia Zander's advice when I was deciding on a program for the recital I planned at semester's end: "You can only sing the songs you know." For the concert, along with the Beethoven sonata I was learning that spring, I'd pulled out of my scant repertoire Schumann's *Papillons* (Butterflies), opus 2, his first suite of fantasy pieces. But in writing poetry, what did I already know? What did I want to remember?

Professor Fitzgerald's shifting domestic arrangements may have prompted him to briefly set aside his latest Olympian translation project, the *Aeneid,* to write a short memoir of his childhood in Springfield, Illinois. "Notes on a Distant Prospect" was published in the *New Yorker* the same week Pusey Library opened its doors, and Fitzy's student admirers felt something like an illicit thrill to be let in on a few scenes from our reticent professor's boyhood. What we learned was almost incalculably sad. The piece was a fond reminiscence of the "humorous and tender, lame personage" who was his father, bedridden with osteotuberculosis the year Robert turned eight and, until his death ten years later, "every evening my companion." Robert Sr.'s crippling illness was not the tragedy, though. Indeed, in surviving so long the disease that had been expected to take him swiftly, "my father was given to me, and the gift was beyond estimation." Robert's mother had died of puerperal fever when the boy was three, and four years later the little brother who'd survived his birth died of influenza — "they had been removed as by a razor." Our professor had discovered early that "the fate of the breathing person was to be hurt and then annihilated." In his father's case there had been a reprieve.

But no father could be only saint, or martyr. In the years immediately following his wife's death, while he could still walk with the aid of crutches, Robert Fitzgerald Sr. had been "one of those Irishmen who when they drink go blindly under some wave that has been mounting inside them . . . and are different men in the violence of the wave." There were times when Robert's father became "a changed and redolent stranger of whom one has to be afraid." Some evenings, the boy was sent by his grandmother, whose home they shared after his mother's death, to fetch his father from a shabby downtown office where he could be found playing cards with "old cronies . . . whisky and syphon bottles beside them." His father's worsening illness brought a reprieve from this too. Never again well enough to go to an office or play a poker game, his father was confined to bed in a second-story room next to Robert's, "not large, with bay windows under a maple tree, and he could look out over a quiet street toward a long slanting lawn where the afternoon sunlight lay, and beyond that to a grove

of elms." No longer "crazed and sodden, cut off from himself," his father had been returned to Robert with "everything to impart, as I had
everything to learn, of the discipline, humility, and humor proper to a
man."

I wished my own father would come back to me, a "personage" from
whom I could learn more than how not to live my life. Perhaps I'd been
drawn to Harvard so I could do it over, differently, for both of us. Sometimes I thought of him arriving in Boston by train at age seventeen for
the start of his freshman year in the fall of 1938, after stopping in Kansas to meet relatives, who'd given him his first drink. He waited tables
in the freshman dining hall, serving his classmates, a requirement of
his scholarship. For spending money he delivered newspapers, running up and down the stairwells of the Harvard dorms in the early
mornings. He'd never owned a raincoat in sunny Southern California,
and he'd bought a cheap slicker that caused him to sweat unbearably
in the humidity on wet days. But I knew little more. He'd won a book
prize for straight A's that year, and the next he'd succumbed to mental
illness, to drink, and been asked to leave.

I was never told to fetch my father from a drunken poker game, but I
remembered the year 1966, when I was twelve and he'd lost his driver's
license. He'd borrowed a neighbor boy's ten-speed bike to get to a bar
(my mother allowed no liquor in the house) and, weaving home late
at night, he'd turned too soon into our driveway, colliding with a concrete lamppost, dislocating his shoulder. If I'd been a year younger, I
wouldn't have been permitted to visit him in the hospital, and I wished
I didn't have to join my mother at his bedside the next evening. He was
groggy and didn't seem to know I was there, the way he often was at
home. But in the hospital with nurses looking on, things should have
been different. I should have been able to wish him a speedy recovery,
to hope he'd get well soon.

I remembered the day I'd come home from school knowing he was
in the house — he'd lost the last of his city planning jobs and stayed
home sleeping much of the day while my mother was at work. I had the
backdoor key tied around my neck on a shoelace, and I'd used it many
afternoons to let myself in. But that day I wanted Dad to let me in. I
knocked on the door. I banged on the glass with the key in my fist until

it broke around my hand. Still no one came, and I swept up the broken glass, mercifully unhurt but afraid to tell my mother what I'd done when she got home. Why hadn't I used my key? Who would knock on a pane of glass? It would cost precious dollars to make the repair.

A few years later I would discover in Professor Fitzgerald's new translation that he had made a bold alteration in the *Aeneid*'s famous opening line, "Arms and the man I sing." His version began, "I sing of warfare and a man at war." He had rendered the epic personal by telling the story of "a man" rather than "the man." In 1977, making my weekly visits to his office, where I found him looking out on an all-too-near prospect, the unlovely courtyard, into shafts of sunlight from the living world above us, I could think only of what it must have cost this small, quiet man, a devout Catholic whose forehead I'd seen marked with ashes on a Wednesday in late February, to cause a rift in the family he had made: the battles that must have preceded and ensued, internal as well as familial. Had he cut himself out of his wife and children's lives "as by a razor" to set up housekeeping with his new, young Penelope? I was grateful I had no part in this drama, and thankful for each afternoon he walked from Fernald Drive to Pusey Library to nod his head over my slight efforts in verse.

I scanned his memoir for clues to his present state of mind. Of long summer days at play with his brother, he'd written, "Imagination like a mercurial fluid ran where it would." And was this sentence, in a passage following the account of his father's drunkenness, a bid for his own forgiveness? "No general view of things would ever seem just to me unless it comprehended Heaven and Hell — a range in experience at least as great as that between my exaltations as a child and my glimpses of anguish and evil." Perhaps the answer lay in his poems: given longer to live than his father, he would not rest content to be a "ghostbody in the sun."

I wrote a love poem for my boyfriend on his birthday in early May and turned it in as the last week's assignment. I called it "The Swing." He was an athlete, adept at racket sports I didn't play, but we'd spent idle hours that spring tossing a softball, joining pickup games on the quad. I admired his form at bat. The poem played with the elements of grammar in the simple sentence so often used as an example in grade school English classes — "the boy hit the ball."

> *... subject and predicate*
> *subject-verb-object,*
> *blackboard diagram*
> *of a primal event —*
> *a child's mind grasps*
> *new relations,*
> *impulse and action,*
> *desire and fulfillment:*
> *the world splits*
> *as he takes his swing. . . .*

The rest of the poem wasn't much good, and Professor Fitzgerald let me know it. But at least I'd written something new, and we had lines to talk about. We parted with a handshake. I might never see him again.

The final acts of the semester played out: my recital, with no hitches since I'd decided to read from the scores rather than perform by memory; a final in psychology, for which I'd filled two blue books; a paper on Edward Taylor and an oral exam in English 270, Early American Writing. The grass in Harvard Yard grew green for commencement, *my* commencement, six years after I'd started at Bennington.

In late May I received a letter from Professor Fitzgerald, handwritten in black ink on a half sheet of English department letterhead:

> 24 May
>
> Dear Megan,
>
> You left me your copy! It's a better poem than anyone listening to my grumbling would think. I've put an A on the record for your 91r and hope this cheerful token will be succeeded by others.
>
> R.F.

Maybe it didn't matter any longer what Miss Bishop thought of me. And if she'd asked Professor Fitzgerald to confirm her suspicions, I'd been forgiven by him.

⊰ 5 ⊱

Miracle

LILLI HAD BEEN the only person in whom Elizabeth could safely confide about Lota's distressing obsession with Flamengo Park and the feuding that preceded her departure for Seattle. Now Lilli was the only one she could speak to frankly about the turmoil during what Lota would call "that dramatic year," 1966.

It hadn't taken Lilli long to sense a cooling in Elizabeth's passion for her "Danish Viking" following the dinner party at which Elizabeth had met the young Roxanne Cumming. There were fewer letters, and in them Elizabeth had begun to "almost enjoy" teaching, thought of Lilli only "a great deal," and reasserted her commitment to Lota. "You know exactly how I feel about you," she wrote to Lilli, "also that I could never leave L — it's my life, I'm afraid, and I wish it weren't so complicated." For the moment, the complications didn't trouble her; she was feeling "pretty cheerful about the future, really." And then the letters stopped, until a June 9 missive from the San Juan Islands, north of Seattle, where Elizabeth was staying in a "weird old cottage" set among fir trees and "great twisted old pines" on the edge of a lagoon. She had made the trip with Roxanne, who was due to have her baby "in about a month" and was setting up house in advance of her husband's arrival to teach at a summer art school. Elizabeth badly needed a rest — "I swear that university makes one work too hard." She'd been suffering from asthma and eczema, she told Lilli, but promised, "I'll be beautiful again when I get back," in early July. She'd be staying away a full month longer than she'd promised both Lota and Lilli.

Lilli would later say that Elizabeth "fell in love easily. She also fell out of love easily." And Lilli may not have minded. She had other companions — "the French ladies," as the villagers referred to Lilli and her cosmopolitan friends in nearby Mariana, Ninita and "GK," women of whom Elizabeth had been intermittently jealous. Elizabeth had never been sure she could count Lilli as *hers,* or, after Seattle, whether she wanted to. So Lilli had chosen to shield Elizabeth, retrieving Roxanne's letters, mailed from Seattle to the Ouro Prêto post office box, and forwarding them in her own envelopes or reading them aloud over the phone. And when Lota, who'd always been a "letter-snoop," discovered one of Roxanne's letters just weeks after Elizabeth's return, Lilli had allowed Elizabeth to retreat to her house in Ouro Prêto after the blowup. Elizabeth's own tumbledown seventeenth-century *casa* wasn't yet habitable.

Had Elizabeth meant to break with Lota over a twenty-three-year-old? Scandinavian by ancestry, Roxanne Cumming really was a "blue eyed fair-headed child," as Elizabeth had once termed Lilli. She'd married at eighteen, leaving a large family in which she was the eldest and most responsible daughter, to keep house for a man in his mid-forties, already the father of four children by previous wives. She'd helped Carolyn Kizer throw the dinner party for Elizabeth, attended mostly by Seattle artists, a crowd that Elizabeth preferred to the scholars on the English department faculty. In the private dining room of a Japanese restaurant, she'd been drawn to Elizabeth's shy, attentive demeanor, as if Elizabeth weren't the guest of honor. Roxanne was good company, jaunty and clever beyond her years, and good at helping people: she'd found Elizabeth an apartment within walking distance of campus and moved her into it, with several of Elizabeth's male students doing the heavy lifting, while Elizabeth spent the afternoon at the hairdresser's. But with her baby due in August, Roxanne wouldn't be leaving Bill Cumming yet, if ever. When Lota discovered Roxanne's letter, Elizabeth was quick to insist, as she'd written to Lilli, that she had no intention of leaving Lota for anyone else. Lota was her life, the affair with Roxanne "just a trifle."

And yet, in the heat of the moment, Lota and Elizabeth had traded accusations that neither could forget. Elizabeth raged that she might have written "better poems" if she hadn't "wasted fifteen years" with Lota. And Lota regretted the "dull, useless days" she'd given to Elizabeth before she'd gone to work in Rio, thinking she was "helping a great poet" overcome alcoholism. In their early years together, love had given Elizabeth the "strength and energy to try to quit drinking and to try to be happy," Lota believed. But those years were in the past.

For Elizabeth, poetry and alcohol had long been twin compulsions. Both brought release from immediate distress, although poetry was the less reliable salve. Elizabeth couldn't count on poems to emerge, especially amid distraction, whereas *cachaça* was easily available at the bakery down the street. Both provided entry to an altered state, a welcome oblivion — unquestionably precious when she was writing well in a days-long daydream; endlessly regrettable when the effects of alcohol wore off after a day or more of binging, leaving her hung over and ashamed. In Brazil a hangover was called a *ressaca,* the term for a storm surge or tidal wave. Elizabeth had seen one of those race up the beach at Copacabana, forcing ocean water along the street below Lota's apartment and leaving behind a thick layer of sand and debris to be cleared away by bulldozers, reminding her of New York City snowplows.

By her fifties, poetry and alcohol had become organizing principles, imperatives more powerful even than love, at least when past the stage of infatuation. Love, too, was irresistible, but could it last? Love was more capricious than the other two, and Elizabeth had returned from Seattle in July 1966 determined to take greater control of both her daemon and her demon. She needed to secure the conditions in which to write, in her own house at Ouro Prêto, she imagined, if Lota would not return with her to Samambaia; and she wanted Lota to quit hounding her about her drinking. Before she'd left for Seattle, Lota had been "almost physically" forcing pills down her throat, in higher doses and with greater frequency than Elizabeth thought necessary. While away, she'd read a news article linking Antabuse with "despondency" and reporting that a feeling of "punishment" associated with taking the pills undercut their effectiveness. Elizabeth already suffered enough from her own "natural melancholia," and she no longer wished to be treated by Lota as a dependent child penalized for bad behavior. She'd sent Lota a copy of the article, but it was lost in the mail, or so Lota said. Instead, when Elizabeth returned from Seattle claiming she'd achieved moderation without the pills, Lota accused her of simply wanting to "keep on drinking." Elizabeth's insistence, in the aftermath of the blowup over Roxanne's offending letter, on her right to continue a friendly correspondence with Roxanne, whose baby was due in less than a month, was, to Lota, the final outrage.

Within days of Elizabeth's flight to Ouro Prêto, Lota wrote to Lilli asking her to tell Elizabeth it was over. She'd written in Portuguese, speaking her mind more eloquently than she could in English, and leaving Lilli to translate. Lota admitted she'd become, as Elizabeth had charged, "impatient and rude, negligent and mindless." She was sorry for "my wrongdoings" and wanted Elizabeth to know "I always admired her and thought that the best thing that ever happened in my life was that I was once honored by being loved by her." But Lota could not be convinced, as Elizabeth had protested, that the "ridiculous love affair" had no meaning; Elizabeth "had proved she can go along by herself, that she can love somebody else, that she doesn't need me anymore." Elizabeth should not come back — "I'd rather be lonely and unhappy than humiliated and desperate." Begging forgiveness for "all this nuisance," Lota asked Lilli to "please" tell Elizabeth: "Living together, when there is no love and respect, is not possible, is not *decent,* and there isn't a ghost of a chance for happiness."

Could Lilli have remained impartial after Elizabeth appeared, bearing chocolates and the lapis lazuli ring from Seattle? Wherever her loyalties lay, Lilli seems to have managed the near-impossible task of guarding the secret of her own brief affair with Elizabeth while consoling both women through a prolonged crisis. For, despite Lota's cool dismissal by letter, there would be no swift end to a relationship of such profound dependency. Neither Lota nor Elizabeth was yet ready to quench the embers of a grand passion that had once provided them both a reason for being.

Soon Lota arrived in Ouro Prêto, driving the flashy blue Willys Interlagos she'd acquired while Elizabeth was in Seattle. Alarmed by Lota's
impulsive purchase and fearing for her safety as she inevitably drove
the lightweight convertible too fast, Elizabeth nevertheless understood why she'd done it. The Interlagos had been one of Brazil's manu-
facturing and design innovations under the now-lamented Goulart
presidency, Brazil's last whiff of democracy for what would be the next
two decades. Production of the Interlagos in São Paulo halted that
"dramatic" year of 1966, after 822 of the Italian-designed sports cars
had reached the market, and just as Lota found herself on the outside
of Flamengo Park's administration for the first time since taking the
job of coordinatress. When Elizabeth returned to Brazil that July,
she'd been shocked by the extreme rightward turn of the new military
government, its clampdown on dissent while she was away. "Everything seems worse, that's all." Carlos Lacerda, she learned, had helped
bring off the 1964 coup she'd feared was a "real" revolution; now Lota
believed he'd sabotaged her efforts to maintain control of the park by
heading up a supervisory commission once the project was completed.
Lota wanted to own a piece of the world she was losing, and she had it
in her Willys.

For years Lota had worked to the edge of collapse, and now, as she
faced the prospect of giving up both her job and her customary life
with Elizabeth, it was here. She'd come to Ouro Prêto to reconcile with
Elizabeth, but she could not forget or forgive Elizabeth's betrayal. She
wasn't eating, she was too agitated to sleep or read, and, while driving one day with Lilli in the Interlagos, distracted by "a bunch of crazy
boys in a Volkswagen," she lost control of the car. The little two-seater
rolled, throwing both women to the roadside, fortunately without injury. The shock of the accident sent Lota to bed and ultimately home
to Samambaia with "what they used to call a 'nervous breakdown,'"
Elizabeth wrote to Cal Lowell from Petrópolis, citing Lota's trials with
the park in Rio — "blow after blow" — as the root cause. To Dr. Anny
Baumann she wrote much the same, adding that Lota "blames an awful
lot on *me,* if not everything, and this makes it very tough" — though not
explaining, beyond her drinking, why.

Elizabeth tried her best to calm Lota and contain the damage. She hoped no one beyond Lilli would find out what she'd done to undermine a relationship she still expected to last, perhaps even to improve, if only Lota could stop raving and accept that "I *have* changed" and "grown up a lot (! — about time) in the past 15 years." What if gossip traveled all the way "back to N Y in a wild and wrong version," Elizabeth worried in a letter to Lilli. Why wouldn't Lota believe her when she swore she'd given up Roxanne, or see that Elizabeth had returned from the United States because "I WANTED to come back, damn it!"

Yet Elizabeth understood it was harder for Lota, and she could hardly bear to see her this way, to feel as if she were "killing L inch by inch." Elizabeth knew exactly what Lota was feeling: she was enduring for the first time in her life the kind of heartbreak "most of us went through ... much younger," Elizabeth wrote to Lilli, "at least I did, a couple of times — so we could get over it quicker." Elizabeth sometimes told the story of walking in on Louise Crane and Billie Holiday in bed together in their shared New York City apartment. Elizabeth had been twenty-eight then. A decade later she suffered again over Jinny Pfeiffer, reconciling herself to Jinny's preference for Laura Archera by telling herself, "Nobody's heart is really good for much until it has been smashed to little bits." Lota had never been wounded this way before, never lacked for a lover. When Mary Morse had decided to move out, Elizabeth was there to take her place.

Now Mary had returned, not as Lota's mate, but to take sides with Lota against Elizabeth. Elizabeth's efforts at containment had not been successful among Lota's intimate coterie — the friends who had been Elizabeth's too. She would soon be reckoning with the power of the de Macedo Soares name, a force that had once also protected Elizabeth. She was feeling "more and more alone on this continent."

But Elizabeth also held fast to her own conditions for a reconciliation. The affair with Roxanne wasn't all that had happened in Seattle to alter her vision of the future. Time and again, as she made her way through "the very worst stretch in my life so far," Elizabeth remembered how much better she'd been treated there, the "friends and gaiety" and how she'd been able to "manage pretty well on my own, and stay sober about 98 percent of the time." Returning from six months away, she could see more clearly that Lota really was — and had been — "very sick." "I was so used to Lota and saw her so constantly that it didn't hit me, really," Elizabeth wrote to Dr. Baumann as she thought back over Lota's "increasing violence and rudeness" of the past several years. "I suppose the person closest is the last one to realize how terribly sick someone is." Now all of Lota's obsessions had "fixed" on Elizabeth — "first love; then hate," in a pattern of rapid mood swings that the psychiatrists Lota began to consult quickly saw required hospitalization.

There was some comfort in learning from Lota's doctors that "it wasn't too wrong of me to suffer so and feel so abused — I really WAS being abused!" But finally, Elizabeth wrote to Dr. Baumann in late September 1966, "I never felt so helpless and ignorant in my life, and unfitted to cope with my life or hers." Madness near at hand was what she hadn't wanted to experience in a closer relationship with Cal, what she had feared long ago in her mother — and what she had counted on Lota's steady good cheer to shelter her from in their mountain aerie at Samambaia, above and away from it all.

Yet she wanted to help, and she was not giving up. Lota had done more for *her* than anyone in her life. Every day Elizabeth phoned Lota at the Clínica Botafogo in Rio where she had finally been hospitalized, but it was Mary Morse who spent the night on the floor of Lota's room, who brought soft clean sheets and home-cooked food. Elizabeth offered to take her place, but Mary said no. When they were apart, all Lota wanted was to have Elizabeth back, but when Elizabeth entered the room, Lota became hysterical and ordered her out.

Lota was given injections and put into an insulin-induced sleep; now it didn't matter who was there, although Elizabeth still wanted to be. When Lota returned to the apartment in Rio with a nurse at the end of December, still heavily sedated, to be woken only every four hours for feeding, Dr. Decio de Sousa, the psychiatrist both Elizabeth and Lota trusted the most, told Elizabeth she'd have to leave. The last time the two women had been alone in the apartment at night, Lota had threatened to jump from the balcony. All Elizabeth wanted now was for Lota to survive. And to live herself. "I hate to leave Lota like this," she wrote to Dr. Baumann, "but it seems almost as if it were a question of saving my own life or sanity, too, now."

Dr. de Sousa, always called Decio by Elizabeth and Lota, had trained in London with the analyst Melanie Klein, whose "grim little book," *Envy and Gratitude*, Elizabeth had read some years before and considered "superb in its horrid way." Klein made much of the "death instinct." She also emphasized the primal importance of the maternal bond, the mother's role in engendering a propensity for either envy or gratitude in her child by offering or withholding her breast. Elizabeth, whose mother had been absent for months during infancy and then vanished altogether, could only have read dire warnings in this philosophy. But Lota wasn't yet ready to take advantage of the analytic theories or skills of Klein's protégé. Insulin shock therapy — like electroconvulsive therapy, its more widely used counterpart in the United States in treating schizophrenia and manic-depressive illness — had left Lota "calmer," Elizabeth wrote to Lilli, "but she just isn't *Lota,* & it is too awful."

Decio instructed Elizabeth to leave the apartment without Lota knowing, while she was out meeting him for an evaluation. Elizabeth must keep her whereabouts secret and never call, perhaps for as long as six months. She left in a hurry with nothing but two suitcases and a box of papers, "all the wrong ones" for her work. It was terrible not to say goodbye, not to know if she'd ever see Lota again. If Lota got better, which Elizabeth sometimes doubted, would she "want me back"?

Elizabeth spent several days in a hotel farther up the beach, and then checked herself into a clinic for exhaustion — it was so "hard to know what to do." She had reached "life's lowest moment," she wrote to Lilli, cautioning her to tell no one where she was. Lota must not be able to find her. "The awful thing is not having any place in the world to go." Lota's nurse paid occasional visits, telling Elizabeth that Lota "talks of me constantly" when awake, "but has no idea where I am in the world." The nurse, Katia, was sworn to secrecy too. Elizabeth put most of the scarcely edible clinic food out on her balcony for the birds, talking to them when they landed to feed, "since there's no one else." No one brought her soft sheets or delicious meals. She lost weight. Yet, free of daily involvement with Lota's case, she began to write again. Among her drafts was a poem she called "Inventory," never finished:

> Bed, birdcage, and a chest of drawers,
> the biggest shell, the flat and foot-shaped
> piece of granite I found myself,
> the paddle, and the portable ink-well;
>
> the baby-book, th¢/ coffe spoons the blue enamm   the cloisonee
> coffe spoons with blue enamel,
>   the living cat
> where   — where can I take them next?   and where
>   do we go next?

Where could Elizabeth go next? Before leaving Seattle, with Cal's assistance, she had secured a $12,000 fellowship from the Rockefeller Foundation to support her work on a book of prose about Brazil — the book she might have written if Time Inc. had let her. She had a title in mind, "Black Beans and Diamonds," and she'd revise the unsold *New Yorker* piece on Brasília and the Uialapiti, and write up her travels on the Amazon along with other trips she still hoped to take. The Rockefeller funds were paid in monthly installments, and she'd been living on the stipend since her return from Seattle. After Decio's orders, Elizabeth realized "the book has to come first now." She made plans for her long-awaited journey on the Rio São Francisco, the continent's fourth-longest river, obtaining free passage through a "powerful friend" of Decio's. She hoped Lilli might come too. Perhaps Elizabeth could devise enough research trips to fill the six months, stretching to June 1967, she was meant to stay away from Lota. Or perhaps she would fly to New York and write the book based on library research. She'd begun to suspect Lota's friends were behind the request that she leave, and to "think it will be a great relief to get back to a country where people are not afraid of the name de Macedo Soares."

Decio wavered in the face of Lota's pleading. He permitted a meeting of the two women in February. Elizabeth had been apprehensive,

but the reunion went well, and Decio relented—they could live together again. They were at Samambaia for Lota's birthday in March,
and Elizabeth baked Lota a *rocambole,* a jelly roll cake. In Rio, both
of them tried sound therapy, a revival of an ancient healing practice,
sonoterapia, in which metal bowls of varying sizes were placed on the
patient's torso and then sounded with mallets by the practitioner, releasing sympathetic tones to resonate through the chest cavity and the
rest of the body. The sessions seemed to have "worked miracles" with
Lota, Elizabeth wrote to Dr. Baumann—"I haven't seen her so much
like her old self in years." But Elizabeth developed a "spectacular" case
of asthma, "useful in getting me LOTS of attention" from the atten-
dants. She planned to devote a chapter in her book to *sonoterapia*—"a
chic touch," she thought.

"All I want to do is WORK WORK WORK," Elizabeth wrote to Lilli
in mid-March. With Lota taking a fresh interest in the renovations
on the Ouro Prêto house, and the Interlagos at last in good repair after the accident—Lota had taken practice spins along the beachfront
roads below their apartment at Copacabana—Elizabeth could foresee
a time when she would be able to work steadily again, either in the *estudio* at Samambaia or in her own "real study" at Ouro Prêto, which

Casa Mariana, Elizabeth's house at Ouro Prêto, under renovation

she planned to line with built-in shelves, painted white, for books and "objects." She counted eighteen months since she'd last settled down at a desk to write.

In April, Lilli visited Lota and Elizabeth in Rio, bringing guava preserves and wearing the lapis lazuli ring, but she would not accompany Elizabeth on her river trip. Before Elizabeth flew to Bahia, and then boarded a seventy-year-old stern-wheeler at Pirapora on the banks of the São Francisco, she made time for two interviews on contemporary poetry with *Time*'s Rio correspondent. She hadn't known, she would write to everyone afterward, that the interview would be used for a cover story on Cal. The trip, during which she tossed all of Roxanne's letters overboard in a private show of renewed commitment to Lota, acted like "a sort of eraser," she wrote to May Swenson. "I lost all track of time and distance — feel as if I'd had amnesia."

To Lilli she confided a grimmer truth: she dreaded the return to Rio. Although Elizabeth had repeatedly promised "everything else *is* All off, forever, really & truly," that there would be no romantic attachments to anyone but Lota, relations between the two were strained at best, and Lota was "still *very* sick." Lota was seeing Decio twice a week for analytic sessions and had become reliant on an array of pills that left her groggy and forgetful and unable to concentrate. Elizabeth wanted to "live with her again and try try to be happy with her — but after every stretch of a few fairly good days comes another explosion — and then I can't be patient enough." To her shame and sorrow, Elizabeth was losing the battle to control her drinking. She would "try and try" again to stay sober, but she had lost confidence in her ability to withstand the "feeling of disintegration and guilt" provoked by each stormy scene, so many of them, stretching back over eleven intolerable months. She had no idea "what I'll find" back in Rio — "if only L will forgive me and BELIEVE me" — "I want only her."

In the villages along the São Francisco there was "ghastly poverty," and she was just as glad Lilli hadn't come along, or Lota, who "wouldn't have liked it a bit." Elizabeth lost her appetite when she learned that the animals brought on board at the start of the journey, including "a big, gentle ram with curling horns," were being slaughtered on the deck below her cabin to feed the ship's fifteen tourist passengers. Nevertheless she took copious notes for her book and dozens of photographs in her Cartier-Bresson style, candid yet composed, bearing witness to scenes of grace amid the squalor.

She remained fearful about her return. Back in Bahia, before boarding the plane to Rio, she picked up the latest issue of *Time* to find Cal's picture on the cover, a cartoonish crayon-and-watercolor portrait of a downcast Caligula, crowned with a laurel wreath.

She hadn't meant to sound stingy, and "maybe I said what they said I said," she wrote to May Swenson. The topic on which Elizabeth had been quoted was "confessional poetry," the new phrase for the auto-biographical turn that both she and Cal had taken in their writing, Cal more explicitly with *Life Studies,* followed by the outpouring of personal and increasingly political lyrics in *For the Union Dead* and *Near the Ocean* that had landed him on *Time*'s cover. He'd spawned a race of imitators — his cohorts John Berryman and Theodore Roethke, and

Riverboat passengers, Rio São Francisco, 1966,
photograph by Elizabeth Bishop

the younger poets Anne Sexton, Sylvia Plath, and Frederick Seidel — whose verses read more like diary entries, Elizabeth often thought. Confessional poetry "is really something new in the world," she'd told the *Time* reporter, offering an apt definition: "the idea is that we live in a horrible and terrifying world, and the worst moments of horrible and terrifying lives are an allegory of the world." But, she quipped, "the tendency is to overdo the morbidity. You just wish they'd keep some of these things to themselves." In recent years, writing to Randall Jarrell and others, she'd gone further, dubbing confessional poetry "The School of Anguish," made up of the "self-pitiers" that Cal seemed "innocently to have inspired."

Elizabeth would not resort to naked retellings of the anguish she now suffered, though what she experienced was as "horrible and terrifying" as any private drama the confessionals might claim. She would not complete and publish "Inventory." Yet Elizabeth had been working on a longer poem, her most openly autobiographical so far, derived from her distressing epiphany as a seven-year-old in an overwarm dentist's waiting room, reading *National Geographic* and studying the adults seated in the room with her: "*I, I, I* . . . was *one* of them too. . . . *Why* was I a human being?" Six years before, in 1961, she'd used the episode to conclude "The Country Mouse," a story about her childhood that she never sent out for publication. The poem would tell it better.

Elizabeth came close to finishing "In the Waiting Room" during the summer of 1967, after another of Lota's explosions prompted Decio to banish Elizabeth once more. This time she packed her bags, gathered up the right papers, and flew to New York City, where she moved into the vacant studio of her old friend Loren MacIver at 61 Perry Street in Greenwich Village. Loren, whose paintings Lota had collected in New York in the 1940s, and her poet husband Lloyd Frankenberg had been living in Paris for most of a decade. Elizabeth was determined to work, and — despite the heat, and a thick layer of dust coating the room making it difficult to breathe, and the aftereffects of a concussion that might have been the result of a drunken fall — she was managing at last. In a first draft, remarkably similar to the final version, the poem began:

> *In Worcester, Massachusetts,*
> *I went with Aunt Consuelo*
> *to keep her dentist's appointment*
> *and sat and waited for her*
> *in the dentist's waiting room.*
> *It was winter. It was already*
> *dark. The waiting room*
> *was full of grown-up people,*
> *arctics and overcoats,*
> *lamps and magazines.*
> *My aunt was inside*
> *what seemed like a long, long time,*
> *and while I waited I read*
> *THE NATIONAL GEOGRAPHIC*
> *(I could read.) and looked at*
> *all the photographs.*

She'd changed Aunt Florence's name to something more fanciful, but little else was altered in the remembered scene. When she checked the appropriate issue of *National Geographic* in the public library that summer, she confirmed a photo essay on the "Valley of 10,000 Smokes" that "has been haunting me all my life, apparently," she wrote to Cal, and triggering other recollected images: a volcano "spilling over / in rivulets of fire" —

> *Babies with pointed heads*
> *wound round and round with string,*
> *naked black women with necks*
> *wound round and round with wire*
> *(like the necks of light bulbs).*
> *Their breasts filled me with awe.*

In later drafts, she would work over that line: "Their breasts terrified me" or "frightened me" or, finally, "were horrifying." Had Elizabeth felt awe or terror forty years later when *she* held a camera to photograph Laura Archera Huxley among the bare-breasted Uialapiti women? That photograph, artfully composed and whimsical, suggests she didn't. By then, in August 1958 at age forty-seven, she was fully "*one* of them," a phrase she borrowed from her unpublished story and inserted, with different emphasis, in the poem; she was a woman with breasts, who loved women with breasts, particularly blonds like Laura. Perhaps the moment on the Xingú brought the memory back, set the story and then the poem in motion.

Now, at fifty-six, evicted from the home she'd known longer than any other, she remembered the earlier forced removal from Great Village to Worcester, the feeling of radical displacement in the months before this "unlikely" waiting room revelation of her unique existence — "you are an *I*, / you are an *Elizabeth*" — which arrived in tandem with a shocking sense of likeness, of being "one of *them*." Hearing her "foolish aunt" cry out from the dentist's chair, the child Elizabeth felt the "*oh!* of pain" as if it rose from her own mouth. She wrote in the finished poem:

> *Without thinking at all*
> *I was my foolish aunt,*
> *I — we — were falling, falling,*
> *our eyes glued to the cover*
> *of the* National Geographic,
> *February, 1918. . . .*

Questions followed:

> *Why should I be my aunt,*
> *or me, or anyone?*
> *What similarities —*
> *boots, hands, the family voice*
> *I felt in my throat, or even*
> *the* National Geographic
> *and those awful hanging breasts —*
> *held us all together*
> *or made us all just one?*

This fall into self-consciousness was almost more than the child could bear. The "bright / and too hot" waiting room carried her "sliding / beneath a big black wave, / another, and another." Yet it was not too much. Thinking saved her; poetry — "a way of thinking with one's feelings" — saved her. She could think then and, decades later, define and contain the unsettling moment in verse:

> *I knew that nothing stranger*
> *had ever happened, that nothing*
> *stranger could ever happen.*

"In the Waiting Room" concludes as the child snaps out of her trance to find herself "back in it," in Worcester, Massachusetts, in February 1918. For Elizabeth as she worked on the poem, "back in it" meant Greenwich Village in 1967, now simply "the Village," and both "wilder" and "hippier" than the shabby-chic neighborhood she'd known in the 1930s and '40s. Perhaps a summer here would "rejuvenate me," she wrote to Cal when she arrived in early July, joking that "I never appear without earrings down to my bosom, skirts almost up to it, and a guitar over my shoulder. I am afraid I am going to start writing FREE VERSE next." "Back in it" meant writing to Lota nearly every day and receiving Lota's daily letters in return. Elizabeth sent her a draft of "In the Waiting Room," and Lota was enchanted. "The poem is a beauty," she wrote in English now, "the kind I like best, that funny sensation between the real and the unreal. Like a sail in the wind but attached by some facts, the National Geographic, Worcester Mass, like nails to the mast." Lota wished she had known Elizabeth at age seven; instead, "we knew each other so late, but lets hope to have more many years to enjoy each others company, so help us God." How Elizabeth must have wanted to believe, in turn, that "nothing / stranger could ever happen" than a rude self-awakening in a dentist's waiting room.

Lota's letters followed the pattern of the days she and Elizabeth had spent together in the months after Decio had permitted their reunion. Desperately loving and apologetic paragraphs dissolved into recrimination and ultimatums, only to end in ardent expressions of longing: "Oh! my darling, my darling what a dreadful waste of time, what a horrible and irrecuperable waste of time this separation is! We are too old to suffer this way." Decio held out the possibility of a visit to New York in September, but in early August he changed his mind; Lota wouldn't be ready to travel until December. Elizabeth could not have been surprised. The doctor, who had met her at the airport in Rio after the river trip to explain that Lota was still in the early stages of convalescence, was communicating separately with Elizabeth that summer. Playing the role of couples therapist, he'd encouraged Elizabeth to take her work to New York; he was well aware of her obligations — not just the book of prose, but a new volume of collected poems that Farrar, Straus and Giroux proposed to follow *Questions of Travel* — and understood her need to complete the projects for her own well-being. Even if Elizabeth hadn't been receiving letters from Decio describing Lota's erratic progress, signs of illness were everywhere in her letters — pills and injections, insomnia and exhaustion, agitation in a crowded movie theater, memory slips about dinner plans or where she'd parked her car, recurrent "very bad mornings" when she woke in a panic that lasted until late afternoon. Most alarming of all, the "terrible depression" Lota referred to in a letter of August 3, "that Decio thinks is increasing."

From afar, Elizabeth often succeeded in providing the affectionate reassurance Lota needed, indeed demanded — "Please write, all the time," Lota urged, and "Tell me again my dearest that you miss me like I miss you," and "I would like to know *more about your feelings,* how are you *feeling,* what you have been thinking about you and me — *It is important.*" Elizabeth signed herself, in a phrase Lota cherished, "your dearest dearest friend and companion and every thing else, family, home and pet." She promised to dedicate her book of prose, now re-titled *Brazil, Brasil,* to Lota. "Nothing could give me more pleasure in the world," Lota answered, "not even a Rolls Royce." Elizabeth sent her "In the Waiting Room" and another poem, "Hen," in the draft that Lota received. Elizabeth had written "Hen," or "Trouvée," as she altered the title for publication in the *New Yorker,* almost as soon as she arrived in the city, mailing the "very, very light poem" to Howard Moss in mid-July. Just before leaving for the United States, she'd asked to revive her first-read contract, and he'd happily answered yes.

Despite its title, "Trouvée" wasn't precisely a found poem, with text adapted from signage or news headlines, although Elizabeth had found her subject in the street:

> Oh, why should a hen
> have been run over
> on West 4th Street
> in the middle of summer?
>
> She was a white hen
> — red-and-white now, of course.
> How did she get there?
> Where was she going?

The poem continued with four more quatrains playing out the unfortunate chicken's ill-timed enactment of the "old country saying." But how "light" was the poem? "How did she get there? / Where was she going?" These were questions Elizabeth had asked of herself in the unfinished "Inventory." Lota found the poem "adorable," perfectly balanced, "like a small Calder." The "poor creature," Lota thought, must have been a "country hen," ignorant of "os sinaes de trafego," traffic signals. Lota showed the poem to Decio and reported his interpretation for Elizabeth: "for him you are the 'hen' . . . white, lovely and crushed by the big city and by the last evenements" — the tumultuous events of the past year. She implored Elizabeth to be careful crossing streets.

Lota knew she was "still turning around the same problems and having nothing to distract me," liable to seek omens everywhere. When she was feeling sturdy, the signs seemed favorable. Elizabeth wrote that May Swenson had broken up with Pearl Schwartz, leaving her for "a new girl called Rosanne," and Lota had "a big laugh." "What a pity for poor Pearl," after nineteen years, but Lota was relieved that Elizabeth had been able to write the name "Rosanne" without comment. Elizabeth must truly have forgotten her own Roxanne. At such times, "I think how lucky we are malgré that dramatic year of 66," Lota wrote, "after all would have been too miraculous if we had spend all our lives without any trouble." Decio had counseled Lota that "we are two different people than we were 15 years ago, that we have to recognise that, and act accordingly." When Lota wasn't in the grips of a morning panic, "I even think that our 'crisis' was good to us, because we can from now on see how much we like each other, and how much better we can get along, and how much more thankful we are going to be with the good things we have."

But Lota saw dark signs too. A close friend had nearly boarded the same airplane that crashed and killed Humberto Castelo Branco in mid-July. (Castelo Branco had resigned the presidency under pressure six months before, to be replaced by a still more repressive army general, Artur da Costa e Silva.) Lota began to update her will and pressed Elizabeth to do the same. Lota wanted to be certain that her sister would not contest her decision to divide her estate between Elizabeth and Mary Morse, who had made substantial loans to Lota and whose adopted daughters — three little girls now — were family to Lota. She knew Marietta was capable of hiring a lawyer to challenge the will; her friend Rachel's "almost death" in the plane crash had given Lota an "urgency." She was filled with "bad ideas about dying . . . and Marietta grabing it all . . . all! all!" But the issue of their wills was also one of *"Faith and Trust."* Lota knew that, after Seattle, Elizabeth had revised her will, leaving a small bequest to help support Roxanne and her son, born in August the year before; Roxanne had decided to leave Bill Cumming, and Elizabeth felt at least partly responsible. Elizabeth also named Catharine Carver, the editor of the British edition of her poems, as her literary executor. Lota had asked Elizabeth to remove both of these provisions before flying to the United States and to put Lota in charge of her literary affairs, but, snooping in Elizabeth's study, she'd found a tightly sealed envelope in a volume of Blake's poetry: a will that Elizabeth hadn't wanted her to read. Its unknown contents tormented Lota.

Lota's tirades about Elizabeth's will, her pleading — "Lets not have *any more secrets*" — filled many pages of her letters. Lota recognized this as another obsession and swore off the subject of wills, then returned to it in the next sentence. She reported fights with Decio, who advised her to let Elizabeth alone. He was right to do so. Leaving her literary legacy in Lota's hands when she was still so unstable could not have seemed wise, and Elizabeth's sense of obligation to Roxanne continued, even though the affair did not. There had been secrets before, but now Elizabeth was reluctant to cede her privacy and independence. Evading Lota's direct pressure, Elizabeth let slip that the recurring topic of their wills was depressing her, only to receive Lota's most abject reply so far. "I cannot bear myself anymore," Lota wrote, bewailing the long separation. "Everything is so against my own temperament, that waiting, and waiting. I spend my morning crying in bed, I only find some consolation talking with Decio — I cannot bear that you feel persecuted by me, that is bad, I only think about dying quickly —"

The letter ended abruptly, to be followed by another written the next day, praising "Hen" once more, worrying over Elizabeth's breathing troubles and loss of appetite — "I love you round not like *A Dama Das Camelias*" — and telling Elizabeth that a friend, hearing how lonely Lota was, had suggested she disregard Decio's advice and "go immediately to see you." The prospect must have been nearly as frightening to Elizabeth as Lota's preoccupation with death, both her own and Elizabeth's. "I hope you think like me," Lota had written, "that if one of us loose the other, that no amount of money, jewells or literary rights can compensated that loss." Remembering other close friends, a historian and his wife, who had died in a plane crash several years earlier, Lota continued, "The only thing I wish for us is to die together like Otavio and Lucia and be happy to the end like they were."

Could Elizabeth be happy with Lota again? Even as she wrote faithfully to her "darling," her "honeybunch," and helped plan the visit in December, suggesting they rent fur coats to withstand the unaccustomed cold, she must have had doubts. Elizabeth and Lota had changed in the past fifteen years, and so had their once-passionate romance. "If sexual love is gone between us," Lota had written to Elizabeth after a session with Decio, "we want it substituted by the feeling that we belong only to each other, that nobody can stand between us, that every thing we have should be shared, that *sleeping peacefully* in each other arms is the reward of the labours of the day." This was what Decio called "tender love." Could Elizabeth be faulted for wanting more?

"I was telling Decio today that he seems to me like a heavy closed door," Lota wrote to Elizabeth in early August, "and I am like a little mouse trying to find a hole in that door, to escape and go to N.Y." Decio continued to urge *"dar tempo ao tempo,"* to give it time, telling Lota this "is our last chance to be able to stand each other." Though December seemed "far away than the moon," Lota pretended to agree. But in her letters to Elizabeth she insisted she would be well soon, as early as November, or even October. "Don't clean any thing any more on that bowl of dust," Lota told Elizabeth, "let me do it when I come — and imagine what a wonderful T.V. dinner I am going to cook for you!! And lots of café espresso." In a postscript she prodded, "Why don't you ask Decio to let me go and spend a month with you in *September* or you don't want it??" Lota would be strong again, she promised, "solid like the Sugar Loaf" that towered above Rio's Guanabara Bay, "fit like a Stradivarius."

Lota's performance began to convince. Decio didn't change his mind about December, but he canceled several appointments with her, busy with the purchase of a new apartment, and Lota didn't object; she canceled once herself. On August 25, Lota brought Elizabeth's sealed will to Decio's office, along with the incendiary letter she'd saved for more than a year, and ripped them to shreds in front of him. "The past is gone and finish," she told Elizabeth. She mailed Elizabeth instructions for the injections she still received and phoned to say she was coming in September after all. She purchased a plane ticket for arrival on Sunday the seventeenth.

How could Lota be well enough to travel? Could Decio really approve, as Lota insisted? Lota had said it would be up to Elizabeth to decide when *she* was ready for Lota's visit, when Elizabeth had gotten enough work done, rested enough from "our Tempest here." But "do you really like to be 'boss'?" Lota had asked. "I thought it was only me." No wonder Elizabeth sounded scared, wary, on the phone when Lota called to announce her plans. Elizabeth sent a cable the next day, reassuring Lota that she wanted her to come — how could she not? That was what Elizabeth knew she must do, prove to Lota that her love was unwavering. She waited for the letter Lota said Decio was writing, but it never came, and when Elizabeth phoned him, the connection was poor.

It was Lota who arrived in New York confused, unable to read the signs. Or perhaps she'd come with the intent to end her life there. Elizabeth could tell right away, when she greeted Lota at the airport after the long flight, that she was "very sick indeed and that Decio had been a damned fool to let her come," she later wrote to Rosinha Leão, her companion years before on the Amazon. Lota was "in a state of extreme depression, and nothing I could say or do seemed to help." Elizabeth made coffee at the apartment; they went out to eat "in a place she *hated.*" Back at Loren's studio, they each had a small glass of Dutch beer and then one Nembutal to sleep. Lota "started in talking about her troubles a bit, the same old cycle," her bitterness over Flamengo Park, *"but we had no quarrel."* First Lota drifted off, complaining of the early bedtime — 9:30 p.m. — on her first night in the city, then Elizabeth. "Everything was very peaceful." But this drugged sleep was not what either Lota or Elizabeth had wished for.

At 6:30 a.m., Elizabeth woke to noises in the upstairs kitchen. Lota was "staggering down those steps" semiconscious, carrying a box of Nembutal, Elizabeth thought, though later the handful of pills Lota had taken turned out to be Valium. Elizabeth "half-carried" Lota to the bedroom and reached for the phone to call Dr. Baumann. Lota tried to grab it from her as Elizabeth begged her to say "how many" pills she'd swallowed. "Ten or twelve."

Lota did not wake up again on Perry Street or in St. Vincent's Hospital, where she lay in a coma. Elizabeth did not see Lota again until she was summoned to the hospital a week later to identify her body. Going through Lota's suitcases during those awful days of waiting, Elizabeth found twelve kilo bags of coffee and her own recent poems, "In the Waiting Room" and "Trouvée," which Lota had read so often "*en cachette,*" in secret, "to console me, and to made me understand you better," Lota had written that summer. "Perhaps she felt some miracle would take place and she'd feel better the minute she got to New York," Elizabeth could only guess. She was always impatient, "my darling Lota — and finally, too impatient to live."

—⁓—

Lota's death, the tragic manner of it — whether accidental overdose or suicide, planned or "sudden impulse," as Elizabeth had conjectured of Randall Jarrell's death two years before — made Elizabeth's very private life excruciatingly public. There were explanations to give to her American friends, some of whom may not have understood or fully sympathized with her love for a woman. It was as if *The Group* had come to life, only this time the Baroness was sacrificed at the end rather than Kay, the novel's central character based loosely on Mary McCarthy. The gossip Elizabeth had feared ran wild, though mostly beyond her awareness. She would not have known of letters exchanged by Mary McCarthy and Cal, chums since the 1940s as members of the *Partisan Review* crowd, in which Mary offered her dark opinions — Elizabeth was a "poet of terror" — and Cal retailed the story of Elizabeth's drunken fall in his house not long after Lota died. Elizabeth had broken her shoulder badly, forcing her to postpone her flight to Rio, which may have been her preference anyway. "I think it cooled her down," Cal wrote to Mary of the injury and several weeks of convalescence, "so that finally she was in very good shape to go back to Brazil, and handled all the very vexing duties and encounters." Elizabeth

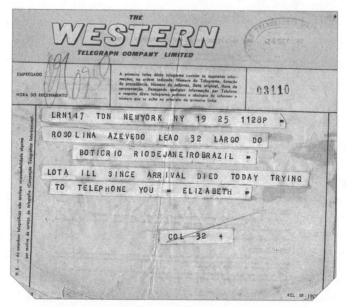

Elizabeth's telegram to Rosinha Leão, September 26, 1967

felt only grateful to Cal, who'd hosted her in his West Side apartment during these loneliest days when "I have no idea what to do with my life any more," and who had called the ambulance; and to May Swenson's Pearl, who visited Elizabeth from the nearby Village apartment the couple once shared. May had moved to suburban Sea Cliff with her newly beloved "Zan." How had May and Pearl managed an amicable breakup after nineteen years?

Back in Brazil, it was worse. Elizabeth felt the coldness right away from nearly everyone but Lilli, to whom she'd keened, "It's not my fault. It's not my fault. It's not my fault," in her first letter after Lota died. Mary Morse, who wouldn't speak to her, had snatched up all of Elizabeth's favorite photographs of Lota and burned Elizabeth's letters. As Lota had anticipated, Marietta hired a lawyer to contest her sister's will. Just months before, Elizabeth had been finalizing plans for renovations on the Ouro Prêto house, drawing a sketch for Lilli of the balcony she wanted widened so that three people — Elizabeth, Lilli, and Lota — could sit comfortably to admire the view of the town and its hillside churches. She knew that Lota had left her the Rio apartment, while Mary would inherit Samambaia; once the estate was settled, if Lota's wishes prevailed, Elizabeth planned to sell the eleventh-floor rooms she had never enjoyed in order to keep the house she'd chosen herself. Lines Elizabeth had written five years earlier while translating Clarice Lispector's story "The Smallest Woman in the World" captured her predicament. Lispector's tiny woman is an African Pygmy, a tree dweller in the satiric fable, whose eyes darken with pleasure at the thought of possessing her own tree. "It is good to own, good to own, good to own," becomes Little Flower's mantra, second only to "Not to be devoured is the secret goal of a whole life." Survival was all Elizabeth could contemplate. "There are times at which one doesn't want to have feelings," she had written in the translation, and this was one of them.

Nearly three years would pass before Elizabeth completed "In the Waiting Room" or any other poem, three years during which she often slid under the waves of oblivion that alcohol provided, and tried but failed to access the reverie that had enabled her as a young girl to know, and then as a mature poet to write, "you are an *I*, you are an *Elizabeth*."

She filled the time with moves, first running away. "I just have to keep going somehow," she wrote Lilli in January 1968, four months after Lota's death. Cal's letter of "gossip" to Mary McCarthy had included news — "I . . . know you won't spread it" — of "a girl, about thirty, in Seattle, divorced, perhaps because of Elizabeth, with a child of two": Roxanne Cumming, just twenty-five. Lizzie Hardwick had been deputized by Dr. Baumann, after Elizabeth's fall in October, to phone Roxanne — "a very decent and good sort" — and let her know that Elizabeth was in need. Someone had to take care of Elizabeth, and it would not be the Lowells. There had been few Decembers in recent years when Cal had not suffered a breakdown.

After considering New York City and Puerto Rico, Elizabeth, Roxanne, and her eighteen-month-old son, nicknamed "Boogie," set up housekeeping in San Francisco early in the new year, renting the second-floor apartment in a "pea green" double-bayed triple-decker at the edge of Russian Hill from a landlord named Mr. Pang. The building at 1559 Pacific Avenue was a "nowhere address," in Roxanne's argot, with a steam laundry on one side and an Italian family's kitchen garden on the other. Across the street was a body painting shop — "CAR, that is," Elizabeth specified in a letter to Cal; this was the winter after 1967's "Summer of Love" brought 100,000 hippies to Haight-Ashbury for a months-long orgy of sex, drugs, and rock 'n' roll.

Elizabeth and Roxanne might have been drawn to the city because of its place at the center of the burgeoning gay rights movement. San Francisco was where, in the mid-1950s, a small group of "homophile" women founded the Daughters of Bilitis, adopting the deliberately obscure name from a nineteenth-century French poet's odes to a fictional lover of Sappho. The organization had gone national, and in 1966, the DOB's publication, *The Ladder,* added a more assertive subtitle, *A Lesbian Review,* in tune with the restive times. But while Roxanne steered Elizabeth toward certain Bay Area radical causes, arranging for her to interview the Black Panther Kathleen Cleaver, Eldridge's twenty-three-year-old wife, for a *New York Review of Books* article that never came to fruition, gay liberation was not one of them. To everyone they met, Roxanne was introduced as Elizabeth's secretary.

Roxanne was more than that. Elizabeth both relied and doted on the tiny dynamo that was Roxanne Cumming. "Not very beautiful, but nice-looking" was how Elizabeth described the blue-eyed Roxanne to Lilli, and she may have called Elizabeth back to her younger, more spirited self. Elizabeth made notes for a poem, "S F," that featured their neighborhood — "the wooden turning fire escapes / such queer clap-boarded faces, ladders - pipes, / and crooked porches" — and trailed off, "it was the moon & not the laundromat / that woke us love." Roxanne's youth and difference in sensibility from Lota's International-style elitism had been attractions from the start; now they were crucial distractions. Elizabeth found they agreed on most things — "music, food, furniture" — but she ceded control of the FM dial to Roxanne, who, while sharing Elizabeth's love of opera, preferred rock to Elizabeth's favored jazz station. Elizabeth let Roxanne shorten her skirt hems above the knee and construct a large writing table for her from a freighter's abandoned hatch cover. Leaving Boogie with a babysitter, Roxanne drove the two of them on a tour of San Francisco's derelict Hunters Point housing projects, in the "Lotus White" Volkswagen Beetle Elizabeth purchased, to prepare for the meeting with Kathleen Cleaver, then transcribed the taped interview and corresponded with Cleaver about the "short prose piece" or "poem" that might result but never did. Roxanne ferried Elizabeth to sessions with a psychotherapist who suggested she join AA. Imagining a basement room crowded with reeking winos, Elizabeth refused. Roxanne drove Elizabeth to the hospital when once again she fell, this time breaking her wrist. She had been "cold SOBER," Elizabeth insisted in a letter to Lilli, had only slipped in her high heels on a wet sidewalk.

Roxanne handled most of Elizabeth's business correspondence, and when Farrar, Straus and Giroux sent a cover design for *Complete Poems* that Elizabeth didn't like, Roxanne drove off to Design Research in Ghirardelli Square and returned with swatches of yellow, blue, and white fabric that she arranged in a simple collage. Elizabeth had not been able to write any new poems or anything more in prose on Brazil since the summer of 1967, but she was reading proof of the collection that brought together the poems from her first three books. Roxanne's tricolor jacket design seemed just right. Still, far from home and responsible for her son as well as Elizabeth, Roxanne had her own periods of despond — "unhappy flower child," Elizabeth wrote in "S F." After more than a year at 1559 Pacific Avenue, both women began to imagine an easier, more picturesque life in Brazil, where Lilli had continued to supervise renovations on Casa Mariana, the name Elizabeth had chosen for her Ouro Prêto house, honoring Marianne Moore and acknowledging the neighboring town reached by the mountain road that separated Lilli's and Elizabeth's houses. They might have moved there sooner if Elizabeth hadn't worried that Lota's friends would look askance at her new housemate. "I keep reminding myself that I am really free to cheer up, free to feel happy, even, if I can," Elizabeth wrote to Cal, but the "very black cloud" of all that had happened when she'd returned to Brazil after Lota's death "hangs over me." Her letters to Lilli were filled with hand-wringing over slights and silences, and messages to the lawyer who was managing her case and finances during the months before Marietta's suit was resolved, finally, in Elizabeth's and Mary Morse's favor.

Elizabeth, Roxanne, and Boogie, now almost three years old, were all living in Ouro Prêto in late February 1970 when word came that *Complete Poems* had won the National Book Award. "It's about time," Elizabeth groused to Roxanne and others, still smarting over her defeat four years earlier. Then she'd been in Seattle gaining self-confidence and hoping to make a victorious appearance in New York City to accept the prize. Now she refused her editor Robert Giroux's offer of a plane ticket for the March 2 ceremony, dreading the prospect of making a speech, unable to retrieve her winter clothes and fur coat from storage in San Francisco. She asked Cal to attend the gala in her place. "You are always doing things for me that I should somehow be able to do for myself, and I am really profoundly grateful," she wrote. The truth was, relations with Roxanne had turned tumultuous in recent months, and Elizabeth couldn't think of traveling with her, or leaving her behind. Elizabeth hinted at problems when she told Cal she'd prefer to move back to San Francisco, where she'd take a separate apartment from Roxanne and "live alone, dismal as it is."

What had she done, bringing Roxanne here, when she'd needed all along to mourn Lota? "I miss her more every day of my life," she wrote to Cal from Ouro Prêto the week the prize was announced. "This is one of the reasons I want to leave Brazil." In an eerie reprise of Elizabeth's last year with Lota, Roxanne appeared to be having a breakdown, alternating rapidly between "adoration & rudeness," spending recklessly from their joint bank account on expensive building supplies and tools she hoarded in her locked room, fighting with the construction crew and firing the maid and babysitter. Roxanne had gone on a "sort of gold & diamonds jag," staying up half the night "hammering rocks," convinced she would find precious ore in the stones of Ouro Prêto, the town that took its name from the "black gold" of its colonial mines. Desperate to rescue the "poor crazy girl" as she had not been able to save Lota, Elizabeth had Roxanne hospitalized, then flown back with Boogie to her family in Seattle. The scenario of an unstable mother and dependent child was "all too much like my own early days," Elizabeth told Cal; she felt "sorriest of all" for "little Boogie, who is so beautiful and was so upset." Elizabeth learned from Roxanne's doctors that she'd been consuming large quantities of Elizabeth's stimulant medication, Anorexyl. Friends in Seattle told Elizabeth that Roxanne had a "long, long history of these breakdowns." Elizabeth paid Roxanne's hospital bill and sent more money to cover psychotherapy back home, even as she removed Roxanne's name from her bank accounts and will.

Truly alone in the hillside *casa* she was suddenly reluctant to leave, Elizabeth turned to a project she'd been contemplating since Lota's death, a "small book of poems for her, or about her," although the prospect of writing it seemed even now, she wrote to Cal, "still too painful." In early 1968, before she broke her wrist in San Francisco, Elizabeth had begun a sonnet sequence, inspired by a new collection of the Brazilian poet and bossa nova lyricist Vinicius de Moraes, a friend through Lilli. Cal too, steadied by a new drug, lithium, had been spinning out sonnets at the rate of four or five per day, quickly filling a volume he would call *Notebook: 1967–68,* capturing his experience of a turbulent year during which he'd joined a group of celebrity writers in Washington, D.C., to protest the draft, and stumped for antiwar Senator Eugene McCarthy in his quixotic bid for the presidency. The sonnet sequence Elizabeth had envisioned in January 1968, when her grief was still fresh, was meant to "remember all the good days only those," she'd written to Lilli. Now she made notes for one long "ELEGY poem" to be composed of "sections, some anecdotal, some lyrical," recounting incidents from Lota's childhood; recalling her physical traits, "small hands, small feet," the "beautiful colored skin — the gestures"; and summing up aspects of her personality, the "reticence — and pride," the "innocent snobbery," her "ability to tease," and her "courage courage to the last, or almost to the last."

Yet when Elizabeth tried to write, grief again overwhelmed her: "For perhaps the tenth time the tenth time the tenth time today / and still early morning I go under the crashing wave / of your death / I go under the wave the black wave of your death." Phrases repeated, collided, and went nowhere: "No coffee can wwake you   no coffee can wakeyou no coffee / can wake you / No coffee." She took solace from the great Spanish elegy by Miguel Hernández, written after the sudden death of his friend and mentor Ramón Sijé, from whom he'd grown estranged. Elizabeth copied the opening lines onto her own pages and began to translate them: *Yo quiero ser llorando el hortelano / de la tierra*

Lota with Sammy the toucan

que ocupas y estercolas. / compañero del alma, tan temprano . . . I want to be the grieving gardener / of the earth you fill and fertilize, / my dearest friend, so soon. Elizabeth's translation strayed from the original: "I want the mint to be weeping / of the land you occupy . . . / companion of the soul." The conceit of the gardener entered Elizabeth's own poem in the person of Lota:

> *Not there.   And not there! !   I see only small hands in the dirt*
> *transplanting Sweet Williams, tamping them down*
> *dirt on the deft hands, the rings, . . .*
>   *small*

Y siento más tu muerte que mi vida, she copied from Hernández's poem onto her page, but did not translate: *I feel your death more than my life.* In a letter to Dr. Baumann, written while Roxanne was still living at Casa Mariana, Elizabeth had admitted, "Since she died, Anny — I just don't seem to care whether I live or die."

Elizabeth may have known Hernández's "Elegía" since its publication in 1936 or learned about it from Pablo Neruda, with whom she'd been staying in Mexico at the time of Hernández's death in prison after the Spanish Civil War. Neruda's influence on Hernández had caused the rift with the politically conservative Sijé, even as Neruda and Hernández drew together as comrades in the Loyalist cause. In 1970, there was still no English translation of the poem, but Elizabeth would not complete her translation or her own "Elegy." The feelings of guilt she shared with the anguished Hernández, who imagined digging up his estranged friend's grave, mining the earth "until I find you, / kiss your noble skull, ungag your mouth, / and bring you back to life," also overwhelmed her. The list of topics she planned to cover in her "Elegy" included "regret and guilt, the nighttime horro[r]s."

What was Elizabeth's responsibility in Lota's death? The difficulty in bearing the silent accusations, in sensing she was blamed and even hated, was an intuition that her accusers were at least partly right. While living with Roxanne, Elizabeth had resumed work on a poem she called "Pink Dog," about a pariah dog wandering the streets of Rio at Carnival, pink because the "poor bitch" was hairless, exposed; pink had been the color Lota thought most becoming to Elizabeth. She resisted self-indictment, put it down to being "just naturally born guilty" or playing the role of scapegoat for Lota's friends and family members, all of whom felt "slightly guilty after a tragic death like that," she wrote to Lilli. Perhaps it was best to give up Roxanne, the innocent flower child who nevertheless had come between Elizabeth and Lota. Elizabeth had quarreled and parted ways with Lilli these past months also. Elizabeth might not write out her love for Lota, her sadness and regret, but at last she was enduring the "great grief" on her own — to her surprise, she wrote Dr. Baumann, *"enjoying* being terribly lonely."

And she had Cal's companionship by letter. He'd just sent Elizabeth three poems dedicated to her, two of them recalling moments they'd spent together in Maine and the third, "Calling," an ode to Elizabeth's "unerring muse": "Do / you still hang words in the air, ten years imperfect, / joke-lettered, glued to cardboard posters, with gaps / and empties for the unimagined word . . . ?" She loved the poems, unrhymed sonnets he would include in his revised *Notebook,* was "dumbfounded." But in this season of renewed mourning Elizabeth clung instead to the final lines of "Obit," the last sonnet in Cal's *Notebook,* in which he reflected on his marriage to Lizzie Hardwick, not yet over but strained to the breaking point by his erratic moods and misdeeds. Somehow, at the end of his rambling diary-in-verse, Cal had composed two lines that "say *everything,"* Elizabeth wrote to him, "and they say everything I wish I could somehow say about Lota":

> *After loving you so much, can I forget*
> *you for eternity, and have no other choice?*

Cal offered another means of rescue. He'd accepted a two-year teaching position at the University of Essex in England, leaving a vacancy at Harvard, where he'd been teaching one semester each year since the fall of 1963. Could Elizabeth fill in for the 1970 and '71 fall semesters? Despite Elizabeth's meager teaching experience, the college was happy to offer the job on the strength of Cal's recommendation and her two major prizes. The invitation arrived just as she'd sent the *New Yorker* the two long poems, "In the Waiting Room" and "Crusoe in England," she'd polished in New York during the summer of 1967 but hadn't found the peace of mind or the will to finish. The first contained a coded acknowledgment of her grief: the "big black wave" that threatened the young Elizabeth of "In the Waiting Room" recurred as the "black wave of your death" in the unpublished "Elegy." The second bade an oblique farewell to Lota in its closing lines, as the repatriated Robinson Crusoe recalls his desert-island exile and the loss of "Friday, my dear Friday," who "died of measles / seventeen years ago come March." Had Lota lived to one more March birthday, the couple would have spent seventeen years together.

Elizabeth accepted the Harvard job without hesitation, and the prospect of regular half-time employment for the next two years buoyed her spirits briefly. But she wasn't writing well. Roxanne sent long letters from Seattle, sometimes daily, and Elizabeth considered urging her to come along to Cambridge where treatment might be better. Roxanne argued that she wasn't sick at all, which seemed to Elizabeth further confirmation that she *was*. Based on Elizabeth's descriptions of Roxanne's condition, Dr. Baumann predicted that "a long hospitalization would be the only hope of curing R."

Elizabeth was still weepy and drinking to excess when James Merrill arrived at Ouro Prêto for a visit in July. Merrill was one of a growing band of younger gay male poets who admired Elizabeth's poetry and sought to know her. He'd met her first over lunch in New York City twenty years before while he was still a college student, inviting her out to discuss a poem that had "bowled" him over, but he'd had to scramble to make conversation when she showed no interest in talking about her work. Jim, as Elizabeth learned to call him — later he was Jimmy — persisted by letter, sending her his books, five by now; he'd won the National Book Award for the fifth, *Nights and Days,* in 1967. Jim had lived abroad too, finding a sybaritic refuge in Greece. As the son of a Merrill Lynch founding partner, he had the money and time to travel. He could afford to accept Elizabeth's invitation to visit in Brazil, as Howard Moss, who'd become a friend as well as her editor, could not.

The rainy winter weather in Ouro Prêto prevented much sightseeing, and they stayed indoors most days, listening to samba records in the high-ceilinged whitewashed main room, where Jim admired the collection of artifacts and bibelots Elizabeth had assembled: the double-sided paddle, a brass tuba cast off by Ouro Prêto's town band, a tiny crucifix enclosed in a lightbulb. At her urging, he'd brought a quantity of duty-free bourbon, not realizing Elizabeth's susceptibility. She often drank alone, and Jim found her one evening settled in her rocking chair by the wood stove in a stupor, books by Robert Lowell and Marianne Moore piled beside her. Another night he'd had to prepare the meal and entertain dinner guests by himself when she failed to emerge from her room. Yet drinking made Elizabeth talkative when she wasn't beyond reach, and she described for Jim the long arc of her romance with Lota, from the invitation to stay at Samambaia with her own studio — "it just meant everything" — to the catastrophic night of Lota's arrival in New York City. She was "only crying in English," Elizabeth apologized to a Brazilian friend who arrived as she wound up her story in tears. Elizabeth told Jim she disliked being "typed as a lesbian," the term woman-loving American feminists now claimed with zeal. Through the 1950s and '60s Brazil had provided for her, as Greece had for Jim, a more fluid and fanciful environment in which to act on her yearnings. One day between rain showers, they'd taken a taxi to the next town, winding through "sparkling red-and-green country, downhill, uphill, then, suddenly, *under* a rainbow," Jim later recalled. Elizabeth spoke in Portuguese to the taxi driver, who burst into laughter. "In the North of Brazil," she told Jim, letting him in on the joke, "they have this superstition, if you pass underneath a rainbow you change your sex."

When Jim left and as the date of her first class approached, Elizabeth sank further into an alcohol-fueled depression, finally checking herself into a hospital in the closest major city, Belo Horizonte. Yet she summoned the nerve to make the trip to Cambridge in September 1970, fighting her instinctive dread of teaching and suppressing memories of her worst students at the University of Washington, "their hatred for my sex, their LSD fantasies, their bluffing." Many of the university's students, most of whom were men whose student deferments kept them out of Vietnam, would have been better off at a trade school, she thought, than on the "big and impersonal" college campus where Elizabeth herself had felt "rather small and much too personal." Harvard, she hoped, would be different. And, despite the boarded-up shop windows in Harvard Square, unrepaired since the previous spring's antidraft riot, and her dreary two-room suite in Kirkland House, a men's dorm favored by varsity athletes, it was.

After a second fall semester of teaching, with a spring and summer in Ouro Prêto intervening, Elizabeth had been promised a full-time "term appointment," two courses each semester, lasting another five years, until she reached sixty-six, retirement age for nontenured faculty. She would continue at Harvard alongside Cal, who was expected back in Cambridge in the fall of 1972. And she had been asked to compose a poem for the Phi Beta Kappa initiation ceremony at commencement in June, one of the most prestigious invitations a poet could receive. Carl Sandburg, T. S. Eliot, Robert Frost, and W. H. Auden were among her predecessors. Elizabeth stayed in Cambridge through the spring of 1972 to work on "The Moose," a poem that had been "hanging in air" for decades.

For "The Moose," Elizabeth drew on memories going back to 1946, recorded in letters to Marianne Moore, who had died in February 1972 at eighty-four after a series of strokes, and to Dr. Ruth Foster, long dead but not forgotten. Perhaps the poem was an homage to both women. If Dr. Foster had been the attentive seal of "At the Fishhouses," then might not Marianne Moore have been, in phantom form, the inquisitive, "grand, otherworldly" creature who appears at the conclusion of

Marianne Moore with elephants at the Bronx Zoo,
photograph by Esther Bubley, ca. 1953–54

"The Moose"? "It's awful plain" and "Look! It's a she!" gasp the passengers on a bus, halted late at night on a country road deep in the Nova Scotia woods to allow the animal to pass. It could not have escaped Elizabeth's notice that switching just one letter in the last name of her former mentor, whose close family members called each other by the names of the woodland characters in *The Wind in the Willows,* would have made Marianne Moore a moose.

Since their first outings to the circus in the 1930s, Elizabeth had known Marianne adored large animals. It was in the letter to Marianne that she described the 1946 bus ride home from Nova Scotia that supplied the poem's title character; she'd quoted to Marianne, who always appreciated a good line of dialogue, the bus driver's remark after the "big cow moose . . . walked away very slowly into the woods, looking at us over her shoulder": "Very curious beasts." In the poem the driver's comment is compressed—"Curious creatures"—and the backward gaze is given to the narrating passenger as the bus moves on, leaving the animal behind in a final stanza with an alliterative M-M phrase at its center:

> by craning backward,
> the moose can be seen
> on the moonlit macadam;
> then there's a dim
> smell of moose, an acrid
> smell of gasoline.

A letter written to Ruth Foster describing the same bus trip omits the moose, but captures the drowsy passenger eavesdropping on gossip through the nightlong journey, the chief subject of the poem's irregularly rhymed six-line stanzas before the animal arrives. In Elizabeth's February 1947 letter to her psychoanalyst, however, she wasn't simply dozing; she'd drunk a glass of rum with her favorite aunt Grace before boarding the bus, and then taken a sleeping pill. The voices she listens to are of "two women seated far back behind me," and their murmuring stirs an aural hallucination. One woman's voice "was a little louder than the other's," she wrote to Ruth Foster, "and had an intonation very much like my Aunt Grace's . . . that same sort of *commiserating* tone." The other voice, less distinct, was her analyst's: "It kept up all night or so I felt, this endless conversation between you and aunt G — I never could quite catch the words but almost. . . . It wasn't about me." For several weeks after she'd returned to New York City from Nova Scotia, Elizabeth continued to hear the voices as she fell asleep at night, until finally she made an appointment with Dr. Foster — "then I came to see you again & yr real voice took up the tale."

In the poem, the pair of women becomes an elderly married couple — "Grandparents' voices / uninterruptedly / talking, in Eternity" —

> *Talking the way they talked*
> *in the old featherbed,*
> *peacefully, on and on,*
> *dim lamplight in the hall,*
> *down in the kitchen, the dog*
> *tucked in her shawl.*

Elizabeth might have chosen to give the poem wider appeal by substituting the set of grandparents for the female couple, a heterosexual decoy. Or perhaps she simply wanted everyone — her Nova Scotia grandparents, Aunt Grace, Marianne Moore, Ruth Foster — with her "in the middle of the road" for that sublime moment when the she-moose enters the scene and the poem's central, heartening question arises: "Why, why do we feel / (we all feel) this sweet / sensation of joy?"

"The Moose," which she completed in time to deliver in her simple BA cap and gown, purchased at the Coop, from the stage of Harvard's Sanders Theatre in June 1972, her first poem written to deadline, was Elizabeth's bus ride home. Boston, she'd written to Cal after accepting the Harvard job, "still seems like home to me in a funny way." Boston was where, despite all that had befallen her as a child growing up in its surrounding suburbs, Grandfather Bishop's stonework still upheld the Boston Public Library and the Museum of Fine Arts, the museum Elizabeth visited with her aunts Grace and Maud; where she'd passed through the cavernous South Station innumerable times to catch trains to summer camp and Walnut Hill School and Vassar College and finally to New York City.

That spring, the first northern spring she'd witnessed since 1952, Elizabeth settled in, marveling at the "*sea* of lilacs" outside her bedroom window and completing more poems in a season than she had in a decade. "I just wish I could keep on like this forever," she'd written to Howard Moss after mailing him a third poem in late May. And she was in love again. Although Elizabeth would follow her vow to live alone through the coming years, this love would last. It had been celebrated early on with a blissful weekend sub rosa at the Hotel Elysée in New York. Was the choice deliberate? Did Elizabeth realize, her lover had asked when she read *The Group* afterward, this was where Lakey had taken the Baroness on her homecoming?

Elizabeth reading "The Moose" at Phi Beta Kappa literary exercises,
Sanders Theatre, Harvard University, 1972

June 14, 1977
SANDERS THEATRE, MEMORIAL HALL

Phi Beta Kappa was for my uncle, my mother's genius older brother, a marine physicist who'd invented a seagoing research vessel that flipped 90 degrees and held its position vertically at the surface, half above and half below, in surging Pacific waters, and the "deep tow" system that revealed hydrothermal vents feeding giant tube worms on the ocean floor. Phi Beta Kappa was not for me, with my A's in courses that asked only for reading and writing, my B in Miss Bishop's class. But then it was — and there I was, seated among the hundred-plus newly elected Phi Beta Kappa scholars in the front pews of Sanders Theatre, my black gown, a rental from the Coop, thrown over white jeans and a navy-blue ribbed tank top. The June day was hot and steamy, and the gown's polyester didn't breathe.

I might have attended the Phi Beta Kappa program on the Tuesday morning before Thursday's graduation anyway, to hear the appointed poet, Robert Penn Warren. A friend had a crush on the red-haired daughter of "Red" Warren, as we knew to call him, and the poet's wife, the writer Eleanor Clark, had been a Vassar classmate of Miss Bishop's. We were curious. Maybe the whole family would come up from Connecticut. But I was separated from my friend and my boyfriend and my visiting parents, listening first to Edwin Land, the day's orator, tell how his young daughter had asked, while walking the beach with him years ago, Why can't we take a snapshot and have the photograph right away? He'd invented the Polaroid camera to answer her question. "The question is itself the answer," he counseled us graduating seniors as we sat, groggy from the revelry of senior week, in our cushioned pews.

If only my questions were as wide-eyed as Land's little daughter's, and I had a scientist's mind to answer them. My mother had taken me aside the day before to tell me she had rented a one-bedroom apartment a few blocks from our family home and would be moving things into it over the summer in preparation for telling my father she wanted a divorce. After that, the house would be sold, and where my long-unemployed father might live next would be up to him. They were staying now in a Harvard dorm room. It was the thirty-fifth reunion of the Harvard class from which my father hadn't graduated, and the college wasn't picky when it came to welcoming potential donors back to campus, though my parents had nothing to spare for Harvard beyond the minimal cost of the lodgings.

My mother had rarely spoken of her unhappiness with my father, and there was no time for elaboration during the fifteen minutes before he joined us for lunch at Piroschka's on Dunster Street. How she would tell him she was moving out and how he might respond was beyond imagining for me. He could talk a blue streak about his favorite novels — *Moby-Dick, Ulysses,* Norman Douglas's *South Wind* — or the ingenious Quincy Market renovation he'd visited the day before, but his grasp on the facts of his situation was weak, and when challenged or even simply interrupted he was quick to anger. He liked to say he believed in the "generation gap" that so many of my age-mates bemoaned. Keeping my mother's secret over the several days they'd allotted to attend my graduation would not be difficult.

But my mother's decision — her decisiveness — surprised me. My parents had operated separately for so long while residing in the same house, I'd stopped wishing for the divorce I'd once thought would bring relief from the painful ambiguity of our lives together. When my father had taken the train back east in May to roam the New England states for several weeks before coming to Cambridge, staying in hostels, I'd thought it was to save the steeper airfare and because he had nothing else to do while my mother worked at her copyediting job and then flew to Boston on the redeye. She must have welcomed the time alone to make her plans. When my father arrived at the café and ordered a sandwich of pâté and lettuce on a baguette, the most expensive item on the menu, we listened to him reminisce about Harry Levin's lectures on Proust, Joyce, and Mann until my mother picked up the check. I felt sorry for him; he hadn't gone to any of the scheduled reunion events. He had only us to tell his stories to, and soon he wouldn't have that either. I doubted there'd be room for me to stay wherever my father lived after our house was sold.

My mother hadn't asked, but she would have been right to believe I had no plans to return home to Pasadena after graduation. I hadn't even visited the summer before when I lived in San Francisco for a work-study job at Laura X's Women's History Research Center in Berkeley. It wasn't until I'd arrived on the West Coast that I learned the WHRC, located in a church basement several blocks from the university campus, was in the process of closing down. Rather than pursuing research projects using the center's collections, I'd spend most of my days packing up files documenting the WHRC's not-so-distant founding in the late sixties and shipping them off to be archived at Radcliffe's Schlesinger Library, a few blocks away from the dorm I'd just left. Laura X, a St. Louis heiress who'd traded in her last name following Malcolm X's lead, had put much of her fortune into acquiring a library to prove a point to her Berkeley history professor, who'd declared there wasn't enough material to support even a semester's course in women's history. But her enterprise had been overtaken by university-backed women's history libraries like the Schlesinger, and the organization shifted focus around the time I arrived, in June 1976, toward contemporary women's issues, developing an informational film strip on the prevalence of rape and sexual assault.

Laura rarely visited the center, and my supervisor warned me to turn down any invitations to visit her at home. I should drop the names of current and former boyfriends when I met her, otherwise our boss might "come on" to me. My supervisor had already "come out" to me one day after work, first extracting my promise not to tell Laura or anyone else in our tiny office her secret: she and her partner were ready to have a child, looking into artificial insemination, maybe using a turkey baster. She didn't want complications on the job either.

It seemed safe enough, though, to accept Laura X's offer to house-sit while she was out of town on vacation. Her sprawling home in the Berkeley Hills may have had views of the Bay and the Golden Gate, but it was stuffed so full of books — the WHRC's library was kept there — I seldom looked out the windows. I pulled some of the slimmer volumes off the shelves, hoping to find samples of recent feminist poetry. One book's author had posed seminude for her jacket photo, arms raised overhead in flamboyant rebellion. Another pamphlet wasn't poetry at all, though its typewritten pages with ragged right margins seemed at first to be some style of verse. It was *Calamity Jane's Letters to Her Daughter,* published by the Shameless Hussy Press. Was Calamity Jane, the frontier heroine, a real person? I hadn't known. Here was a record spanning nearly three decades, from 1877 to 1903, letters written from Coulson, Deadwood, Stringtown, and New York City to a girl who grew to become a woman, cared for by others while her mother was on the road. I felt no qualms about taking the little book with me, a totem of the greater knowledge I'd hoped to gain that summer, but I wouldn't go back to California except to clear out my bedroom.

When Red Warren stepped to the podium in Sanders Theatre, I had to wonder whether his nickname derived from his ruddy complexion as much as the hair that now fell in white wisps from a balding pate. Academic regalia hadn't camouflaged Edwin Land's straight edges, his businessman's verve. But Warren's flowing robes, along with his impressive height, beaklike nose, and regal bearing, set him on a plane with the toga-clad heroes that flanked him on the stage — the patriot orator James Otis and the antebellum Boston mayor and Harvard president Josiah Quincy — pale marble though they were.

Then his voice split the air, a rasping Kentucky twang as startling as a Confederate saber rattling in the hall, paneled in honey-colored hardwoods and dedicated to the memory of Harvard's Union dead. We knew Robert Penn Warren as the author of *All the King's Men,* his novel of political demagoguery in the Depression-era South, and after that as coauthor of dusty English textbooks with his colleague Cleanth Brooks at Yale — reason enough to view him as an intruder in Crimson territory. What kind of poet was he? None of my teachers had ever mentioned him; his six books of verse were not on our reading lists.

He was nearly spitting out the lines of a poem called "Red-Tail Hawk and Pyre of Youth," but his stretched and battered words were at first unintelligible. I picked up the outlines of a reminiscence: he'd been out hunting as a boy, climbed a ridge where the red-tail flew at him, "a shadowy vortex of silver," then closed in —

> *I pressed the cool, snubbed*
> *Trigger. Saw*
> *The circle*
> *Break.*

The boy carries the bloodied corpse home, "cuddled / Like babe to heart, and my heart beating like love," to stuff and mount his prey —

> *I knew my business. And at last a red-tail —*

> *Oh, king of the air!*

> *And at that miraculous range.*

> *How my heart sang!*

I knew Miss Bishop had read at this ceremony five years before. Her poem, "The Moose," one of my favorites in *Geography III,* told a vastly different story of a wild creature's surprise appearance at close range. That "curious" beast had been cautiously admired, then allowed to go her own way. How I wished for an end to Warren's savage bluster, to listen instead one last time to my teacher's softly musical voice as she spoke her poems, as if in conversation with herself or just a few intimates. There had been the time in Robert Lowell's class when, after reading "Poem," she'd flipped back through her binder to find "Crusoe in England" and started in with a little laugh: "A new volcano has erupted, / the papers say, . . . / But my poor old island's still / un-redis-covered, un-renamable. / None of the books has ever got it right." She'd taken us on a journey of the imagination, *her* imagination.

> *My island seemed to be*
> *a sort of cloud-dump. All the hemisphere's*
> *left-over clouds arrived and hung*
> *above the craters . . .*
> *The turtles lumbered by, high-domed,*
> *hissing like teakettles. . . .*
>
> *The sun set in the sea; the same odd sun*
> *rose from the sea,*
> *and there was one of it and one of me.*

And there had been the evening this past winter when, basking in the rosy glow her walls of exposed brick seemed to emit, she'd read from her rocking chair: "practice losing farther, losing faster." I had disappointed Elizabeth Bishop, but she could never, I realized, disappoint me.

Our poet continued. The stuffed bird took up residence "year after year, in my room, on the tallest of bookshelves," presiding over prized volumes of Blake, Milton, Hardy, and Shakespeare, "unsleeping," glass eyes staring into the night as the boy slept, until "I slept in that room no more." I was listening now —

> *Years pass like a dream, are a dream, and time came*
> *When my mother was dead, father bankrupt, and whiskey*
> *Hot in my throat while there for the last*
>
> *Time I lay, and my heart*
> *Throbbed slow in the*
> *Meaningless motion of life, and with*

My eyes closed I knew
That yellow eyes somewhere, unblinking, in vengeance stared.

Or was *it vengeance? What could I know?*

The grown man hunts down his childhood trophy, relegated to the cellar along with his books, and douses the bird with gasoline. "Flames flared. Feathers first. . . . I / Did not wait" —

What is left
To do but walk in the dark, and no stars?

———

My bid for the Rockefeller fellowship had failed, and little wonder. Writing poetry in Paris, exotic as it seemed to me, couldn't compete with the winning students' proposals for travel in Africa and Poland. I hadn't won any of the big-money creative-writing prizes that might have permitted time off from the research assistant jobs I'd recently pushed to full time, or simply boosted my confidence, the jolt I most needed. As it was, the award I would receive at Thursday afternoon's diploma-granting ceremony had me blushing with something like the opposite of pride: the Harvard Monthly Prize for "the student in the most advanced course in English composition who shows the greatest literary promise." Miss Bishop ordinarily selected the winner from among her Advanced Verse Writing students, but this year she'd given up the task, unwilling to do anything more than teach her classes when the college hadn't renewed her contract. Certainly the prize would not have been mine if Miss Bishop had kept her job. Professor Fitzgerald stepped into the breach and chose me.

The purse, $140.44, belied the commendation's windy grandeur. I'd already spent the money: $5 on an oak bookcase another graduating senior was selling on the street, and the rest for a sleek new silver ten-speed bicycle outfitted with red panniers. My boyfriend and I had planned a bike trip in Nova Scotia, stopping first to visit a friend of his on North Haven Island, a short ferry ride off the Maine coast. Then we'd be back in it.

Sun

T HE POOR HEART doesn't seem to grow old at all," Elizabeth had written to Alice Methfessel from Ouro Prêto in March 1971, a month after her sixtieth birthday and two weeks past Alice's twenty-eighth. But their age difference was nearly always on her mind, from the moment Alice first laid her head on Elizabeth's shoulder when Alice had stopped in to see her after a "beery party" with the boys of Kirkland House, where Elizabeth was living in an apartment reserved for visiting scholars during the fall of 1970, and "stayed & stayed, like a child who couldn't bear to go to bed." Alice Methfessel was the otherwise entirely sensible, slim and athletic Kirkland House secretary, with "blue blue blue" eyes and a disposition as bright as the "Sunny-Side Up" formula she used to lighten her cropped hair, who had helped move Elizabeth into her second-floor rooms in I-Entry in early October, showed her how to use the basement washing machines, and soon was handling Elizabeth's mail, meeting her at the airport after a late return from New York City, and bringing her home to the fifth-floor studio apartment on Chauncy Street where Alice lived just outside Harvard Square.

Alice's apartment was "the most electrified place" Elizabeth had ever seen: "hi-fi, radios (2), color TV, hair dryers (2), electric blanket, electric clock, electric 'Water Pik'" for tooth-brushing, along with an electric stove and refrigerator, "just normal here," in contrast to Brazil, Elizabeth supposed, as she watched Alice dress for work in the morning from the large blue bed that took up more space than anything else in the room. She'd loved the lock of hair that Alice allowed Elizabeth to smooth back from her forehead, and "those nice satiny eyelids shut tight" as Alice slept. She loved the coffee Alice brought to her now in bed, and looking out the window to see nothing but bare branches when Alice drew back the curtains, and the sound of Alice's voice, "nice & loud and cheerful," as she spoke the words that became their waking-up ritual, "Good-morning I love you." Elizabeth adored "the way you pull on your stockings in the morning — very American, careless and extravagant," and she'd never forget the sight of Alice wrapping her beautiful neck with a bright red scarf against the cold. Later that fall and winter they would plan ahead for more indulgent breakfasts of croissants from C'est Si Bon and foamy cappuccinos that Elizabeth taught Alice to make with Medaglia d'Oro coffee.

When they parted at the end of Elizabeth's first Harvard semester in February 1971, following a magical weekend at New York's posh Hotel Elysée — Elizabeth did *not* remember this was where "the ladies" stayed in *The Group* — both were in tears, neither sure that the other's love could last through the seven months before Elizabeth returned to teach again in September. Alice, who was used to chatting up Harvard professors and assorted dignitaries passing through Kirkland House, had still been "taken aback at your loving little me"; Alice was tall, Elizabeth was the little one, but she was so much older, and a famous poet. For her part, Elizabeth knew "I'm wrong in every way, except as a 'dear older friend,'" she wrote to Alice from Ouro Prêto, and that "you are much too young for me; have many many things you must do"; surely Alice's admirable practicality would cause her to break things off, to "do what's right for you, and I'll *know* it's right for you — but I dread it terribly at the same time." Troubled by the "beaux" in Alice's past, and having witnessed the attraction Alice held for Kirkland House boys and even the avuncular housemaster, Professor Arthur Smithies (he'd given Alice a book called *Nymphos and Other Maniacs* for her birthday), Elizabeth wooed Alice as best she could in letters she feared were "indiscreet" and asked her to please destroy "after a while." She conjured a scene: Alice arriving home from work, where "all your electrical gadgets will be waiting for you and they will turn themselves on & begin throbbing and singing: 'Alice, we love you . . . we love you . . . we love you — Please let us warm your little body and dry your hair and make ice for your bourbon." But Elizabeth didn't really have to try so hard. Her sensible lover would not be shaken off course, despite the occasional dinner out with "Bob the Boring" or the sighting of a former beau, Toby. She signed her letters, "For Always, Alice."

Elizabeth sent Alice "love — housefulls, churchfulls, airportsfull," slept with Alice's letters, carried her photo buttoned into her shirt pocket. Alice lay in bed at night watching slides of Elizabeth she'd taken on late-fall excursions, projected on the white wall of her studio apartment. Still Elizabeth worried, dreamed they met by chance in a foreign airport, but had only three hours together before catching separate planes. She began taking a nightly Nembutal to sleep. Then, in Ouro Prêto, where bottles of *cachaça* and Old Crow were plentiful, and having the "best breakfast for hundreds of miles around" (her own cornbread toasted, plum jam she'd made from fruit in the garden) was "no fun at all, alone," Elizabeth had "two collapses, one on top of the other" — binged twice in quick succession, she admitted after failing to write for more than two weeks, frightening Alice. Elizabeth could not

Elizabeth with Alice Methfessel

stop envisioning a dreadful end to their pleasure and the saving grace of Alice's love.

It was now Elizabeth learned she could tell Alice anything — and Alice, "less neurotic than anyone else" Elizabeth knew, would remain unfazed, continue to love Elizabeth "unreservedly" and, unlike Elizabeth, who was "morbidly given to borrowing trouble & expecting the worst," confine her own worries to "things I can actively do something about." That was Alice: grateful to know the much older Elizabeth, or "I'd be really hung up on the generation gap"; literary enough to quote Wordsworth — "the child is father of the man" — but taking the adage to define the child's responsibility for his parents, "the Ageds," as she called hers. The senior Methfessels were Elizabeth's age, but conservative Pennsylvania country-club Republicans with whom Alice had nothing in common but "our mutual past," and declining, Alice thought, into a nattering senescence. Both Elizabeth and Alice agreed that, despite the "vast difference in our ages," they shared a sense of humor, a yen for travel (Alice had already proposed a trip to Brazil for that August of 1971 to relieve Elizabeth's exile), and a circumspection about romance that was increasingly rare as the 1970s gave birth to "women's lib" and, before long, radical lesbian separatism. They had "the same way of looking at things."

So when Elizabeth confided that her two collapses had come as she sank once again into "just plain grief" after "so many sad deaths the past few years, so much insanity, so many god-awful experiences, & so much time lost forever," fearing above all that her new "unsuitable" love was only likely to "bring more grief & loss," she was testing Alice, even as Elizabeth insisted she didn't mean to burden the younger woman. This "awful tail-spin" was "not *your fault*." How would Alice respond when Elizabeth foretold the worst — a day, probably soon, when "I'll have to see you going off with someone more suitable — and I'll have somehow to turn into just being a 'good friend' etc."? Elizabeth loathed the thought of "your coming to call on me in my 'flat' in Boston, & bringing me a bunch of flowers or something. Or your feeling you have to be 'nice' to an old lady because she is fond of you — & you'll be dying to get away & go skiing or swimming or love-making with your young man — I really hope I die first."

Of course Alice aced the exam. When Elizabeth worried that she'd be left sitting on shore holding Alice's terry-cloth beach wrap while her young lover swam in the Pacific on the tour of the Galápagos Islands they'd tacked onto the planned August visit, Alice brushed those worries aside and then made certain they both went swimming on Charles Island — "a nice beach, flamingos" — and mingled with the blue-footed boobies, sea lions, and albatrosses they'd flown all that way to see together. When Elizabeth returned to Cambridge in September, Alice had a one-bedroom apartment waiting for her in the Brattle Arms, a solid brick building at 60 Brattle Street, just past Design Research and next door to the Window Shop bakery, its walls freshly painted by Harvard boys Alice had hired, and with Alice's new red-yellow-and-blue-striped terry-cloth bathrobe, purchased in the men's department of Lord & Taylor, ready for lounging on Sunday mornings. Writing to Elizabeth that spring about her discovery of the Brattle Street apartment, Alice had crowed, "If Elizabeth lived here I'd be home now!," mimicking the twin billboards aimed at harried commuters on Boston's Storrow Drive advertising luxury rentals in the new Charles River Park complex: *"If You Lived Here . . ."* *". . . You'd Be Home Now!"* Elizabeth's surprise phone call from Brazil just days before had left Alice in a state of "blissful shock" — "Your wonderful laugh will ring through my dreams."

Elizabeth warned Alice there might be setbacks, future collapses when "the horrors set in." She copied out a long passage from Melanie Klein's *Love, Guilt and Reparation* on female friendship and sent it to Alice. Klein, whom Elizabeth described as Freud's "best successor," no longer seemed "grim" to her. Klein's "books are wonderful — and she *looks* wonderful," Elizabeth told Alice. The passage she excerpted, in which Klein observed that "a successful blending of a mother-attitude and a daughter-attitude seems to be one of the conditions for an emotionally rich feminine personality and for the capacity for friendship," made the "Lib Ladies" and "their talk about actually *liking* their own sex" seem "pretty shallow," Elizabeth thought, despite having been "written by a wonderful *old* woman, and quite some time ago." But Klein also noted occasions when the past presses "strongly upon the present," and "early situations of unsatisfied desires" for nurture break through, bringing up "feelings of dissatisfaction and loneliness," and "we . . . expect the friend to make up for our early deprivations." Such "excessive unconscious demands lead to disturbances in our friendships, exact repetitions," Klein wrote. Few knew this better than Elizabeth, after her difficult last years with Lota.

Alice might feel she had little in common with "the Ageds," her parents, Elizabeth allowed, but they had not abandoned her, and "you seem to have come through your years so far pretty unscathed." For Elizabeth — "well, so many things just happened to fail for me." She did not enumerate: her father's early death, her mother's insanity, the orphan childhood spent shuttling between households, boarding school, and summer camp with no sure guardian. But if things had been different, "I'd undoubtedly be a different person, maybe happier and easier to love." Still, "I'll do my best," Elizabeth promised Alice. "I am *aware* of all this, at least — & really trying, baby." "Baby" was the way she addressed Alice in letters, and Alice, who called Elizabeth "Darling," thought the name was sweet. Elizabeth had not typed out for Alice the footnote to the passage from Klein's book, in which Klein remarked that "the subject of homosexual love relations is a wide and very complicated one," beyond the scope of the study, and stated simply that "much love can be put into these relationships." She didn't have to.

Elizabeth taught a second and then a third fall semester at Harvard, in 1972, without a serious collapse, living at the Brattle Arms, where she'd installed a ping-pong table for exercise that could double as a dining table for the occasional dinner party. Alice stayed with her many, if not most, nights. Bravely, Elizabeth accepted an offer to return to the University of Washington for one highly paid quarter in the spring of 1973, to raise money for future travels abroad with Alice. They'd cruised in Scandinavia on a Norwegian mail boat the summer before, after Elizabeth's successful reading of "The Moose." Now she booked a roomette on the Empire Builder from Chicago to Seattle.

Elizabeth had always wanted to see the Rockies rise up from the Great Plains, and the new Amtrak's Vista Dome car promised dramatic views. She was traveling alone, but Alice would meet her at the end of term to explore the Olympic Peninsula by rental car. As always when they were apart, Elizabeth jotted down her every move in letters to

Alice, typing her first one on a portable machine she'd settled on the roomette's closed toilet lid, an awkward stretch from her single seat by the window. In Chicago, the line for the Renoir show at the entrance to the Art Institute had been too long, so she'd skipped her planned museum visit and ordered the taxi driver straight on to Union Station, where she sat on a bench in the glorious waiting room modeled after Rome's Baths of Caracalla, reading the *New York Times* and a lurid tale of a sex-obsessed centenarian dowager by Tennessee Williams in the latest issue of *Playboy* — "SICK is the only word for it, or maybe DECADENT." An article on Colorado River trips caught her eye, and she urged Alice to consider joining her on one with motorized rafts; a seventy-six-year-old woman had managed that. Or the twelve-day "*rowed* trip? I could make it, probably." With Alice as guide, she'd recently learned to cross-country ski. Why not this?

But what Elizabeth wanted to tell Alice most of all was about taking off on the first leg of her journey, the flight from Boston to O'Hare, the day before. "Yesterday as we whooshed up above the rain and gloom of Boston into the bright blue sunlight above it," Elizabeth wrote, "I thought it was exactly what your coming into my life has done for me, Alice — not that fast, maybe, but pretty fast — and the wonderful difference is just the same."

As a result of taking Cal's place at the head of English S — "Writing (Advanced Course) Primarily poetry. *Note:* For students actively engaged in creative writing" — Elizabeth became the first woman to teach an advanced writing class at Harvard and the first woman poet to have her name published in a course catalogue. It might not have happened without Cal's intercession for Elizabeth, or any woman, for quite some time. Harvard's English department simply was not welcoming to female faculty members. The poets May Sarton and John Ciardi had been hired for brief stints in the early 1950s, but only Ciardi was permitted to teach a poetry course or named in the catalogue; Sarton taught freshman composition. No woman had been appointed to the Briggs-Copeland Lectureship held by Ciardi and Sarton since. These were the years when Archibald MacLeish held sway as the Boylston Professor of Rhetoric, establishing a beachhead for creative writing at the college by claiming English S, initially offered to students "with a professional interest in writers' problems," and fostering introductory courses in fiction and poetry, such as Ciardi's English G.

When MacLeish retired in 1963, Cal had come on, but his erratic health and reluctance to settle again in Boston stood in the way of the named professorship, which went to poet and translator Robert Fitzgerald, the faculty member who welcomed Elizabeth to Harvard in 1970. She had an early taste of the college's stodgy ways when she learned from department chairman Morton Bloomfield that, although he'd altered the title of the graduate literature seminar she would also teach, from Cal's Types of Modern Poetry to Subject Matter in Twentieth-Century Poetry, at her request (substance, what actually transpired in a poem, was what she aimed to teach), he would not be able to publish her name in the catalogue this first year. That would require a vote of the Harvard Corporation, which wouldn't meet until the semester began in September. He resolved the matter by entering "Miss _____" under both her classes, perhaps a nod to the times. By now the Radcliffe students who had access to all of Harvard's courses had begun to agitate for female professors.

Not that Elizabeth wanted to be known as the first woman poet to teach creative writing at Harvard, or as a woman poet at all. She'd always been irked when described in reviews or introduced at readings as one of America's best women poets or "the greatest feminine poet of the decade." Men and women "do not write differently," she insisted. But hers was a position increasingly under attack. First May Swenson wrote urging her to give permission for a poem, preferably "In the Waiting Room," to appear in a new "scholarly and significant" anthology, *The Women Poets in English*. Hoping to overcome Elizabeth's resistance, May described the volume, the first such collection to be published since 1825, as "*not* propagandist or 'womans lib.'" Still Elizabeth refused, and on "Women's Lib." grounds: "Why not *Men Poets in English*? Don't you see how silly it is?" She didn't like to have "things compartmentalized like that" — "I like black & white, yellow & red, young & old, rich and poor, and male & female, all mixed up." Segregation, whether social or artistic, could only work against women's acceptance as equal to men. "Literature is literature, no matter who produces it."

Then a younger poet, Adrienne Rich, pressed her to contribute to an anthology devoted to American women poets. The occasion was a dinner party with writers in Harvard's orbit. As a Radcliffe senior in 1951, Adrienne's first book of poems had been selected by W. H. Auden for publication in the Yale Series of Younger Poets, and another book followed four years later. But it wasn't until the 1960s that Adrienne, who'd married a Harvard economics professor and given birth to three sons in quick succession, turned prolific, finding freer expression in the language of the antiwar and women's movements she joined after moving to New York City, then leaving her husband, and finally coming out as a lesbian in 1976. To Adrienne's request, Elizabeth answered no again; she didn't want to be classified as a "woman poet."

But privately Elizabeth expressed to Adrienne Rich an urge to follow her path, to write more openly about "the situation of woman." Along with other vexations of her teaching job — coping with the fragile egos of students who, she noted in her journal, viewed C's as failing grades, and deliberating over which student to select for the Harvard Monthly Prize (one year she chose a freshman, "an Irish boy who looks like the sun"; another an older married student not even enrolled in the college) — she particularly disliked being seen as a female role

Adrienne Rich,
photograph by Thomas Victor, 1974

model. Speaking to a group of students at Dartmouth College following a reading in the fall of 1973, one year after the Ivy League school went co-ed, she'd been asked by a "militant young lady" whether she felt like a *"woman — (of all things!),* when I write poetry." The question seemed to her absurd. But when it came to subject matter, the aspect of contemporary poetry Elizabeth was willing to teach in her graduate seminar, she thought she might *"try"* to be more "frank," she wrote to Adrienne after reading *Diving into the Wreck,* the book that won its author a National Book Award a year later in 1974. (When her book was announced the winner at the awards ceremony, Adrienne read an acceptance speech written jointly with the two other women finalists, Audre Lorde and Alice Walker, "refusing the terms of patriarchal competition and declaring that we will share this prize among us, to be used as best we can for women.")

Elizabeth and Adrienne had met at parties in New York City and Cambridge as early as 1971, and shortly before *Diving into the Wreck* was published in 1973, Adrienne gave Elizabeth a ride from New York back to Boston, where Adrienne was living while teaching for a year at Brandeis. The conversation turned confiding. Adrienne had not known, during the 1950s when she'd struggled in her marriage, that Elizabeth, a poet she deeply admired, had a female lover in Brazil. In 1970, Adrienne's husband had killed himself after she'd left him to explore her sexuality. Now in the whirring car, enveloped by darkness, "we found ourselves talking of the recent suicides in each of our lives," Adrienne later recalled, "telling 'how it happened' as people speak who feel they will be understood." Absorbed by the conversation, Adrienne missed the exit at Hartford and drove all the way to Springfield, thirty miles ahead, before realizing her mistake and turning east toward Boston.

Elizabeth's departure for Seattle soon after, and Adrienne's move back to New York City at the end of her Brandeis appointment, prevented a friendship from developing. Or perhaps the women had too many differences to remain close. Elizabeth's decades-long friendship with May Swenson would fade as May, like Adrienne, became more open about her lesbian identity and "militant" in her feminism. But Elizabeth's instinct to confide continued by letter for several months.

First Elizabeth sent Adrienne a postcard of de Chirico's surreal pair, *The Disquieting Muses,* apologizing for "having TALKED so much on our drive back" and causing the younger poet to miss the turnoff. She invited Adrienne to a "Brazilian lunch" — *feijoada* — featuring a traditional stew Elizabeth would serve to a half-dozen friends on her ping-pong table at 60 Brattle Street the following weekend.

Later that spring Elizabeth wrote from her teaching job in Seattle to thank Adrienne for sending her *Diving into the Wreck,* and to respond to a passage from Adrienne's 1972 essay "When We Dead Awaken: Writing as Re-Vision," which had been reprinted in a special issue of the *Harvard Advocate,* the college's literary journal, on "Feminine Sensibility." The essay was an invitation to women writers to unite in "refusal of the self-destructiveness of male-dominated society," and "to see — and therefore live — afresh." The portion published in the *Advocate* referred to Elizabeth directly: "Much of woman's poetry has been in the nature of the blues song: a cry of pain, of victimization, or a lyric of seduction. (Or, like Marianne Moore and Elizabeth Bishop, she kept human sexual relationships at a measured and chiselled distance in her poems.)"

"Today, much poetry by women — and prose for that matter — is charged with anger," Adrienne continued. She applauded the development: "I think we need to go through that anger." The effort to achieve "objectivity" or "detachment" — "to sound as cool as Jane Austen or as Olympian as Shakespeare" — was pointless, could only "betray our own reality." In the past, "every woman writer has written for men," she argued, establishing a central tenet of feminist literary criticism in the coming decades, while men rarely wrote with the opinions of women foremost in their minds. It was time for women to "stop being haunted" by "internalized fears of being and saying themselves."

Elizabeth wrote to assure Adrienne she had no objections: "I don't mind what you say of me at all — probably perfectly true." And as for the anger, "I'm sure you're absolutely right." Elizabeth conceded, "I must have felt the same way many years ago — but my only method of dealing with it was to refuse to admit it." One of the poems Elizabeth praised in *Diving into the Wreck* was Adrienne's "The Phenomenology of Anger," which read in part:

"The only real love I have ever felt
was for children and other women.
Everything else was lust, pity,
self-hatred, pity, lust."
This is a woman's confession.

Yet Adrienne's poems weren't so much confessional as they were polemical. Like her essay, whose title, borrowed from Ibsen, she also gave to a poem in her collection, they framed arguments, putting Elizabeth in mind of Marianne Moore's long poem "Marriage." Elizabeth had assigned "Marriage" to her students in Seattle that semester, though few sympathized with Moore's critique or appreciated her humor: "I wonder what Adam and Eve / think of it by this time."

In avoiding direct confession, Elizabeth and Adrienne shared a reluctance to join "The School of Anguish," and a determination to keep the specific details of their intimate lives private. Elizabeth attributed her instinctive reticence, which had prompted her to apologize to Adrienne for confiding, even in the seclusion of a car's front seat, to her "Scotch-Canadian-Protestant-Puritan" temperament. Elizabeth sometimes wished, as she'd written to Alice after her double collapse in Ouro Prêto, that she could be more like other writers she knew, who "drink worse than I do, at least badly & all the time, and don't seem to have any regrets or shame — just write poems about it." But these were all men. Would Elizabeth, as she hinted to Adrienne, write something more "frank" on the situation of women?

In a sense she already had, with "In the Waiting Room," adapting the principle of confessional poetry she'd outlined years before in the *Time* interview — "the idea is that we live in a horrible and terrifying world, and the worst moments of horrible and terrifying lives are an allegory of the world." The astonishment Elizabeth remembered feeling at being "one of *them*," after viewing pendulous breasts in *National Geographic,* scanning the room's adult female inhabitants, hearing her "foolish" aunt's cry of pain, was an allegory of every girl's shocking realization of what growing up to become a woman could mean. Yet Elizabeth *had* managed the Olympian distance and objectivity, along with a charged immediacy, that her younger colleague thought impossible or inauthentic in these angry times. "In the Waiting Room" was a poem written by a woman about a girl's perceptions, but the "subject matter" — growing up, experiencing self-consciousness — was universal.

And although Adrienne had no way of knowing, Elizabeth was fully capable of writing poems that celebrated "human sexual relationships." She wrote one now for no one but Alice to see, called "Breakfast Song," expressing her love and the fear she could not shake:

> *My love, my saving grace,*
> *your eyes are awfully blue.*
> *I kiss your funny face,*
> *your coffee-flavored mouth.*
> *Last night I slept with you.*
> *Today I love you so*
> *how can I bear to go*
> *(as soon I must, I know)*
> *to bed with ugly death*
> *in that cold, filthy place,*
> *to sleep there without you,*
> *without the easy breath*
> *and nightlong, limblong warmth*
> *I've grown accustomed to?*
> *— Nobody wants to die;*
> *tell me it is a lie!*
> *But no, I know it's true.*
> *It's just the common case;*
> *there's nothing one can do.*
> *My love, my saving grace,*
> *your eyes are awfully blue*
> *early & instant blue*

Even as she confided in Alice her fears of death and aging, Elizabeth scolded Cal, six years her junior, "Please, *please* don't talk about old age so much, my dear old friend!" Recurrent breakdowns had left him pale and haggard, his white hair, grown long in the fashion of the times, a hazy corona. In his late fifties, Cal felt himself to be "de-effervescing," inclined toward what Elizabeth considered premature lament. "If only age could stop; and inspiration be an irregular constant," he'd written to her in March 1973. For Cal's benefit Elizabeth claimed to have no such qualms — "in spite of aches & pains I really don't feel much different than I did at 35 . . . I just *won't* feel ancient" — although inspiration eluded her once again after the spurt of productivity during the spring of "The Moose." She had not offered the *New Yorker* another poem since. By contrast, Cal had three books going to press at once: *History,* a substantially revised, expanded, and rearranged version of the unrhymed sonnets that had appeared in *Notebook; For Lizzie and Harriet,* a compilation of the sonnets on family life extracted from *Notebook;* and an entirely new volume, *The Dolphin.* "The three books are my magnum opus, are the best or rather they'll do," he'd written as his ambitions for them rose and sank along with his moods.

The third of these had given Elizabeth a great deal more to scold Cal about. Ever since his appropriation of Jean Stafford's complaints against him for use in *The Mills of the Kavanaughs,* she'd been troubled by Cal's magpie tendency to scavenge materials from the lives and writings of those close to him and reshape them for his own ends. Elizabeth herself had not been immune. May Swenson had been resentful on Elizabeth's behalf ten years before when Cal had lifted whole phrases "word by word" from her story "In the Village" and recast them as a

Cal at Milgate House,
photograph by Walker Evans, 1973

poem he called "The Scream." "Of course it's a compliment in a way," May had written after reading the poem in the *Kenyon Review,* "but in another way it's an unnecessary adaptation — why do it?" In that instance, Elizabeth told May, Cal had asked her approval, sending a draft in advance, and she'd decided to take the compliment; in both the *Kenyon Review* and Cal's book *For the Union Dead,* in which "The Scream" was published in 1965, Cal had credited Elizabeth and her story. She was content, as well, to be the unnamed companion in his poem "Water," which described their day alone in Stonington in 1948, although "I swear he has my dream wrong," she wrote to May. "One night you dreamed / you were a mermaid clinging to a wharf-pile, / and trying to pull / off the barnacles with your hands," Cal had written. She did not object to his summary of their mutual resignation to a platonic love, that day and since:

> *We wished our two souls*
> *might return like gulls*
> *to the rock. In the end,*
> *the water was too cold for us.*

But Cal had given Elizabeth no warning of the sonnet published in late 1970, one of a quartet "For Elizabeth Bishop" in the British edition of his revised *Notebook.* The first three had lifted her spirits when Cal sent them to her in draft during the dark months in Ouro Prêto the previous February; but not the fourth. There was no mistaking the source of phrases cribbed, once again word for word, from a letter describing her anguish as relations with Roxanne Cumming deteriorated and her mourning for Lota intensified: ". . . the worst situation I've ever / had to cope with. I can't see the way out." It was just the kind of nakedly confessional poem Elizabeth herself would never have written, and now he'd done it for her.

Cal wrote when it was too late, after publication, admitting, "I may owe you an apology for versing one of your letters." But he defended himself: "what could be as real" — Cal's highest aim — "as your own words . . . ?" He claimed the portrait of Elizabeth that emerged as he quoted further from the letter, a passage in which she pictured herself seeking the "faint blue glimmer" of daylight ahead "after hours of stumbling along" in a cave — "air never looked so beautiful before" — only "does you honor." But these weren't precisely Elizabeth's words. Inevitably he'd altered her sentences to fit his sonnet's blank verse meter and to suit his own purposes, as with the final lines in which Elizabeth addressed Cal gratefully: ". . . Your last letter helped, / like being mailed a lantern or a spiked stick." The imagery of Elizabeth's original letter had been still more "real," or realistic: "like being handed a lantern or a spiked walking stick."

Elizabeth never responded to his letter of apology, but when Cal asked her to read the manuscript of *The Dolphin* a year later, in February 1972, saying "I am going to publish, and don't want advice, except for yours," she did not hold back. Seventeen months before, in September 1970, as Elizabeth had been preparing for her first semester at Harvard, Cal had written with news from England: "I have someone else." He'd fallen in love with Lady Caroline Blackwood, a younger writer and an heir to the Guinness brewery fortune; he intended to leave his marriage. This Elizabeth could accept. She could even sympathize with the troubles that doubtless lay ahead; she'd had "someone else," and would soon have Alice. Both Cal and Elizabeth had sought young lovers. Then Cal began writing yet more sonnets, a verse diary of his marital collapse and simultaneous self-rejuvenation with Caroline, quoting passages from Lizzie's bitter, grief-stricken letters to achieve the crucial realism. These became *The Dolphin.*

Elizabeth had never been especially fond of Lizzie Hardwick, though like all of Cal's friends she understood that his second wife's loyalty through his many breakdowns and affairs had kept Cal alive and writing. Now her heart went out to Lizzie and Harriet, who could hardly take comfort in the companion volume of poems bearing their names that may have been Cal's idea of appeasement: republished sonnets of familial affection that marked, at best, a lull before the storm. *The Dolphin,* which would win Cal his second Pulitzer Prize, was where his energy was concentrated. Yet, while recognizing the strength of the poems, Elizabeth tried her best to persuade him not to publish — or to delay until the crisis had passed. The book was set to appear less than a year after his divorce and remarriage, two years after Sheridan, his son with Caroline, was born. Cal would not listen — "I couldn't bear to have my book (my life) wait inside me like a dead child."

Reading the manuscript of *The Dolphin,* named for Caroline — "My Dolphin, you only guide me by surprise," ran the first line of the closing sonnet — Elizabeth could see that Cal would do plenty of damage even without quoting his ex-wife's letters. Caroline, fifteen years younger than Lizzie, was also "my fresh wife," and a "Mermaid" of Cal's own dreams: "Alice-in-Wonderland straight gold hair, / fair-featured, curve and bone from crown to socks." But Elizabeth, who shared Cal's devotion to the real, or the "true," in her preferred term — "Poetry has got to be true," she'd once said in explaining her efforts to accurately represent a goat's eyes in "Crusoe in England" — built her case on the cannibalized letters, and Cal's deliberate alterations of them.

He'd written "magnificent," "honest poetry — *almost,*" she said of *The Dolphin* in manuscript. Elizabeth loved reading writers' letters; she'd taught a course in them at Harvard her second year. But Lizzie was still alive, she had not given permission — "aren't you violating a trust?" To use "personal, tragic, anguished letters" in this way — "it's cruel." And worse, Cal had "*changed* her letters" to fit his lines and to alter meaning, "loading the dice so against" Lizzie. In some passages the words didn't sound like Lizzie's; in others Elizabeth could read excisions and emendations on the page. "In general, I deplore the 'confessional,'" she told him, "when you wrote *Life Studies* perhaps it was a necessary movement, and it helped make poetry more real, fresh and immediate." But now, "anything goes," and Cal had gone too far, with borrowed lines like:

> "*I think of you every minute of the day,*
> *I love you every minute of the day;*
> *you gone is* hollow, bored, unbearable.
> *I feel under some emotional anaesthetic,*
> *unable to plan or think or write or feel . . .*"

Once again Cal was forcing someone else into public confession with words that purported to be her own, when in fact many were "made up." The damage to Lizzie, the wrong done to her as a writer as well as a devoted wife, would be irreversible — *"art just isn't worth that much."*

Cal responded defensively, insisting it was "the revelation" that troubled Elizabeth, not the misleading "mixture of truth and fiction" as she had charged. He claimed to have softened the letters already, and that by cutting them "drastically" he had painted Lizzie in a better light — "the original is heartbreaking, but interminable." He would re-arrange and revise yet again, turn Lizzie's words "milder," but "making the poem unwounding is impossible." Still, Elizabeth's emphatically phrased warning — "I love you so much I can't bear to have you publish something that I regret and that you might live to regret, too" — had pierced him. "Who can want to savage a thing," he asked, unable to find an answer. "How can I want to hurt?"

Elizabeth made her point about the letters one last time — "you've changed them — & you had no right to do that" — and then let the "painful subject" rest. Cal asked Elizabeth to be Sheridan's godmother, and Elizabeth was "delighted" to accept. They exchanged letters of concern and affection for Frank Bidart, "our Frankie" to Elizabeth, the young Harvard doctoral student and poet who knew Cal's sonnets so well he'd spent months in England with Cal, sorting out revisions and devising a proper sequence for more than five hundred poems, "gone over for about the thousandth time." In Cal's absence in Cambridge, Frank — a tall, clean-shaven Californian, whose urbanity belied his Ba-kersfield upbringing — had become Elizabeth's most reliable compan-ion after Alice. Frank had been the one to visit "every single day" while Alice was at work, bringing "quarts of vanilla ice-cream" and "$$$$$$ worth of coffee from the French coffee shop" during a week's hospital-ization for asthma at the end of Elizabeth's second term at Harvard, staying while she "talked his ear off" and "even wept" under the ef-fects of cortisone. But now Cal was returning to teach again at Harvard in the fall of 1973. In the end, he'd wangled a three-year leave. With the contract extending her employment through retirement age still unsigned, Elizabeth worried that her position might be in jeopardy. "Please, please don't let any of this academic stuff come between us to the slightest degree," she wrote to Cal when inquiring about his plans.

"I think we both need to keep our old friends — for the rest of our lives — don't you . . . ?" "We (you & I) are together till life's end," Cal replied. Elizabeth's contract was signed. She was a full-time professor now, with health benefits year-round.

Cal's three books appeared, and Lizzie *was* wounded. The influential weeklies — *Time, Newsweek,* the *New Republic* — reviewed *The Dolphin,* and the damage spread as Lizzie's versed letters were quoted and the marriage was dissected. Cal understood, as he hadn't before, that Lizzie didn't want to "think of herself as being injured," or have others see her that way. She became distraught; her friends sat suicide watch. "We dread the telephone," Cal wrote to Elizabeth from Milgate House, the centuries-old country house he'd bought with Caroline in Kent, forty miles from London. "Your old letter of warning — I never solved the problem of the letters," he admitted now. Indeed there was confusion over "fact and fiction," and Cal had willfully ignored the potential for "big circulation" magazines to "reduce my plot to news or scandal." It was "not enough," he knew, that Lizzie came off as "brilliant and lovable more than anyone in the book," and Cal as flawed, an errant husband. *The Dolphin* was as great a betrayal as his desertion of wife and daughter: "My sin (mistake?) was publishing."

Cal's admission of guilt, or of *feeling* guilty, earned Elizabeth's sympathy. "We all have irreparable and awful actions on our consciences," she wrote, commiserating. "I just try to live without blaming myself for them *every* day." Elizabeth knew she had wronged Lota, and perhaps also Lilli and Roxanne, who had followed her to Cambridge in hopes of a reconciliation, only to be firmly rebuffed. She'd disappointed herself, leaving books unfinished, essays unwritten, poems incomplete. "But for God's sake don't quote me!" Elizabeth made Cal promise. She could not quite trust him to leave her letters alone.

Elizabeth was writing her own poem now on the subject of shame and guilt, a "short, sad poem," she called it in her accompanying letter to Howard Moss in December 1973. "Five Flights Up" was based on a dream of Alice's treehouse apartment, as well as on a recollection of a neighbor, "the weird man who raises Corgies," shouting at his dogs on a summer day when Elizabeth had been writing at the Chauncy Street apartment with the windows open — "You ought to be ashamed of yourselves!" "Still dark," the poem begins, evoking the predawn hour she'd always loved:

> The unknown bird sits on his usual branch.
> The little dog next door barks in his sleep
> inquiringly, just once.
> Perhaps in his sleep, too, the bird inquires
> once or twice, quavering.
> Questions — if that is what they are —
> answered directly, simply,
> by day itself.

Later —

> The little black dog runs in his yard.
> His owner's voice arises, stern,
> "You ought to be ashamed!"
> What has he done?
> He bounces cheerfully up and down;
> he rushes in circles in the fallen leaves.
>
> Obviously, he has no sense of shame.
> He and the bird know everything is answered,
> all taken care of,
> no need to ask again.
> — Yesterday brought to today so lightly!
> (A yesterday I find almost impossible to lift.)

Cal had written five hundred confessional sonnets, baring his soul and others'. Everything Elizabeth wished to confess in a published poem was contained in a single parenthetical line. One day she would make it the final line in her last book of poems, *Geography III*.

She mailed a copy of "Five Flights Up" to Loren MacIver on the first day of January 1974, thanking her for putting up with "my ridiculous gloom last night," New Year's Eve, when Elizabeth had made a lonely, perhaps drunken, phone call. Alice was away visiting family friends in

Munich. Elizabeth asked Loren if she thought the new poem wasn't "just too sad & awful." Two days later Elizabeth was in Harvard's Stillman Infirmary, recovering from a fall on the staircase leading down from the bar at Casablanca, a restaurant near her Brattle Street apartment. She'd broken her shoulder again.

Sometimes a poem had to sneak up on her, emerging from a dream or an odd occurrence that sparked associations, or a combination of both, like "Five Flights Up," presenting an unlooked-for opportunity to set down preoccupations: the persistent feelings of regret and shame she'd acknowledged in her letter to Cal and found "almost impossible" to bear. In the poem, as in her letter, the feelings are both personal (though undisclosed) and part of the human condition. Unlike the barking dog or chirping bird — "We all have" them.

   Other times Elizabeth had to fool herself into writing, as with "Under the Window: Ouro Prêto," which began as a remembrance of her early stays with Lilli, a thank-you gift that took hold of her imagination and finished as a fully realized poem, the original impulse of gratitude left behind. Since returning to the United States, Elizabeth had revived old friendships with Frani Blough and Louise Crane, and

Snapshot of Cambridge backyards,
from Elizabeth's photo collection

deepened those with James Merrill and the poet John Malcolm Brinnin, whom she had first met at Yaddo in the 1940s. Frani had a husband
and grown children. Jimmy, John, and Louise, who'd finally settled
down with Victoria Kent, a Spanish Civil War exile with whom she'd
founded the journal *Iberica,* all had longtime romantic partners of the
same sex. All four had country homes that Elizabeth and Alice visited
frequently, especially John Brinnin's cottage on Duxbury Bay, an hour
south of Boston. After the spring of 1974, when there had been weekend visits to Duxbury as Elizabeth nursed her painful shoulder, and a
longer stay of nearly a month while John and his partner, Bill Read,
were away, Elizabeth began writing a poem that "started out as a sort
of joke thank-you-note" but turned serious.

She called the poem "The End of March," and she would dedicate
it to the couple in the pages of the *New Yorker,* once again persuading
Howard Moss to override the ban on dedications, especially "intramural" ones naming contributors to the magazine, like John Brinnin. The
poem had much in common with "At the Fishhouses" and "The Bight,"
Elizabeth's shoreline poems of the 1940s, opening with description
before turning to fanciful brooding and metaphysics — "thinking with
one's feelings," as she'd described the poet's task to May Swenson years
ago. But in "The End of March" she is not alone, not lonely. "It was cold
and windy," she recalls of an afternoon walk on the beach at Duxbury,
when the "rackety, icy, offshore wind / numbed our faces on one side."
The walkers — perhaps John, Bill, Alice, and Elizabeth — trek "along
the wet sand, in rubber boots" at low tide, following a trail of dog-prints
"so big / they were more like lion-prints." They come across "lengths
and lengths" of what appears to be kite string, wet and white, "looping
up to the tide-line, down to the water," finally ending in "a thick white
snarl, man-size, awash, / rising on every wave, a sodden ghost."

Passing the tangled apparition, she hopes to reach a remembered
house, one she'd seen on warmer days when walking the beach wasn't
so arduous: "my proto-dream-house / my crypto-dream-house, that
crooked box / set up on pilings, shingled green." Pressing on with her
friends, but thinking her own thoughts, she imagines making the house
hers:

I'd like to retire there and do nothing,
or nothing much, forever, in two bare rooms:
look through binoculars, read boring books,
old, long, long books, and write down useless notes,
talk to myself, and, foggy days,
watch the droplets slipping, heavy with light.

She'd make herself a *"grog à l'américaine"* and, to warm the drink, set the rum ablaze with a kitchen match and watch the "lovely diaphanous blue flame / . . . waver, doubled in the window." A solitary existence contemplated while among friends held no threat, even permitted the old fantasy that drinking alone would bring revelation rather than ruin.

Elizabeth had in fact just acquired a proto–dream house at the water's edge — in Boston's Lewis Wharf, a granite warehouse on a pier jutting out into the harbor, built at the height of the port's prosperity in the nineteenth century and fallen into disrepair in the twentieth. "The whole Boston waterfront is being renovated," she'd written to Anny Baumann, "and it is the *one* beautiful place to live." The massive four-story structure had been gutted by a developer who was selling luxury condominiums, a fresh concept in 1970s Boston real estate, with eighteen-inch-thick walls of exposed brick, beamed ceilings, and rusted iron bolts protruding from ancient oak uprights as innovative decor. Elizabeth had selected a top-floor apartment with a view east across the harbor and north to the mouth of the Mystic River.

When she'd signed the purchase agreement the year before, in March 1973, the apartment was still only a blueprint: bedroom, study, living room, galley kitchen, and six-by-twelve-foot "verandah." She'd visited the wharf and taken snapshots of the building's shell, learning that the granite blocks had been quarried in Quincy, Massachusetts, where her Bishop grandmother's family first settled; her seafaring Nova Scotian great-grandfather might have unloaded his ship's cargo at this very dock. Elizabeth knew she couldn't retire to Lewis Wharf and "do *nothing*" yet. The cost of the apartment was almost beyond her means (she'd been irked, on "women's lib" grounds, to find that banks were reluctant to grant mortgages to single women); she had not managed to sell Casa Mariana, though she'd made up her mind to let the Ouro Prêto house go. But Elizabeth would have her binoculars to observe passing ships, mostly tankers, and the smelt fishermen who worked at night under gasoline flares — "very pretty." She would read long books and watch the tide rise and fall.

And Alice, who would take over Elizabeth's Brattle Arms apartment in September when construction at Lewis Wharf was finished, would stay overnight and they'd have breakfasts in bed or on the verandah in warm weather. Alice, and all the new and old friends in her new American life, had made this possible. In their company she could walk past the floating "man-size" shroud — "falling back, sodden, giving up the ghost" — perhaps a reminder of the father she'd never known, and whose early death, possibly hastened by drink, had set in motion the cascade of events that "just happened to fail for me," as she'd summarized for Alice. To Alice she could admit, as she rarely had before to herself or anyone, always denying the early feeling and claiming each new instance as the first, that she had suffered from "homesickness"

View of East Boston from Elizabeth's Lewis Wharf
condominium, under construction, 1973

as a child: "once, age 6 — a constant heavy sensation in the pit of the stomach." This was how she'd felt when carried off to Worcester, leaving behind the grandparents she loved and the weekly packages it was her sad duty to mail, which nevertheless enabled her to maintain a tie to her mother. She'd wanted to hide the address of the asylum on those packages; she'd felt ashamed. But she'd been protected from shame as a small child in Great Village — "all taken care of" — before she was sent to live alone among strange family members and homesickness brought on the precocious self-awareness of "In the Waiting Room" that marked her for a poet.

In Duxbury at the end of March, the walkers turned back before reaching Elizabeth's proto-crypto dream house; "our faces froze on the other side." Surprising them all, the sun came out "for just a minute," and —

> *For just a minute, set in their bezels of sand,*
> *the drab, damp, scattered stones*
> *were multi-colored,*
> *and all those high enough threw out long shadows,*
> *individual shadows, then pulled them in again.*
> *They could have been teasing the lion sun,*
> *except that now he was behind them*
> *— a sun who'd walked the beach the last low tide,*
> *making those big, majestic paw-prints,*
> *who perhaps had batted a kite out of the sky to play with.*

Elizabeth wrote Howard Moss that "The End of March" was "my version of The Lake Isle of Innisfree," Yeats's masterpiece inspired by Thoreau's removal to Walden: "I will arise and go now, and go to Innisfree / And a small cabin build there," and "live alone in the bee-loud glade." Though Elizabeth considered herself much less the "hermit-type" than she once had been, like Thoreau and Yeats she heard the call to solitary creation "in the deep heart's core," and she could still respond, now and then, with a poem.

—⁓—

"I'd be a wreck without you," Elizabeth told Alice, and it seemed to be true. Collapses were nearly inevitable when Alice was away or when Elizabeth spent weeks or months alone in Ouro Prêto or Seattle. Alcohol wasn't the only problem. Bouts of asthma and recurrent dysentery, contracted in Brazil, weakened her system and made her susceptible to colds and flu; her teeth bothered her and required extractions, root canals, and bridges; rheumatism made walking or typing painful at times. For allergies she endured a series of weekly cortisone injections, only to find they'd aggravated her tendency to anemia. And she'd grown reliant on a combination of Nembutal for sleep and Dexamyl — "pep-up cheer-up pills" — to lift her spirits and dull her appetite. Elizabeth didn't want to risk losing Alice's interest by putting on pounds — "my age and physical decay" were bad enough. Metrecal was a staple, cigarettes a habit, and when Dexamyl was withdrawn from the market as a diet drug, she persuaded Dr. Warren Wacker at Harvard's University Health Services to continue prescribing the stimulant as an energy booster to ward off melancholy. Early in their love affair, by letter from Ouro Prêto, Elizabeth had warned Alice, too, not to get fat. She loved Alice's slim body, scarcely minded that she had "no breasts." Alice's "build" seemed attractively American, and Alice herself reminded Elizabeth pleasurably of "the north and Massachusetts ... and all those old things I used to know."

Though so much younger, Alice was the more practical of the two, "brave & sensible," as Elizabeth readily acknowledged. From afar Alice did her best to organize Elizabeth's daily life and manage her health problems: ordering her to take Antabuse pills regularly and go easy on the cigarettes and Nembutal; paying her bills (Elizabeth complained that "my mind closes up like a clam when business is discussed"); coaxing her to complete writing assignments, though Elizabeth never did turn in any reviews to the *New Yorker* after volunteering to serve as poetry critic when Louise Bogan died in 1970. Nor did Elizabeth finish her "long-procrastinated" book on Brazil, or complete the introduction to a volume of Sylvia Plath's letters to her mother, due for publication in 1975. In the last case, Elizabeth had been startled to find that so talented a poet could write such "insipid" and "superficial" letters; Elizabeth had not had a mother to humor with chatty letters like

Plath's. She could find nothing kind to say about them, and she jotted down several pages on letter writing in general before scrawling on her draft, "Gave up on this!"

But Elizabeth's needs organized Alice's days too, and Elizabeth had plans for Alice, who admitted to being in an Erik Erikson–style "identity crisis" over what to do with her life. Though she enjoyed the freedom of working on an academic calendar and having only genial "Uncle Arthur" Smithies to answer to, Alice was unsure whether to stay on as Kirkland House secretary. Should she go for an advanced degree in business or law? And there was the lure of family life, a direction her parents strongly favored. Alice wrote glowingly of time spent with friends who had children, and of touring Boston with a young godson.

Elizabeth told Alice she was "much too good for the job you have," even if she was "wonderful" at it, and she sympathized with Alice's quandary. "Being extremely interested in any one thing," as Elizabeth was in writing poetry, was a great advantage — "one of my really lucky breaks in this world" — but rare. Yet Elizabeth couldn't "imagine that just 'being married' . . . would be what you'd want to do, or be, most." Would Alice really like having "2 awful little American children who won't let the grown-ups talk," as in one family Alice had described? Alice was ambivalent about children herself. By the summer of 1974, four years into their alliance, Alice had quit her job at Harvard and enrolled in Boston University's new School of Management for the fall. At a time when women were agitating for equal access to medical, law, and business schools, it was a bold "Woms. Lib." move, yet one that could still satisfy Alice's Republican parents.

With Frank Bidart, who was teaching now at Wellesley College, Elizabeth split the cost of a summer rental on Maine's North Haven Island for two weeks in July. She'd answered a classified ad in the newspaper and come up with a vacation spot that was "almost too good to be true." The property was called Sabine Farm, and it offered "magnificent views" of Penobscot Bay and the Camden Hills from a capacious two-story gray-shingled house full of "high-brow books in 1st editions," she wrote to Howard Moss, with access to a rocky beach, rowboat, and sailing dinghy. The island had "one general store — the rest is fields and woods, very much like Nova Scotia — and birds & wildflowers." North

Haven proved to be "a haven for the *very* rich," but the island's summer people were inclined toward a familiar New England–style shabby gentility, and "somehow we have infiltrated."

Elizabeth, Alice, and Frank, who had brought over "bags and bags" of groceries on the ferry, kept mostly to themselves anyway. Frank became absorbed in the drama of the House Judiciary Committee's impeachment hearings against Richard Nixon unfolding on Sabine Farm's television set, while Elizabeth and Alice sampled the island's pebbled beaches. Relieved that impeachment seemed "pretty certain," Elizabeth nevertheless cursed the "*god damn TV*" blaring all day and the "false rhetoric, bombast, self-righteousness, *repetition*" of the lawyers and politicians. "If this is 'witnessing history' — I'd rather not," she wrote in her journal, and ran a bath in the late afternoon, happy to soak "in a hot tub — the wind blowing the curtains — dazzling light — drinking a Bloody Mary at the same time! — oh!"

A new friend, Lloyd Schwartz, a poet in Frank's graduate school class at Harvard, arrived to distract Frank with games of anagrams — "at least A's are *silent*," Elizabeth sighed in relief. The only one of her circle to have remained in Cambridge over the previous Christmas holiday, Lloyd had visited Elizabeth in Stillman Infirmary after her fall on

Frank Bidart and Elizabeth on the ferry from Rockland
to North Haven Island, Maine, 1974

the stairs at Casablanca, and their friendship deepened; soon he would ask Elizabeth's permission to write his doctoral dissertation on her poetry, the first at Harvard. Elizabeth's career still wasn't what she'd hoped — she could still be "cast into gloom" by the thought of her more prolific peers, as she once confessed to Jimmy Merrill — but her reputation had gained luster since her return from Brazil. She'd received honorary degrees from Brown and Rutgers; a scholar was at work on a bibliography. She'd had her portrait taken by celebrity photographer Thomas Victor for a glossy coffee-table book called *Preferences,* edited by Richard Howard, in which "fifty-one American poets choose poems from their own work and from the past." Elizabeth had selected "In the Waiting Room" and George Herbert's "Love Unknown," but she tore her photo out of the book when it arrived in the mail, believing she looked old and bloated from cortisone treatments.

Often Elizabeth fought the feeling that it might be "too late," as she wrote of her desire to master the Peterson Field Guides to birds and wildflowers, and another volume on beach pebbles she'd brought with her to Maine. "I want now — now that it's too late — to learn the name of *everything.*" She satisfied herself that summer of 1974 with identifying every flower she could see growing in the meadow within several feet of her front porch: yellow goat's-beard, lesser stitchwort, Queen Anne's lace, white clover, ox-eye daisy, red clover, rabbit's-foot clover, lobelia, blue-eyed grass, wild radish, creeping bellflower, wild lupine, mullein, purslane, chicory, common morning glory, beach pea, white rosa rugosa, rosa rugosa, fragrant bedstraw, cow or tufted vetch, common Saint John's wort, eyebright, lesser pyrola.

Still suffering insomnia, Elizabeth found herself waking at dawn while her young lover, a heavy sleeper, and their two friends slept on. Frank often couldn't be roused until past noon. Elizabeth made notes for a poem, "Late Sleepers": "Dreams they'll never need or use. . . . But they are busy, busy their eyelids move // They are at work, these dreamers — . . . sorting, discarding."

> *The dreams are working, working —*
> *discarding love*

She'd had a premonition, or was it only her inclination to borrow trouble? Alice started graduate school; her mind was filled with numbers, tax laws — she said she liked the work. At Christmas, Elizabeth and Alice took their holiday together, visiting the once-gamine, now — appallingly, to Elizabeth — overweight Louise Crane at her seaside estate in Fort Myers Beach, Florida. There was no collapse. Instead, with Alice, there had been a "sailing trip — 3 days, 2 nights — Saw the *white pelicans,*" Elizabeth recorded in her journal. They made plans to come back next year. Only Elizabeth returned.

Elizabeth had first brought up the subject of her will with Alice in the late spring of 1971, writing from São Lucas Hospital in Belo Horizonte where she was recuperating from dysentery that had been diagnosed, erroneously she would learn, as typhoid fever. Her love for Alice was new; they hadn't yet made their first trip together, to the Galápagos. Nevertheless Elizabeth asked: would Alice agree to be "one of the trustees . . . (or whatever it is)"? Alice consented, "on the condition that you not die for a long, long time." The prospect of going on without Elizabeth in her life was "so scary & awful I refuse to consider it further." Even at a distance, Elizabeth was powerfully alive to Alice. A year later, when Elizabeth was in Ouro Prêto for what would be her last extended stay, Alice wrote with the direct but demure passion they both indulged in their letters, "Could I be suffering from a bad case of LUST? Likely . . . My body wants yours!"

Before leaving for Seattle in the spring of 1973, Elizabeth named Alice in her will as sole beneficiary of all but her library, which would go to Frank Bidart. The bequest, including future royalties on Elizabeth's books, Casa Mariana and the Lewis Wharf condominium, and the Bishop trust that had provided Elizabeth a small but steady income for so long, took Alice by surprise. "Just knowing you is enough of a legacy for me," she wrote to Elizabeth finally. "I love you and admire you and enjoy you and have learned from you — that is enough." The night she wrote, Alice had been watching *The Waltons,* the "syrupy" family drama, on television and she'd had a good cry: "Goodness knows what the future will bring." Having Elizabeth's love meant so much more than real estate or money, which Alice, an idealistic thirty-year-old, promised to donate to a cause Elizabeth would approve if she didn't "really" need it. And "you know I will always care and do what I think you will want done." Elizabeth had appointed Alice literary executor along with Frank, giving Alice the final word in case of dispute. "So, thank you, Darling, for your confidence in me," Alice wrote. "I will try with all my might to live up to it."

But that was nearly two years ago. Turning thirty-two in the spring of 1975, after five years together, Alice still loved Elizabeth "best" and "For Always." Yet Elizabeth was drinking to the point of collapse even with Alice nearby. Her apologies and vows to reform, passionately expressed, had become predictable and unconvincing, almost worse than not saying she was sorry: "Please forgive me for being such a mess sometimes, Alice," "I wish I had as much self-discipline as you have," "I am going to try to respect myself a little more, honestly," "I am sorry — terribly sorry." The "excessive unconscious demands" Elizabeth had warned Alice against by quoting Melanie Klein were breaking through beyond Elizabeth's control and overwhelming Alice.

In July 1975, Elizabeth returned for a second summer on North Haven, while Alice stayed behind in Cambridge to attend summer classes, visiting on weekends. An old friend from Walnut Hill School, Rhoda Wheeler, divorced and living with her children on family property in Rhode Island, drove Elizabeth to Maine, but after Rhoda left, Elizabeth felt helpless with no car or driver. When Alice arrived, she brought guests, and the two were rarely alone. Elizabeth rationed her remaining green pills, the Dexamyl that her doctors were increasingly reluctant to prescribe. She was tired and fell asleep in the evening. She attempted a poem:

> — *To have no personal moods at all, to have*
> *only the same moods that the weather has*
> *here on North Haven Island — that would be*
> *the (perfect) temperament, ~~for the rest of life~~ the rest of life)*

Her journal entries were sparse. She added to the list of wildflowers in the front meadow: common evening primrose, bladder campion, harebell. But when she sat on the front porch her eyes were fixed on the line of fir trees "between us & the water" that her landlady "hates so" for obstructing the view. Elizabeth studied them: "the *last reality,* looking out to the bay — which is quite unreal. Vaporous, dream-like — an unknown. Only the fir trees are real — & *alive,* too — in the strong winds we've been having — moving, rushing, sometimes trying to get away — next to, against the sudden change to an atmospheric, imaginary world —" What was fixed, permanent, real — and what was not? Even the trees, the *last reality,* seemed poised for escape.

Before she left for North Haven, Elizabeth had written down further instructions to Alice about her will. "Frank gets the books. . . . But you take out whatever you want first . . . & a book or two to Lloyd." Alice was free to "sell all my papers — if you can!" Something impelled her to write out the half page in longhand of hardly necessary advice: "*Keep* Loren's paintings if you want them" — Loren MacIver's portrait of Elizabeth, and those Lota had collected — "Or *sell,*" signing her full name, Elizabeth Bishop.

Three months later, on October 8, Elizabeth typed two long pages, another addendum to her will, addressed to "Dearest Alice." Now there *was* need. The two women had separated. Alice had someone else, a man named Peter.

"Don't be alarmed," Elizabeth told Alice. "I'm not expecting to die today or even tomorrow — right now I'm planning no drastic changes in my life at all." Yet the letter must have weighed heavily on Alice as she attempted to make a break the only way she knew how, the only way Elizabeth would accept as final. "Forgive me," Elizabeth wrote. "Love me if you can and remember me as kindly as you can."

Elizabeth wanted Alice to know that she would remain her sole beneficiary. "This holds good no matter where you are or what you are doing, etc. — married or single, etc., at the time I die." Did Alice hear in these words the echo of a poem Elizabeth had written long ago and dedicated to Louise Crane, "Letter to N.Y.," after the first painful rejection Elizabeth had suffered, the one she sometimes said had inured her to all others?

> *In your next letter I wish you'd say*
> *where you are going and what you are doing;*

how are the plays, and after the plays
what other pleasures you're pursuing . . .

"I want you to be happy and good and loved," she wrote to Alice now, feigning good cheer. Happiness was mostly "a matter of luck," Elizabeth thought, "even with a happy disposition like yours." Elizabeth herself had been prone to "bad luck — but it couldn't be helped, really." And "until quite recently I think I've managed to cope with disasters, etc. fairly well."

Elizabeth turned to Alice now as "the only 'family' I have and like these days." She'd neglected to specify in her will the wish to be cremated, then buried with "no services at all, please" in the "cheapest kind of pine box" next to her parents in Worcester's Hope Cemetery. It would fall to Alice, as well, to administer the twenty Nembutal that Elizabeth planned to store away in the event of an incapacitating accident, stroke, or terminal cancer. Elizabeth wasn't feeling well, "at least I never seem to feel the way I know I shd. & used to." Perhaps something was seriously wrong. She was sixty-four; neither of her parents and few of her aunts or uncles had lived so long. Alice must please "let me — or if necessary — *help* me, die." Or let Dr. Baumann "pull the plug" — "I'm serious about this — *practical,* I hope, not morbid." As for a good "cause," if Alice wanted to give away some of her inheritance, Elizabeth asked her to consider the Charles Darwin Research Center in the Galápagos Islands, where Alice and Elizabeth had swum from a beach populated by flamingos and Elizabeth had been the first to spot a tiny, "ruby-like" vermilion flycatcher — "my one triumph" — on their trip four years earlier.

The will gave Elizabeth an excuse to write to Alice, who urged Elizabeth to become less "attached." Perhaps Elizabeth also hoped the letter — a dignified, legalistic pleading — could change Alice's mind. It didn't.

The week before Elizabeth wrote her letter, perhaps before Alice delivered her awful news, Elizabeth had sketched a "self-portrait" for a collector who was gathering hand-drawn images from eminent poets, among them her friends — Jimmy Merrill, May Swenson, Howard Moss — and new acquaintances, Octavio Paz, Richard Howard,

John Ashbery. Though she had skill as an artist, Elizabeth chose not to sketch her face but instead to trace the outline of her left hand. The fingers were crooked and swollen, and she'd signed the sketch, "With best wishes, rheumatically, Elizabeth Bishop." But on her ring finger she'd whimsically drawn an enormous sparkling diamond, labeling it "imaginary"; on her fifth finger she'd outlined a heavy ring of woven metal.

Was the "real" ring the gold one Lota had given her to mark their commitment to each other in 1951, the one she still often wore? Or another, a gift from Alice? Elizabeth had selected a moss agate for Alice at a gem shop in Ouro Prêto during their second summer apart, to be set in a ring with small diamonds on either side. Alice might have reciprocated with a ring of her own. In Elizabeth's self-portrait, the large diamond was fantastical, both in its size and in its presence, marking an engagement she'd never had or wanted. After October 8, the woven metal ring was no more real than the diamond—whether it marked a lost attachment to Lota or to Alice.

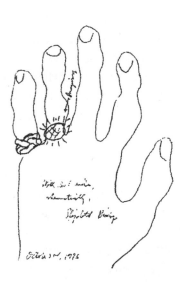

Elizabeth's self-portrait, October 2, 1975, from the
self-portrait collection of Burt Britton

"I wish I'd been able to write more and better poems these last few years," Elizabeth mourned in her October 8 letter to Alice. "And poems *for* you. Well, who knows, something may come along. . . ." And something did. "One Art" began with a prosy first draft titled "How to Lose Things": "One might begin by losing one's reading glasses / oh 2 or 3 times a day — or one's favorite pen." The list lengthened and gathered mass with lost houses, an island and a peninsula, an entire continent, until reaching a plaintive coda —

> *One might think this would have prepared me*
> *for losing one average-sized not exceptionally*
> *beautiful or dazzlingly intelligent person*
> *(except for blue eyes)*
> *But it doesn't seem to have, at all . . .*

Here was the poem *for* Alice, now that it was too late.

In the second of seventeen drafts Elizabeth turned out rapidly during the month of October, the poem took shape as a villanelle — Elizabeth's "one and only," she later said — with its first stanza nearly finished:

> *The art of losing isn't hard to master:*
> *so many things seem to be meant*
> *to be lost that their loss is no disaster.*

The first line remained the same in each successive draft, and it was repeated almost exactly at regular intervals through six stanzas, following the villanelle form, in the final version she mailed to Howard Moss at the end of the month. It was the third line, also required by the form to repeat, that Elizabeth varied, just as the disasters in her life had varied. Some were insignificant, like the minor mishaps Brazilians called *desastres*. She listed lost door keys, misspent hours, forgotten travel plans: "None of these will bring disaster." Then, as in her first draft, the stakes escalated, "losing farther, losing faster," and the losses mounted: my mother's watch, three loved houses, two cities, two rivers, a continent. "I miss them, but it wasn't a disaster."

As late as draft eleven, the loss of Alice still registered in the poem's concluding stanza as the one misfortune Elizabeth could not withstand: "My losses haven't been too hard to master / with this exception (Say it!) this disaster." Or, in an alternate version of the same draft:

> *I wrote a lot of lies. It's evident*
> *the art of losing isn't hard to master*
> *with one exception.* (Write it!) *Write "disaster."*

But, though she later described "One Art" as "pure emotion," Elizabeth guarded her feelings in the final version's last stanza, pretending bravery. And she merged the two great disasters of her adult life, leaving out Alice's blue eyes and selecting physical characteristics she'd loved in both Alice and Lota:

> *— Even losing you (the joking voice, a gesture*
> *I love) I shan't have lied. It's evident*
> *the art of losing's not too hard to master*
> *though it may look like* (Write *it!*) *like disaster.*

By draft fifteen, the poem had acquired its title, "One Art." Elizabeth had been practicing the art of losing since infancy; art had become her one means of mastery. "One Art" was the elegy she had wanted for so long to write.

"Upsetting and sad" as the poem was, Howard Moss wrote in early November 1975 accepting "One Art" for publication, Elizabeth had established "just the right amount of distance." Yet once it was finished, Elizabeth had nothing left to defend against her loss, no way of maintaining that distance. She sent the poem in typescript to friends, but their reactions — "it makes everyone weep, so I think it must be rather good," she wrote to Katharine White — weren't enough. And by December she'd received another "blow." Alice planned to marry Peter.

Alice drove Elizabeth to the airport in a snowstorm on December 21, letting her go alone to Fort Myers Beach, where Louise Crane, who was vacationing elsewhere this year, had offered her guesthouse to

Elizabeth as a warm-weather refuge. Alice may have offered to drive Elizabeth after receiving yet another "Postscript" to Elizabeth's will, dated December 18. Or she might have returned to the Brattle Arms to find Elizabeth's letter waiting for her there. Something caused Alice to initiate phone contact with Elizabeth, calling to check on her three times during the first week of Elizabeth's planned monthlong vacation.

The brief letter was alarming. Elizabeth's pretext was forwarding a packet of information on the Galápagos foundation, but she returned to the grim instructions of her longer letter of October 8: "Since I'll be taking my ten or eleven sleeping pills with me — I can't give you a supply for the emergencies referred to. However, I still count on you always to do the humane and sensible thing by me, *somehow*." And: "One morbid afterthought — if I shd. happen to die in Florida — not that I expect to," Alice should have her cremated there and the ashes sent to Worcester. Finally: "Please love me and try to forgive me. I have loved you — and love you now — more than anything in the world."

At first it was easier to be "*away* from it all," as she wrote Anny Baumann from Florida, and for ten days she had the company of Rhoda Wheeler, "a good sailor," who'd flown down in hopes of a three-day cruise like last year's with Alice. But the weather was "too cold and windy," and they managed only an afternoon's sail. Elizabeth mailed a Christmas card on December 24 to Robert Fitzgerald, who'd helped arrange a medical leave when Elizabeth realized she couldn't face teaching in the spring: "It's cold for here, but sunny. Best wishes & love to you and Penny & *many thanks*." Two weeks later, she sent Robert a postcard; Elizabeth had been relieved to learn that Cal, too, had obtained a semester's leave after suffering "another really bad breakdown." The postcard, purchased at a wildlife sanctuary she'd visited with Rhoda, pictured a stuffed and mounted red-tailed hawk: the "handsome" birds were frequently killed as "chicken hawks," the caption read. "Help conserve them." The swamplands were "*beautiful*," Elizabeth reported to Robert, "it's been lonely since."

Elizabeth was on her own now and intending to "WORK," she wrote to Anny Baumann, but she was "desperately unhappy; can't work, can't sleep — & can't *eat*." Dr. Baumann's "idea of being cheerful, ignoring everything, and pretending that nothing is wrong," typical of the firm-handed physician, wasn't helping at all — "much too optimistic!" Without Alice, there was no one in whom she could confide. Elizabeth still kept the facts of her private life secret. Though her friends in Boston were anxious about her, "they don't know the story," she told Dr. Baumann, "or perhaps *do* intuitively, I don't know." Even in letters to Anny, Elizabeth would not refer to Alice by name, only as "the friend I am so concerned about." Of course Elizabeth drank. Of course she consumed too many pills in one nearly lethal dose.

Since Lota's death, thoughts of suicide had rarely been far from Elizabeth's mind, though her concern was nearly always for the bereaved. Even with an ambiguous death brought on by an "accident of an unconscious-suicide kind, a sudden impulse," as she'd judged Randall Jarrell's fatal walk on the highway and possibly Lota's overdose, Elizabeth knew how feelings of responsibility and guilt inevitably spread to survivors. After John Berryman leapt from a bridge in 1972 and Anne Sexton succumbed to carbon monoxide poisoning in her garage in 1974, she'd moaned to Howard Moss, "Oh dear, oh dear — I wish people would *stop* doing this." Yet Elizabeth harbored a recurrent desire, she'd once confided in Alice, "to pass quite out of the picture from time to time," to perform a vanishing act without serious consequences. During the season of her double collapse in Ouro Prêto, she'd welcomed a "stupendous thunderstorm" that descended with biblical force on the town, she'd written to Alice, hoping "I might get struck by lightning — a dramatic demise, don't you think — & so good for book-sales." Alice had easily read the desperation in Elizabeth's fantasy and scolded her: wishing to be struck by lightning was "*not* ok. . . . Cut that out!"

In the past year, Elizabeth's attitude toward suicide had shifted as she looked ahead to old age and increasing "decrepitude." Her longtime friend Lloyd Frankenberg, Loren McIver's husband, who had been in and out of hospitals for years with a seemingly uncontrollable mania, had died that spring after taking an overdose of sleeping pills. "I think this was a wise decision for him, really," she'd written to Jimmy Merrill, who knew the couple too. There were times when suicide was the rational, even honorable choice. Elizabeth had translated a poem by her Brazilian friend Manuel Bandeira called "My Last Poem," in which he envisioned his final opus: it would have "the purity of the flame in which the most limpid diamonds are consumed," and "the passion of suicides who kill themselves without explanation." Was Elizabeth ready to leave "One Art" as her last work?

Elizabeth's brush with death in Florida in mid-January 1976 was not the result of a "decision," or she would have succeeded. That month, Elizabeth called Frank Bidart to say she was fighting an impulse to throw herself under a passing car. She did not do it. "One Art" was no suicide note. The poem's concluding lines underscored Elizabeth's fortitude. On January 13, neighbors discovered Elizabeth passed out on the floor in Louise Crane's beach house and rushed her to the hospital. Soon Elizabeth was apologizing again for "having behaved so stupidly," for being "an awful fool," as she had after so many drunken collapses. She returned to Boston earlier than planned, and pled with Robert Fitzgerald and Dr. Wacker, who'd approved her medical leave, for the chance to teach in the spring after all, though it was too late.

In the months after Lota's death, Cal had written to Mary McCarthy of Elizabeth's "ox-like power of character and imagination which nothing can break"; Elizabeth herself had told Alice in the early months of their love affair that she need never worry about her, she was "made of iron." Elizabeth wasn't that strong anymore; her recurrent dysentery or some unnamed ailment lingered. But she had plans — to write a "more cheerful poem," as she told Anny Baumann. Elizabeth's bleak December "Postscript" to her will mentioned her "modest" expectations for a new book, *Geography III*. She'd like to see it in print.

And Elizabeth didn't want to lose Alice. Although it had once seemed an unbearable prospect, they could still be friends. Elizabeth would manage as long as "you'll *talk* to me," she wrote to Alice from Florida while recovering from her collapse. "I DO want you to be free, darling — that wouldn't ever make me stop loving you." And: "You can always have me back if ever you should want me . . . truly."

No one could say what changed Alice's mind. It wasn't Elizabeth's near suicide. As late as the end of February, Elizabeth was still weepy, writing to Robert Fitzgerald that she'd cried over his memoir in the *New Yorker.* Robert's fond recollection of his father, a sometime alcoholic who'd died in Robert's adolescence, struck a chord. Elizabeth's own father's terminal illness might have been aggravated by drink. Now here she was, ruining her life the same way, and with no child — no "Baby" — to forgive her.

Lloyd Schwartz heard later that Elizabeth "promised everything" to Alice — no more drinking. Perhaps Alice never really wanted to marry, only to escape the wearying cycle of Elizabeth's binge drinking, and to please the "Ancients," her parents. In early March, at the end of a week's stay in New York for the premiere of Elliott Carter's song cycle *A Mirror on Which to Dwell,* with six of her poems as lyrics, and to see an infectious disease specialist, Elizabeth sprained her ankle badly on the sidewalk. Alice met her at the airport in Boston, drove her to Stillman Infirmary for x-rays, and brought her home. Alice would not marry. They were together again.

By late spring they'd made a plan to travel to Europe that summer — Alice with her parents on a family vacation, Elizabeth to visit Cal in England — and then meet in Lisbon afterward to tour Portugal by rental car. Elizabeth had won a $10,000 prize — the Neustadt International Prize for Literature — a first for a woman or an American, and she could afford the trip. "I like being with you more than anyone else in the whole world," Alice wrote Elizabeth in early June from a Norwegian cruise ship packed with senior citizens. She wondered if she liked being with her parents *"least —* it's close."

Elizabeth's reunion with Alice and other boons of 1976 — the Neustadt Prize, her European trip, the upcoming publication of *Geography III,* and a "very smart" Advanced Verse Writing class in the fall, the last she was scheduled to teach — almost compensated for the imminent termination of her Harvard contract at the end of the spring 1977 semester. After six years in the job, Elizabeth no longer thought of herself as "a scared elderly amateur 'professor,'" as she had during her first term in Cambridge. No longer did she wake in the night with dreams like the one she'd reported to Alice, in which she'd ordered her students to go spend an hour in the Harvard Square Woolworth's, then come back to write about the items they'd seen. Their poems "lacked 'reality,'" she'd railed at them.

In the classroom during waking hours, Elizabeth addressed her students by surname — Miss Agoos, Mr. Sorensen — and tried to be tactful, believing that "the more polite the teacher, the more polite the students." Teaching writing, a phrase she placed in quotation marks, still seemed a dubious enterprise. "Group reading, group discussion, all this going over and over and over, usually strikes me as a wasteful form of time-passing or therapy, with little or no connection to writing," she'd groused in a teaching evaluation for a faculty member under review at MIT in December 1976. But she admitted that "some students do learn a lot in writing classes and . . . their writing does improve." The class she observed met her standards for decorum: "no one seemed aggressive or rude and no one's feelings seemed to get hurt." She hoped the MIT students, all male, might in the end "produce better-written scientific papers, or letters to their wives, or read a few good books a year, or at least feel respect for people who chose to spend their lives writing prose or poetry rather than working at more 'practical' things."

This year in Elizabeth's Harvard class there were "two really witty boys" for whom she held out hope, and she'd maintained friendships with other promising students, mostly young men — Jonathan Galassi; the angelic Irish boy, Mark O'Donnell; and her favorite, John Peech, a graduate student in physics whose poems she pressed on Howard Moss at the *New Yorker* with some success. Why, Elizabeth wondered in a letter to Alice, had she been "scared to death of 'boys' when I was at the age I should have been wild about them — was afraid to talk to them, etc — and suffered hells," and now, "forty years too late," she found herself perfectly at ease. In January she invited the class to Lewis Wharf for a first-ever semester's end party, along with the older young men who were her close friends — Frank Bidart, Lloyd Schwartz, and the Brazilian poet Ricardo Sternberg, a junior member of Harvard's elite Society of Fellows.

The day after the party, she flew to New York on the 3 p.m. shuttle for the National Book Critics Circle Awards reception in the Time-Life Building's auditorium, then caught an 8 p.m. flight home. Elizabeth had won the prize in poetry for *Geography III*. It was the first time she'd accepted a book award in person. The slender volume was made up of the nine extraordinary poems of the past decade, among them "In the Waiting Room," "Poem," "The Moose," "Crusoe in England," "Five Flights Up," "The End of March," and "One Art." As May Swenson had written after reading "Questions of Travel" in the *New Yorker,* "Those are bulls' eyes only E.B. can hit." Maybe now she'd have a chance at an extension on her Harvard contract.

But it was not to be. Not even Robert Fitzgerald could successfully appeal Dean Henry Rosovsky's decree that, since "Miss Elizabeth Bishop will pass her 66th birthday during the academic year 1976–77 . . . no further appointment should be recommended." Elizabeth had been a diffident teacher of "creative writing," another phrase she despised, along with the trendy term "creativity," and her literature seminars attracted only a handful of students each year. Many were scared off by her requirement to memorize poetry each week and unimpressed by her attention to the surface action — the "subject matter" — of the poems discussed in class. She refused to teach the poetry of John Ashbery, whose *Self-Portrait in a Convex Mirror* won the Pulitzer Prize in 1976, saying she couldn't understand him. This was the "age of poet-teachers," Cal had once said, but Elizabeth wasn't one of them. Her poetic gift had come to her early in a time of need, and

Elizabeth's portrait by Thomas Victor, in *Preferences,* 1974

she had nurtured it, as it had nurtured her, not in the classroom but in solitude — in libraries and apartments in New York City, in rented rooms and a white house in Key West, in an *estudio* in Brazil, and now in a "new home, alone, and on the ocean," as Cal described her Lewis Wharf apartment. How could she advise students to do otherwise?

Cal was younger — just sixty that spring of 1977. Retirement wouldn't catch up to him for another six years, and he'd "looked awfully well — younger even," when she visited him at Milgate House outside London the past summer, although it was his breakdown two months later that had given Elizabeth her verse-writing class. She never taught a workshop the same semester as Cal, not wishing to compete for the top students or spread thin the ranks of the talented. But they compared rosters, and inevitably "a lot of your ex-es" found their way into her courses, Elizabeth told Cal. The creative writing students at Harvard were a self-selecting and sometimes cliquish bunch, accustomed to anointing each other with membership in the college's literary societies — the Signet and the *Advocate*'s staff. It paid to follow Cal's lead, she'd learned at the start of her first semester in 1970 when James Atlas came to see her at Kirkland House with his girlfriend, Peggy Rizza, pleading her case after Elizabeth failed to admit her to the class when she'd been accepted to Cal's twice before. Peggy "looked tragic," Elizabeth relented, and the girl held her own with what Cal had judged "quite sensitive, low-keyed poems" in a group that included Atlas, R. D. Rosen, Jonathan Galassi, and Ezra Pound's grandson, Siegfried Walter "Sizzo" de Rachewiltz. Still, Elizabeth had been annoyed to discover, when students moved from her class to Cal's, that "my best pupils are now handing in their poems — the ones I know by heart, almost — all over again, to him." She didn't fault Cal for this, rather the students, who seemed to "think if they can only manage to take the course enough times, *some* poet is going to like the poems."

Cal's health had deteriorated by the time he reached Cambridge to teach in the spring, making up for the fall semester he'd forfeited because of a late-summer breakdown. He'd arrived without Caroline, who'd proved nearly as psychologically unstable and prone to drink as he. Alcohol combined with mania to make Cal delusional; Caroline turned hostile, vituperative. In the fall they'd attempted to live and write together in the Cambridge house they'd rented for what was meant to be Cal's teaching semester, bringing five-year-old Sheridan and Caroline's daughters along, but tensions ran so high Cal soon moved out to Frank Bidart's apartment. Caroline had taken the children back to England in December. Cal still loved his "dolphin," he told Lizzie, with whom he was back on speaking terms, and wanted the marriage to work, but the strain had been enormous. He missed his first classes of the semester, hospitalized for congestive heart failure.

Cal recovered, after doctors drained the fluid from his lungs that his heart, weakened by a mild heart attack the previous fall, could no longer pump efficiently. Elizabeth cooked him a birthday dinner — "LAMB," she recorded in her datebook — on March 1, and they shared other meals through the spring as Elizabeth finished out her year, teaching a prose-writing class as well as her customary seminar, Subject Matter in Twentieth-Century Poetry. Often when they met, "it seemed as if almost thirty years had rolled back," as Cal had written after the summer's visit at Milgate House. The two poets, shy about "talking emotionally," experienced a "lonely warmth," Cal thought, as on the day in Stonington so many years ago: "no need to stop talking, and always when the talk stops it starts." But Elizabeth's own failing health kept her from visiting Cal's class that spring to give a reading, as she had two years before when an imbalance of lithium made Cal's attendance erratic, bringing both Frank Bidart and Elizabeth to his aid. Five days after the lamb dinner, Elizabeth had vomited in a way that *"hurt,"* and by the end of term in May, she was under observation in Phillips House, the private-care wing at Massachusetts General Hospital where Cal had been treated in February. She remembered convalescing there after her appendectomy at age twelve, sponsored by her wealthy Bishop grandfather and under the watchful care of Aunt Grace Bulmer, who'd risen to become superintendent of the Phillips House nursing staff before returning to Nova Scotia to marry.

The previous summer Elizabeth had spent twelve days in Cambridge Hospital after an attack of asthma on the flight home from Lisbon left her gasping for breath and unable to walk. Frank, who'd met Elizabeth and Alice at Logan Airport, was sure she was dying in her wheelchair. But Elizabeth, who knew that particular menace intimately, had been certain she'd survive. This was different. Doctors discovered a hiatal hernia, the cause of the ongoing discomfort she'd taken for dysentery or some lingering tropical disease. The disturbance in her lower esophagus had gone undiagnosed for so long that she'd become severely anemic; the hernia had begun to bleed. Transfusions helped restore the balance of red blood cells, and iron pills were prescribed in high doses.

On Mother's Day, Alice, Lloyd, and Frank (for whom she'd once confessed "*motherly*" feelings to Cal) visited her room overlooking the Charles. The next day a freak snowstorm blanketed New England, but the following Sunday she'd been permitted an afternoon with Alice at Mount Auburn Cemetery — "trees & lilacs wonderful." They'd hunted unsuccessfully for the graves of Henry, William, and Alice James in the family plot at Cambridge Cemetery across the road. Two days later she was "allowed OUT!" and by June Elizabeth was taking in a screening of *Star Wars* and preparing for the annual North Haven vacation, expanded to two months this year.

Cal was in Maine that summer too, staying with Lizzie and Harriet, taking refuge from the new life he'd chosen. "I think on clear days you can see Castine from the northern shore" of North Haven, he'd written to Elizabeth, though they did not visit each other. She'd been working on a poem called "Santarém," after the village where the Amazon and the Tapajós Rivers flow together, "grandly, silently." She remembered the place vividly from her first Brazilian river trip almost twenty years before: "That golden evening I really wanted to go no farther." Lingering in the town of "stubby palms, flamboyants like pans of embers," and one-story "blue or yellow" stucco houses, and wading through streets "deep in dark-gold river sand / damp from the ritual afternoon rain," she'd heard about a thunderstorm the week before. Lightning struck the cathedral tower, leaving "a widening zig zag crack all the way down." The priest's house next door had been hit too, his brass bed "galvanized black." By a "miracle" — "*Graças a deus* — he'd been in Belém."

As Elizabeth worked over the poem in early September and prepared for a verse-writing course she'd agreed to teach that fall at New

York University, she learned the dreadful news. Cal had flown to Ireland, where Caroline had bought an apartment in a grand country house outside Dublin, for a ten-day visit during which he'd hoped to settle matters between them, only to have Caroline depart in a rage. Returning to the United States, Cal succumbed to a heart attack in the back seat of the cab carrying him to Lizzie's Manhattan apartment. "When you are dying, and your faith is sick," Cal had quoted one of Lizzie's accusatory letters in *The Dolphin,* "you will look for the love you fumbled."

The City of Boston installed a historic marker on Cal's boyhood home at 91 Revere Street even before he died. Robert Lowell was a celebrity. *Time* sent a reporter, Elizabeth's and Cal's former student James Atlas, to cover the funeral. Six hundred mourners and curiosity seekers filled Beacon Hill's Church of the Advent. Elizabeth sat up front with the two wives, Lizzie and Caroline, and her godson Sheridan. The hymns were not hers, and she would not receive communion in the solemn high-church Episcopal requiem service; Caroline took Sheridan outside during the ritual. Elizabeth passed up a place in the caravan to the private graveside ceremony at the family burial ground in New Hampshire, and instead held a reception at Lewis Wharf, crowded with friends not invited to the interment, among them the critic Helen Vendler and the poet Alan Williamson. Elizabeth had once told Alice she never got drunk at her own parties, and she was true to her word. But at a second gathering late in the day, at the home of Cal's old friend and distant cousin, the documentary film maker Bob Gardner, one of ten pallbearers along with Frank Bidart and Robert Fitzgerald, she gave in.

Since their first meeting at Randall Jarrell's New York apartment in 1947, there had been an unquenchable attraction. Cal was Elizabeth's opposite, and her double. On that day Elizabeth, who'd been awarded rare A-pluses at Walnut Hill School for neatness, was charmed by slovenly, rakish, thirty-year-old Cal — "your dishevelment, your lovely curly hair." Cal remembered Elizabeth, at thirty-six, as "shy but full of des[cription] and anecdote as now." Three decades and more than four hundred letters later, writing Elizabeth to declare the manuscript of his *Day by Day* "done," Cal told her his last book was "the opposite" of her *Geography III,* "bulky, rearranged, added-to, deleted two months after submission — as though the unsatiated appetite were demanding a solid extra course when dinner was meant to be over." Even as Cal predictably feared he was "spoiling" his poems by reworking them, "I already miss their presence pressing on me to change, polish, do more." By contrast, he wrote Elizabeth after reading "One Art," "You command your words." She always knew when a poem was "done." Cal was rarely without a poem of Elizabeth's folded in his wallet as talisman.

Long ago when they were starting out, when "we were swimming in our young age, with the water coming down on us, and we were gulping," Cal's memoir, "91 Revere Street," had seemed to him "thin and arty" compared with Elizabeth's own autobiographical "In the Village." But it was 91 Revere Street, not the Bulmer house on the corner of Cumberland and Old Post Roads in Great Village, that bore a plaque now. Cal's brashness, his sloppiness when it came to others' feelings, had won him an audience in the age of poetic self-revelation he'd ushered in with *Life Studies.* "One does use 'painful experiences' — ALL experiences — how else could one write anything at all?" Elizabeth had consoled Cal in the depths of his regret over having hurt Lizzie with *The Dolphin.* But Cal envied a quality in Elizabeth's verse, and perhaps in her life as a writer, that he could never achieve: "the pleasure of pure invention," as if the poems had sprung entire from her imagination. Elizabeth had never published a poem "one would usually hesitate to read before an audience," in the end Cal's best definition of a "confessional poem."

The difference was in what Elizabeth hesitated to — *could not* — reveal. Elizabeth once boasted to Cal that she'd "never met a woman I couldn't make." Like Cal, she'd had numerous dalliances with "other" women and a late-life partnership with a younger woman. Cal could, and did, take the line and use it in a poem, "White Goddess," in *History.* Elizabeth could not. Keeping secrets made her poems *tell* more than Cal's outright confessions.

Elizabeth labored over a valedictory, "North Haven," during the summer of 1978, a year after Cal's death. She celebrated the island she'd so quickly come to love, naming the wildflowers she catalogued each year from her front porch, those with "gay" colors she found in "Shakespearian" profusion every July:

> ... Buttercups, Red Clover, Purple Vetch,
> Hawkweed still burning, Daisies pied, Eyebright,
> the Fragrant Bedstraw's incandescent stars,
> and more, returned, to paint the meadows with delight.

But Cal was her subject. He'd told her he'd "discovered *girls*" on North Haven during one "classic summer" in boyhood when he "learned to sail, and learned to kiss." She concluded her elegy —

> You left North Haven, anchored in its rock,
> afloat in mystic blue ... And now — you've left
> for good. You can't derange, or re-arrange,
> your poems again. (But the Sparrows can their song.)
> The words won't change again. Sad friend, you cannot change.

The two had been closest when apart. It was then they could "talk" in letters "with confidence and abandon and delicacy." No longer was she "My Darling receding Elizabeth," as Cal had once addressed her. Cal was gone.

"Hadn't two rivers sprung / from the Garden of Eden?" Elizabeth had asked in "Santarém," then corrected herself: "No, that was four / and they'd diverged. Here only two / and coming together." Elizabeth would soon follow Cal, and perhaps she sensed it. At the end of a grueling 1978 fall semester commuting to New York City to teach at NYU, she was back in the hospital, this time at Lenox Hill in Manhattan, where Dr. Baumann had admitting privileges, stricken once again with internal bleeding from the hernia that surgeons deemed too risky to repair. Suspecting more grim news, Elizabeth begged Anny Baumann to deliver the "truth." But there was nothing more to be said. Rest and the prospect of a year off from teaching, subsidized by a Guggenheim fellowship she was awarded that spring, revived her.

Sensibly, Elizabeth deepened friendships with young people with whom Alice felt at ease. Rosalind Wright, a novelist at Radcliffe's Bunting Institute, and Amram Shapiro, a poet who'd enrolled in Harvard Business School, were new to Cambridge during Elizabeth's last years at the college and found their way to her literature class as auditors. The couple, who joined Elizabeth and Alice in games of Boggle after dinners at Lewis Wharf, lived in an apartment over a pharmacy in East Boston's Maverick Square on the opposite side of the harbor. With binoculars, the friends could spot each other across the water and wave. "It had a bit of the feel of *bon voyage,*" Amram thought. "We were on the dock; they were on the ocean liner." Sitting on her top-floor verandah in the late afternoon, looking toward her young friends' apartment as the sun set behind her, Elizabeth might have felt she was living out the last lines of the first sestina she'd written forty years ago: "A window across the river caught the sun." Did it still seem "as if the miracle were working, on the wrong balcony"? Four miles beyond Maverick Square was the house at 55 Cambridge Street in Revere where Uncle George had once dangled her by the hair over the second-floor back porch railing. Then it must have seemed a miracle would be required to transport that little girl to safety.

In the winter of 1979, Elizabeth asked a student from her last Harvard verse-writing class, Mildred Nash, a young mother of two, to help winnow her vast library of books. Forty cases had arrived from Ouro Prêto in early 1975, after she'd moved into the condominium at Lewis Wharf, and the shelves in her bedroom had been crammed so full, two of them snapped off, scattering "books everywhere, and lots of broken *objets d'art,*" she'd written to Jimmy Merrill. Mercifully, Elizabeth had been out at the opera — Sarah Caldwell's production of *Così fan tutte* — when it happened, and most of the broken bibelots were "things I should have got rid of anyway." Her student John Peech had come to repair the faulty brackets.

By February 1979, Elizabeth was ready to get rid of more things, and her mood as she and Millie Nash sorted through the books — twenty feet of art books, six of philosophy, and nearly a full wall of novels in the living room alone — was retrospective. They paused to look at photographs of Casa Mariana, the "house of my dreams" Elizabeth hadn't seen for five years and was still trying to sell, and an album labeled "unknown relatives" shelved next to Elizabeth's scarlet grosgrain baby book — "I was my loveliest at nine months." Hunting among the volumes for a prized recording of South American birdsong, Elizabeth recalled Cal's visit to Brazil and how "only the gaudy birds" had kept him from "going crazy with boredom."

A coffee break prompted a disquisition on the medical establishment's contradictory recommendations on caffeine and hiatal hernias; she would not give up her daily cup of Medaglia d'Oro. Elizabeth, who'd met one of Millie's daughters when she'd come along to class on a public school snow day, spoke of family life, remarking that marriage "just never worked out for me, but I don't regret — all things considered — it's not happening." She'd come to believe, too, after observing her friends' difficulties with their mothers, that she'd been better off without one.

Elizabeth continued to dread a "decrepit" old age, or one dimmed by senile dementia such as her aunt Grace had suffered. She resented now being taken for "someone's grandmother" or "a great aunt," as she'd been described at two recent readings and in a New Jersey newspaper account — "It makes one very feminist." "Robert Fitzgerald's older," she complained to Millie, "and no one tells him, 'You look like anyone's grandfather.'" Robert was one year older, to be precise, and as a tenured professor in an endowed chair at Harvard, he'd been allowed to keep his job until age seventy. Elizabeth still relied on him for favors, such as a recommendation for the Guggenheim fellowship, but she would rebuke him teasingly in a letter that spring for his immunity to being described as "a grandfather or great-uncle" — "Lady poets are supposed to die young, I think." She closed the letter announcing her intention to walk up to Boston's Government Center to have a passport photo taken for the trip to Greece she and Alice planned as the culmination of Elizabeth's fellowship year.

The Lewis Wharf apartment had begun to drag on her. Elizabeth had never liked living in city apartments, even ones with spectacular views; she craved whole houses in rural landscapes. What she appreciated most about Lewis Wharf was its proximity to Boston's North

End, the Italian neighborhood across Atlantic Avenue, with its narrow cobblestone streets lined with flat-front brick row houses and shops that sold olive oil, cured meats, and spumoni by the slice for takeout if you asked for it right. She walked to Giuffre's Fish Market for the daily catch, Drago's Bakery for long loaves of bread called *flutes*, Caffé Pompei for cappuccino, Martignetti's for deals on "booze and groceries." Elizabeth still drank herself into a stupor many nights. She *was* "that dreadful thing" she'd once told Ruth Foster she feared becoming, an alcoholic. Despite her promises to Alice, Elizabeth could not stop. Truth be told, Alice often drank with her.

Of necessity, Elizabeth had agreed to teach at MIT in the fall of 1979, and the two women spent as much time as possible out of the city before then, staying at friends' country homes for weekends, and longer stretches at John Brinnin's in Duxbury — "stray dogs — pink sky, blue sea, red boat," Elizabeth noted in her diary after another chilly walk on the beach. Again she rented Sabine Farm for two summer months on North Haven. Except for skipping the climb up Santorini's steep stone "Steps to Heaven," Elizabeth had kept up with Alice on the Swan cruise they joined in late May, paying close attention to the variety in size and color of wild poppies, from blood red to California orange, on the six Greek islands they toured. But she'd been "in a sort of daze" since their return, she wrote to Howard Moss from Sabine Farm in July. She could no longer manage the walk across the meadow past the line of fir trees and down the hill to "our beach." Instead, in the late afternoon on an "intensely quiet, slightly hazy" day, they drove north on the island to "3rd Beach," where Alice "went in naked — water very clear, lap-lapping. *Drifts* of mussel shells." Elizabeth remained on shore, ready to offer Alice a towel when she emerged from the frigid water, beautiful as ever to Elizabeth at thirty-six. Elizabeth was sixty-eight.

That summer, Elizabeth conducted her annual wildflower census, and made jam from the "millions of blueberries" growing near the house. On July 20, the tenth anniversary of *Apollo 11*'s landing on the moon, she produced a molded blancmange to please Alice, who'd asked to celebrate the day with a "Moon Pudding." Searching Sabine Farm's bookshelves, Elizabeth picked out Aldous Huxley's last novel, *Island,* and skimmed through it — "badly written — very sad ending — he was discouraged." She wasn't impressed by Huxley's "illumination by use of drugs" at the book's conclusion: "one shd. be able to see that much by simple concentration, absorption, self-forgetting, etc. — without eating mushrooms or taking LSD." Huxley, with whom Elizabeth had traveled to Brasília and the Xingú River in 1958, had died of laryngeal cancer in 1963, a year after the book was published. At age sixty-nine he'd been eased out of the world with an injection of LSD administered by his wife, Elizabeth's old friend Laura Archera. Laura had written a book about it, *This Timeless Moment,* which, like *You Are Not the Target,* sold "in many editions, and in paperback," a "rather embarrassing" fact for Elizabeth, since the women shared Farrar, Straus and Giroux as publisher.

The next day, while picking raspberries along the road that ran in front of the house, Elizabeth found herself "eye to eye — about 18 inches apart — with a Lesser Fly-Catcher (I think) — 2 of them." Cedar waxwings and goldfinches arrived too, attracted by the ripe berries. Overhead, the barn swallows, whose nests she and Alice had knocked down from the eaves after the young were launched, could be seen "mating wildly in the air . . . eager to begin over again."

Day followed day, each as foggy as the last. Even Elizabeth's typewriter began to feel damp. "Such fogginess seems to make one sleepy, lazy, and extra-remote," she wrote to Frani, who'd visited Sabine Farm the year before in better weather. This was "The Foggy Summer," as Elizabeth titled one journal entry. Her last letter to Howard Moss, written August 17, ended with a handwritten postscript: "The sun has come out!"

Elizabeth never got to meet her verse-writing class at MIT. Illness kept her away from the first sessions, though she read through a sheaf of submissions to select students for English 582. On October 6, the night before she was due to give a reading, along with the short story writer Mary Lavin, to benefit the literary journal *Ploughshares,* Alice had driven to Lewis Wharf to pick up Elizabeth for a Saturday-night dinner party at Helen Vendler's apartment with Frank Bidart, Harvard English professor Harry Levin, and his wife, Elena. Alice and Elizabeth still loved each other; Alice was not just being "'nice' to an old lady because she is fond of you," as Elizabeth had so often feared. They were a couple with plans for a night out, though, as was their custom, they would not hold hands or display affection in the company of others, even close friends. The condominium at 437 Lewis Wharf was silent. Alice found Elizabeth on the floor of her bedroom, where she'd been dressing for dinner. There was no mistaking this collapse for a drunken fall. Elizabeth was dead of a cerebral aneurysm.

In recent years Elizabeth had changed her mind about being buried in Worcester and asked to be interred in one of the rustic cemeteries on North Haven Island. But Alice soon learned that the right to burial on the island was reserved for those born there. On October 25, a handful of mourners, including Alice, Frank Bidart, Amram Shapiro, and Rosalind Wright, gathered in Worcester's Hope Cemetery, a lush park of rolling hills covered with slate headstones, sculptured memorials, and granite family vaults, to bury Elizabeth beside the parents she hadn't known. Within the year, an inscription was chiseled into the monument that marked Gertrude and William Bishop's earlier deaths, the last line of the poem Elizabeth had written as a present to herself on a lonely birthday in 1948: "All the untidy activity continues, awful but cheerful."

Perhaps Elizabeth *had* been better off without her parents. There had been no one to admire her, no one to please, but also no one to disappoint by not marrying or raising a family, to shock by her decision to live with and love women. Elizabeth had staked her life on "the pleasure of pure invention," and she could depart unencumbered — "Yesterday brought to today so lightly!" — leaving the choice fruits of her gift in the hands of her readers.

Elizabeth left behind a puzzle in the form of one last poem, published in the *New Yorker* the week after her young friends buried her in Hope Cemetery. Elizabeth's biographer of the 1990s, Brett Millier, speculated that Howard Moss, to whom Elizabeth sent "Sonnet" the year before, in the fall of 1978, delayed publication, worried about Elizabeth's "veiled confession" of homosexuality in the poem. Was "Sonnet" Elizabeth's declaration that she, like Howard Moss and Bob Giroux and so many in her literary circle who remained circumspect, was "gay" — her way of "coming out," as many later critics and readers have interpreted the poem?

Elizabeth had written numerous sonnets during her high school and college years when she was practicing her craft, but few since. This late sonnet, with its brief lines and unpredictable rhyme scheme, utterly defied convention:

> *Caught — the bubble*
> *in the spirit-level,*
> *a creature divided;*
> *and the compass needle*
> *wobbling and wavering,*
> *undecided.*
> *Freed — the broken*
> *thermometer's mercury*
> *running away;*
> *and the rainbow-bird*
> *from the narrow bevel*
> *of the empty mirror,*
> *flying wherever*
> *it feels like, gay!*

Certainly defiance in form supported defiance in "subject matter." But what convention was Elizabeth defying?

In 1973 Elizabeth had told Adrienne Rich that she hoped to write something more "frank" about the situation of women, but she had hardly done so. Feminist as she was, marking advances toward the passage of the Equal Rights Amendment in her journal, wearing her "Woms. Lib." button to a "Sapphic" tea at Lilli's in Ouro Prêto, railing against Norman Mailer's misogynist *American Dream* as "really a sick book" in a letter to Alice, Elizabeth had not joined any crusade. As in her response to May Swenson's plea to contribute a poem to the women's verse anthology — "I like black & white, yellow & red, young & old, rich and poor, and male & female, all mixed up" — Elizabeth was an integrationist, a position falling out of fashion in the 1970s with the emergence of Black Power, Gay Pride, and lesbian separatism. The sentiment found its way into the opening stanza of "Santarém," the poem on "the conflux of two great rivers":

> ... *Even if one were tempted*
> *to literary interpretations*
> *such as: life/death, right/wrong, male/female*
> *— such notions would have resolved, dissolved, straight off*
> *in that watery, dazzling dialectic.*

"Sonnet," too, aimed to "resolve, dissolve" arbitrary and constricting divisions. The creature "caught" in the opening line — divided, wobbling, wavering — is later "freed" to fly wherever it pleases: a "rainbow-bird" of all colors, perhaps all genders — "gay." But was that what Elizabeth meant by "gay"?

In the previous decade, following the bloody Stonewall riots of 1969 on the streets outside a bar that had been a meeting place for lesbians when Elizabeth first lived in Greenwich Village, there had been a rapid shift toward public acceptance of homosexuality, along with the rise to prominence of the term "gay," embraced as a positive identity label by both male and female homosexuals. Through the early 1970s, half of American states acted to repeal anti-sodomy laws; the American Psychiatric Association removed homosexuality from its manual of mental disorders. In 1975, the U.S. Civil Service ended its ban on employing homosexuals. In 1978, the rainbow flag was designed and flown by San Francisco Gay Pride activists. Would Elizabeth have known, as she wrote "Sonnet" that same year?

On October 11, 1978, the day before Howard Moss wrote a "delighted" letter accepting "Sonnet" for publication, Elizabeth recorded a frightening incident in her daily diary. She and Alice had been eating dinner at Francesca's, a favorite North End restaurant, when their meal was disturbed by "a gay drunken party behind me — 2 men, 1 woman." The noisy trio got up to leave, but "one man (tall, good-looking) rushed — well, 2 or 3 ft. — toward A[lice] (facing me) & shouted: '*You're a good-looking son of a bitch!*'" This man — not "gay" in the new sense of the word — had caught on to Alice's boyish charm, what others sometimes referred to in Alice as "butch," and he was making just the sort of public scene Elizabeth had always hoped to avoid.

When the couple first visited New York City together, they'd stayed at the elegant Hotel Elysée, whose rooms were stocked with stationery and blue pens bearing the motto "Where Courtesy Prevails." After that, they'd visited only friendly households, and they'd established separate residences. In Brazil, Elizabeth had lived openly with Lota, but her life in America had to be different. Elizabeth believed her job and reputation were on the line. There were closeted gay men on Harvard's English department faculty, but there had been scandals as nearby as Smith College and as recent as 1960, when a popular English professor, Newton Arvin, was forced into retirement after police raided his Northampton apartment and arrested him for possession of homosexual pornography. "Closets, closets, and more closets" was what she told the openly gay poet Richard Howard she wanted in her new Lewis Wharf apartment, knowing he'd get the double meaning. Ironically, increased public awareness of the gay "life-style" (a coinage Elizabeth despised) meant an increased likelihood of confrontations such as the one at Francesca's. In years past, Alice and Elizabeth would have been just two women out to dinner. Now, much as Elizabeth wished otherwise, they appeared to be a gay couple asserting their rights in public.

Elizabeth told Lloyd Schwartz, whose questions about her poetry she'd come to welcome during the writing of his dissertation, that with "Sonnet" she had wanted to "restore" the word "gay" to its "original" meaning. The lighthearted little monosyllable had been unfairly pressed into service for a cause. The word itself could have been the "rainbow-bird" Elizabeth wished to set free. Gay liberation was developing its own orthodoxy, appropriating words like "gay" and "rainbow," the very tools of her trade. "Rainbow" had been a favorite image of Elizabeth's since "The Fish," carried forward in a vision of refracted brilliance in "Under the Window: Ouro Prêto," in the "multi-colored" stones illuminated by the "lion sun" in "The End of March," and still evident in her writing notebook during her last summer on North Haven. As Alice swam naked at "3rd Beach," Elizabeth was dazzled by the heaps of broken mussel shells shimmering "just under water showing iridescent streaks, green & blue." That summer, too, she'd felt "a bit sad" on an August day, recollecting how "much more gay — 'youthful'" the colors of Sabine Farm's wildflowers had been in late June and July than the "almost autumnal" hues of Queen Anne's lace, loosestrife, fireweed, and steeplebush then in bloom.

Another phrase Elizabeth defended, this time in a letter to Lloyd Schwartz, was "making love." Elizabeth scolded him for the use of the trendy "to have sex" in one of his own poems: "it may be what everyone says at present, but it always offends me. . . . If it isn't 'making *love*' — what other way can it be put?" The newly popular phrase, which she remembered hearing decades before from the fan dancer Sally Rand, in reference to her pet snake's mating habits, "seems like such an ugly, generalized sort of expression for something — love, lust, or what have you — always unique, and so much more complex than 'having sex.'" Elizabeth's closeted romantic life had never prevented her from full experience of that "much more complex" passion. She'd written about it too, though privately, as in this untitled poem, shared with close friends in Brazil, one of whom read the verses aloud to a young documentary filmmaker in Ouro Prêto in 1987:

> *Close close all night*
> *the lovers keep.*
> *They turn together*
> *in their sleep,*
>
> *close as two pages*
> *in a book*
> *that read each other*
> *in the dark.*
>
> *Each knows all*
> *the other knows,*
> *learned by heart*
> *from head to toes.*

Elizabeth had kept back the most explicit quatrain, which survived, nevertheless, in a notebook:

Once in the night
the lovers turned over
tightly, together,
under the cover,

Elizabeth Bishop wrote love poems, and poems about lovemaking, and one of the best poems ever written in English about the loss of love, but she had made her way through life as an orphan, a solitary. Reticence wasn't the reason she'd become a poet of the self — of a singular "mind in action," as she'd once described the effect she hoped to achieve in her poems. She had discovered early on, perhaps too early, that she was "an *I* . . . an *Elizabeth*" — and she'd treasured that painful, "unlikely" self-awareness ever since, knowing it was the same thing as her imagination.

As an ambitious but still fanciful sixteen-year-old at Walnut Hill School, Elizabeth had written a poem in which she imagined she heard an elf "go whistling by," whose "singing echoed through and through" and "split the sky in two" —

The halves fell either side of me,
And I stood straight, bright with moon-rings.

As she wrote "Sonnet" a half century later, Elizabeth could no longer look ahead to a vibrant future, standing tall, with songs echoing through her, splitting the sky. The writer's life — her life — had turned out to be so much more difficult. Often she had felt "caught," like the spirit-level's bubble, or internally "divided" — painfully "undecided." At the end of a long letter she'd written to her first biographer, one of a dozen letters summarizing her family history, education, and development as a poet, Elizabeth had apologized: "This is just the sketchiest of armatures, really, leaving out so many friends, people, places, events — false beginnings, retreats, mistakes, and so on." She knew how important the "left out" could be — the townspeople gathered by the fountain in Ouro Prêto, the aspiring shaman on the Amazon, the squatter's children in Rio, the proprietors of a roadside filling station, the moose or armadillo that crossed her path and caught her attention.

These made her poems, which would not have come into being without her own false starts, retreats, and mistakes.

Even if her writing had not shaken the world, or so far claimed a wide readership, writing had always saved her. "What one seems to want in art," she'd also told her biographer, "is the same thing that is necessary for its creation, a self-forgetful, perfectly useless concentration. (In this sense it is always 'escape,' don't you think?)" Characteristically, she had rendered her most important statement as a parenthetical aside, followed by a question. But she knew the answer. Poetry had been her refuge, her escape — had "freed" her. Elizabeth was the rainbow-bird, as she had been the sandpiper, only now it was time to stop "looking for something, something, something" and run away to wherever she felt like. She too was gone.

Envoy

January 23, 2014
PATOU THAI, BELMONT CENTER

I didn't see Elizabeth Bishop on North Haven in the summer of 1977, although our host's boyfriend, who'd taken one of Miss Bishop's classes several years before me, had heard she was renting on the island and fantasized about running into her at the general store, picnicking at Mullin's Beach, or in line at the ferry. I hoped we wouldn't. I'd tossed out my notes for the poetry classes I'd taken my last year at Harvard, and nearly all the poems as well. I was still ashamed of what I'd done, or what Miss Bishop thought I'd done. I was twenty-three years old, and it was hard to know the difference between what others thought of me and what I knew to be true.

I saved the poem I now called "Birthdays," the one with the line Frank Bidart had praised, about capturing the spawning grunion at high tide on the night of my twenty-first birthday, and sent it to the *New Yorker,* receiving an answer by return mail. The magazine's "poetry department" was closed for the summer. I fared better with the *Atlantic Monthly.* "The manuscript we are returning to you is one in which we have taken a special interest," the editors' form letter told me; "we are grateful for the chance to consider your work, and hope you will try us again."

Soon after, I found myself in the position of issuing those same form letters, which I learned to code as *R,* signifying "rather enjoyed reading," instead of the more usual *D,* meaning simply "dump." That fall, the *Atlantic* had a sudden need for a "first reader" of short fiction and poetry submissions, and Robert Fitzgerald put in a good word for me with the poetry editor, Peter Davison, who may have read my "Birthdays" poem. Once a week I borrowed my boyfriend's car and drove to the magazine's offices in a lofty brownstone on Arlington Street facing Boston's Public Garden, picked up a cardboard carton filled with envelopes of all sizes, and returned with them a week later, having made my decisions. Poems that I rated *R* were read by Peter Davison for serious consideration, the others were returned with the *D* form letter, which I never got to read.

The short fiction submissions were all considered "over the transom," or "slush" — unsolicited manuscripts by unknown authors without literary agents. But poets didn't have literary agents, and I read every poem that came to the magazine. It was an important job, and it turned out I did it badly. I hadn't recognized the work of my boss's friends. Writers with three names and what I considered fussy poems, like John Frederick Nims and John Hall Wheelock, had been receiving *D* form letters. Peter Davison was outraged, and I was fired. I might write good poems someday, the burly blustering poet informed me in an exit interview in his book-lined corner office, but I'd never be an editor. There would be no second chance: I learned afterward from the fiction editor that Mary Updike, John Updike's ex-wife, who had given up the job earlier that fall, wanted it back. Who could say no to a recently divorced mother of four? Mary Updike was another of Peter Davison's friends.

I never wrote another poem after that, and scarcely read one. I didn't want to be one of *them.* Or maybe, as I read in an interview Elizabeth Bishop had done with the London *Times,* I was one of those female poets who quit because they "get discouraged very young." When I came across the line years later, I appreciated its double meaning. Both could have applied to me back then.

I did send "Birthdays" to a friend of a friend who worked as a bookstore clerk in Manhattan and was starting a poetry journal called *Other Islands.* He'd borrowed the phrase from Elizabeth Bishop's "Crusoe in England," a poem he loved even more than I did. "Dreams were the worst," the stanza began, as Crusoe recalled his long nights in exile:

> *. . . I'd have*
> *nightmares of other islands*
> *stretching away from mine, infinities*
> *of islands, islands spawning islands,*
> *like frogs' eggs turning into polliwogs*
> *of islands, knowing that I had to live*
> *on each and every one, eventually,*
> *for ages, registering their flora,*
> *their fauna, their geography.*

My poem appeared in the first issue of *Other Islands*. By letter, the young editor praised my poem's "wonderfully sculptural lines" and technique "subsumed by the intention." Neither the journal nor my career nor my friend's took off. That wasn't the way our story went. I saved the small pamphlet, tucked away with the rhyming dictionary my mother had given me in grade school and the versification texts from Professor Fitzgerald's class, its title an unwelcome reminder of the way ambitions tease and proliferate.

I was even a tiny bit glad I'd been dismissed from the *Atlantic Monthly* when I learned that another first reader, Mary Jo Salter, an earlier student of Elizabeth Bishop's who took over the slush pile from Mary Updike, had plucked out work by the little-known poet Amy Clampitt and helped make her career. Would I have seen the promise in lines like these, at the opening of Clampitt's "Fog"?

> *A vagueness comes over everything,*
> *as though proving color and contour*
> *alike dispensable: the lighthouse*
> *extinct, the islands' spruce-tips*
> *drunk up like milk in the*
> *universal emulsion; houses*
> *reverting into the lost*
> *and forgotten; granite*
> *subsumed, a rumor*
> *in a mumble of ocean.*

Miss Bishop would have liked them, I felt sure. The poem reminded me of my stay on North Haven. It could have described her "Foggy Summer."

Peter Davison thought I was a poor judge of poetry, and I'd come to doubt my opinions. As if to compensate, I began writing book reviews, nearly always finding fault with the writers whose books I'd been assigned — historians, biographers, novelists, but never poets. I stayed away from them. I wrote, but not poetry. I meant to get back to it. And then I lost the knack for knowing what makes a poem. "I really don't know *how* poetry gets to be written," Elizabeth Bishop told an inquiring reader at about the time I first met her in Robert Lowell's class. "There is a mystery & a surprise, and after that a great deal of hard work."

The last time I felt that mystery and surprise was when I was well into my thirties. My boyfriend and I had married. We had a four-year-old daughter, and I'd taken her for a walk in a nearby nature preserve. The ranger handed us a slip of pale blue paper headed "Scavenger Hunt," with a list of items for preschoolers to identify along the trail:

Find:
Something green
Something blue
Something that moves in the water
Something that flies in the air
Something that makes a sound
Something that crawls on the ground
Something that reminds you of you

The list was almost a poem, and maybe at some future time I could make it into one. I kept the list on the windowsill above the kitchen sink in our suburban home until it was too watermarked to read.

My marriage ended badly at the same time I finished writing a book I'd been working on for twenty years. Maybe there was a connection between the two culminations, or maybe not. I do know that I'd struggled with what Adrienne Rich identified in a famous essay as the "discontinuity of female life with its attention to small chores, errands, work that others constantly undo, small children's constant needs." I'd wanted to do all that for my family, had not wanted my two daughters to come home from school to an empty house, or one with a parent inside but too far off to hear them knocking on our front door's glass windowpane with key in hand. I'd have agreed with Rich, if I'd picked up the essay again during that time and read: "For a poem to coalesce, for a character or an action to take shape ... a certain freedom of the mind is needed — freedom to press on, to enter the currents of your thought like a glider pilot, knowing that your motion can be sustained, that the buoyance of your attention will not be suddenly snatched away." I closed my ears to freedom's siren song, and opened my heart to my husband and daughters. I was not willing to conclude, as Elizabeth Bishop had, "I am just not made for 'family life.'"

Then there was the way I went about writing when I found the time for it. The book was as far from a poem as one could imagine — a six-hundred-page biography of three nineteenth-century sisters tracing their involvement with Transcendentalism, the intellectual movement my junior honors adviser had told me I didn't know how to define. When people asked about my preparation for the work, I told them I'd learned to write in poetry workshops in college. But of course, I joked, you can't write a six-hundred-page book with the same attention to every word and sentence that I'd been taught to give to each line of a poem. Or maybe that's what I *had* done, and why it took so long.

Newly divorced, I found myself looking for a teaching job in my mid-fifties, as Elizabeth Bishop had after her marriage ended. I didn't think of myself as elderly, but I was a scared amateur professor counting myself lucky to find work when I did. A second biography, written faster than the first or I'd have lost my job, brought tenure and the Pulitzer Prize the year I turned sixty. My children were grown. My marriage was over. My parents were dead: seventeen years apart, both suffered falls resulting in fatal head injuries, my mother at sixty-eight on a freshly waxed concrete floor in the lobby of her apartment building, my father at eighty-eight, stumbling over the threshold of his favorite bar. Assuming my own fatal fall was in the distant future, I was free to write what I wanted. I had time to follow up on an email from Mildred Nash, a student I hazily remembered from the class I'd taken with Elizabeth Bishop in 1976.

I'd been thinking of writing about our professor, but Millie Nash couldn't have known that when she wrote to me, curious about whether the author of two biographies she'd read was the same Megan Marshall she'd known in Miss Bishop's class. I was eager to meet, and Millie was too. I hoped she might have saved her notes from our class, maybe even some of the poems I'd passed around in photocopies for discussion.

A retired public school teacher of the gifted and talented, and an active poet, Millie Nash arrived for lunch at Patou Thai in Belmont Center bearing several folders stuffed with papers and wrapped in a plastic shopping bag. She had all my poems, including the one that had earned me my B, along with pages of notes covering both poetry classes I'd taken that fall; Millie had audited Professor Fitzgerald's versification class too, paying closer attention than I had to his lectures. She'd kept a diary describing encounters with Miss Bishop over three years: our first class session, coffee and hot chocolate at Piroschka's in Harvard Square when her daughter came to class on a snow day, the party at Lewis Wharf, precious hours spent culling Elizabeth Bishop's library during the spring before her death.

From Millie's notes and diary entries I was able to reconstruct a chronology, and I found more of my poems in a file at Yale's Beinecke Library, part of the Robert Fitzgerald collection. But my story quickly took a back seat to what I was discovering about Miss Bishop. There was so much I hadn't known, that almost no one else knew. In Elizabeth Bishop's archive at Vassar, a trove of letters had appeared, locked away in a file box until Alice Methfessel's death in 2009. What I read brought tears: in letters written to her psychoanalyst, Elizabeth described in alarming detail her harrowing childhood and the car wreck that severed Margaret Miller's arm; letters to and from Lota de Macedo Soares recorded the crises of the last years in Brazil. Hundreds of pages of letters exchanged with Alice Methfessel showed what the couple had never revealed in public or even to close friends: a passionate and abiding love.

I was falling in love, too, with the Elizabeth Bishop I began to know in her letters and manuscript drafts and in snapshots: the little girl sitting in wet sand on a beach in Nova Scotia, the grown woman swimming nude in a private pool at Samambaia, each offering up the same pleased grin; the unseen photographer capturing Cartier-Bresson–style images on the Xingú, along the Amazon, and down the Rio São Francisco. I admired what Elizabeth Bishop called her "geographic curiosity," so deep it pervaded her dreams. She'd described one such dream to Howard Moss: "There was a narrow road that began at Tierra del Fuego and went straight north, and I had started to walk it, quite cheerfully. A large primitive stone coffin was being carried on muleback alongside of me, ready for me when I gave out."

If Miss Bishop had been snappish with me, she had been equally severe with others. I took a perverse pleasure in her cracks, always in private letters, at Robert Frost ("something slightly unpleasant under that lichen-covered stone"), E. E. Cummings ("you have to pretend you've never seen a Cummings poem before, and that's difficult"), and J. D. Salinger ("Henry James did it much better in one or two long sentences"). Robert Bly and Octavio Paz were "all too vague," and Allen Ginsberg "just can't write."

What would she have said of herself? Elizabeth knew the worth of her own poems. She never sought advice as Cal had, as "dear Frankie" Bidart did so sweetly in repeated phone calls — "Have you a few minutes? Could I read you something?" — as I had, in fishing for compliments on my Catullan hendecasyllabics. Elizabeth sent her poems to editors and friends when she considered them finished. But she also knew she should have written more and simply could not, despite vowing to "grit my teeth and write another poem, that's all." And she knew when she'd "behaved badly." She begged forgiveness of those she'd hurt or offended so often they grew impatient with her. I sometimes tired of reading her apologies and excuses too. And then I felt sad about the futility of her always broken promises — to write more, drink less.

But could it have been otherwise? I thought of the poems she *did* write, almost improbably — how the writing of them was what she'd lived for, and how they'd made her reputation after her death. Would Elizabeth have been happy to know how famous she'd become, that movies were made about her, and scholarly societies established in her name? Disturbed to find that Cal, her dear friend, was comparatively neglected? Cal had seen that Elizabeth could write the "immortal" poem, as she had yearned to do from her earliest days as a writer: one "short, but immortal, poem," she'd imagined in her 1938 story "In Prison." With "One Art," Elizabeth Bishop had done that. Could any other American poet of her generation claim as much? And I had been there, by lucky chance, to sport among these gods of verse on an ivied Mount Olympus.

Millie Nash had a message for me that day in Patou Thai. She put it delicately, not naming names. When Millie and Elizabeth had taken a coffee break on one of those long mornings of book-sorting in 1979, Elizabeth spoke of something that had troubled her since the time of Millie's class three years before. There had been a student who turned in a poem written for another professor, and Miss Bishop had to lower her grade. She felt sorry about it to this day. Millie eyed me as she told the story. Millie knew the student was me.

Forty years late, this unsought apology felt like an invitation, a call. It carried me back to autumn hours spent in a hushed classroom, when I'd wanted more than a teacher could give.

In the weeks and months ahead, as I pored over manuscripts, letters, and journals, as I read and reread one hundred perfect poems, I sometimes paused and let myself imagine Elizabeth Bishop: sitting on her balcony with Millie or Alice — or possibly even me — brushing crumbs from a tablecloth on which coffee cups sat half full next to a plate of croissants or homemade corn bread, taking in the view of brick and stone dormitories at the Charlestown Navy Yard where Cal's commander father had once been quartered, gazing farther north in the bright morning sun toward the conflux of two great rivers, the Mystic and the Charles, and witnessing the daily miracle. "If you *squint* a little," Elizabeth would turn and say, "it looks almost like the Grand Canal in Venice — really."

ACKNOWLEDGMENTS

This book could not have been written without the foundational work of previous scholars, editors, and biographers of Elizabeth Bishop and her circle, including Sandra Barry, Frank Bidart, Joelle Biele, Peter Brazeau, Bonnie Costello, Gary Fountain, Robert Giroux, Langdon Hammer, Saskia Hamilton, David Hoak, Jill Janows, David Kalstone, Linda Leavell, Candace MacMahon, Brett Millier, George Monteiro, Carmen L. Oliveira, Barbara Page, Alice Quinn, Camille Roman, Lloyd Schwartz, Thomas Travisano, and Helen Vendler. I am grateful to those who welcomed my questions and offered guidance. Important conversations with friends and acquaintances of Elizabeth Bishop in her last years — Frank Bidart, Roxanne Cumming, Jonathan Galassi, Rachel Jacoff, Alexandra Johnson, Gail Mazur, Pamela Painter, Grace Schulman, Amram Shapiro, Jane Shore, Deborah Weisgall, Rosalind Wright, and Ross Terrill–helped immeasurably. I am indebted to Lloyd Schwartz for his patience with my queries by email and over lunches at Changsho, and his careful reading of an early draft of this book; and to James Atlas, whose guest appearance in Jane Shore's poetry workshop at Harvard inspired me to follow the biographer's path. Four decades later, Jim set my work on Elizabeth Bishop in motion.

My memories of English Sar, Fall 1976, have been tested and augmented by classmates Julie Agoos, Mildred Nash, David Owen, and William Sorensen. Other students who worked with or encountered Elizabeth Bishop memorably at Harvard — April Bernard, Paula Bonnell, Steven Fenichel, and Elise Partridge — generously shared recollections and notes, and Isabel Swift recalled a North Haven summer. Elizabeth Bishop's own school communities welcomed and supported my research: at Walnut Hill School for the Arts, Sarah Banse, Jennifer TumSuden, Bruce Smith, and Charlotte Hall; at Vassar College's Archives and Special Collections Library, Dean Rogers and Ronald Patkus.

An extraordinary year as a fellow at the Dorothy and Lewis B. Cullman Center for Scholars and Writers at the New York Public Library under the directorship of Jean Strouse pushed the book toward completion. Several NYPL librarians provided important research leads: Elizabeth Denlinger, Karen Gisonny, Denise Hibay, and Carmen Nigra. The companionship of writers at the Cullman Center as well as members of the New England Biography Seminar of the Massachusetts Historical Society, the 40 Concord Group of the Radcliffe Institute for Advanced Study, the faculty of Emerson College's Department of Writing, Literature and Publishing, and my longstanding biographers group — Joyce Antler, Frances Malino, Susan Quinn, Lois Rudnick, Judith Tick, and Roberta Wollons — made lonely work less so. Emerson College supported my research and writing on Elizabeth Bishop with a grant from the Faculty Advancement Fund and in many other ways.

For help with Brazilian lore and translation from Portuguese and Spanish, I relied on the expert advice of Carlos Dada, Stefanie Kremser, Jordi Punti, Larry Rohter, Katherine Vaz, and Andrew Zingg. Dr. Carol Zuckerman advised on the treatment of asthma in the mid-twentieth century; Deborah Cramer on the shore birds of South America; Gary Wolf on architectural details; Kenneth Gross on the history of lyric poetry; David Hopkins on North Haven nomenclature. Anne Gray Fischer offered research assistance on short notice when my tech capabilities failed. For information on Elizabeth Bishop's psychoanalyst, Dr. Ruth Foster, I consulted Lucy Claire Curran, Maxwell Foster Jr., Nancy Foster, Joyce A. Lerner, Susan McGrath, Susan Twarog, Roger Warner, Brenda Lawson of the Massachusetts Historical Society, Nellie Thompson of the New York Psychoanalytic Institute, and Margaret Warren, archivist of The Winsor School. At other archives and for grants of permission I was aided by Marylène Altieri and Sarah Hutcheon of the Arthur and Elizabeth Schlesinger Library on the History of Women in America, William Minor of Washington University Libraries' Department of Special Collections, Bernard Schwartz of the Unterberg Poetry Center at the 92nd Street Y, Christina Davis of the Woodberry Poetry Room at Harvard University, Catherine Fancy of the Elizabeth Clark Wright Archives of Acadia University, Victoria Fox of Farrar, Straus and Giroux, Rosanna Warren, and Carole Berglie, representative of the May Swenson estate. In my travels for research and writing, I was fortunate to experience the generous hospitality of Lithgow Osborne and Chuck Burleigh, Emily and Jay McKeage, and the North Haven Library and Symposium.

My longtime editor at Houghton Mifflin Harcourt, Deanne Urmy, along with Larry Cooper, Jenny Xu, and Jackie Shepherd, helped make this book beautiful and true. Neil Giordano's expertise with rights and permissions made it all possible. My literary agent, Katinka Matson of Brockman Inc., has enabled me to write books over nearly four decades. Friends and family, not all named here, tolerated and even encouraged the past several years of intense effort, bordering on obsession: Carol Bundy, Natalie Dykstra, Mark Edmundson, Rebecca Goldstein, Anne C. Heller, Carla Kaplan, Louise Knight, Diane McWhorter, Patricia O'Toole, Stacy Schiff, Lorraine Shanley, Amanda Vaill, Susan Ware, Mary Liz and George DeJong, Amy Marshall and Tim Zenker, Scott Harney, Josephine Sedgwick, and Sara Sedgwick Brown. Their gifts of attention and love are the miracle I had not looked for, but receive with intense gratitude and the will to respond in kind.

NOTES

In quotations from primary sources I have retained the original spelling and punctuation, except in some instances where I have altered capitalization at the start of sentences for ease of reading. I have also used, both in quotations and in my text, Elizabeth Bishop's preferred spelling of her maternal family name — Bulmer, rather than Boomer — and of her aunt Maude Bulmer Shepherdson's first name — Maud.

ABBREVIATIONS

Names

AB: Dr. Anny Baumann
AM: Alice Methfessel
EB: Elizabeth Bishop
LA: Lilli Correia de Araújo
LS: Lota de Macedo Soares
MM: Marianne Moore
MS: May Swenson
RF: Dr. Ruth Foster
RL: Robert Lowell

Books and Manuscript Collections

BNHJ: The North Haven Journal, 1974–1979, Elizabeth Bishop, ed. Eleanor M. McPeck (North Haven, ME: North Haven Library, Inc., 2015)

BNY: Elizabeth Bishop and The New Yorker: *The Complete Correspondence,* ed. Joelle Biele (New York: Farrar, Straus and Giroux, 2011)

BP: Poems, Elizabeth Bishop (New York: Farrar, Straus and Giroux, 2011)

BPPL: Poems, Prose, and Letters, Elizabeth Bishop, ed. Robert Giroux and Lloyd Schwartz (New York: Library of America, 2008)

BPR: Prose, Elizabeth Bishop, ed. Lloyd Schwartz (New York: Farrar, Straus and Giroux, 2011)

EAP: Edgar Allan Poe & The Juke-Box: Uncollected Poems, Drafts, and Fragments, Elizabeth Bishop, ed. Alice Quinn (New York: Farrar, Straus and Giroux, 2006)

EBC: Conversations with Elizabeth Bishop, ed. George Monteiro (Jackson: University Press of Mississippi, 1996)

EBHA: Elizabeth Bishop and Her Art, ed. Lloyd Schwartz and Sybil P. Estess (Ann Arbor: University of Michigan Press, 1983)

EBL: Elizabeth Bishop: Life and the Memory of It, Brett Millier (Berkeley, Los Angeles, Oxford: University of California Press, 1993)

LL: The Letters of Robert Lowell, ed. Saskia Hamilton (New York: Farrar, Straus and Giroux, 2005)

LP: Collected Poems, Robert Lowell, ed. Frank Bidart and David Gewanter (New York: Farrar, Straus and Giroux, 2003)

LPR: Collected Prose, Robert Lowell, ed. Robert Giroux (New York: Farrar, Straus and Giroux, 1987)

OA: One Art: Letters, Selected and Edited, Elizabeth Bishop, ed. Robert Giroux (New York: Farrar, Straus and Giroux, 1994)

REB: Remembering Elizabeth Bishop: An Oral Biography, Gary Fountain and Peter Brazeau (Amherst: University of Massachusetts Press, 1994)

SL: Arthur and Elizabeth Schlesinger Library on the History of Women in America, Radcliffe Institute for Advanced Study, Harvard University

VC: Elizabeth Bishop Papers, Special Collections, Vassar College; access codes refer to box and file numbers

WIA: Words in Air: The Complete Correspondence Between Elizabeth Bishop and Robert Lowell, ed. Thomas Travisano and Saskia Hamilton (New York: Farrar, Straus and Giroux, 2008)

WU: May Swenson Papers, Special Collections, Washington University, St. Louis

YCAL: Yale Collection of American Literature, Beinecke Rare Book and Manuscript Library, New Haven

OCTOBER 21, 1979: AGASSIZ HOUSE, RADCLIFFE YARD

page

1   *Waiting to sing:* The recording of Elizabeth Bishop's memorial service can be heard at Harvard University's Woodberry Poetry Room "Listening Booth" website: http://hcl.harvard.edu/poetryroom/listeningbooth/poets/bishop .cfm.

     "Unbeliever": BP 24.

2   *"I ordered the book": OA* 256.

4   *"A Miracle for Breakfast": BP* 20–21.

CHAPTER 1: BALCONY

7   *recorded in a baby book:* "The Biography of Our Baby" and other quotations on these pages from EB's baby book: VC 113.1.

8   *another cherished album:* honeymoon album of William and Gertrude Bishop, VC 119.18.

     "What it is": Ellery Bicknell Crane, ed., *Historic Homes and Institutions and Genealogical and Personal Memoirs of Worcester County, Massachusetts,* Vol. I (New York and Chicago: Lewis Publishing Company, 1907), 174.

9   *"being brave":* EB to RF, Saturday morning, February 1947, VC 118.33.

10   *"a homely old white house":* EB quoted in William Logan, "Elizabeth Bishop at Summer Camp," *Guilty Knowledge, Guilty Pleasure: The Dirty Art of Poetry* (New York: Columbia University Press, 2014), 296. Logan's chapter on EB's friendship with Louise Bradley at Camp Chequesset has been enormously helpful to my understanding of EB's adolescence.

     rose-patterned carpet: EB, "Reminiscences of Great Village," Part I, VC 54.13.

     "blur of plants": *EBC* 126.

     view her mother: EB to RF, February 24, 1947, VC 118.33; EB, "A mother made of dress-goods . . ." *EAP* 156.

     Her mother hit her: EB to RF, February 24, 1947, VC 118.33.

11   *"held specks of fire":* EB, "The Drunkard," *BP* 317.

12   *she jumped out:* *REB* 4.

     holding a knife: *REB* 3.

     "pure note": EB, "In the Village," *BPR* 63, 69. EB changed "Mate" to "Nate" in the story.

     "gasoline . . . Vaseline": *EBC* 71.

     "Holy, Holy": "Elizabeth Bishop: Influences," *American Poetry Review,* January/February 1985, 14. This article is described as "an edited version of a talk Elizabeth Bishop gave on December 13, 1977 in a series of 'Conversations' sponsored by The Academy of American Poets," 11.

13   *"made a satisfying":* EB, "Primer Class," *BPR* 80, 85.

     she didn't say: When enrolling EB at Walnut Hill School, EB's uncle Jack Bishop told the assistant principal, Helen Farlow, "no one has ever spoken to her about her mother and she has never mentioned her." *REB* 29.

14   *"permanently insane":* EB to Anne Stevenson [EB's first biographer], January 8, 1964, *BPR* 410.

     "wet red mud": EB, "In the Village," *BPR* 71.

     "kidnapped": EB, "The Country Mouse," *BPR* 87, 86.

     "was another grandfather": EB to RF, February 24, 1947, VC 118.33.

     "silver stubble": EB, "For Grandfather," *EAP* 154.

     she was lucky: *EBL* 180, *REB* 314.

     "didn't know anything": EB to RF, February 24, 1947, VC 118.33.

15   *"good manners":* EB, "Manners," *BP* 119.

16   *"bitterly unhappy and lonely":* EB to RF, February 24, 1947, VC 118.33.

     "hideous craving": EB, "The Country Mouse," *BPR* 98.

     "someone needed a spanking": EB to RF, February 24, 1947, VC 118.33.

     "foolish": EB, "In the Waiting Room," *BP* 180.

     "others waiting": EB, "The Country Mouse," *BPR* 99.

     latest National Geographic: See Jim Powell, "Bishop's *Arcadian Geographic,*" *TriQuarterly* 81, Spring/Summer 1991, 170–74, on EB's "poetic confabulation" of images from several issues of the magazine, published in February 1918 and preceding years, in "In the Waiting Room."

     "a feeling of absolute": EB, "The Country Mouse," *BPR* 99.

     "sliding / beneath": EB, "In the Waiting Room," *BP* 181.

17   "myself": EB, "The Country Mouse," *BPR* 99.

"inside looking out": EB, "The Country Mouse," *BPR* 99, 96, 95.

"aging, even dying": EB, "The Country Mouse," *BPR* 98.

"in another two months": EB to RF, February 24, 1947, VC 118.33.

Gertrude's sister Maud: EB always spelled her aunt Maude Bulmer Shepherdson's name as "Maud," and I have retained her spelling here and elsewhere.

18   *"suddenly very uncomfortable"*: EB to RF, February 24, 1947, VC 118.33. In this letter to her psychoanalyst, EB describes the workings of her memory in regard to such painful incidents: "another thing that I'd remember and then forget for stretches of years sometimes I think."

"very tall man": EB to RF, February 24, 1947, VC 118.33.

"Maybe lots of people": EB to RF, February 1947, VC 118.33.

"I got to thinking": EB to RF, February 24, 1947, VC 118.33.

19   *"wheezing and reading"*: EBC 112.

"harder & harder": EB to RF, February 24, 1947, VC 118.33; *"small, worried"*: EB, "Mrs. Sullivan Downstairs," *EAP* 203.

"the most natural": EBC 99.

"aliens, dreamers": EB, "Mrs. Sullivan Downstairs," *EAP* 204.

20   *"From the icy"*: EB, "Autobiographical Sketch," July 22, 1961, VC 53.6.

"The First Snow-Fall": James Russell Lowell, *The Poetical Works of James Russell Lowell* (Boston: Houghton Mifflin & Co., Riverside Press, 1890), 350.

easily rattle off: OA 83.

"say good-bye": EB, "First Death in Nova Scotia," *BP* 123–24.

21   *"just temporarily"*: EB, "Mrs. Sullivan Downstairs," *EAP* 202.

"by heart": WIA 135.

"no apparatus": EB mentions *Soap Bubbles, EBC* 121; quotations: C. V. Boys, *Soap Bubbles and the Forces which Mould them* (London: Society for Promoting Christian Knowledge; New York: E. & J. B. Young & Co., 1890), 7, 9.

"Observation is a great joy": EBC 101.

"dreaming deliberately": from EB draft poem recalling Aunt Maud — "when you talked so much / to my young deaf dreaming deliberately ears." *EAP* 307.

22   *"an idiot child"*: EB to RF, Sunday morning, February 1947, VC 118.33. The girl Elizabeth met on the train may have been Louise Bradley, with whom she quickly formed a lasting friendship. See Logan, "Elizabeth Bishop at Summer Camp," 264.

"tomboy": EBC 43.

"other children": EB to RF, Sunday morning, February 1947, VC 118.33.

"the new poetry": Harriet Monroe and Alice Corbin Henderson, eds., *The New Poetry: An Anthology* (New York: Macmillan, 1917), vi.

"simple dignity": EB quoting Coleridge in "Elizabeth Bishop: Influences," *American Poetry Review,* January/February 1985; *"very deep emotion"*: EB in "Elizabeth Bishop: Influences."

23   *"extremely popular"*: EB to RF, Sunday morning, February 1947, VC 118.33.

turned physical: "all the little girls were falling in love with each other right and left," EB to RF, Sunday morning, February 1947, VC 118.33.

"I haven't any": EB quoted in Logan, "Elizabeth Bishop at Summer Camp," 254.

forty-seven-foot sloop: Logan, "Elizabeth Bishop at Summer Camp," 253; *Ark:* EB to Maude Shepherdson, July 1, 1928, quoted in Sandra Barry, "Lifting Yesterday:

Elizabeth Bishop and Nova Scotia" (unpublished ms., copyright 2014), chapter 5, 24. I am grateful for Sandra Barry's careful research into EB's Nova Scotia roots in this book and other publications, including "Elizabeth Bishop and World War I," *WLA: War, Literature and the Arts: An International Journal of the Humanities* 11, no. 1 (Spring/Summer 1999), 93–110.

24   *"should have known better":* EB to RF, Sunday morning, February 1947, VC 118.33.

she detested the book: "I've detested [Gibran] since my counselor at camp gave me *The Prophet* to read when I was 14 or 15," EB to AM, July 1, 1972, VC 115.12.

"There was a white": EB to RF, February 24, 1947, VC 118.33.

25   *"always trying to feel":* EB to RF, February 24, 1947, VC 118.33.

26   *"beautiful girl":* EB quoted in Logan, "Elizabeth Bishop at Summer Camp," 287.

"liked to feel": EB to RF, Sunday morning, February 1947, VC 118.33.

"normal": REB 23.

drives and picnics: EB to RF, Sunday morning, February 1947, VC 118.33.

dressed up in bedspreads: REB 28.

27   *regulation that required hats:* "Student Government Regulations," E. Farrington scrapbook, 1926–27, Walnut Hill School archive.

"dreadful little house": EB to RF, Sunday morning, February 1947, VC 118.33.

burst into tears: EB to RF, Sunday morning, February 1947, VC 118.33.

"on more or less": EB to Anne Stevenson, "Answers to your questions of March 6 [1964]," *BPR* 429.

28   *"Ridge," visiting Judy Flynn:* EB to RF, Sunday morning, February 1947, VC 118.33.

Elizabeth rated poorly: Walnut Hill School register of student grades, 1929–30, Walnut Hill School archive.

"social terrors": EB to Anne Stevenson, "Answers to your questions of March 6 [1964]," *BPR* 430.

"worried . . . a lot": EB to RF, Sunday morning, February 1947, VC 118.33.

"Behind Stowe": BPPL 184. The poem's title has been adopted for the campus alumni magazine.

29   *"On Being Alone": BPR* 451–52.

"Roof-Tops": BPPL 321.

30   *"handicapped by an unusual": REB* 39–40.

"good musician": REB 39.

her information card: REB 59; *"independent":* EB to Anne Stevenson, "Answers to your questions of March 6 [1964]," *BPR* 429.

"too self-conscious self": REB 40.

31   *"Two Noble Emancipists":* Matthew Vassar quoted in Barbara Miller Solomon, *In the Company of Educated Women: A History of Women and Higher Education in America* (New Haven and London: Yale University Press, 1985), 48.

A next generation: see Helen Lefkowitz Horowitz, *Alma Mater: Design and Experience in the Women's Colleges from Their Nineteenth-Century Beginnings to the 1930s* (Amherst: University of Massachusetts Press, 1993), 218–22.

Hallie Flanagan at Vassar: See Susan Quinn, *Furious Improvisation: How the WPA and a Cast of Thousands Made High Art out of Desperate Times* (New York: Walker, 2011), 3–5.

blue chip stocks: I am grateful to Sandy Barry for sharing the results of her study of Bishop family probate records held at the courthouse in Worcester, Massachusetts. Sandra Barry email to the author, May 6, 2016.

32   *"really 'red'"*: EB to Anne Stevenson, "Answers to your questions of March 6 [1964]," *BPR* 432.

       "Then Came the Poor": *BPR* 465.

       "wax-faced": EB, "Hymn to the Virgin," *BP* 219–20.

33   *$26.18, a princely sum*: *EBL* 58.

34   *"looked exhausted"*: *EBC* 107.

       "spontaneous": EB, "Eliot Favors Short-Lived Spontaneous Publications," *Vassar Miscellany News* 17, no. 46 (May 10, 1933).

       loosen his tie: *EBC* 108.

       "Any man has to": T. S. Eliot, "Sweeney Agonistes," *Complete Poems and Plays* (Boston: Houghton Mifflin, 1952), 83.

       "ever done," "I am not": EB, "Eliot Favors Short-Lived Spontaneous Publications."

       "scared out of my wits": *EBC* 57.

35   *"Mortal and sardonic"*: MM quoted in "First Production of Sweeney Brings T. S. Eliot Here," *Vassar Miscellany News* 17, no. 45 (May 6, 1933).

       "impersonal," "goes right on": *OA* 21.

       "I hadn't known": EB, "Efforts of Affection: A Memoir of Marianne Moore," *BPR* 117, 118.

       "I too, dislike it": MM, "Poetry," *Observations,* ed. Linda Leavell (New York: Farrar, Straus and Giroux, 2016), 28.

       "relentless accuracy": MM, "An Octopus," *Observations,* 91.

       "the self-portrait": Glenway Wescott quoted in Leavell's introduction to MM, *Observations,* xi.

       dressed impeccably: For details of EB's dress on the day of their meeting as recalled by MM, see Leavell, *Holding On Upside Down: The Life and Work of Marianne Moore* (New York: Farrar, Straus and Giroux, 2013), 278. EB's recollection of what she wore that day is less explicit: "my new spring suit," EB, "Efforts of Affection," *BPR* 119.

       "quaint . . . but stylish": EB, "Efforts of Affection," *BPR* 119.

36   *"it went very well"*: *EBC* 57.

       "ability and technical," "It is almost": MM quoted in Leavell, *Holding On Upside Down,* 279, 278.

       "having affairs": EB to RF, Sunday morning, February 1947, VC 118.33.

       Music as a Literature: EB, College Notes: Music 140, VC 69B.9.

       "A ladder goes up": *OA* 14.

37   *"The chimney pots"*: *OA* 22.

APRIL 29, 1975: NINTH-FLOOR CONFERENCE ROOM, HOLYOKE CENTER

42   *in an uncanny way*: One poem I brought to class that semester, about my father's arrival at Harvard as a freshman, contained the lines "1938. / A train traveling east." Professor Lowell was stunned when he read the poem aloud to open discussion, remarking, "I just wrote that line myself. It will be in the *New York Review* next week. I'll have to change it." His poem, about his first marriage, to

Jean Stafford, then titled "1938–1975," began: "1938, our honeymoon train west." In revision the poem became "Since 1939," with the opening lines altered: "We missed the declaration of war, / we were on our honeymoon train west." RL, "Three Poems," *New York Review of Books,* May 29, 1975; LP 740.

43   *"About the size":* EB, "Poem," BP 196–97.

CHAPTER 2: CRUMB

45   *"I guess I should":* OA 24.

"Apoplexy": Gertrude Boomer Bishop "Certificate of Registration of Death," May 29, 1934, Nova Scotia Archives. In her unpublished ms., "Lifting Yesterday: Elizabeth Bishop and Nova Scotia" (copyright 2014), chapter 4, 28, Sandra Barry offers evidence from Gertrude Bishop's case file suggesting she may also have suffered from hypothyroidism, "undiagnosed and untreated for decades."

"constantly": EB to RF, February 24, 1947, VC 118.33.

46   *"no hereditary tendency":* REB 30.

"The past / at least": EAP 23.

"mystical": EAP 273.

47   *"howling away":* EB to RF, February 24, 1947, VC 118.33.

48   *"wonderful, romantic":* EBC 127.

"island feeling": EB journal, "Cuttyhunk, July 1934," quoted in *EBL* 62.

sharing a room: EB to RF, February 24, 1947, VC 118.33.

berating: EB, "In a cheap hotel . . . ," *EAP* 83.

"I'd like him better": EB to RF, February 24, 1947, VC 118.33.

"cheap hotel": EB, "In a cheap hotel . . . ," *EAP* 83. See also editor Alice Quinn's note, 291.

49   *"Elizabeth, Go to hell":* REB 68.

"figuring up": EB to Frani Blough, July 29, 1934, quoted in Barry, "Lifting Yesterday," chapter 6, 12.

"riding around aimlessly": OA 26.

one in four: Edward Robb Ellis, *The Epic of New York City* (New York: Coward-McCann, 1966), 533.

50   *Early Keyboard Music:* EB College Notes, VC 71.3.

"sex desire": Casal quoted in John D'Emilio and Estelle B. Freeman, *Intimate Matters: A History of Sexuality in America* (New York: Harper & Row, 1988), 228.

"an ideal friendship": Mary Casal, *The Stone Wall: An Autobiography* (Chicago: Eyncourt Press, 1930), 165.

"When at its best": Casal, *The Stone Wall,* 211.

51   *while she was drunk:* EB to RF, February 24, 1947, VC 118.33.

after two weeks: Concluding her story based on her experience teaching in the correspondence school, "The U.S.A. School of Writing," EB writes: "I stood the school for as long as I could, which wasn't very long." *BPR* 108. In a chronology written for her psychoanalyst Ruth Foster, circa 1947, EB records that she'd spent "about two weeks" working for the school in 1935, VC 118.33.

52   *"very nice":* OA 33. George Platt Lynes also photographed EB in the 1930s, VC 100.2.

53   *"wade / through black jade"*: MM, *Observations,* ed. Linda Leavell (New York: Farrar, Straus and Giroux, 2016), 41.

      "never try to publish": EB, "Efforts of Affection," *BPR* 128.

      "like a bucketful": EB New York City notebook, quoted in *EBL* 65.

      "painful": *REB* 111–12.

      "TERRIBLE": *EAP* 254.

      "I've always felt": *WIA* 81.

54   *"The Map"*: *BP* 5.

      "in action, within itself": *OA* 11.

      "tentativeness can be": *EBHA* 179.

      "oiled": EB, "The Map," *BP* 5.

55   *"These peninsulas," "Are they assigned"*: EB, "The Map," *BP* 5.

      "archaically new": *EBHA* 175.

      "A Little Miracle": EB New York City notebook, quoted in *EBL* 79–80.

56   *"homesickness"*: EB travel journal, quoted in *EBL* 87, 88.

57   *"picturesqueness is just"*: *OA* 34.

      "I looked for the kiss": *EAP* 250.

      cost only $155: *REB* 62.

58   *half-dozen lessons*: *OA* 478.

59   *"thoughts that were"*: EB, "Sleeping Standing Up," *BP* 31.

      "Some surrealist poetry": *EAP* 272.

      "surrealism of everyday life": EB to Anne Stevenson, January 8, 1964, *BPR* 414.

      "I cannot, cannot": *OA* 45; *She signed herself*: *EBL* 106.

60   *"enviable"*: MM quoted in *EBL* 106.

      By return mail: *EBL* 107.

      "something needn't be": *EBC* 24.

      more recent attempts: Pound, "Sestina Altaforte," 1909; Auden, "Paysage Moralisé," 1934.

      "colorless": *OA* 54.

      "my Depression poem": *EBC* 25.

      almost 20 percent: Ellis, *The Epic of New York City,* 533.

61   *communion rite*: Thirty years after "A Miracle for Breakfast" was published, EB wrote to a friend, "I didn't even mind, because I suppose it is obvious, although I'd never thought of it consciously, when two different critics pointed out that 'A Miracle for Breakfast' referred to the Mass." *OA* 477.

      "A Miracle for Breakfast": *BP* 20–21.

62   *"is in the eye"*: Hallie Tompkins Thomas quoted in *EBL* 97.

      "boisterousness": *OA* 54.

      Margaret remembered: *EAP* 260.

63   *"freakishly cruel"*: *OA* 61. EB seemed to believe that Louise Crane really was "an awfully good driver" with "a very large safe car," as she wrote to MM when proposing the outing to Coney Island. *OA* 33.

      "what resides in the right": *OA* 62.

      "To keep 'going'": *OA* 61.

"I know now": EB to Frani Blough, August 9, 1937, quoted in *EBL* 124.

"it would have been better": EB to RF, February 24, 1947, VC 118.33.

64 *"condemned to death"*: *EAP* 35. Although *EAP* editor Alice Quinn gives this passage the title "Villanelle," it is possible that EB's notes on the villanelle's rhyme scheme that appear on the same notebook page may not apply to the journal entry recounting the dream.

"Lizzie and Louise": *REB* 71.

65 *"perfectly beautiful"*: *OA* 74.

"coffee concerts": *REB* 84.

"I can scarcely": *BPR* 18.

"Many years ago": *BPR* 24.

"attract to myself": *BPR* 24; *"inscriptions"*: *BPR* 23.

"twelve or fifteen": *BPR* 20; *"a short, but immortal"*: *BPR* 23.

66 *"We hadn't meant"*: *EAP* 41.

it had been Billie Holiday: *REB* 328. EB had known Billie Holiday through Louise Crane, and was proud to have introduced her to the harpsichordist Ralph Kirkpatrick at one of their parties. *REB* 104. Her set of four poems, "Songs for a Colored Singer," were written with Billie Holiday in mind.

infidelity was unforgivable: See EB to AM, March 31, 1971, VC 114.40: "I was only jealous in this awful way once, when I was 28 years old — for about two weeks — and in that case, since I was sensible, and *was* being treated dishonestly, I simply broke the thing off. . . . It's the worst feeling in the world, & the most disgusting, and I wish I could be all for promiscuity and free love and menages à trois and not give a damn whom you sleep with. But I can't."

"huge blue eyes": *REB* 41.

"See, here, my distant": EB, "Valentine," *EAP* 40.

"scaled, metallic": EB notebook quoted in *EBL* 117.

67 *"submarine / toadstools"*: MM, "The Fish," *Observations*, 42.

"I caught a tremendous": EB, "The Fish," *BP* 43–44.

68 *"nothing"*: EB notebook entry, February 8, 1941, quoted in *EBL* 164.

69 *"Sex Appeal"*: *OA* 86.

"militarism": *OA* 96.

"more and more Navy ships": *OA* 91.

"almost every boy": EB to Anne Stevenson, "Answers to your questions of March 6 [1964]," *BPR* 426. A more accurate census is provided by Sandra Barry, "Lifting Yesterday," chapter 1, 45: "seventy men . . . enlisted between 1914–1918. Many of them were wounded, twenty-one died."

"command and terrorize": EB, "Roosters," *BP* 36, 37.

"purified": *EBL* 159.

"The Cock": *OA* 96.

"water-closet door": EB, "Roosters," *BP* 36.

70 *"cranky"*: *OA* 97.

"perhaps some early": EB to Anne Stevenson, March 18, 1963, *BPR* 393.

"I took Marjorie": EB to RF, February 24, 1947, VC 118.33.

"drunkenness is an excuse": *OA* 76.

71　*"would drip on the screens":* EB to RF, February 24, 1947, VC 118.33.

　　"It is marvellous": EAP 44.

　　"just starting to get light": EB to RF, February 24, 1947, VC 118.33.

　　population rapidly doubled: Stephen Nichols, *A Chronological History of Key West: A Tropical Island City* (Key West: Key West Images of the Past, Inc., 2000), 1941–1945 entry.

72　*Blackouts curtailed:* See Abraham H. Gibson, "American Gibraltar: Key West During World War II," *Florida Historical Quarterly* 90, no. 4 (Spring 2012), 393–425.

　　"translucent-looking": EB notebook quoted in *EBL* 169.

　　becoming her lover: EB to RF, February 1947, and Sunday Morning, February 1947, VC 118.33.

73　*"seem to comb": OA* 115–16.

74　*"stupider and stupider": OA* 116.

　　"six bedraggled old poems": OA 113.

　　she no longer found: EBL 179.

　　"lovely brand-new": OA 122.

75　*"scenery":* EB, "Chemin de Fer," *BP* 10. For an account of the influence of EB's Camp Chequesset years on her mature writing, especially "Chemin de Fer," see William Logan, "Elizabeth Bishop at Summer Camp," *Guilty Knowledge, Guilty Pleasure: The Dirty Art of Poetry* (New York: Columbia University Press, 2014), 299.

　　"with birds, with bells": EB, "Anaphora," *BP* 52.

　　"trying to make": Marjorie Stevens letter quoted in *EBL* 179.

　　"Miss Bishop's": Barbara Gibbs review in *Poetry* quoted in *EBL* 184.

　　"honest in its wit": Randall Jarrell, "On *North & South," EBHA* 181.

　　"this small-large book": MM, "A Modest Expert," *EBHA* 178–79.

76　*25 percent premium: EBL* 188, *BNY* xviii.

　　"one of the best": RL, "Thomas, Bishop, and Williams," *EBHA,* 186–88.

77　*"her most important":* RL, "Thomas, Bishop, and Williams," *EBHA* 187.

　　"rumpled": EB notebook quoted in *EBL* 186–87.

　　"certain things": OA 54.

　　"Every magazine or paper": OA 163.

　　"makes one write": EB letter quoted in *EBL* 126–27.

78　*Karen Horney: OA* 108.

　　"the quiet heroisms": MM, *Selected Letters,* ed. Bonnie Costello, with Celeste Goodridge and Cristanne Miller (New York: Penguin Books, 1998), 405.

　　"I really do": EB to RF, Saturday [February 1947], VC 118.33.

　　estranged from her: author's interviews and correspondence with Foster family members.

　　That education: "Dr. Ruth Foster," *Biographical Directory of Fellows and Members of the American Psychiatric Association* (New York: American Psychiatric Association, 1950), 253.

79　*"Dear Dr. Foster": EAP* 77. Editor Alice Quinn chose not to give Dr. Foster's name, and published the draft with the title "Dear Dr. ——"; cf. *EBL* 180.

"in my cups": EB to RF, Sunday morning, February 1947, VC 118.33.

account of her sexual history: In a letter to RF dated "February 1947," VC 118.33, EB confides her worry, amounting to a conviction, that "I have no clitoris at all." Two women "I have lived with," Loren MacIver and Marjorie Stevens, had "commented" on this. In an article titled "Approaching Elizabeth Bishop's Letters to Ruth Foster," scholar Lorrie Goldensohn writes, "There seems to be no good reason to dismiss Bishop's description of her anatomical abnormality." *Yale Review* 10, no. 1 (January 2015), 15. Yet there is no record of RF's reaction to EB's stated worry, which she admits "may be all nonsense," or the conversation that followed from this confession; EB's later relationships with women, documented in private correspondence and unpublished poems, show her taking a great deal of pleasure in sexual relations. When asked about the "February 1947" letter, EB's former lover Roxanne Cumming, with whom EB lived from 1968 to 1970, laughed and said, "She must have been having a bad day." Interview with the author, December 13, 2015.

"it was all": EB to RF, February 24, 1947, VC 118.33.

80 *"a few weeks old":* EB to RF, chronology [February 1947], VC 118.33.

"Heavens do you": EB to RF, February 1947, VC 118.33.

three quarts: EB to RF, Saturday [February 1947], VC 118.33.

premenstrual symptom: EB to RF, February 24, 1947, VC 118.33.

the year her mother died: EB to RF, February 24, 1947, VC 118.33.

"hours of hangover": EB to RF, "Saturday" [February 1947], VC 118.33.

"that dreadful thing": EB to RF, Sunday morning, February 1947, VC 118.33.

"more or less drunk": EB to RF, February 1947, VC 118.33.

81 *Department of Health, "I had the feeling": REB* 100.

strange behavior, "seldom speaks": Barry, "Lifting Yesterday," chapter 4, 34, 36, 38.

And delusions: Barry, "Lifting Yesterday," chapter 4, 21, 20.

delivered by forceps: Barry, "Lifting Yesterday," chapter 4, 12.

"so nice": OA 206.

"tight": EB to RF, Feburary 1947, VC 118.33.

82 *"excitement":* RL, "Thomas, Bishop, and Williams," *EBHA* 188.

free-flowing iambs: I am grateful to Lloyd Schwartz for a discussion of the meter of "At the Fishhouses," in which he described the poem's "loose iambs."

"The day I saw": EB to RF, February 1947, VC 118.33.

"big old seal": EB to RF, February 1947, VC 118.33.

"curious about me": EB, "At the Fishhouses," *BP* 62.

"started feeling": EB to RF, February 1947, VC 118.33.

"regarded me / steadily": EB, "At the Fishhouses," *BP* 63.

"seal," "double meaning": EB to RF, February 1947, VC 118.33.

"Cold dark deep": EB, "At the Fishhouses," *BP* 64.

83 *"Knowledge is historical":* EB to RF, February 1947, VC 118.33.

"she hardly knew": REB 339–40.

addressed her as "Elizabeth": WIA 7.

"a psychiatrist friend": WIA 16.

84   *"your poetry is as different":* WIA 273.

    "There's a side": WIA 380. RL was referring to EB's poem "First Death in Nova Scotia."

85   *"shake so I can't":* OA 211.

86   *"literary":* EBC 95.

    draining all the bottles: Published accounts of this episode vary slightly. Compare *REB* 109–10 and David Kalstone, *Becoming a Poet: Elizabeth Bishop with Marianne Moore and Robert Lowell* (New York: Farrar, Straus and Giroux, 1989), 146–47.

    "constant menace," "morality and decency": quoted in David K. Johnson, *The Lavender Scare: The Cold War Persecution of Gays and Lesbians in the Federal Government* (Chicago and London: University of Chicago Press, 2004), 57, 2; *Six thousand workers:* Jill Lepore, "The Last Amazon: Wonder Woman Returns," *New Yorker,* September 22, 2014, 72.

    "all those piles": OA 194.

    unsteady foundation of her appointment: For an extensive discussion of EB's year in Washington, see Camille Roman, *Elizabeth Bishop's World War II — Cold War View* (New York: Palgrave Macmillan, 2001).

    "purge of the perverts": quoted in Johnson, *The Lavender Scare,* 2.

87   *"terrible flop":* OA 199.

    helpless to draw them out: REB 119.

    "all this recording": OA 202.

    "hopeless": OA 199.

    "the high point": WIA 99.

88   *locked themselves in the butler's pantry:* REB 120.

    "go back on the parish?": WIA 99.

    three simple pieces: OA 207.

    blowing bubbles: OA 190; Pearl K. Bell, "Dona Elizabetchy: A Memoir of Elizabeth Bishop," *Partisan Review,* Winter 1991, 29.

    "so fast I expect": OA 207.

    "sort of 'Pub'": OA 206.

    survived by her mother: "Dr. Ruth Foster," obituary, *New York Times,* September 30, 1950.

    pancreatic cancer: coroner's report, Case No. 7247, City of New York, Office of Chief Medical Examiner.

    variety of . . . medications: OA 198–99.

    an inhaler that made: OA 204.

89   *"for about a week":* OA 198.

    "this side of going": OA 199.

    "helped me more than": OA 206.

    five-day hospitalization: REB 119.

    "Well, go ahead": OA 210.

    "She had been promiscuous": EB, "Homesickness" (unfinished short story), *EAP* 190.

90   *"worst year":* EB notebook quoted in Roman, *Elizabeth Bishop's World War II — Cold War View,* 139.

    "not even realizing": EB, "Homesickness" (unfinished poem), *EAP* 86.

OCTOBER 5, 1976: ROBINSON HALL, HARVARD YARD

96 *"The Colder the Air"*: BP 8.

97 *"Please try your hands"*: EB, "Assignments for English Sar Fall Term, 1976," Mildred Nash papers, private collection.

"PLEASE USE": EB, "Assignments for English Sar Fall Term, 1976."

CHAPTER 3: COFFEE

98 *"large apartment"*: WIA 109.

99 *"a smallish sand"*: WIA 116.

"tax tangle": WIA 119.

"85% at Houghton Mifflin": WIA 122.

"crazy trip": WIA 129.

"But no!": EB, "I introduce Penelope Gwin . . . ," EAP 4, 3.

100 *"harrowing," "a girl can bear"*: WIA 112, 113.

New York rental: BNY 65.

"mostly fairies": WIA 116.

"a very nice tall bony": OA 278.

101 *"frank conversational"*: EB to RF, Sunday Morning, February 1947, VC 118.33.

hadn't caught on: EB to RF, February 24, 1947, VC 118.33.

"a lot to me": EB notebook quoted in EBL 238–39.

journal letters: See M. Eleanor Prentiss, "Leaves from an Oxford Notebook," *Blue Pencil*, March 1927, 14–16.

"day-dreams": WIA 130.

102 *"all very luxurious"*: OA 226.

"driving to the interior": EB, "Arrival at Santos," BP 88.

"very sour": OA 231.

"large red-hot mushrooms": OA 232.

103 *"A love letter"*: EAP 296.

"fearful and wonderful": OA 236.

"I call to you": EAP 296.

leaving Lota: EB to Maria (Maya) Osser, January 4, 1968: "I lived with Lota all that time — much longer than Mary did, and I never *left* Lota (*she* did, and rather decisively, you know, even if she continued to live nearby)." OA 490. Mary Morse, quoted in REB 132: "we were staying at a friend's when Elizabeth came to stay with us at Christmas time [in 1951]. I had begun building my house because I had decided to adopt children. [When] Elizabeth went to live with Lota in the new house, I was living down [the hill from Lota's new house] in the house that I was finishing."

"I believe": EB notebook quoted in EBL 244.

"made that kind": EB quoted by James Merrill in REB 266.

"died and gone to heaven": OA 246.

104 *"alive forever," "those pure blue"*: EB, "In the Village," BPR 62.

"leaning willows": EB, "In the Village," BPR 77.

"unbelievably impractical": OA 234.

"brilliant, brilliant": *OA* 243.

"I am a little": *BNY* 85. EB wrote similarly to Yaddo friends Kit and Ilse Barker two days later, on October 12, 1952: "It is funny to come to Brazil to experience total recall about Nova Scotia — geography must be more mysterious than we realize, even." *OA* 249.

"You have an ally": *BNY* 142.

"20-12-51": *OA* 551.

"or my perpendicular": *BNY* 165.

"my hostess": *BNY* 74.

"coming in my bedroom": *OA* 237.

"like waterfalls": *OA* 243.

"much too attached": *OA* 240.

105   *"rarely without"*: *OA* 358.

samba competitions: *OA* 292.

"getting used to be": *OA* 264.

"wonderful you are": LS to EB, Morning Sunday [June 21, 1964], VC 114.20.

106   *"real," "very tame"*: *OA* 236.

"lifelong dream": *OA* 234.

"in a chauvinistic outburst": *WIA* 136.

"For Lota": *BPPL* 911.

"Lota likes luxury": *OA* 259.

"the last six or seven": *OA* 238.

107   *"is really interested"*: *OA* 245.

"the friend with whom": *BNY* 85.

"sociopathic personality": *Diagnostic and Statistical Manual of Mental Disorders* (American Psychiatric Association, 1952), 7, 38–39.

"functional references": *OA* 251.

"definitely out as humor": *BNY* xxiv.

"fundamentally": *WIA* 140.

"a masochist, a Lesbian": Elizabeth Hardwick, "The Subjection of Women," *A View of My Own: Essays on Literature & Society* (New York: Ecco Press, 1962), 170.

"a fine job": *WIA* 140.

"she wanted me to stay": *WIA* 143.

108   *"fantastic"*: *OA* 289.

how happy: EB to RL: "Here I am extremely happy, for the first time in my life." *WIA* 143.

"happier than I have felt in ten years": *OA* 232.

or twenty: *OA* 280.

or ever: *OA* 143.

"It is so much easier": *OA* 247.

"the really lofty": *OA* 237.

"seasons, fruits": *OA* 243.

"nice & relaxing": *OA* 232.

"complete confusion": *OA* 243.

"extremely affectionate": *WIA* 143.

"wonderful . . . likes to read": *OA* 257.

"mens": *OA* 359.

"superb": *OA* 250.

109 *"once or twice a month"*: *OA* 246.

"wander around the world": *WIA* 143.

"so beautiful": *OA* 243.

"rather elderly": *OA* 273.

"enormous": *OA* 241.

"way up in the air": *OA* 252.

110 *"stupendous mountain scenery"*: *OA* 256.

"neck-deep": *WIA* 191.

"delicious": *OA* 293.

"black with white feet": *OA* 256.

"Wishes seem to come true": *OA* 244.

"super-bathroom": *OA* 267.

"running, rushing water": *OA* 272.

"The still explosions": EB, "The Shampoo," *BP* 82.

111 *"Giving you what"*: Luís de Camões quoted in translation in George Monteiro, *Elizabeth Bishop in Brazil and After: A Poetic Career Transformed* (Jefferson, N.C., and London: McFarland & Company, 2012), 15.

"This sort of small," "It won't make": *BNY* xxv.

"I never thought": Karl Shapiro quoted in *BNY* xvi.

"winter . . . when I thought": *WIA* 143.

112 *"something indecent"*: *BNY* xxvi. In responding to MS's approving letter, EB writes a rare explanation of her poem: "I am awfully pleased with what you say about the little Shampoo & you understood exactly what I meant and even a little bit more — it's a nice thought that perhaps the shampoo will arrest Time. . . . The Shampoo is very simple: — Lota has straight long black hair. — I hadn't seen her for six years or so when I came here and when we looked at each other she was horrified to see I had gone very gray, and I that she had two silver streaks on each side, quite wide. Once I got used to it I liked it — she looks exactly like a chickadee — remember them at Yaddo? & it's quite chic. Shiny tin basins, all sizes, are very much a feature of Brazilian life — you see them hanging in graduated sizes outside the little hovels people live in — various degrees of shininess — we used an enormous one before we got our now more-or-less-hot-running-water in the bathroom — And I am surrounded with rocks and lichens — they have the sinister coloration of rings around the moon exactly, sometimes — and seem to be undertaking to spread to infinity, like the moon's, as well —." EB to MS, September 19, 1953, WU.

sanctified by rings: Paul Swenson, "A Figure in the Tapestry," *Body My House: May Swenson's Work and Life,* Paul Crumbley and Patricia M. Gantt, eds. (Logan: Utah State University, 2006), 33.

"the little poem": *BNY* xxv.

"a good spell": *OA* 289.

"old bronchitis-asthma": EB to Pearl Kazin Bell [writer and editor, EB's friend since Yaddo], November? 1953, VC 24.3.

"ride": *WIA* 146; "this euphoria is wonderful": *WIA* 150.

"intimacy with clouds": *OA* 237.

$1,200 for "Gwendolyn": *OA* 259.

"stop being the passenger-type": *OA* 273.

113　*"I don't like"*: EB to Anne Stevenson, January 8, 1964, *BPR* 413.

　　　"Well done, daughter!": EB to MS, August 10, 1953, WU.

　　　"the few people": *WIA* 164.

　　　"who just can't 'produce'": *OA* 296.

　　　"CANNOT PROMISE": *OA* 288.

　　　"getting used to": *OA* 249.

　　　"Elizabeth is the slowest": *OA* 264.

　　　"so at home": *OA* 262.

　　　"dead low tide": *OA* 250.

　　　"hesitated": EB, "A Cold Spring," *BP* 55.

　　　"The Bight": *BP* 59.

114　*"world inverted"*: EB, "Insomnia," *BP* 68.

115　*"collected poems"*: Candace W. MacMahon, *Elizabeth Bishop: A Bibliography, 1927–1979* (Charlottesville: University Press of Virginia, 1980), 12.

　　　"misbegotten book": *OA* 304.

　　　yellow-green leaf: Loren MacIver told EB she'd chosen a violet leaf for the cover, EB to MS, September 6, 1955, *BPPL* 805.

　　　"the best, or maybe first": *BNY* 165.

　　　"maybe gradually making up": *OA* 327.

　　　"almost a new book": *OA* 312.

　　　"theoretically and practically": Randall Jarrell, *Randall Jarrell's Letters: An Autobiographical and Literary Selection,* ed. Mary Jarrell (Boston: Houghton Mifflin, 1985), 420.

　　　"Exile seems to work": *OA* 312.

116　*grant of $2,700: OA* 317.

　　　"Never has so little": *OA* 318.

117　*"pointedly uninterested"*: *OA* 275.

　　　she was dating men: EB to Pearl Kazin Bell, November 28, 1953, VC 24.3.

　　　disliking his poetry: EB to MS, September 6, 1955, *BPPL* 809.

　　　"NO MIDDLE CLASS": *OA* 271.

118　*home address:* At graduation from Vassar, EB had listed Great Village rather than Cliftondale as her hometown, although she hadn't visited Great Village since age sixteen.

　　　drafted a poem: EB, "Hannah A.," *EAP* 53.

　　　"Squatter's Children": *BP* 83.

119　*"Squatter's Children" published in* Anhembi: See Monteiro, *Elizabeth Bishop in Brazil and After,* 58.

　　　subscribing to the Sunday: EB also subscribed to these publications: *New*

American Writing, Botteghe Oscure (a free subscription), *Partisan Review, Poetry, Hudson Review, Kenyon Review, New York Times Book Review, Times Literary Supplement, New Statesman, The Listener,* and *Farmer's Digest.* LS subscribed to *House & Garden, Interiors, Psychoanalytic Quarterly,* and *Ellery Queen's Mystery Magazine.* EB to MS, March 20, 1953, WU.

"bi-localization": WIA 135.

"deep river of red mud": OA 261.

"my hostess": OA 244.

"secret beaches": EB letter quoted in *EBL* 299.

120 *"living poetry":* EB, "On the Railroad Named Delight," *BPPL* 442.

"Rio de Janeiro": EB translation, "On the Railroad Named Delight," *BPPL* 443.

"Come, my mulatta": EB translation, "On the Railroad Named Delight," *BPPL* 444.

"beautiful colored skin": EAP 219.

"Anglo-Saxon blood": OA 243.

"underdeveloped-yet-decadent": OA 271.

Elizabeth looked "wise": OA 316.

121 *"young Negro cook":* EB, "On the Railroad Named Delight," *BPPL* 448.

"half squatter": EB, "Manuelzinho," *BP* 94.

"United we shall be happy": BNY 167.

"Judy": EB notebook, VC 73.2.

122 *"no one knows":* EB to MS, December 26, 1953, WU. Aware of her confusing syntax, EB wrote: "You can arrange this to please yourself — it is beyond me right now." MS responded (January 25, 1954, WU) with the following series of "arrangements. I can't decide which I like best":

> *No one knows a child, whether is a boy or a girl.*
> *Or a girl — whether is a boy, a child — no one knows.*
> *A child or a girl, no one knows whether is a boy.*
> *A child, whether is a boy, no? One knows, or a girl . . .*
> *A child is a boy or a girl? No one knows whether.*
> *Is a boy or a girl a child whether no one knows?*
> *A child? No. No one knows whether. Or a girl is a boy.*

"Are you": Gene Stratton-Porter, *The Keeper of the Bees* (New York: Doubleday, Page & Co., 1925), 90.

"on bended knee": Stratton-Porter, *The Keeper of the Bees,* 69.

"particular bright": EB to MS, November 20, 1953, WU.

kill a five-foot snake: OA 331.

"combined being asthmatic": WIA 250.

"hydraulic cannon": EB to MS, May 10, 1956, WU.

"wild Atlantic Ocean": EB to MS, April 11, 1956, WU.

123 *"on parade with such":* MS to EB, May 8, 1956, WU.

Poets Since 1945: MS to EB, May 22, 1958, WU.

repeated "crack": OA 320.

"feminine": EB to MS, November 14, 1954, WU.

"our best women poets": MS to EB, May 8, 1956, WU.

124 *"When the muse":* EB to MS, September 6, 1955, WU. The full letter also appears in *BPPL* 805–10.

Kylso: REB 131–32.

"Filling Station": BP 125–26.

"Love's the main thing": EB letter quoted in *EBL* 266.

"magnificent with child-problems": WIA 255.

125		*"discovering her voice":* EB letter quoted in *EBL* 267, 266.

"best results": EB to MS, February 18, 1956, WU.

"Early Sorrow": MS to EB, October 28, 1955, WU.

"inscrutable": EB, "Sestina," *BP* 121.

"a way of thinking": EB to MS, September 6, 1955, *BPPL* 809. MS did not initially recognize the poem, titled "Early Sorrow" when EB mailed it to her in manuscript, as a sestina: "It's hypnotic. It's wonderfully organized, and yet so casual in tone. What do you call it when a set of the same words are used to end the lines in each stanza? I never studied prosody." MS to EB, October 28, 1955. EB replied: "I'm very pleased that you liked my sestina — which is what it is and what I think I'll call it now instead of that hammy title. And I think I'll send you [Clement] Wood's *Complete Rhyming Dictionary and Handbook of Poetry* for Christmas!" EB to MS, November 4, 1955. Perhaps MS's inability to recognize the sestina form played a role in EB's decision to choose an informative generic title, setting a precedent for the later "Poem" and "Sonnet."

"forever": MS to EB, December 9, 1955; also RL to EB, November 6 [1955]: "don't stay away for ever," *WIA* 171.

"everybody is so intent": OA 276.

126		*"inter-communication": WIA* 143.

"start sounding": EB to MS, July 27, 1953, WU.

"sometimes I get": EB to MS, July 2, 1955, WU.

"I'd like to hear": EB to MS, May 10, 1956, WU.

"the way I got around": EB to MS, July 2, 1955, WU.

"Sorry I can't": EB to MS, October 28, 1956, WU.

nearly four-hundred-page: EB to MS, November 4, 1955, WU.

"finicky": EB to MS, September 25, 1956, WU.

twenty-six pieces: EBL 293.

"bang-up party": WIA 233.

"svelte and chic": I am grateful to Joelle Biele for directing me to this letter from Katharine White to Mary McCarthy, August 19, 1957, in the *New Yorker* correspondence held by the Manuscript Division of the New York Public Library.

127		*"almost off the rails": WIA* 213.

Linked in the popular imagination: see *BNY* 27n. Joelle Biele writes of a column by Lewis Gannett, "Books and Things," *New York Herald Tribune* (December 13, 1946): "Gannett reported that Selden Rodman had written him in response to his statement that 1946 'was the most arid year in American literature since our renaissance began thirty-odd years ago.' Rodman believed Gannett would not have made the claim had he read Bishop's *North & South* and Robert Lowell's *Lord Weary's Castle.*"

"I think of you": WIA 175.

"real": WIA 243, 315.

"genuine": *WIA* 137.

"firmly new": *WIA* 262.

"to get things straight": *WIA* 161.

"great ruminating": *WIA* 151.

"as though you weren't": *WIA* 174.

"growing-up novel": *WIA* 151.

128   *"sat through"*: *WIA* 188.

"purple panes," "delicate bay": RL, "91 Revere Street," *LPR* 315.

"less than fifty yards": RL, "91 Revere Street," *LPR* 313.

"Weelawaugh": RL, "91 Revere Street," *LPR* 317.

"freedom to explode": RL, "91 Revere Street," *LPR* 326.

"keep it up": *WIA* 188.

129   *"in the upstairs"*: EB, "Mrs. Sullivan Downstairs," *EAP* 197. See also other draft memoirs EB may have begun writing at this time, "Primer Class" and "The Country Mouse," dated 1960 and 1961 in *BPR*.

"psycho-therapy": RL to EB, November 18, 1949, *WIA* 92.

"what we imagine": EB, "At the Fishhouses," *BP* 63, 64.

"similar difficulties": *WIA* 121.

130   *"Thomas wanted to live"*: *WIA* 152.

"really just love": EB to Pearl Kazin Bell, November 28, 1953, VC 24.3.

"Oh what a gap": *WIA* 182.

"We seem attached": *WIA* 151.

"A Valediction: Forbidding Mourning": John Donne, *The Complete Poetry and Selected Prose of John Donne,* ed. Charles M. Coffin (New York: The Modern Library, 2001), 38–39.

"armored heavy": RL quoted in David Kalstone, *Becoming a Poet: Elizabeth Bishop with Marianne Moore and Robert Lowell,* ed. Robert Hemenway (New York: Farrar, Straus and Giroux, 1989), 174.

"glistening": EB, "The Armadillo," *BP* 102. "The Armadillo" was not a poem that EB associated with RL initially. EB, who by May 1956 had let the correspondence with RL lapse for more than six months, describes the sighting of the animal to MS: "Well — last night I saw an armadillo in the car headlights — I hadn't known we had them around here before, but there he was, crossing the road with his head down, quite glisteny and very lonely-looking." EB to MS, May 10, 1956, WU. EB also wrote to MM in a letter of the same date: "After all this time, I've just found out we have armadillos here — I see one crossing the road in the headlights at night, with his head and tail down — very lonely and glisteny." Quoted in *EBL* 275.

"breaking through": *LPR* 227.

131   *amorousness:* Kalstone, *Becoming a Poet,* 174.

had a fling: Edmund Wilson, *The Fifties: From Notebooks and Diaries of the Period,* ed. Leon Edel (New York: Farrar, Straus and Giroux, 1986), 452–53.

"Italian girl": Jarrell, *Randall Jarrell's Letters,* 414.

nearly broken up his marriage: See Jeffrey Meyers, *Robert Lowell in Love* (Amherst and Boston: University of Massachusetts Press, 2016), 129–35.

"more constructive": *WIA* 217.

"with ALL his heart": *WIA* 214n.

"scherzo," "rich in undramatic mishaps": WIA 219.

"second ex-": WIA 220.

"anti-manic pills": WIA 213.

132 *"our relations": WIA* 225–26.

"Oh heavens": WIA 211.

"one great might-have-been": WIA 108.

"delighted": WIA 180.

"I read you": WIA 204.

"we might almost claim": WIA 226.

133 *"the whole thing":* Virginia Woolf and Lytton Strachey, *Letters,* ed. Leonard Woolf and James Strachey (New York: Harcourt, Brace and Company, 1956), 37; also, Lytton Strachey quoted in Charles Poore, "Books of the *Times," New York Times,* December 29, 1956.

"of course there was": WIA 226.

"all has come right": WIA 225.

"great block": WIA 226.

"distance makes the heart": OA 325.

"As you must know": OA 481.

"red fox stain": RL, "Skunk Hour," *LP* 191.

"short line stanzas": RL, "On 'Skunk Hour': How the Poem Was Written," *LPR* 227.

134 *"best" of the new group: WIA* 243.

"My mind's not right": RL, "Skunk Hour," *LP* 191–92.

"all seem real": WIA 243.

JANUARY 12, 1977: 437 LEWIS WHARF, BOSTON

137 *"couldn't get started":* Mildred Nash diary, November 3, 1976, private collection.

138 *"For Once, Then, Something":* Robert Frost, *The Poetry of Robert Frost,* ed. Edward Connery Lathem (New York: Henry Holt & Co., 1923, 1969), 225.

141 *fled the conference center:* Lloyd Schwartz email to the author, August 25, 2016.

"My god, Elizabeth": William Sorensen recollection, email to the author, January 6, 2014.

"the famous eye": RL quoted in *EBL* 415.

"The art of losing": EB, "One Art," *BP* 198.

CHAPTER 4: RIVER

142 *"I am NOT":* EB to MS, September 28, 1961, WU.

"Graveyard of the Grand Banks": BNY 66.

"projected fact pieces": BNY 172.

143 *"up to me": OA* 288. EB repeated this 1954 statement in a 1960 letter to RL: "I think it is up to me to earn $$$$ somehow or other," *WIA* 310.

"created from scratch": OA 360.

"missionaries, land speculators": EB to MS, August 25, 1958, WU.

"go ahead": BNY 202.

"rather highbrow": EB, "A New Capital, Aldous Huxley, and Some Indians," *BPR* 310.

"the River of Souls": EB to MS, August 25, 1958, WU.

144   *"medicine, mysticism"*: *WIA* 265.

"all quite naked": EB to MS, August 25, 1958, WU.

"rounded behinds": EB, "A New Capital," *BPR* 317.

"small": EB, "A New Capital," *BPR* 300.

145   *"tall," "well-modeled"*: EB, "A New Capital," *BPR* 300.

"from his great height": EB, "A New Capital," *BPR* 316.

"manioc patch," "only attempt": EB, "A New Capital," *BPR* 318.

"most primitive": EB, "A New Capital," *BPR* 310.

"do no work": EB, "A New Capital," *BPR* 318.

"they rarely miss": EB, "A New Capital," *BPR* 317.

"messed about with": EB, "A New Capital," *BPR* 316–17.

146   *"they are gentle"*: EB, "A New Capital," *BPR* 318.

becoming one family: See Ruth A. Hawkins, *Unbelievable Happiness and Final Sorrow: The Hemingway-Pfeiffer Marriage* (Fayetteville: University of Arkansas Press, 2012), 277. Aldous Huxley had also entered into a "tripartite relationship" in the early years of his first marriage to Maria Nys, whom he'd met as she was extracting herself from a love affair with Lady Ottoline Morrell. Nicholas Murray, *Aldous Huxley: A Biography* (New York: Thomas Dunne Books, St. Martin's Press, 2002), 141.

"swooping": EB, "A New Capital," *BPR* 301.

"everything 'tails off badly'": *BNY* 208.

147   *"rather* dumb": *OA* 369.

"what a relief": EB to MS, August 25, 1958, WU.

"dingy and dark": *OA* 343.

place to retire: *OA* 379.

"I wonder": *WIA* 275.

"inoffensive": *WIA* 256.

"I killed you!": EB, "Sammy," *EAP* 179.

148   *"up to our necks in babies"*: *WIA* 255.

"stretch" of fluent composition: *WIA* 246.

"assurance," "all you have to do": *WIA* 247.

"I feel awful": *LP* 176.

149   *"It is hell to realize"*: *WIA* 247.

"behave": Behaving badly was EB's euphemism for her drinking spells. See *EBL* 515; EB to LA, June 3 [1967], VC 112.6.

"seems to feel": EB to MS, August 10, 1953, WU.

"um grande poeta": LS to LA, July 28, 1966, included in letters from EB to LA, VC 112.5.

"my natural melancholia": *OA* 367.

"a great letter-snoop": EB to MS, June 1, 1956, WU.

150   *Lota hated*: "Lota hates it," *WIA* 315; "Lota hates that poem and I don't like it too much myself," EB to MS, the day after Christmas [1960], WU.

"anthropological number": BNY 209.

"just crumbs": EB to MS, March 26, 1959, WU.

"The Riverman": BP 103.

learned from Wagley's book: Charles Wagley, *Amazon Town: A Study of Human Life in the Tropics* (Oxford and New York: Oxford University Press, 2014), 228–34.

151 *"Why shouldn't I"*: EB, "The Riverman," BP 105.

"green cheroots," "tall, beautiful": EB, "The Riverman," BP 104.

"travelling fast": EB, "The Riverman," BP 110.

"for each of the diseases": EB, "The Riverman," BP 106; *"it stands"*: BP 105.

"behind her back": EB, "The Riverman," BP 104.

"You can peer": EB, "The Riverman," BP 106–7.

"magical poem that casts": BNY 210.

"long arid stretch": BNY 211.

152 *dedicate the poem:* In the end, EB did not dedicate the poem to Katharine White. The *New Yorker* would not print a dedication to one of its staff members, and when the poem appeared in *Questions of Travel* (1965), EB omitted the promised dedication. BNY 212.

"the best fairy story": WIA 321.

"very powerful": WIA 591.

she wasn't interested: "Lota flatly refuses to travel in Brazil," EB to MS, May 10, 1956, WU; "I can't interest Lota in our scenery," EB to MS, October 27, 1964, WU.

"roughing it": EB to MS, the day after Christmas [1960], WU.

"refuses to have anything": WIA 318.

sixteen-year-old nephew: In a letter dated March 22, 1960, from the time of the trip, EB says Manoel was sixteen years old. *OA* 380. In a retrospective account given nearly three decades later, Rosinha Leão stated that her nephew was "about twelve." *REB* 164.

"like weak café": EB to LS, February 21, [1960], VC 32.8.

"RIVER VERY BIG": EB telegram to LS, VC 118.44.

153 *"Pink ones are lucky"*: WIA 313.

"against a dark": EB journal, "Trip on the Amazon," February 1960, p. 8, VC 55.2.

"authentic, post-Amazon": WIA 315.

154 *"I want to go back"*: WIA 316.

"I . . . am living": EB to Howard Moss, BNY 229.

read "all" the mail: EB to LS, February 21 [1960], VC 32.8.

"we think that": EB to LS, February 28 [1960], VC 32.8.

"my dream": EB to LS, February 22 [1960], VC 32.8.

"Love, love, love": EB to LS, February 22 [1960], VC 32.8.

"Love and devotion": EB to LS, February 28 [1960], VC 32.8.

"sticking up": EB to LS, February 21 [1960], VC 32.8.

bought it from a boatman: See James Merrill, "Elizabeth Bishop (1911–1979)," *Collected Prose,* ed. J. D. McClatchy and Stephen Yenser (New York: Alfred A. Knopf, 2004), 233. Rosinha Leão's somewhat different account of the acquisition confirms that it took place on the Amazon trip, rather than on the Rio Negro, where Merrill places the incident. *REB* 164–65.

155 *"On the Amazon": EAP* 124–25. EB also wrote to RL about a poem called "January River" that she worked on at this time. She thought of giving her next book of poems that title: "there's a poem of that name, or with that in it at least." *WIA* 354. The editors of *WIA* identify "January River" as EB's unfinished "On the Amazon." *WIA* 354n. But "January River" was most likely an early title for "Brazil, January 1, 1502," EB's poem about the Portuguese landing on the coast of Brazil at what became the port of Rio de Janeiro (River of January). *BP* 89–90. EB refers to that poem as "the 'January' one" in correspondence with the *New Yorker. BNY* 218.

"*everything seems nearer": WIA* 327.

"*cleaning up the attic": WIA* 260.

"rumba *rhythm": WIA* 346.

"*Hidden, oh hidden":* EB, "Song for the Rainy Season," *BP* 99.

"*he can count":* EB, "Song for the Rainy Season," *BP* 99.

156 "*love will unexpectedly":* EB journal quoted in *EBL* 244.

"*I always thought": OA* 367.

"*It is marvellous": EAP* 44.

stanzas added: "I wrote stanzas one and four in one day and then worked on it all off and on for six years — heavens." EB to MS, June 9, 1961, WU.

"*without water":* EB, "Song for a Rainy Season," *BP* 100.

157 "*we are delightedly": BNY* 231–32.

"*one of my greatest worries": WIA* 317.

"*I don't want to": BNY* 233.

Mrs. White conceded: The poem appeared as "Song for a Rainy Season" in the *New Yorker,* October 8, 1960, with no accompanying note situating the poem. When it was republished in *Questions of Travel* in 1965, EB changed the title to "Song for the Rainy Season" and added a detailed note locating the poem precisely: Sitio da Alcobaçinha, Fazenda Samambaia, Petrópolis.

"*too damp":* EB to MS, "the day after Christmas" [1960], WU.

158 "*twice as tall":* EB to MS, October 28, 1956, WU.

"*Let Shakespeare": BPPL* 245.

"*It rains and rains":* EB to MS, March 8 [1961], WU.

hair had gone gray: EB to MS, September 19, 1953, WU; "*retired" from "society": OA* 271.

159 "*darling baby":* EB to MS, February 9, 1961, WU.

"*useful days":* EB postcard to MS, n.d. [before June 9, 1961], WU.

"*big excitements":* EB to MS, February 9, 1961, WU.

"*Chief Coordinatress": OA* 398.

"*just the kind," "macho":* EB to MS, February 9, 1961, WU.

160 "*backyards":* EB to MS, July 26, 1964, WU.

"*wonderful in action": OA* 393.

"*doing something at last": OA* 397.

"*everyone involved":* EB to MS, March 8 [1961], WU.

"semi-revolutions": EB to MS, July 31, 1962, WU.

"anti-revolution revolution": *OA* 309.

"very bloody": *OA* 401.

"find herself in politics": *OA* 397.

"a real old crook": *OA* 401.

"We might even leave": *OA* 401.

"as usual": *OA* 401.

"strange": *OA* 396.

"up & down life": EB to MS, June 9, 1961, WU.

"the word for even": *WIA* 164.

161　*"beaches & mts."*: EB to MS, March 17, 1955, WU.

"awful but cheerful": EB, "The Bight," *BP* 59.

"Rio de Janeiro": EB, "On the Railroad Named Delight," *BPPL* 443.

"amazing first aid": *WIA* 329.

"hates to be alone": EB to MS, February 25, 1961, WU; *more than once:* "hates to be alone," EB to MS, July 26, 1964, WU.

compile an "anthology": EB to MS, January 7, 1963, WU.

"made her coffee": EB to MS, February 25, 1961, WU.

"sick of cooking": EB to MS, day after Christmas [1960], WU.

162　*"go down and heat up"*: *OA* 326.

"get busy cooking": *OA* 397.

"seemed to have one hand": MS to EB, October 28, 1955, WU.

"fear it could": *BNY* 234.

"You are about the only": *WIA* 331.

"their Republican readers": *BNY* xxxvii.

"several poems": *OA* 357.

"almost ready": *WIA* 353.

163　*"Sandpiper"*: *BP* 129; *compare herself:* "Laureate's Words of Acceptance," on receipt of Neustadt International Prize for Literature, April 9, 1976, *World Literature Today,* Winter 1977, 12.

164　*"finical"*: EB, "Sandpiper," *BP* 129.

"bitter telephone fights": *OA* 404.

"Radcliffe girl": EB to MS, May 15, 1962, WU.

"attack of pathological": RL, "Near the Unbalanced Aquarium," *LPR* 346.

five breakdowns: WIA 303.

"very dangerous": EB to MS, January 7, 1963, WU.

tearing off his clothes: Jeffrey Meyers, *Robert Lowell in Love* (Amherst and Boston: University of Massachusetts Press, 2016), 82; *accompanied by a doctor:* Ian Hamilton, *Robert Lowell: A Biography* (New York: Random House, 1982), 303.

"the knot inside": *WIA* 295.

"psych-a": *WIA* 303.

165　*"the seemingly dispassionate"*: *LL* 491.

"the most natural": *EBC* 99.

"think I may be able": *WIA* 303.

Calling it an "elegy": WIA 380.

"about snow": WIA 260.

resemblance to an earlier: RL did compare "First Death in Nova Scotia" favorably to John Crowe Ransom's "Bells for John Whiteside's Daughter" and Ben Jonson's "On Salathiel Pavy." *WIA* 380.

"a little frosted cake": EB, "First Death in Nova Scotia," *BP* 124–25.

rattled it off: OA 83; *"heaping field":* James Russell Lowell, "The First Snow-Fall," *The Poetical Works of James Russell Lowell* (Boston: Houghton Mifflin & Co., Riverside Press, 1890), 350.

166 *"immortal":* WIA 380.

the most "distrait": EB postcard to MS, n.d. [after December 12, 1962], WU.

"I have been minding": WIA 439.

"lost in admiration": OA 398.

"shrieking": EB to MS, November 10, 1965, WU.

167 *Time offered $9,000: OA* 400.

"material possessions": EB to MS, February 24 [1962], WU.

"homesick": EB to MS, January 22 [1962], WU.

"I can't see or hear": EB to MS, December 27, 1961, WU.

"so blue-eyed": OA 404.

"fight with LIFE": EB to MS, February 24 [1962], WU.

"ghastly 'slanting'": EB to MS, April 10 [1962], WU.

168 *"that blasted book":* EB to MS, April 10 [1962], WU.

"Groups and Individuals": EB, "Brazil," *BPR* 230.

"A Changing Social Scene": EB, *Brazil* (New York: Time Inc., 1962), 113.

"marriage at seventeen": EB, "Brazil," *BPR* 235.

"LIFE-slicked": OA 413.

"customary": EB, *Brazil,* 117.

"I have no confidence": EB to MS, Valentine's Day [1962], WU.

"I've never seen": WIA 259.

"what I like": EB to MS, January 7, 1963, WU.

"if I can": EB to MS, February 2, 1962, WU.

169 *Clarice Lispector:* "She is better than J. L. Borges — who is good, but not all that good!" EB to Ilsa and Kit Barker [writer and artist, friends from Yaddo], October 29, 1962, quoted in Benjamin Moser, *Why This World: A Biography of Clarice Lispector* (Oxford and New York: Oxford University Press, 2009), 257.

"Practicing Poets": EB to MS, March 5, 1963, WU.

"I can't write": EB to MS, October 3, 1963, WU.

"Work's the thing": OA 276.

"set-fire-works-sex-pieces": WIA 506.

"foreign woman": Mary McCarthy, *The Group* (New York: Harcourt, Brace & World, Inc., 1963), 369.

"This woman": McCarthy, *The Group,* 370.

"the convention": McCarthy, *The Group,* 371.

"not to think": McCarthy, *The Group,* 372.

170   *"short sandy-haired":* McCarthy, *The Group,* 100.

"Mary lets her off," "I was not": EB to MS, October 3, 1963, WU.

"I'm thankful": EB to MS, November 11, 1963, WU.

resemblance to Margaret Miller: OA 614n.

"stocky": McCarthy, *The Group,* 369.

carbon copy: In a letter to EB that she never received, McCarthy claimed the resemblance to Lota was unintentional; the letter was written in Paris and dated three weeks after EB's death. *OA* 614.

eighteen-hour days: EB to MS, November 10, 1965, WU.

except to sleep and shout: EB to MS, May 22, 1963, WU.

"I admire her gall": EB to MS, October 3, 1963, WU.

"commercial success": WIA 495.

"What DOES California": WIA 480.

"recipes for living": Laura Archera Huxley, *You Are Not the Target* (New York: Farrar, Straus and Co., 1963), table of contents.

171   *"craving for a good":* EB to MS, December 12, 1964, WU.

"no escape": EB to MS, July 2, 1963, WU.

"self-preservation's": EB to MS, December 12, 1964, WU.

"whether I'm there": EB to MS, March 24, 1963, WU.

"I don't mind": EB to MS, September 19, 1953, WU.

"I scarcely seem": EB to MS, May 22, 1963, WU.

"We're all silent": EB to MS, August 27, 1963, WU.

"This isn't *my world": WIA* 531.

"I feel like": WIA 350.

172   "capsula": *WIA* 415.

"golpe": *WIA* 515.

spent every night: EB to MS, August 4, 1963, WU.

"awful brown slime": EB to LS, July 7 [1964], VC 118.49.

"scared to death": EB to MS, October 3, 1963, WU.

"rest home": EB to MS, October 3, 1963, WU.

"great low pink": EB to MS, October 27, 1964, WU. EB hadn't known that the Flamengo (Flemish) district of Rio was named for a Dutch sea captain, Olivier van Noort, who'd attempted to invade the Portuguese settlement in the colonial era, and not for the elegant shorebird, called "flamingo" in both English and Portuguese. In Spanish, which EB had studied in Mexico, *flamengo* means "flamingo."

a "real" revolution: EB to MS, April 8, 1964, WU.

173   *"acutely anxious":* EB to LS [June 30, 1964], VC 118.48.

"YE GODS": EB to LS, June 25 [1964], VC 118.48.

"Oh so many poets": WIA 547.

"I wish you were": EB to LS, June 29 [1964], VC 118.48.

"GORGEOUS": EB to LS, July 10, 1964, letter #16B, VC 118.50.

"light as a feather": EB to LS, June 24 [1964], VC 118.48.

"excellent for ladies' use": EB to LS, July 7 [1964], VC 118.49.

"*a thousand*": LS to EB [June 15, 1964], English translation by Carmen L. Oliveira, VC 114.18.

Antabuse twice a week: EB to LS, July 3 [1964], VC 118.49.

"*my love*": LS to EB [June 21, 1964], English translation by Carmen L. Oliveira, VC 114.20.

"*slow boat*": EB to MS, May 5 [1964], WU.

"*I am dying*": *WIA* 549.

"*back to the Brazilian*": *WIA* 546.

"minha querida": EB to LS, July 15 [1964], VC 118.50.

"*inferiorities*": LS to EB, Morning Sunday [June 21, 1964], VC 114.20.

174   "*near-canonisation*": Edward Lucie-Smith, "No Jokes in Portuguese," *Sunday Times* (London), July 26, 1964, photo by Erich Auerbach.

"*Dear, my compass*": *EAP* 140. I have inserted an em dash at the start of the final quatrain, which is the way EB punctuated the poem in her handwritten version, not reproduced in *EAP*. Lloyd Schwartz email to the author, March 19, 2016. See also Lloyd Schwartz, "Annals of Poetry: Elizabeth Bishop in Brazil," *New Yorker*, September 30, 1991, 86.

175   *marked a star:* EB to LA, Friday Thursday AM [1965], p. 23a, VC 112.3.

"*reluctant*": EB to LA, January 18 [1966], VC 112.4.

small notebook: EB notebook, Ouro Prêto 1961–1965, VC 73.5.

"*good old*": *OA* 332.

"*If happiness*": Charles Berg and Clifford Allen, *The Problem of Homosexuality* (New York: Citadel Press, 1958), 53.

176   "*psychological deviation*": Berg and Allen, *The Problem of Homosexuality,* 52.

"*we make such a fuss*": Berg and Allen, *The Problem of Homosexuality,* 115.

"*psychopathology*": Berg and Allen, *The Problem of Homosexuality,* 151–53.

"*The socially accepted*": Wilhelm Reich quoted in Berg and Allen, *The Problem of Homosexuality,* 124.

wrote out the lines by hand: See Schwartz, "Annals of Poetry," 86. EB's typed copy, also illustrated, is reproduced in facsimile in *EAP* 140.

"*My dear Aurora Borealis*": EB to LA, April 9 [1965], VC 112.2.

"*Darling Lilli*": numerous letters from EB to LA, VC 112.2 and 112.3.

"*The more I give you*": Luís de Camões, quoted in translation in George Monteiro, *Elizabeth Bishop in Brazil and After: A Poetic Career Transformed* (Jefferson, NC, and London: McFarland & Company, 2012), 15.

177   "*killing herself with work*": *BNY* 278.

"*mean abandoning Lota*": EB to MS, January 26, 1965, WU.

"*THE Baroque town*": *WIA* 218.

"*strange assortment*": EB to MS, May 21, 1965, WU.

"*do all kinds of things*": EB to MS, February 24, 1962, WU.

"*hard hands*": EB to LA, November 18 [1965], VC 112.3.

"*my dearest blue eyed*": EB to LA, June 17 [1965], VC 112.2.

178   "*Tell me*": EB to LA, Sunday 13 [1965], p. 4, VC 112.2.

"*small water-fall*": EB to MS, May 21, 1965, WU.

"*a single iron pipe*": EB, "Under the Window: Ouro Prêto," *BP* 175–76.

"*simple" talk:* EB, "Under the Window: Ouro Prêto," *BP* 175–76.

"Women!": EB to MS, February 9, 1961, WU.

"*Somebody loves us all":* EB, "Filling Station," *BP* 126.

179 "*The seven ages":* EB, "Under the Window: Ouro Prêto," *BP* 176.

"*I feel human":* EB to LA, June 17 [1965], VC 112.2.

"*full of poetry":* EB to LA, "Sunday 13" [1965], VC 112.2.

"*all kinds of bits":* EB to LA, June 22–25 [1965], VC 112.3.

"*I wake up frightened":* EB to LA, July 2 [1954], VC 112.3.

"*split personality":* EB to LA, June 22–25 [1965], VC 112.3.

180 "*my lovely hot":* EB to LA, July 2 [1965], VC 112.3.

"*my appletree":* EB to LA, "Sunday 13" [1965], VC 112.2.

"*who gives everything":* EB to LA, June 17 [1965], VC 112.2.

"*dear danish pastry":* EB to LA, "Sunday 13" [1965], VC 112.2.

"*hideously guilty":* EB to LA, June 22–25 [1965], VC 112.3.

"*studying":* EB to LA, Friday Thursday AM [1965], VC 112.3.

"*We speak of shipwrecks":* EB notebook, 1962–64, VC 73.6.

"*Oh white":* EB, "Mr. and Mrs. Carlyle," *EAP* 180.

"*abrupt and rude":* *OA* 446.

"*violent . . . manner":* *OA* 450.

"*bossy":* *OA* 446.

studied Thomas Hardy's: OA 434.

"*Here is the ancient floor":* Thomas Hardy, "The Self Un-Seeing," *The Complete Poems of Thomas Hardy,* ed. James Gibson (New York: Macmillan, 1976), 166.

181 "*finally came":* EB to MS, November 10, 1965, WU.

secret plan: EB to LA, January 18 [1966], VC 112.4.

"*is always very happy":* *OA* 359.

15 percent contractor's fee: EB to LA, Saturday Morning [October 8, 1966], VC 112.5.

"*big old-fashioned":* EB to MS, May 21, 1965, WU.

"*it is almost":* *BNY* 281.

182 "*and it makes me feel":* EB to LA, November 12 [1965], VC 112.3.

"*not just a fling":* EB to LA, November 18 [1965], VC 112.3.

"*fat round pigs":* EB to LA, Monday afternoon [November? 1965], p. 21a, VC 112.3.

"*lavishly run kitchen":* EB to LA, June 22–25 [1965], VC 112.3.

183 "*nice and big":* EB to LA, January 1 [1966], VC 112.4.

diet pills: EB to LA, November 18 [1965], VC 112.3; *Metrecal:* EB to LA, Thursday 25th [1965], p. 8, VC 112.2; *Danish Coffee flavor:* EB to LA, February 21, 1966, VC 112.4.

"*both my grandmothers":* *WIA* 594.

"*pretty thin":* *BNY* 281.

"*cool, eely":* "Poetry in English," *Time,* March 9, 1962, quoted in *EBL* 334.

"*some of the finest":* "The Passing Strange," *Time,* December 24, 1965.

"*one of the shining":* reviews of *Questions of Travel* quoted in *EBL* 373.

"loves *it when I":* EB to LA, November 12 [1965], VC 112.3.

"feeling too many things": WIA 505.

"gumboils": EB to MS, November 10, 1965, WU.

"now she's had a taste": OA 438.

"soothing presence": EB to LA, June 22 [1965], VC 112.3.

"great comfort": EB to MS, November 10, 1965, WU.

184 *"accident of an unconscious-suicide"*: WIA 593.

"determined . . . that I am": EB to LA, June 22 [1965], VC 112.3.

"some of the Lost World": OA 434–35.

"passive forever": EB to LA, November 12 [1965], VC 112.3.

"make a fool": EB to LA, November 12 [1965], VC 112.3.

"keeps telling me": EB to LA, December 14 [1965], VC 112.3.

"sad scene": WIA 595.

"the courage to make": EB to LA, November 12 [1965], VC 112.3.

185 *"get some"*: EB to LA, December 31, 1965, VC 112.3.

"not my line at all": WIA 555.

"lists and lists": EB to LA, November 22 [1965], VC 112.3.

"I don't want": EB to LA, Friday Thursday AM [1965], p. 23b, VC 112.3; EB to LA, December 26 [1965], VC 112.3.

"How wonderful": EB to LA, January 8 [1966], VC 112.4.

"I go around": EB to LA, January 1 [1966], VC 112.4.

"wonderful rich": EB to LA, February 5, 1966, VC 112.4.

186 *"strange"*: EB to LA, January 6 [1966], VC 112.4.

Elizabeth tossed: Roxanne Cumming interview with the author, June 11, 2015.

SPRING 1977: PUSEY LIBRARY, HARVARD YARD

187 *"dime"*: Julie Agoos recollection, email to the author, January 14, 2014; "Assignment #5," Julie Agoos, ms., in Mildred Nash papers, private collection.

188 *"What should"*: Robert Fitzgerald, "Elegy," *In the Rose of Time* (Norfolk, CT: New Directions, 1956), 21.

189 *"brief but intense"*: http://uraf.harvard.edu/michael-c-rockefeller-memorial -fellowship.

191 *"humorous and tender"*: Robert Fitzgerald, "Notes on a Distant Prospect," *New Yorker,* February 23, 1976, 39–42. Reprinted in Robert Fitzgerald, *The Third Kind of Knowledge: Memoirs and Selected Writings,* ed. Penelope Laurans (New York: New Directions, 1993), 3–10.

193 *"I sing of warfare"*: Virgil, *Aeneid,* trans. Robert Fitzgerald (New York: Random House, 1983), 1.

"Imagination," "No general view": Fitzgerald, "Notes on a Distant Prospect," 42, 40.

CHAPTER 5: MIRACLE

195 *"that dramatic year"*: LS to EB, July 17 [1967], VC 118.8.

"almost enjoy": EB to LA, January 12 [1966], VC 112.4.

"a great deal": EB to LA, February 5, 1966, VC 112.4.

"You know exactly": EB to LA, February 13, 1966, VC 112.4.

"weird old cottage": EB to LA, June 9, 1966, VC 112.4.

196 *"fell in love easily"*: LA interview quoted in *EBL* 378.

"the French ladies": *ELC* 362; *"GK"*: EB to LA, June 17, 1966, VC 112.4.

"just a trifle": LS to LA, July 28, 1966, translated by Carmen L. Oliveira, VC 112.5.

197 *"better poems"*: LS to LA, July 28, 1966, translated by Carmen L. Oliveira, VC 112.5.

ressaca: EB to MS, April 25, 1963, WU.

"almost physically,": *OA* 449.

"despondency," "punishment": *OA* 448.

198 *"natural melancholia"*: *OA* 367.

"keep on drinking," Elizabeth's insistence: LS to LA, July 28, 1966, translated by Carmen L. Oliveira, VC 112.5.

"impatient and rude": LS to LA, July 28, 1966, translated by Carmen L. Oliveira, VC 112.5.

199 *"Everything seems worse"*: EB letter quoted in *EBL* 381.

"a bunch of crazy": *WIA* 609.

"what they used," "blow after blow": *WIA* 607, 608.

"blames an awful lot": *OA* 451.

200 *"I have changed"*: *OA* 450.

"grown up a lot": *OA* 449.

"back to N Y": EB to LA, September 1, 1966, VC 112.5.

"killing L inch by inch": EB to LA, September 1, 1966, VC 112.5.

"Nobody's heart is really": *OA* 191.

"more and more": EB to LA, September 1, 1966, VC 112.5.

"the very worst": EB to LA, October 23, 1966, VC 112.5.

"friends and gaiety": EB to LA, January 10, 1966 [really 1967], VC 112.6.

"manage pretty well": *OA* 449.

201 *"very sick"*: EB to LA, September 1, 1966, VC 112.5.

"I was so used to": *OA* 457.

"increasing violence": *OA* 451.

"I suppose the person," "fixed" on Elizabeth: *OA* 457.

"it wasn't too wrong": EB to LA, January 10, 1966 [really 1967], VC 112.6.

"I never felt so helpless": *OA* 451.

"I hate to leave": *OA* 458.

202 *"grim little book"*: *OA* 371.

"calmer": EB to LA February 19, 1967, VC 112.6.

"all the wrong ones": *OA* 457.

"want me back": EB to LA, January 4 or 5 [1967], VC 112.6.

"hard to know": EB to LA, January 4 or 5 [1967], VC 112.6.

"talks of me constantly": EB to LA, January 10, 1966 [really 1967], VC 112.6.

"since there's no one": EB to LA, January 12 [1967], VC 112.6.

203 *"Inventory"*: *EAP* 143.

"the book has to": EB to LA, January 14, 1967, VC 112.6.

"powerful friend": EB to LA, January 10, 1966 [really 1967], VC 112.6.

"think it will be": EB to LA, February 22, 1967, VC 112.6.

204 *"I haven't seen her"*: *OA* 458.

"All I want to do": EB to LA, March 14, 1967, VC 112.6.

"real study": EB to LA, March 4, 1967, VC 112.6.

205 *wearing the lapis lazuli ring*: EB to LA, April 25, 1967, VC 112.6.

"a sort of eraser": EB to MS, June 8, 1967, WU.

"everything else is All off": EB to LA, June 3 [1967], VC 112.5.

"feeling of disintegration": EB to Rosinha Leão and Magú Ribeiro [Rosinha's sister], June 3 [1967], VC 113.7.

"what I'll find": EB to LA, June 3 [1967], VC 112.5.

"I want only her": EB to Rosinha Leão and Magú Ribeiro, June 3 [1967], VC 113.7.

"ghastly poverty": EB to LA, June 3 [1967], VC 112.5.

"wouldn't have liked": EB to MS, June 8, 1967, WU.

206 *"maybe I said"*: EB to MS, June 8, 1967, WU.

race of imitators: "If I were a critic and had a good *brain* I think I'd like to write a study of 'The School of Anguish' — Lowell (by far the best), Roethke, and Berryman and their descendents like Anne Sexton and Seidel, more and more anguish and less and less poetry." EB letter quoted in *EBL* 361.

207 *"is really something"*: EB quoted in "Poetry in an Age of Prose," *Time,* June 2, 1967, 68.

"The School of Anguish": EB letter quoted in *EBL* 361.

"self-pitiers": *OA* 432.

"I, I, I": EB, "The Country Mouse," *BPR* 99.

208 *"In Worcester"*: EB, "In the Waiting Room," draft 1, VC 58.14.

"Valley of 10,000": *WIA* 630. See also *BNY* 319 for another report by EB on her library visit, and Jim Powell, "Bishop's *Arcadian Geographic*," *Tri-Quarterly* 81, Spring/Summer 1991, 170–74, for a discussion of EB's remembered images from various issues of *National Geographic.*

"Babies with pointed": EB, "In the Waiting Room," draft 1, VC 58.14.

"Their breasts": EB, "In the Waiting Room," drafts, VC 58.14.

209 *"unlikely"*: EB, "In the Waiting Room," *BP* 180–81.

210 *"the Village"*: EB to Rosinha Leão and Magú Ribeiro, July 10, 1967, VC 113.7.

"rejuvenate me": *WIA* 625.

"The poem is a beauty": LS to EB, August 16, 1967, VC 118.21.

"we knew each other": LS to EB, August 17, 1967, VC 118.22.

"Oh! my darling": LS to EB [August 2, 1967], VC 118.15.

211 *"very bad mornings"*: LS to EB, August 8, 1967, VC 118.19.

"terrible depression": LS to EB, n.d. [after August 3, 1967], VC 118.17.

"Please write": LS to EB, n.d., p. C, VC 118.9.

"Tell me again": LS to EB, August 8, 1967, VC 118.18.

"I would like to know": LS to EB, August 12, 1967, VC 118.20.

"your dearest dearest": EB quoted in LS to EB, July 19, 1967, VC 118.5.

"Nothing could give": LS to EB, August 8, 1967, VC 118.19.

"very, very light poem": BNY 295.

first-read contract: BNY 291.

212   *"Trouvée"*: BP 172.

"adorable": LS to EB, n.d. [1967], p. D, VC 118.9.

"for him you are": LS to EB, n.d. [1967], VC 118.17.

"still turning around": LS to EB, July 19, 1967, VC 118.6.

"a new girl called Rosanne": LS to EB, [July] 17 [1967], VC 118.8.

"we are two different": LS to EB, n.d. [1967], VC 118.17.

213   *"I even think"*: LS to EB, August 17, 1967, VC 118.22.

"almost death": LS to EB, July 28, 1967, VC 118.11.

"Lets not have": LS to EB, July 28, 1967, VC 118.11.

214   *"I cannot bear myself"*: LS to EB, August 2, 1967, VC 118.15.

praising *"Hen"*: LS to EB, August 3, 1967, VC 118.16.

"I hope you think": LS to EB, August 2, 1967, VC 118.14.

"honeybunch": EB to LS, July 10, 1964, letter #16B, VC 118.50.

"If sexual love": LS to EB, July 19, 1967, VC 118.5.

215   *"I was telling"*: LS to EB, August 2, 1967, VC 118.14.

"far away than the moon": LS to EB, n.d. [1967], VC 118.24.

"Don't clean any thing": LS to EB, August 28, 1967, VC 118.26.

"Why don't you," "solid like": LS to EB, August 8, 1967, VC 118.18.

"fit like a Stradivarius": LS to EB, August 28, 1967, VC 118.26.

"The past is gone": LS to EB, September 7 [1967], VC 118.28.

"our Tempest here": LS to EB, July 29, 1967, VC 118.10.

"do you really like": LS to EB, n.d. [1967], p. C, VC 118.9.

216   *"very sick indeed"*: EB to Rosinha Leão and Magú Ribeiro, September 23, 1967, VC 113.7.

identify her body, twelve kilo bags: OA 471.

"en cachette": LS to EB, n.d. [1967], VC 118.17.

"Perhaps she felt": OA 471.

217   *"sudden impulse"*: WIA 593.

"poet of terror": LL 491–92.

218   *"I have no idea"*: OA 470.

"It's not my fault": EB quoted in Lloyd Schwartz, "Elizabeth Bishop and Brazil," *New Yorker,* September 30, 1991, 94.

burned Elizabeth's letters: OA 526.

sketch for Lilli: EB to LA, June 16, 1967, VC 112.6.

"It is good," "There are times": "The Smallest Woman in the World," trans. EB, BPR 384, 383.

219   *"I just have to keep"*: EB to LA, January 13, 1968, VC 112.7.

Cal's letter of "gossip": LL 491–92.

few Decembers: Ian Hamilton, *Robert Lowell: A Biography* (New York: Random House, 1982), 370.

"Boogie": EB to LA, January 13, 1968, VC 112.7.

"pea green": *WIA* 636.

interview: EB's interview with Kathleen Cleaver on February 1, 1969, a remarkable document of the era, survives in Roxanne Cumming's transcript. VC 53.12.

220 *"Not very beautiful"*: EB to LA, January 13, 1968, VC 112.7.

"S F": *EAP* 147–48.

"music, food, furniture": *WIA* 640.

abandoned hatch cover: EB to LA, January 25, 1968, VC 112.7.

"Lotus White": *WIA* 652.

"short prose piece": Roxanne Cumming to Mrs. Eldridge Cleaver, April 11, 1969, included in folder with transcript of the February 1, 1969, interview, VC 53.12.

suggested she join AA: Elizabeth refused: Roxanne Cumming interview with the author, June 11, 2015.

"cold SOBER": EB to LA, February 8, 1968, VC 112.7.

drove off to Design Research: Roxanne Cumming interview, June 11, 2015.

221 *"unhappy flower child"*: *EAP* 148.

"I keep reminding myself": *WIA* 640.

"It's about time": Roxanne Cumming interview, June 11, 2015; "About time," *WIA* 668.

"You are always": *WIA* 668.

"live alone, dismal": *WIA* 664.

"I miss her more": *WIA* 665.

222 *"adoration & rudeness"*: *WIA* 675.

spending recklessly: EB to AB, June 10, 1970, VC 23.7.

"sort of gold": EB to AB, Washington's Birthday, 1970, VC 23.7.

"poor crazy girl": *WIA* 677.

"all too much like": *WIA* 673.

Elizabeth learned from: EB to AB, June 10, 1970, VC 23.7, and *OA* 529.

"long, long history": *WIA* 677. It is difficult to establish precisely what happened between EB and Roxanne Cumming in the months of February through May 1970. EB was also taking Anorexyl and drinking to excess; Cumming told EB's 1993 biographer Brett Millier that she never had a breakdown. *ECL* 426. EB provided a detailed account in EB to AB, June 10, 1970, VC 23.7; she describes behavior "totally unlike R's more normal self," as well as EB's own distress over Cumming's accusations that "I was 'throwing her out' . . . that I 'use up' my friends 'like old gloves' and 'throw them away,' or drive them to suicide." Nevertheless, EB wrote, "I am fond of Roxanne, and the worse she got the more I realized how terribly lonely and friendless she is in this world and how much she needs someone to help her." For some months after Cumming's departure, EB still hoped to be that person. In later years, Cumming attended medical school and worked as a doctor.

"small book of poems": *WIA* 677.

begun a sonnet sequence: EB to LA, January 3, 1968, VC 112.7

"remember all the good": EB to LA, January 3, 1968, VC 112.7.

223 *"ELEGY poem"*: *EAP* 219.

"For perhaps the tenth": *EAP* 149, 220–21. Lines in Spanish and English translation from "Elegía," Miguel Hernández, *The Unending Lightning: The Selected Poems of Miguel Hernández,* trans. Edwin Honig (Riverdale-on-Hudson, NY: Sheep Meadow Press, 1990), 12, 44.

224 *"Since she died"*: EB to AB, Washington's Birthday, 1970, VC 23.7.

"until I find you": Hernández, "Elegía," *The Unending Lightning,* 13.

"regret and guilt": *EAP* 219.

"poor bitch": EB, "Pink Dog," *BP* 212; poem begun in 1963: *EBL* 519, 545; EB worked on "Pink Dog" in San Francisco: Roxanne Cumming interview, June 11, 2015; "Lota likes me in pink," EB to MS, May 22, 1963, WU.

225 *"just naturally born"*: *WIA* 673.

"slightly guilty": EB to LA, January 3, 1968, VC 112.7.

"great grief": EB to LA, January 3, 1968, VC 112.7.

"enjoying *being terribly lonely"*: EB to AB, June 10, 1970, VC 23.7.

"Calling": *WIA* 663n2. After considerable revision, this poem became "For Elizabeth Bishop 4" in RL's 1973 volume *History, LP* 595, concluding: " . . . Do / you still hang your words in air, ten years / unfinished, glued to your notice board, with gaps / or empties for the unimaginable phrase — / unerring Muse who makes the casual perfect?"

"dumbfounded": *WIA* 663.

"say everything": *WIA* 677.

"After loving you": RL, "Obit," *LP* 642.

226 *"Friday, my dear"*: EB, "Crusoe in England," *BP* 186.

"a long hospitalization": EB to Dorothee Bowie [assistant to English department chair, Washington University], December 7, 1970, VC 114.5.

"bowled" him over: James Merrill, "Memories of Elizabeth Bishop," *Collected Prose,* ed. J. D. McClatchy and Stephen Yenser (New York: Alfred A. Knopf, 2004), 243.

collection of artifacts: Langdon Hammer, *James Merrill: Life and Art* (New York: Alfred A. Knopf, 2015), 483.

227 *"it just meant"*: Merrill, "Memories of Elizabeth Bishop," *Collected Prose,* 244.

"only crying": Merrill, "Elizabeth Bishop (1911–1979)," *Collected Prose,* 233.

"typed as a lesbian": Merrill, "Memories of Elizabeth Bishop," *Collected Prose,* 245.

"sparkling red-and-green": *EBHA* 260.

"their hatred for": EB to Rosinha Leão and Magú Ribeiro, May 31, 1966, VC 113.7.

228 *"term appointment"*: *OA* 553.

229 *"It's awful plain"*: EB, "The Moose," *BP* 193.

would have made Marianne Moore: "You are *not* the moose," EB wrote of the poem to her aunt Grace, to whom she dedicated "The Moose." *OA* 568. RL was not alone in asking, about Marianne Moore, "aren't all her animals her?" — as he wrote to EB in regard to "The Pelican," and Moore's many other significant poems about wildlife. *WIA* 739.

"big cow moose": *OA* 141.

alliterative M-M phrase: In April 1972, as she was composing "The Moose," EB wrote to RL, "I am still struggling to put down all my Marianne Moore recollections." *WIA* 716. EB ultimately concluded her memoir of Moore with an alliterative rhapsody, another M-M goodbye: "I find it impossible to draw conclusions or even to summarize. When I try to, I become foolishly bemused: I have a sort of subliminal glimpse of the capital letter *M* multiplying. I am turning the pages of an illuminated manuscript and seeing that initial letter again and again: Marianne's monogram; mother; manners; morals; and I catch myself murmuring, 'Manners and morals; manners *as* morals? Or is it morals *as* manners?' Since like [Lewis Carroll's] Alice, 'in a dreamy sort of way,' I can't answer either question, it doesn't much matter which way I put it; it *seems* to be making sense." EB, "Efforts of Affection," *BPR* 140.

"by craning backward": EB, "The Moose," *BP* 193.

"two women seated": EB to RF, February 1947, VC 118.33. Note also EB's lines in "The Moose" describing the experience of eavesdropping: "A dreamy divagation / begins in the night, / a gentle, auditory, / slow hallucination...." *BP* 191. For an analysis of the poem that places EB in the tradition of English lyric poetry, see Helen Vendler, "The Numinous Moose," *London Review of Books* 15, no. 5 (March 11, 1993), 6–8.

230   *"Grandparents' voices"*: EB, "The Moose," *BP* 191–93.

purchased at the Coop: OA 567.

"still seems like home": *WIA* 677.

231   *"sea of lilacs"*: *OA* 565.

"I just wish": *BNY* 342.

JUNE 14, 1977: SANDERS THEATRE, MEMORIAL HALL

233   *"The question is"*: Edwin Land quoted in Francis J. Connolly, "Land Speaks on Science, Metaphysics," *Harvard Crimson,* June 15, 1977.

236   *"Red-Tail Hawk and Pyre of Youth"*: Robert Penn Warren, *New Yorker,* July 18, 1977, 32–33; also reprinted, with minor alterations, in Robert Penn Warren, *Now and Then: Poems, 1976–1978* (New York: Random House, 1978), 17–21.

237   *"A new volcano"*: EB, "Crusoe in England," *BP* 182–83.

"practice losing farther": EB, "One Art," *BP* 198.

CHAPTER 6: SUN

239   *"The poor heart"*: EB to AM, March 31, 1971, VC 114.40.

"beery party": EB to AM, March 26, 1971, VC 114.39.

"blue blue blue": EB to AM, July 1, 1972, VC 115.12.

"Sunny-Side Up": EB to AM, March 23 or 24, 1971, VC 114.37.

"the most electrified": *OA* 543.

240   *"those nice satiny"*: EB to AM, March 23, 1971, VC 114.36.

"nice & loud": EB to AM, February 14, 1971, VC 114.32.

"Good-morning": EB to AM, February 19, 1971, VC 114.32.

"the way you pull on": EB to AM, March 23 again 8:30 PM, 1971, VC 114.36.

"the ladies": EB to AM, March 23, 1971, VC 114.36.

"taken aback": AM to EB, March 20, 1971, VC 116.14.

"I'm wrong in every way": EB to AM, February 22, 1971, VC 114.33.

"you are much too young": EB to AM, February 19, 1971, VC 114.32.

"beaux": EB to AM, February 24, 1971, VC 114.34.

"indiscreet": EB to AM, February 14, 1971, VC 114.32.

"all your electrical": EB to AM, February 17, 1971, VC 114.32.

241   *"Bob the Boring"*: AM to EB, July 2, 1971, VC 116.20.

"For Always, Alice": AM to EB, Feburary 22, 1971, VC 116.12.

"love — housefulls": EB to AM, April 1, 1971, VC 115.1.

"best breakfast": EB to AM, February 16, 1971, VC 114.32.

"two collapses": EB to AM, March 22, 1971, VC 114.36.

242   *"less neurotic"*: EB to AM, March 23 or 24, 1971, VC 114.37.

"unreservedly": AM to EB, March 2, 1971, VC 116.13.

"morbidly given to": EB to AM, March 31, 1971, VC 114.40.

"things I can actively": AM to EB, March 12, 1971, VC 116.14.

"the Ageds": AM to EB, February 15, 1971, VC 116.10.

"our mutual past": AM to EB, March 12, 1971, VC 116.14.

"vast difference in our ages": EB to AM, March 31, 1971, VC 114.40.

"the same way": EB to AM, February 20, 1971, VC 114.32.

"just plain grief": EB to AM, March 31, 1971, VC 114.40.

"awful tail-spin": EB to AM, March 19, 1971, VC 114.36.

"I'll have to see you": EB to AM, March 31, 1971, VC 114.40.

243   *beach wrap*: "your terry-cloth beach-wrapper," EB to AM, July 9, 1971, VC 115.5.

"a nice beach": *OA* 591.

"If Elizabeth lived here": AM to EB, April 20, 1971, VC 116.17.

"blissful shock": AM to EB, April 15, 1971, VC 116.7.

"the horrors set in": EB to AM, March 23 or 24, 1971, VC 114.37.

"a successful blending": Melanie Klein, *Love, Guilt and Reparation and Other Works, 1921–1945* (New York: Free Press, 1975), 331.

"Lib Ladies": EB to AM, March 23 or 24, 1971, VC 114.37.

"strongly upon the present": Klein, *Love, Guilt and Reparation,* 332.

244   *"you seem to have"*: EB to AM, March 23 or 24, 1971, VC 114.37.

"the subject of homosexual": Klein, *Love, Guilt and Reparation,* 331.

245   *"SICK is the only"*: EB to AM, March 23, 1973, VC 118.36. Tennessee Williams's story was "The Inventory at Fontana Bella," published in *Playboy,* March 1973, and collected in Williams's *Eight Mortal Ladies Possessed* (New York: New Directions, 1974), 21–29.

"rowed trip?": EB to AM, March 23, 1973, VC 118.36.

"Yesterday as we": EB to AM, March 23, 1973, VC 118.36.

"Writing (Advanced Course)": Harvard University Catalogue, 1970–71.

These were the years: Harvard University Catalogues, 1949–50, 1951–52. Isabel G. MacCaffrey, a scholar of Milton and Spenser, became Harvard's first female tenured professor of English literature, with an appointment in the Department of History and Literature, in July 1971. Formerly a professor at Bryn Mawr College, MacCaffrey had followed her husband, historian Wallace MacCaffrey, to Cambridge when he accepted a professorship at Harvard five years earlier. She taught at Tufts University in the interim.

246 *Subject Matter, vote of the Harvard Corporation:* Morton Bloomfield to EB, June 16, 1970, VC 40.8.

"Miss_____": Harvard University Catalogue, 1970–71.

"the greatest feminine": EBC 53.

"scholarly and significant": MS to EB, November 3, 1971, WU. *The Women Poets in English: An Anthology,* ed. Ann Stanford (New York: McGraw-Hill, 1972).

"Women's Lib.": EB to MS, November 7, 1971, WU; also published in *BPPL* 883–85.

247 *"woman poet":* REB 329.

"the situation of woman": EB to Adrienne Rich, April 25, 1973, Rich Papers, Series II, Folder 126, SL.

C's as failing grades: "*C*'s are failing grades for good students." EB small notebook, College Teaching Notes, VC 71.6.

"an Irish boy": OA 552.

older married student: Anne Hussey, *REB* 311.

248 *"militant young lady":* BNY 353.

"try" to be more: EB to Adrienne Rich, April 25, 1973, Rich Papers, Series II, Folder 126, SL.

"refusing the terms": W. W. Norton press release with text of speech, April 18, 1974, National Book Foundation archives.

"we found ourselves": Adrienne Rich, "The Eye of the Outsider," *New Boston Review,* June 1984.

249 *"having TALKED":* EB to Adrienne Rich, February 3, 1973, Rich Papers, Series II, Folder 126, SL. By selecting de Chirico's *The Disquieting Muses* for her postcard to Adrienne Rich, Elizabeth might have been offering an oblique commentary on Sylvia Plath's well-known poem of the same title, her 1957 complaint against her mother. If so, Elizabeth's intent may have been both whimsical and corrective. De Chirico's painting represents the Greek muses Melpomene and Thalia (tragedy and comedy), with a shadowed Apollo looking on. In her poem, Plath had wrongly taken the figures in the painting to be three females, turning them into three fairy godmothers appointed by her mother; perhaps she'd confused the muses with the three fates of Greek myth. Elizabeth did not refer to the postcard image in her note except to say that the colors in the reproduction "are all wrong — shd. be more orange, I think." Yet on the car ride, Elizabeth and Adrienne had discussed the "recent suicides in each of our lives" at a time when suicide among American poets was also rampant (Plath, Jarrell, Berryman, soon Anne Sexton). In apologizing for "having TALKED so much" about their twin losses, Elizabeth sent Adrienne a card depicting two sturdy, if outré, female literary figures, survivors who put Apollo in the shade.

"refusal of the self-destructiveness": Adrienne Rich, "When We Dead Awaken: Writing as Re-Vision," *College English* 34, no. 1 (October 1972), 18.

"Much of woman's": Adrienne Rich, "Feminine Sensibility: A Forum," *Harvard Advocate,* Winter 1973, 16. The *Advocate* excerpt was culled from several parts of Rich's essay. The sentence beginning "Much of woman's poetry" appears to have been written expressly for the *Advocate,* substituting for a sentence that concluded: "... until recently this female anger and this furious awareness of the Man's power over her were not available materials to the female poet, who tended to write of Love as the source of her suffering, and to view that victimization by Love as an almost inevitable fate." The following sentence on Moore and Bishop was not parenthetical in the essay. Rich, "When We Dead Awaken," 19.

"Today, much poetry": Rich, "Feminine Sensibility: A Forum," 16.

"I don't mind": EB to Adrienne Rich, April 25, 1973, Rich Papers, Series II, Folder 126, SL. Although EB conceded Rich's point that, along with Marianne Moore, she had "kept human sexual relations at a measured and chiselled distance in her poems," EB expressed a different opinion to May Swenson, writing of Moore, "I'm afraid she never can face the tender passion." *BPPL* 807.

250   *"The only real"*: Adrienne Rich, "The Phenomenology of Anger," *Diving into the Wreck: Poems, 1971–1972* (New York: Norton, 1973), 30. Rich italicized the quoted lines in later editions.

"I wonder what": Marianne Moore, "Marriage," *The Poems of Marianne Moore,* ed. Grace Schulman (New York: Penguin, 2005), 155; *assigned "Marriage"*: EB to Adrienne Rich, April 25, 1973, Rich Papers, Series II, Folder 126, SL.

"Scotch-Canadian": EB to AM, Tuesday, March 23, 1971, VC 114.36.

251   *"Breakfast Song"*: *BP* 327.

"Please, please *don't"*: *WIA* 778.

"de-effervescing": *WIA* 739.

252   *"If only age could stop"*: *WIA* 740.

"in spite of aches": *WIA* 778.

"The three books": *WIA* 704.

"word by word": MS to EB, October 30, 1962, WU.

253   *"I swear he has"*: EB to MS, November 7, 1962, WU.

"One night you dreamed": RL, "Water," *LP* 321–22.

British edition: *WIA* 687n.

"the worst situation": RL, "For Elizabeth Bishop 3. Letter with Poems for Letter with Poems," *LP* 594.

"I may owe you": *WIA* 687.

254   *"faint blue glimmer"*: RL, "For Elizabeth Bishop 3. Letter with Poems for Letter with Poems," *LP* 594.

"does you honor": *WIA* 687.

"Your last letter": RL, "For Elizabeth Bishop 3. Letter with Poems for Letter with Poems," *LP* 594.

"like being handed": *WIA* 665.

"I am going to publish": *WIA* 704.

"I have someone else": *WIA* 681.

255   *"I couldn't bear"*: *WIA* 752.

"My Dolphin": RL, "Dolphin," *LP* 708.

"my fresh wife": *WIA* 712.

"Mermaid": *LP* 665.

"Poetry has got to be": *REB* 377.

"magnificent": *WIA* 707–8.

"I think of you": RL, "Marriage," *LP* 656.

256   *"made up,"* "art just isn't": *WIA* 709, 708.

"the revelation": *WIA* 714.

"milder": *WIA* 715.

"I love you so much": *WIA* 707.

"Who can want": WIA 715.

"you've changed them": WIA 716.

"delighted" to accept: WIA 725.

"our Frankie": WIA 731.

"gone over for about": WIA 735.

"every single day": WIA 696.

"Please, please don't let": WIA 730.

257 *"We (you & I)": WIA* 733.

"think of herself": WIA 740.

"We dread the telephone": WIA 752.

"We all have irreparable": WIA 753.

"short, sad poem": BNY 354.

"the weird man": OA 583.

258 *"Still dark":* EB, "Five Flights Up," *BP* 203.

"my ridiculous gloom": OA 582.

259 *"just too sad":* EB to Loren MacIver, January 1, 1974, VC 31.6.

Two days later: "Stillman," January 3, 1974, entry, EB datebook, 1973–74, VC 120.4.

260 *"started out as a sort of joke": WIA* 767.

"intramural": BNY 361.

"thinking with one's": EB to MS, September 6, 1955, WU; *BPPL* 809.

"It was cold": EB, "The End of March," *BP* 199–200.

261 *"The whole Boston waterfront": OA* 578.

"verandah": OA 578.

262 *possibly hastened by drink:* EB to Pearl Kazin Bell, November 28, 1953. "My father died at about the same age [as Dylan Thomas] — previous drinking was supposed to have had something to do with it, too — but I really don't know much about it and I was a few months old at the time." VC 24.3.

"homesickness": EB to AM, July 2, 1971, 6 PM, VC 115.4.

263 *"our faces froze":* EB, "The End of March," *BP* 200.

"my version": BNY 360.

"I will arise and go": William Butler Yeats, "The Lake Isle of Innisfree," *The Collected Works of W. B. Yeats, Volume One: The Poems,* ed. Richard Finnerman (New York: Scribner, 1997), 35.

"hermit-type": EB to AM, February 16, 1971, VC 114.32.

"in the deep": Yeats, "The Lake Isle of Innisfree," *The Collected Works of W. B. Yeats, Volume One: The Poems,* 35.

264 *"I'd be a wreck":* EB to AM, April 24, 1973, VC 118.37.

"pep-up cheer-up pills": WIA 798.

"my age and physical": EB to AM, February 21, 1971, VC 114.32.

"no breasts": EB to AM, March 23, 1971, again 8:30 PM, VC 114.36.

"brave & sensible": EB to AM, February 22, 1971, VC 114.33.

"my mind closes up": EB to AM, March 26, 1971, VC 114.39.

"long-procrastinated": BNY 355.

"insipid": REB 276.

265 *"Gave up on this":* EB draft for Sylvia Plath's *Letters Home: Correspondence, 1950–1963,* ed. Aurelia Schober Plath (New York: Harper & Row, 1975), VC 54.20.

Erik Erikson–style: AM to EB, March 3, 1971, VC 116.13.

"much too good": EB to AM, March 28, 1971, Sunday again, VC 114.39.

"Being extremely interested": EB to AM, May 6, 1971, VC 115.2.

"imagine that just": EB to AM, March 28, 1971, Sunday again, VC 114.39.

"Woms. Lib.": EB to AM, February 21, 1971, VC 114.32.

"almost too good": BNHJ 12.

"magnificent views": BNY 360.

"one general store": OA 587.

266 *"a haven for": BNY* 360.

"bags and bags": BNY 360.

"pretty certain": BNHJ 15, 14.

"at least A's": BNHJ 18.

267 *"cast into gloom": OA* 597.

"fifty-one American": Richard Howard, ed., *Preferences* (New York: Viking, 1974).

tore her photo out: Lloyd Schwartz recalls, "I was visiting her the day her copy of Richard Howard's coffee-table anthology *Preferences* arrived. . . . She excused herself, went into her bedroom, and tore the page with the photograph out of the book." Schwartz, "Elizabeth Bishop: Sonnet," *Atlantic Online,* March 29, 2000. http://www.theatlantic.com/past/docs/unbound/poetry/soundings/bishop.htm.

"I want now": BNHJ 12.

"Late Sleepers": BNHJ 20–21.

268 *"sailing trip": BNHJ* 22.

"one of the trustees": EB to AM, May 6, 1971, VC 115.2.

"on the condition": AM to EB [May 15, 1971], VC 116.19.

"Could I be suffering": AM to EB, July 15, 1972, VC 116.28.

"Just knowing you": AM to EB, March 22, 1973, VC 116.29.

269 *"best":* AM to EB, February 1, February 7, February 9, 1971, VC 116.9 and more.

"Please forgive me": EB to AM, April 24, 1973, VC 118.37.

"— To have no personal": BNHJ 24.

added to the list: BNHJ 12.

270 *"between us & the water": BNHJ* 25–26.

"Frank gets the books": EB to AM, June 25, 1975, VC 118.38.

"Dearest Alice": EB to AM, October 8, 1975, VC 118.39.

"Letter to N.Y.": BP 78.

271 *"I want you to be":* EB to AM, October 8, 1975, VC 118.39.

"the only 'family'": EB to AM, October 8, 1975, VC 118.39.

"ruby-like": OA 591.

"attached": EB to AM, January 16, 1976, VC 118.41.

272 *"With best wishes":* EB, in "Self-Portraits" from the collection of Burt Britton, *Antaeus* 23, Autumn 1976, 87.

moss agate: EB to AM, July 7, 1972, VC 115.14.

273 *"I wish I'd been able":* EB to AM, October 8, 1975, VC 118.39.

"How to Lose Things": EB, "One Art," draft 1, *EAP* back matter, unpaginated.

"one and only": BNY 378.

"The art of losing": EB, "One Art," draft 2, *EAP* back matter, unpaginated.

"None of these": EB, "One Art," *BP* 198.

274 *"My losses haven't been":* EB, "One Art," draft 11, *EAP* back matter, unpaginated.

"pure emotion": EBC 66.

"— Even losing you": EB, "One Art," *BP* 198.

"Upsetting and sad": BNY 373.

"it makes everyone weep": BNY 378.

received another "blow": EB to AM, December 18, 1975, VC 118.40.

275 *calling to check on her:* EB to AB, December 24, 1975, VC 23.8.

"Since I'll be taking": EB to AM, December 18, 1975, VC 118.40.

"away from it all": OA 602.

"too cold and windy": OA 603.

"It's cold for here": EB to Robert Fitzgerald, December 24, 1975, Robert Fitzgerald Papers, Box 4, Folder 131, YCAL.

"another really bad": EB to Robert Fitzgerald, December 5, 1975, Robert Fitzgerald Papers, Box 4, Folder 131, YCAL.

"handsome": EB to Robert Fitzgerald, January 12, 1976, Robert Fitzgerald Papers, Box 4, Folder 131, YCAL.

"WORK": OA 603.

276 *"the friend I am so":* EB to AB, December 24, 1975, VC 23.8.

"accident of an unconscious": WIA 593.

"Oh dear, oh dear": BNY 364.

"to pass quite out": EB to AM, April 2, 1971, 10:30 AM, VC 115.1.

"stupendous thunderstorm": EB to AM, February 21, 1971, VC 114.32.

"not ok": AM to EB, March 2, 1971, VC 116.13.

"decrepitude": EB to AM, May 6, 1971, VC 115.2.

"I think this was": OA 595.

277 *"My Last Poem":* BP 241.

fighting an impulse: REB 333.

rushed her to the hospital: There are conflicting accounts of this day. In *EBL,* Brett Millier mentions a hospital stay connected with the overdose. *EBL* 525. In *REB,* Louise Crane's caretaker, A. L. Francis, recalls that EB was left to sleep it off. *REB* 334.

"having behaved": EB to AB, January 16, 1976, quoted in *EBL* 515.

"an awful fool": OA 604.

"ox-like power": LL 495.

"made of iron": EB to AM, March 31, 1971, VC 114.40.

"more cheerful": OA 602.

"Postscript": EB to AM, December 18, 1975, VC 118.40.

"you'll talk to me": EB to AM, January 16, 1976, VC 118.41.

"I DO want you": EB to AM, January 15, 1976, VC 118.41.

she'd cried over his memoir: EB to Robert Fitzgerald, February 23, 1976, Robert Fitzgerald Papers, Box 4, Folder 131, YCAL.

278 *"promised everything"*: Lloyd Schwartz interview with the author, January 8, 2016.

"Ancients": AM to EB, May 29, 1976, VC 116.32.

"I like being": AM to EB, June 10 [1976], VC 116.32.

"very smart": BNY 380.

"a scared elderly": OA 535.

"lacked 'reality'": EB to AM, March 25?, 1971, VC 114.38.

279 *"the more polite"*: EB teaching observations, December 1976, VC 71.7.

"two really witty": BNY 380.

"scared to death": EB to AM, Sunday again — noon [March 28, 1971], VC 114.39.

flew to New York: EB datebook, 1977, VC 120.6.

280 *"Those are bulls' eyes"*: MS to EB, February 13, 1956, WU.

"Miss Elizabeth": Henry Rosovsky to David Perkins, May 13, 1976, VC 40.8.

"creativity": EB, "IF YOU WANT TO WRITE *WELL* ALWAYS AVOID THESE WORDS," facsimile in *BPR* 252. The word "creativity" is underlined in this 1975 list for EB's prose-writing class.

refused to teach: EBC 141.

"age of poet-teachers": *WIA* 202.

281 *"new home, alone"*: *WIA* 757.

"looked awfully well": OA 606.

"a lot of your": *WIA* 761.

"looked tragic": *WIA* 684.

"quite sensitive, low-keyed poems": *WIA* 686.

group that included: WIA 685.

"my best pupils": BNY 353.

282 *"LAMB"*: EB datebook, 1977, March 1 entry, VC 120.6.

"it seemed as if thirty": *WIA* 793.

"talking emotionally": *WIA* 780.

"lonely warmth": *WIA* 764.

"hurt": EB datebook, 1977, March 5 entry, VC 120.6.

superintendent: Sandra Barry, "Lifting Yesterday: Elizabeth Bishop & Nova Scotia," (unpublished ms., copyright 2014), chapter 5, 23.

283 *"motherly" feelings: WIA* 766.

"trees & lilacs": EB datebook, 1977, May 15 entry and following, VC 120.6.

"I think on clear": *WIA* 793.

"Santarém": BP 207–8.

284 *"When you are dying"*: RL, "Artist's Model 2," *LP* 682.

historic marker: WIA 791.

"your dishevelment": *WIA* 778.

"shy but full of": *WIA* 776.

285   *"done"*: *WIA* 796–97.

     "spoiling": *WIA* 757.

     "I already miss their presence": *WIA* 793.

     "You command your words": *WIA* 785.

     folded in his wallet: "The Armadillo," *WIA* 324; "Under the Window: Ouro Prêto," *WIA* 613; "Five Flights Up," *WIA* 762.

     "we were swimming": *WIA* 776.

     "thin and arty": *WIA* 181.

     "One does use": *WIA* 758.

     "the pleasure of pure": *WIA* 760.

     "never met a woman": Frank Bidart in conversation with the author, April 20, 2015.

     "White Goddess": *LP* 432.

286   *"gay . . . Shakespearian"*: *BNHJ* 41.

     "Buttercups, Red Clover": EB, "North Haven," *BP* 210–11.

     "talk . . . with confidence": *WIA* 298.

     "My Darling receding": *WIA* 234.

     "Hadn't two rivers": EB, "Santarém," *BP* 207.

     "truth": *OA* 618.

287   *"It had a bit of"*: Amram Shapiro email to the author, December 1, 2015.

     "books everywhere": *OA* 594; Così fan tutte: Daniel Kessler, *Sarah Caldwell: First Woman of Opera* (Lanham, MD: Scarecrow Press, 2008), 231.

     "house of my dreams": EB to AM, July 9, 1971, VC 115.5.

288   *"unknown relatives"*: Mildred J. Nash, "Elizabeth Bishop's Library: A Reminiscence," *EBC* 136.

     "just never worked out": Nash, "Elizabeth Bishop's Library," 136.

     "decrepit": EB to AM, March 31, 1971, VC 114.40.

     "someone's grandmother": EB to Robert Fitzgerald, March 1, 1979, Robert Fitzgerald Papers, Box 4, Folder 131, YCAL.

     "Robert Fitzgerald's older": Nash, "Elizabeth Bishop's Library," 136.

     "a grandfather": EB to Robert Fitzgerald, March 1, 1979, Robert Fitzgerald Papers, Box 4, Folder 131, YCAL.

289   *"booze and groceries"*: *OA* 628.

     "stray dogs": EB datebook, 1978, December 6 entry, VC 120.7.

     wild poppies: EB travel journal, Greece, 1979. This small Vassar College notebook has a "blood-red" poppy pressed into it, along with other notes on the color of poppies. VC 121.3.

     "in a sort of daze": *BNY* 397.

     "our beach": EB datebook, 1978, July 18 entry, VC 120.7.

     "intensely quiet": *BNHJ* 41.

     "millions of blueberries": *BNHJ* 41.

     "Moon Pudding": *BNHJ* 44.

     "badly written": *BNHJ* 42.

290 *"in many editions":* OA 498.

"eye to eye": BNHJ 43.

"Such fogginess seems to make": OA 637.

"The Foggy Summer": BNHJ 47.

"The sun has come out!": BNY 400.

English 582: OA 637.

"'nice' to an old lady": EB to AM, March 31, 1971, VC 114.40.

291 *on the floor of her bedroom:* Brett Millier writes that Alice Methfessel found Elizabeth collapsed in her Lewis Wharf study, "the telephone off the hook beside her, when she arrived to take her to dinner at Helen Vendler's." *EBL* 550. Frank Bidart, who was called to the scene, confirms the account given in *REB:* "Bishop died in her apartment . . . while she was dressing for dinner at Helen Vendler's. Methfessel found her on the floor in her bedroom when she came to Lewis Wharf to pick her up." *REB* 349. Frank Bidart email to Lloyd Schwartz, March 14, 2016. Bidart adds: "Her face was calm, wiped of any expression of pain or dismay."

"veiled confession": EBL 545.

292 *"Caught — the bubble":* EB, "Sonnet," BP 214.

"Woms. Lib.": EB to AM, February 21, 1971, VC 114.32.

"Sapphic": EB to AM, July 4, 1972, VC 115.13.

"really a sick book": EB to AM, March 23, 1971, VC 114.36.

293 *"Santarém":* BP 207.

Through the early 1970s: John D'Emilio and Estelle B. Freeman, *Intimate Matters: A History of Sexuality in America* (New York: Harper & Row, 1988), 324.

"delighted": BNY 391.

"a gay drunken party": EB datebook, 1978, October 11 entry, VC 120.7.

294 *"Where Courtesy Prevails":* EB to AM, February 25, 1971, VC 114.34.

"Closets, closets": REB 330.

"life-style": EB, "IF YOU WANT TO WRITE *WELL* ALWAYS AVOID THESE WORDS," BPR 252.

"restore . . . gay": Schwartz, "Elizabeth Bishop: Sonnet."

"just under water": BNHJ 41.

295 *"it may be what everyone":* BPPL 896. EB also included "to have sex" on her list, "IF YOU WANT TO WRITE *WELL* ALWAYS AVOID THESE WORDS," BPR 252.

documentary filmmaker: Jill Janows, *Elizabeth Bishop: One Art.* Written, produced, and directed by Jill Janows. Produced by the New York Center for Visual History for *Voices & Visions,* its thirteen-part documentary film series on modern American poetry. Running time: 60 minutes. PBS broadcast: 1988. Distributor: Annenberg Learner.

"Close close all night": EAP 141.

296 *"Once in the night":* EAP 336.

"mind in action": EBC 26.

"go whistling by": EB, "Behind Stowe," BPPL 184.

"This is just the sketchiest": EB to Anne Stevenson, March 23, 1964, BPR 433.

297 *"What one seems":* EB to Anne Stevenson, January 8, 1964, BPR 414.

"looking for something": EB, "Sandpiper," BP 129.

ENVOY: JANUARY 23, 2014, PATOU THAI, BELMONT CENTER

298 *"poetry department"*: letter from "The Editors" of the *New Yorker* ("To Our Contributors") to the author, May 23, 1977.

"The manuscript we are returning": The Editors of the *Atlantic Monthly* to the author, November 15, 1977.

299 *"Crusoe in England"*: *BP* 185.

300 *"wonderfully sculptural"*: Joe Gonnella to the author, postmarked February 6, 1977.

"Fog": Amy Clampitt, *The Collected Poems of Amy Clampitt* (New York: Alfred A. Knopf, 1999), 7.

301 *"I really don't know"*: *OA* 596.

nature preserve: Habitat Education Center and Wildlife Preserve, Belmont, Massachusetts.

302 *"discontinuity of female"*: Adrienne Rich, "When We Dead Awaken: Writing as Re-Vision," *College English* 34, no. 1 (October 1972), 23.

"I am just not made": EB to AB, Washington's Birthday, 1970, VC 23.7.

303 *Hundreds of pages:* EB's letters to AM from the early 1970s were not among those locked in the file box, although they were withheld by AM from the collection she sold to Vassar College in 1981. These were acquired by VC from AM's heir in 2010, the contents of the locked file box in 2011. David Hoak emails to the author, October 4, 5, and 8, 2016.

304 *"geographic curiosity"*: *OA* 386.

"something slightly unpleasant": *OA* 283.

"you have to pretend": *OA* 363.

"Henry James did it": *OA* 375.

"all too vague": EB to AM, May 7, 1971, VC 115.2.

"just can't write": EB to AM, April 1, 1971, VC 115.1.

"Have you a few minutes?": EB to AM, June 26, 1972, VC 115.11.

"grit my teeth": *OA* 314.

305 *"immortal"*: *WIA* 380.

"short, but immortal, poem": EB, "In Prison," *BPR* 23.

"If you squint *a little"*: *OA* 601.

INDEX

Page numbers in italics refer to illustrations.

TEXT PERMISSION ACKNOWLEDGMENTS

Excerpts from *Edgar Allan Poe & The Juke-Box* by Elizabeth Bishop, edited and annotated by Alice Quinn. Copyright © 2006 by Alice Helen Methfessel. Reprinted by permission of Farrar, Straus and Giroux, LLC. Excerpts from *Poems* by Elizabeth Bishop. Copyright © 2011 by The Alice H. Methfessel Trust. Publisher's Note and compilation copyright © 2011 by Farrar, Straus and Giroux, LLC. Reprinted by permission of Farrar, Straus and Giroux, LLC. Excerpts from *Prose* by Elizabeth Bishop. Copyright © 2011 by The Alice H. Methfessel Trust. Editor's Note and compilation copyright © 2011 by Lloyd Schwartz. Excerpts from *One Art: Letters by Elizabeth Bishop,* selected and edited by Robert Giroux. Copyright © 1994 by Alice Methfessel. Introduction and compilation copyright © 1994 by Robert Giroux. Reprinted by permission of Farrar, Straus and Giroux, LLC. Excerpts from *Words in Air: The Complete Correspondence Between Elizabeth Bishop and Robert Lowell,* edited by Thomas Travisano with Saskia Hamilton. Copyright © 2008. Reprinted by permission of Farrar, Straus and Giroux, LLC.

Excerpts from unpublished letters written by Elizabeth Bishop to May Swenson, Alice Methfessel, Robert Fitzgerald, Anny Baumann, Loren McIver, Dr. Ruth Foster, Rosinha Leão, Magú Ribeiro, Lilli Correia de Araújo, Lota de Macedo Soares, Pearl Kazin Bell, and Randall Jarrell. Copyright © 2017 by The Alice H. Methfessel Trust. Printed by permission of Farrar, Straus and Giroux, LLC, on behalf of the Elizabeth Bishop Estate.

Excerpts from unpublished material written by Elizabeth Bishop, including journal entries, draft of poem (26 lines, "In the Waiting Room"), datebooks, teaching observations, college teaching notes, "Trip on the Amazon," telegraph to Lota de Macedo Soares, draft of introduction to Sylvia Plath's letters home, unfinished poem "Judy," autobiographical sketch, Bishop family baby book/photo album. Copyright © 2017 by The Alice H. Methfessel Trust. Printed by permission of Farrar, Straus and Giroux, LLC, on behalf of the Elizabeth Bishop Estate.

"Fog" from *The Collected Poems of Amy Clampitt* by Amy Clampitt, copyright © 1997 by the Estate of Amy Clampitt. Used by permission of Alfred A. Knopf, an imprint of the Knopf Doubleday Publishing Group, a division of Penguin Random House, LLC. All rights reserved.

Excerpts from "Notes on a Distant Prospect" by Robert Fitzgerald, from *The Third Kind of Knowledge,* copyright © 1984 by Robert Fitzgerald. Reprinted by permission of New Directions Publishing Corp.

"For Once, Then Something," from *The Poetry of Robert Frost,* edited by Edward Connery Lathem. Copyright 1923, 1969 by Henry Holt and Company, copyright © 1951 by Robert Frost. Used by permission of Henry Holt and Company, LLC. All rights reserved.

Excerpts from *Collected Poems by Robert Lowell.* Copyright © 2003 by Harriet Lowell and Sheridan Lowell. Reprinted by permission of Farrar, Straus and Giroux, LLC. Excerpts from *Words in Air: The Complete Correspondence Between Elizabeth Bishop and Robert Lowell,* edited by Thomas Travisano with Saskia Hamilton. Copyright © 2008. Reprinted by permission of Farrar, Straus and Giroux, LLC.

Excerpt from "The Eye of the Outsider: Elizabeth Bishop's Complete Poems, 1927–1979," from *Blood, Bread, and Poetry: Selected Prose 1979–1985* by Adrienne Rich. Copyright © 1986 by Adrienne Rich. Used by permission of W. W. Norton & Company, Inc.

Excerpt from "The Phenomenology of Anger," from *Diving into the Wreck: Poems 1971–1972* by Adrienne Rich. Copyright © 1973 by W. W. Norton & Company, Inc. Used by permission of W. W. Norton & Company, Inc.

Excerpts from "'When We Dead Awaken': Writing as Re-Vision," from *Arts of the Possible: Essays and Conversations by Adrienne Rich.* Copyright © 2001 by Adrienne Rich. Used by permission of W. W. Norton & Company, Inc.

Lines from "Red-Tail Hawk and Pyre of Youth" by Robert Penn Warren quoted with permission of the Estate of Robert Penn Warren.